Birds

A GUIDE BOOK TO BRITISH BIRDS

THE AUTHOR

Jonathan Elphick is a writer, editor and consultant specializing in ornithology and has been a keen birdwatcher for over 40 years. The innovative Collins *Atlas of Bird Migration*, of which he was General Editor, won *Bird Watching* magazine's award for the best general reference book about birds for 1996.

JONATHAN ELPHICK

Birds

A GUIDE BOOK TO
BRITISH BIRDS

Approved by the RSPB

BBC BOOKS

To Melanie, Becky, Alys, Tom and Callum,
and to my parents, Walter and Mimi,
for their love and support

AUTHOR'S ACKNOWLEDGEMENTS

Thanks to Rob Hume, Christine King, Martin Hendry, David Robinson, Linda Blakemore, Judit Budinszky, Martha Caute and Sheila Ableman for helping to make this book what I wanted it to be; to all the artists, for a superb set of illustrations that are as beautiful as they are accurate; to John Sparks for helping to set the ball rolling; and to all those who have given me help and encouragement from my earliest birdwatching days, especially Tony Angell, Richard and Michael Elphick, Peter Hope-Jones and Peggy Walton.

PICTURE CREDITS

Illustrations are by the following artists:
Richard Allen 8, 9 (tail and wing details), 10-14, 15 bottom right, 16 bottom left, 192-7, 236-9, 274-9, 286-9; Robert Gillmor 7 centre right, 16 bottom right, 44-63, 280-5; Ren Hathway 7 centre left, 9 top left, 212-19, 256-73, 298-9, 312-17; Peter Hayman 9 centre right, 15 centre left, top right (except Wigeon), 17, 19, 120-69, 198-205, 220-35, 240 top, 300-11; David Quinn 170-91; Owen Williams 7 top left, 9 bottom left, 15 top right (Wigeon), 64-119, 290-7; Martin Woodcock 15 centre right, 240 bottom, 241-55; Colin Woolf 206-11

Cover illustration by Gill Tomblin; Insets on front cover: Kingfisher, Ren Hathway; Barn Owl, Colin Woolf; Redwing, Martin Woodcock

Photographs are from the following sources:
Bruce Coleman 27 (Geoff Dore), 32-3 (Robert Glover), 36 (Gordon Langsbury); FLPA 21 (Frank Lane), 26 (Hugh Clark), 30 (Leo Batten); Jennifer Fry 40; S. and O. Matthews 25; NHPA 22, 23 (both E. A. Janes), 24 (Stephen Dalton), 29, 35 (David Woodfall), 31 (Nigel Dennis), 34 (Roger Tidman); RSPB 28 (Frank Blackburn), 38 bottom (Robert Glover), 39 (C. H. Gomersall)

Maps by Technical Art Services
The information for the maps and population figures was drawn chiefly from *The New Atlas of Breeding Birds in Britain and Ireland 1988-1991*, Poyser 1993, and *The Atlas of Wintering Birds in Britain and Ireland*, Poyser 1986

Consultant: Rob Hume
Editor: Christine King
Art Editor: Martin Hendry
Designer: David Robinson

© Jonathan Elphick 1997
The moral rights of the author have been asserted
First published in 1997 by BBC Books, an imprint of BBC Worldwide Publishing
BBC Worldwide Limited, Woodlands, 80 Wood Lane, London W12 0TT

ISBN 0 563 36954 X

Set in Plantin
Printed and bound in Great Britain by
Butler & Tanner Limited, Frome and London
Colour separations by Goodfellow & Egan Limited, Peterborough and Cambridge
Cover printed by Clays Limited, St Ives plc

This book is accompanied by the BBC's *Birds: A Video Guide to British Birds*, presented by Tony Soper. It features film of over 200 of the species described here, arranged by habitat. So that you may quickly refer to relevant film and sound recordings, each bird in the video is given a number, in order of appearance; this is printed in the top left-hand corner of its distribution map in the book (if a map has no such number, that particular species does not feature in the video). Likewise, the video shows page numbers on screen, so that you may easily find individual birds in the book.

CONTENTS

INTRODUCTION

THE FIELD GUIDE

THE BIRDS, ARRANGED BY FAMILY

HOW TO USE THIS BOOK

The first part of this book gives information on both how to identify birds and where to find them; it also provides advice on choosing and using binoculars and telescopes, birdwatching techniques and recording your observations, and includes details of societies and publications.

With the field guide itself, it is a good start to leaf through it and familiarize yourself with the different groups of birds. (Their essential details, including identification tips, are summarized in introductory panels.) Then, when you see an unfamiliar bird, you can judge whether it is a gull or a tern, or a pipit or a wagtail, for instance. Turn to the relevant section and see if you can match your bird to any illustration within that group. Check the text description against your own notes for common features. Always check similar species, mostly illustrated on facing pages.

THE BIRDS IN THIS BOOK

Every one of the 260 or so species that occur most regularly in the British Isles is described and illustrated in this book. Although over 500 different species have been recorded in these islands, and new species are being seen every year, almost half this total is made up of rare wanderers (vagrants) from far away in southern and eastern Europe, Asia and North America, most of which turn up after being blown off course during their annual migrations. A selection of rarities you may be lucky enough to encounter is also included in the field guide.

COMMON NAMES

Whether the bird you have seen is an abundant species or a rarity, you will want to put a name to it. The common names of birds in this book are those generally used by birdwatchers. You may see slightly different names in other books, because there is no standard list. However, a bird's scientific name represents its place in the scheme of classification, and is the same in every modern field guide – and in every country in the world.

CLASSIFYING BIRDS

Scientists classify all animals in a series of groupings, which are given names derived from Latin and Greek. These groupings form a hierarchy, according to how closely the animals within a grouping are related to one another. The first level in this hierarchy that need concern us is called the order. The names of orders always end in the suffix -iformes. There are 28 orders of birds in the world, of which 18 are represented in the British Isles and thus appear in this book. They include such familiar bird groups as the swans, geese and ducks (wildfowl), in the order Anseriformes, and the owls (order Strigiformes). More than one-third of the bird species in this book (and over half the world total) belong to a single order, the

Passeriformes or perching birds. All the birds in a particular order are more closely related to one another than to the birds in other orders.

The second level is the family. There are 165 families of birds in the world, of which 56 are included in this book. The names of families always end in -idae. All the birds in a particular family are more closely related to one another than to the birds in other families. Some large orders contain several families.

The Charadriiformes, for instance, includes various families of waders – notably the Charadriidae (plovers) and Scolopacidae (sandpipers and snipes) – as well as the Stercorariidae (skuas), Laridae (gulls), Sternidae (terns) and Alcidae (auks). In the order Passeriformes, 21 families are included in this book, such as the Troglodytidae (wrens), Paridae (true tits) and Corvidae (crows). Other orders, such as the Gaviiformes (divers) and Podicipediformes (grebes), contain only a single family.

Next comes the genus (plural genera) – birds in the same genus are closely related. For example, within the warbler family (Sylviidae) the group known as leaf warblers all belong to the genus *Phylloscopus*. Each unique species is distinguished by a specific name. Thus, the Willow Warbler is *Phylloscopus trochilus*, the Chiffchaff *Phylloscopus collybita*, and so on.

Thus each species of bird has its own, unique scientific name, which is a unique combination of the generic name and specific name. This is normally written in italics, the genus name with an initial capital, the species name all in lower case letters. You can learn a lot by looking at the scientific names of birds – in the example above, you would not realize from its common name that the Chiffchaff is a warbler, but knowing that it belongs to the same genus tells you that, like the Willow Warbler and all the other *Phylloscopus* warblers, it is a leaf warbler.

Although they are merely races of the same species, **Corvus corone,** *Carrion and Hooded Crows look very different*

SPECIES AND SUBSPECIES

A bird normally breeds only with other members of its species. So despite their great similarity in appearance, the Willow Warbler and Chiffchaff may nest near each other and yet they do not interbreed, because they are separate species. Their very different songs help to keep them apart.

Contrast this with the case of domestic dogs, where breeds may look very different (e.g. a corgi and an Irish setter) and yet, because they are just variations of a single species, they could interbreed to produce fertile offspring. One sometimes reads in the newspapers about a 'variety' or 'breed' of wild birds when what is really meant is a species.

Most species can be further subdivided into subspecies, or geographical races. By virtue of a wide geographical range or long isolation on islands, different populations of a species evolve slight differences in appearance, voice and so on. As with dog breeds, they can interbreed to produce fertile hybrids because they belong to the same species. Most subspecies are indistinguishable in the field, but those that can be identified are described and illustrated in this book.

A subspecies has a third part to its scientific name – for example, the Scandinavian race of the Chiffchaff is *Phylloscopus collybita abietinus*, usually abbreviated to *P.c.abietinus*, or just *abietinus*. Sometimes a species is given a separate common name, for example, the White Wagtail (a Continental race of the Pied Wagtail), and the Hooded Crow (a race of the Carrion Crow).

KNOWING BIRD FAMILIES

One of the main keys to successful bird identification is to know to which family a bird belongs. Suppose you are walking through a wood and you see a small bird flitting about in the branches. To the uninitiated, it is just a 'little brown bird'. But if you look closer, you may notice that it has a rounded head and body, a stubby bill and a black cap, and that it hangs acrobatically from the tips of branches – all features that give you a clue that this is a member of the tit family.

Often, deciding which family 'your' bird belongs to will narrow the choice of species from a bewildering number down to just a handful, though there are families – such as waders, gulls or warblers – where there is much more choice and many species look very similar. But take heart, because there are not many of these real 'problem' groups, and even the experts find them difficult!

Also, the larger, more complex families can generally be broken down further into smaller groupings, such as the different sorts of ducks (shelducks, dabbling ducks, diving ducks and so on) or warblers (grass warblers, scrub warblers, leaf warblers etc).

These two species look superficially similar, but belong to completely different families (warblers and tits)

THE SEQUENCE OF BIRDS IN THIS BOOK

The arrangement of bird families, genera and species in this book follows the generally accepted scientific scheme proposed by the Dutch ornithologist Dr Karel Voous in his *List of Recent Holarctic Bird Species* (1977) – except where it has been necessary to make slight alterations to ensure that similar-looking species are shown together.

The great advantage of this method of arrangement, rather than listing the birds in some other manner (e.g. alphabetically, by size or by colour), is that similar species within a family are grouped together and can easily be compared.

HOW TO IDENTIFY BIRDS
Field characters

Each species of bird has its own distinctive features – field characters. These include size, shape and structure, colour and shape of bill, legs and feet, plumage marks and the sounds it makes.

The major field characters of a Wren, for example, are its rotund shape, small size, barred brown plumage, short, often cocked, tail, whirring flight on short wings and distinctive calls and song, while those of a Red Kite are its wing shape, flight action, often twisted, forked tail and reddish-brown plumage, with white wing patches and black wingtips.

The field guide section of this book will help familiarize you with the important field characters of each species. Start off with common species that you can watch easily, and progress to birds that are not so readily accessible and identifiable.

SIZE

Judging the size of a bird in the wild can be surprisingly difficult, and it should not be relied on too much in identification. It is impossible to make a dependable size estimate of birds seen at a distance, or against a featureless sky. In mist and haze, birds can look bigger than they really are. If you are looking through binoculars or a telescope, an optical illusion, resulting from the distortion of perspective, causes you to see the further away of two birds as larger than it actually is relative to the nearer bird; the greater the magnification, the more pronounced the effect. This can cause problems, for example, if you are using a telescope at high magnification to watch a Common Gull standing behind a Herring Gull, when the smaller Common Gull could look almost as large as its bigger relative. If the birds are the same distance from you, the effect does not occur, and it is minimal when the birds are in a flock on the ground or in the air.

Judging size is most reliable if you can compare the bird with another species alongside but, failing that, you can use your knowledge of familiar species as a yardstick and see it as 'slightly bigger than a House Sparrow' or 'Blackbird-sized'. Otherwise, you should not rely too much on estimates of size for identification.

SHAPE AND STRUCTURE

A bird's shape and the relative proportions of its bill, head, wings and tail, etc – its structure – can provide useful clues to its identity. For example, pipits and buntings are both small streaked brown birds, but buntings are plumper, with shorter, thicker necks and stubby bills; Goshawks are much bulkier and deeper-chested than Sparrowhawks; Rooks are deeper-bodied than Carrion Crows, more untidy-looking, with looser plumage over the thighs making it look as if they were wearing baggy trousers.

It is as well to be aware that a bird's shape can vary quite dramatically with weather conditions and with its mood; for instance, compare the plump, neckless shape of a Song Thrush's head and body huddled on a branch on a cold winter's day with its much more elongated appearance as it runs across a lawn in spring, searching for worms. Despite this, most species do have a reasonably consistent overall shape and characteristic postures that help in identifying them.

The bird's structure can be a particularly useful and reliable aid to identification. Sometimes, these differences can be appreciated most readily when the bird is perched, with its wings neatly folded.

The distance the primary flight feathers of the wingtips extend beyond the longest of the

Changing shapes: in this flock of Knots, some are sleeping, heads tucked into 'shoulders', while others are alert and look much slimmer

Icterine Warbler   *Melodious Warbler*

Closed wings, showing primary projection

The Icterine Warbler's longer wings have a greater primary projection than those of the very similar Melodious Warbler

tertials (inner flight feathers) is known as the 'primary projection'. This is important in distinguishing some species. For example, Glaucous and Iceland Gulls are both large, pale gulls breeding in the far north, scarce winter wanderers to our shores; a major difference is that the wingtips of the Iceland extend beyond its tail, but in the Glaucous they only reach the end of its tail.

WING SHAPE

The shape of the wings is important when identifying flying birds. For example, both the Swift and the unrelated Swallow and martins have pointed wings, but those of the Swift look much longer and slimmer, less broad-

Buzzard   *Peregrine*

Swift   *Swallow*

Wing shape can help distinguish a Buzzard from a Peregrine, for example, or a Swift from a Swallow

based, adapting it for a life spent almost entirely on the wing. A Sparrowhawk's wings are broad, with rounded tips, enabling it to manoeuvre at speed to surprise its prey in the dense cover of a wood or along a hedge, while a Kestrel, which hunts in open country, has more distinctly pointed wings (though wings may alter shape somewhat; the Kestrel's look rather blunter-tipped when soaring).

TAIL SHAPE

Tails, too, are distinctively shaped. Some are long, others short, some narrow, others broad, some square-tipped, others notched or deeply forked. A Skylark and a Woodlark look very different in flight because of the latter's extremely short tail. The tail of a Swallow is much more deeply forked than a House Martin's, and a female Pintail can be distinguished from the similar female Mallard by its longer, pointed tail.

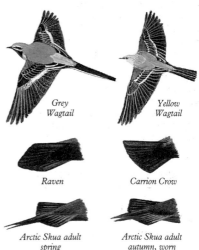

Grey Wagtail   *Yellow Wagtail*

Raven   *Carrion Crow*

Arctic Skua adult spring   *Arctic Skua adult autumn, worn*

Tail length helps distinguish Yellow and Grey Wagtails, for instance; tail shape is distinctive for many species

Even more so than with wings, the tail shape can alter depending on what the bird is doing. Birds spread their tails when soaring or landing and a rounded tail can appear square-ended or even notched in some postures. Be aware, also, that young birds often have distinctly shorter tails than their parents, and that feathers can be broken off or lost by moult. Skuas are one group of birds that present such problems.

BILLS

Birds use their bills for a huge range of tasks: preening feathers; digging out nest holes in river banks, or carrying and weaving nest material; as a weapon in territorial disputes; to caress a mate during courtship. But above all the bird's bill is used for feeding: both to obtain food (in those species that do not seize prey with their feet) and to deal with it. As birds live in every habitat and on widely different foods, their bills are adapted accordingly.

A wide range of unrelated birds, such as divers, gannets, herons and terns, have long dagger-like bills adapted for seizing and holding struggling fish.

Ducks have broad bills, flattened from top to bottom, equipped with little projections called lamellae. In dabbling ducks, these are fine and form a sieve for filtering tiny animals or seeds from the water. Some of the sea ducks, such as eiders and scoters, eat mainly shellfish, and their bills have larger, stronger lamellae at their edges for grasping and dislodging molluscs from the seabed. Another group of ducks that dive for their food, the aptly named sawbills, feed mainly on fish, grasping them in their long, slender bills with serrations like saw teeth and a hook at the tip.

Waders have bills of various lengths, adapted to the depth at which they need to probe in mud for their particular prey. Thus plovers and stints have shortish bills for picking food from the surface of the mud, while those of Dunlin and Knot are longer, used for shallow probing. Redshank and Greenshank have longer, deeper-probing bills; and the longest bills, those of the snipe, curlews and godwits, are able to reach deepest. By eating prey from different layers of mud, a variety of species avoid competing for food on the same stretch of estuary.

Many small birds are primarily insect-eaters, with neat, slender bills for dealing with their prey. Some, such as warblers and tits, take insects mainly from foliage or bark. Others specialize in catching flying insects. Flycatchers fly out from a perch to snap up an insect in mid-air. Their bills are broad-based, giving them a wide gape to stand the best chance of seizing a fast-moving insect. The most highly adapted insect-eaters are those, such as swifts, swallows and nightjars, that feed only on the wing, and have tiny, weak-looking bills but huge gapes for scooping up their prey. Swifts and nightjars have stiff bristles (modified feathers) fringing the mouth to enlarge the area for prey capture and perhaps also to protect the eyes from being damaged by the tough bodies of the insects.

Some birds, such as sparrows and finches, have short, strong, conical bills for opening seeds. This basic plan varies from the delicate tweezers of the Goldfinch, with which it extracts small seeds from thistle heads, to the powerful nutcrackers of the Hawfinch, capable of cracking cherry stones.

Identifying birds by bills

Looking at the bill of a bird will often provide useful clues to its identity. Shape is particularly important; for instance, Dunnocks and House Sparrows may seem quite similarly plumaged, similarly sized brown birds if you are not familiar with them, but the slender, pointed bill of the Dunnock instantly distinguishes it from the House Sparrow, which has a short, conical bill.

As well as shape, bill length can be useful in identification, especially in waders. Colour, too, is often distinctive (see box, right).

It helps when judging the length of a bird's bill to compare it with the length of the head. For smaller birds, it may be easier to compare it with the distance between the base of the bill and the eye.

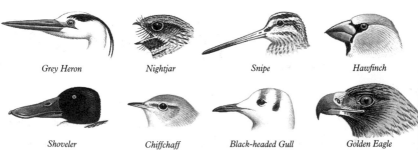

Grey Heron   *Nightjar*   *Snipe*   *Hawfinch*

Shoveler   *Chiffchaff*   *Black-headed Gull*   *Golden Eagle*

Bills come in all shapes and sizes, adapted to birds' different diets

LEGS AND FEET

All birds' legs share the same basic general plan, but differ in length, colour and degree of feathering. Feet, like bills, vary greatly according to the bird's way of life. They are used, naturally enough, in walking, running, hopping, perching, clinging and climbing, but also in swimming and digging.

No bird has more than four toes, but some have fewer. Most birds have feet primarily adapted for perching, with three toes pointing forwards and one backwards. In birds of prey and owls, the feet are modified for seizing and subduing prey, with rough soles and powerful, sharp claws. Some feet are adapted for life on the ground: gamebirds like grouse have strong, short, blunt claws, with which they scratch for seeds on the ground, while larks and pipits have long hind claws to help them balance as they run among vegetation.

A woodpecker's foot has two toes pointing forwards and two backwards, giving it a firm grip as it climbs a tree; it can rotate one of its hind toes sideways for a wider grasp on a branch. Swifts have all four toes on their tiny feet pointing forwards, allowing them to cling to vertical surfaces when breeding.

Most birds that swim, such as divers, cormorants, ducks, gulls and auks, have webbed feet that propel them through the water. Grebes and Coots achieve the same end with lobed feet.

Identifying birds by legs and feet

Colour (see box, right), length and, sometimes, other features are often distinctive. Leg length is important in several groups, especially waders; for instance, the Spotted Redshank has longer legs than the much more common Redshank. Feathering (or lack of it) may be a useful clue: Rough-legged Buzzards, true to their name, have feathered legs, while the legs of Buzzards are bare.

BARE PARTS

The term 'bare parts' is used collectively for the legs, bill and areas of bare skin around the eye, as in gulls; on fleshy structures on the head (combs or wattles) in gamebirds; on the forehead (the frontal shield) in the Coot and Moorhen; or at at the base of the bill (the cere) in pigeons and birds of prey.

These have distinctive colours that are often useful in identification. For instance, they can help distinguish some species of waders, such as the scarce Little Ringed Plover, which has duller legs than the common Ringed Plover, a yellow eyering and an all-black, not mainly orange, bill. Among terns, three similar species have different-coloured bills in the breeding season. The colours of bare parts can also help distinguish young from adults: the legs and bill base of a juvenile Redshank, for example, are orange, not red.

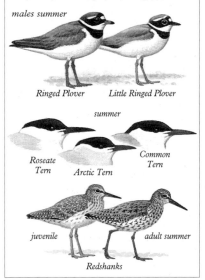

males summer

Ringed Plover   *Little Ringed Plover*

summer

Roseate Tern   *Arctic Tern*   *Common Tern*

juvenile   *adult summer*

Redshanks

Barn Owl   *Ptarmigan*   *Coot*   *Moorhen*   *Cormorant*

Great Spotted Woodpecker   *Garden Warbler*   *Swift*   *Kingfisher*   *Meadow Pipit*

Some of the range of different feet in birds, adapting them for different lifestyles

THE PARTS OF A BIRD

These diagrams of the parts of a bird show the precise positions and names of the feather groups making up a bird's plumage, as well as the structure of the bill, eyes, legs and feet.

The feather groups of the wings are complex: it is important to understand how they change position relative to one another when the bird opens and closes its wings. Equally important, in certain groups of birds such as waders, gulls and terns, some large feather groups become hidden when they close their wings, obscuring vital identifying marks. In the Redshank, for instance, the bold white panel on the trailing edge of each wing, which is so striking in flight, is completely hidden when it lands and folds its wings (see also page 15). In thrushes, warblers, tits and other perching birds, most of the feather groups of the upperwing remain visible when the wings are closed, though some of the smaller wing coverts may be concealed by the feathers of the scapulars, sides of the breast, and flanks.

PERCHING BIRD (Passerine)

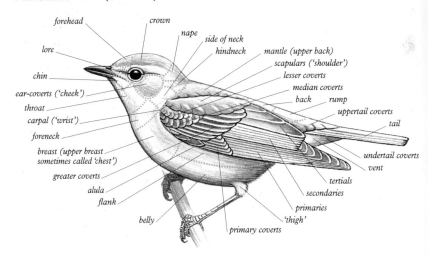

WADER

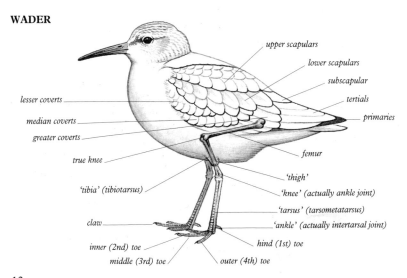

BILL DETAILS (Gull)

upper mandible
nostril
loral point
culmen
cutting edges
gonys
lower mandible
mouth
malar point
gape

HEAD DETAILS (Falcon)

cere
nostril
gape
moustache stripe
orbital ring

HEAD STRIPES (Bunting)

crown stripe
lateral crown stripe
supercilium ('eyebrow')
eyestripe
moustachial stripe ('moustache')
malar stripe
submoustachial stripe

EYE DETAILS (Gull)

eyering (feathered)
orbital ring (bare skin)
iris
pupil

UPPERWING

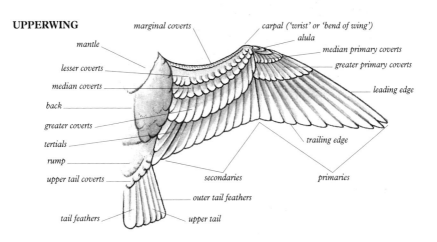

marginal coverts
carpal ('wrist' or 'bend of wing')
alula
mantle
median primary coverts
lesser coverts
greater primary coverts
median coverts
leading edge
back
greater coverts
tertials
trailing edge
rump
upper tail coverts
secondaries
primaries
outer tail feathers
tail feathers
upper tail

UNDERWING

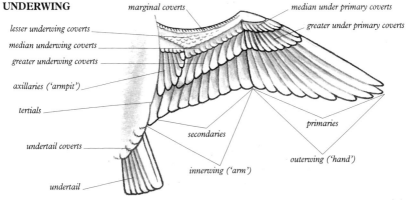

marginal coverts
median under primary coverts
greater under primary coverts
lesser underwing coverts
median underwing coverts
greater underwing coverts
axillaries ('armpit')
tertials
primaries
undertail coverts
secondaries
outerwing ('hand')
undertail
innerwing ('arm')

PLUMAGE PATTERNS

In identifying birds by plumage, half the battle lies in getting to know the names of the different feather groups that are common to all birds, from the Mute Swan and Golden Eagle to the Kingfisher and Wren.

The number of feathers in each group varies between species, but the names are standard – though there are both scientific and popular versions. For example, the patch of feathers above the eye is known formally as the supercilium, or more popularly as the eyebrow. This is a precise term referring to a particular feather area, but some other popular names – such as 'wingtip' – can be ambiguous. For this reason, although I have tried to make terms 'user-friendly', in some cases the 'official' term has been unavoidable. Even so, most of these are relatively easy to comprehend – and it is a good idea anyway to get to know the 'official' names for all the feather groups. If you go on to use more specialist field guides and read journals, you will find that these terms are used there rather than the simplified ones.

Familiarize yourself with the positions and names of all the feather groups in the diagrams on pages 12-13 and try to relate them to the birds you see. As ever, start off with easily observed, relatively approachable species in your garden or local park. For example, look for the bold yellow *eyering* of the male blackbird, the white *nape* of the Coal Tit or the greenish *rump* of the Chaffinch. You could also compare the plumage diagrams with the artworks in the field guide section of this book, or with photographs of the birds.

The great secret of bird identification is knowing what to look for. Faced with an unfamiliar bird, the novice is often bewildered by trying to make out distinguishing features, and may only remember unimportant features rather than the key ones that will clinch a correct identification. For instance, it is little use noticing that a Great Tit has a black cap, for this is a feature shared by most other members of the tit family; whereas observing that its black bib runs into a broad black stripe extending down its breast and belly distinguishes it from the rest.

Try to be as precise as possible when noting details: you are much more likely to make a correct identification if you notice that a bird has a dark crown and eyestripe contrasting with a pale eyebrow, than if you merely observed that it had a striped head.

As you get to know the birds with the help of the field guide section of this book, you will eventually find it second nature to look out for the unique pattern of upperwing bars and tail markings in a flying wader, or the colours on the head and back of a woodpecker.

Head patterns

Some species have a distinctive pattern on their crowns – for instance, the Great and Lesser Spotted Woodpeckers are differentiated by these markings, which also differ according to the sex and age of the bird. The pattern of stripes on the heads of many birds, such as waders, thrushes and some warblers, help distinguish close relatives. Thus a Whimbrel can be distinguished from a Curlew by its pale eyebrow and two dark crown stripes, and a Firecrest from a Goldcrest by the black eyestripe running through its eye and white eyebrow. Some birds have distinct 'moustaches'; among the falcons, for example, the Peregrine and Hobby have bold black moustache stripes, much more distinct than those of the Kestrel or Merlin.

Some head markings – or their absence – can give a bird a distinct 'expression', along with bill shape, eye colour and so on. Thus the pale eyebrow of the Redwing can make it look 'angry' compared to the more benign, open-faced appearance of the Song Thrush.

summer   *winter*

Common Terns

male   *female*

Blackcaps

Firecrest   *Goldcrest*

males

Pintail   *Mallard*

Many birds have distinctive patterns on their heads or necks, including contrasting caps, stripes and bands

Body patterns

Breast bands are found in some species, such as the Shelduck, Ringed Plover and Bluethroat, while others have streaks or spots on their underparts. These may be largely restricted to the upper breast, as in the Short-eared Owl, or cover most of the underparts, as in the Long-eared Owl. The size or density of the markings can help to distinguish similar species: the Tree Pipit has a cleaner, more evenly streaked breast and fewer, thinner streaks on its flanks than the Meadow Pipit.

If you can see it, the undertail of many species is distinctively coloured or patterned – variations on black and cream in Teal and Pintail, patterns of barring in many of the rails, or red in the Great Spotted Woodpecker.

Ringed Plover   *Mistle Thrush*

Body patterns include breast bands, as in the Ringed Plover, or spotted underparts, as in the Mistle Thrush

Wing patterns

A Redshank can be distinguished from a Spotted Redshank or Greenshank as soon as it takes to the air: its open wings reveal broad white trailing edges. Single or double wingbars – often pale but sometimes dark – formed by the contrastingly coloured tips of the covert feathers help identify such birds as waders and finches. Wing patterns are important in identifying other birds, too, especially ducks in flight. Most have well-marked wings, with bold wingbars or patches (sometimes called panels) of white or distinctive colours. The speculum is a patch of iridescent brightly coloured secondary feathers, often framed by narrow white bands on one or both sides, in the dabbling ducks.

Wingtips are important when identifying gulls. Most have a black tip broken up by white 'mirrors' – the size of which helps distinguish species.

In some species, such as the ducks, it is the upperwings that are distinctive, but in birds of prey, the underwing pattern is more important; most birds of prey are seen soaring from below, when dark carpal bars (at the 'wrist' of the wing) or other features are significant.

Siskin, double wingbars

Sanderling winter, single wingbar

Redshank, wing panel

Wigeon male 1st-winter, speculum

Wing patterns include various kinds of wingbar, broad panels and the glossy speculum of many ducks

Tail and rump patterns

Many birds are distinguished by bold tail markings. Various species, including some waders, wagtails and pipits, have white outer tail feathers; in others, the pattern is restricted to the sides of the tail base, as with the red patches of the Bluethroat; some have white only at the tip, as in the Hawfinch.

The pattern of bars on the tails of many birds of prey can be distinctive; the Buzzard's tail is densely barred, while the Rough-legged Buzzard's has a broad black band at the tip. Similar patterns help distinguish Bar-tailed and Black-tailed Godwits in flight.

Some birds have a white rump that contrasts strikingly with a dark tail. Its extent and shape may be important, as with the larger, undivided white rump of the Storm Petrel compared to the divided one of Leach's Petrel. Coloured rumps are also distinctive; for example, Cirl Buntings can be distinguished from Yellowhammers by duller, olive to greyish (not chestnut) rumps.

Chaffinch   *Wheatear*

Bar-tailed Godwit   *Black-tailed Godwit*

Tail patterns include white outer feathers, barring or dark bands, sometimes with a white rump

15

PLUMAGE AND MOULT

Birds replace their feathers regularly, and in many cases the different plumages are distinctive, depending on the bird's age or sex, or the time of year. For instance, young Starlings are greyish-brown, very different from the glossy black adults; female Tufted Ducks are dark brown, much less dramatic-looking than the bold black and white males; Black-headed Gulls lose their neat chocolate-brown face masks in winter, except for a small spot behind the eye.

You will need to familiarize yourself with the names used to describe the different plumages (see below). It is also helpful to understand something of the moulting processes by which they are produced.

Moult

A bird's feathers are beautifully evolved to cope with the demands of flight, as well as keeping their owner warm, protecting it from the heat of the sun, repelling water, and providing an astonishing variety of colours and patterns for courtship display, alarm signals or camouflage. Although they are remarkably tough structures, feathers wear out or become damaged, and must be replaced. This process of feather replacement is called moult.

Birds do not lose all their feathers simultaneously, or they would be cold and unable to fly. They do so over a period of time. Larger species take longer to moult than smaller ones; a warbler or a tit may moult all its feathers in about six weeks, while one of the large gulls may take six months or more. The large and important wing and tail feathers are moulted in a regular sequence. Most birds, for instance, moult their primary wing feathers in strict progression from the innermost to the outermost.

Young birds

A bird's first set of feathers, after it has left the nest, is known as its *juvenile* plumage. This may look very like the *adult* plumage of the mature bird (as in the Kingfisher or the Wren) or may be quite different (as with the spotted plumage of the juvenile Robin). In species where the sexes look different, juveniles resemble the drabber females – helping to camouflage them from predators.

Most small perching birds remain in juvenile plumage for a short time only. Then they undergo a second moult into *first-winter* plumage. This is usually a partial moult, involving only the feathers of the head, body and smaller wing coverts. In many species, such as the Robin, the first-winter plumage is indistinguishable in the field from the adult plumage. In others, such as the Blackbird, first-winter birds can be distinguished because the juvenile wing and tail feathers, which they retain, are differently coloured from an adult's.

Some large birds take much longer to reach maturity; the Gannet and many gulls, for instance, pass through a series of speckled brown stages before attaining the adult's white, or grey and white, plumage. A Common Gull takes about two years to do this, and the first-winter stage is followed by *first-summer* plumage, then *second-winter* and *second-summer* before adult plumage is acquired. Smaller gulls, such as the Black-headed, take only 13-16 months to reach adulthood, while larger ones, such as the Great Black-backed, take three or more years to do so.

When it is difficult to decide the age of a young bird, or when a group of plumages is being referred to, the term 'immature' is used. Sometimes 'first-year' is used to refer to the juvenile, first-winter and first-summer plumages collectively.

Great Black-backed Gull

This moulting gull shows a mix of new, old and missing wing and tail feathers

juvenile

3rd-year

It takes a Gannet 4–6 years and several moults to attain adult plumage

Adults

As adults, some birds, such as waders, gulls and some small perching birds, have two moults each year. A partial moult early in the year, called the pre-breeding moult, and involving just the body feathers, produces the *summer* plumage; this is often brighter or bolder than the *winter* plumage, especially in males – for example in the Grey Wagtail and Pied Flycatcher. A later, complete moult, called the post-breeding moult, produces the winter plumage. The timing and duration of these moults vary considerably between species, and sometimes within a single species, according to the sex of the bird. The pre-breeding moult usually occurs in spring, but may begin as early as the beginning of winter in some species; the post-breeding moult may start as early as late spring or as late as early winter, though it usually happens in autumn.

Other birds do not have a pre-breeding moult, and, in many cases, such as the thrushes and tits, their plumage looks the same all year round. Some of these birds do, however, acquire a distinct summer plumage without the energy-demanding process of moulting. Instead, the pale fringes of the winter feathers wear away to reveal brighter or darker colours beneath; the effect is particularly noticeable in the males. This happens, for instance, in the male House Sparrow, Brambling, Linnet and Reed Bunting. In some species both sexes acquire a distinctive summer plumage.

Wildfowl (swans, geese and ducks) and some other groups, such as divers and grebes, moult their flight feathers all in one go, over a period of a few weeks. The males of many ducks, which have brightly coloured plumage, acquire a much duller, *eclipse* plumage, similar to that of the females. This helps to camouflage them during the vulnerable period while they are grounded. The moult that produces this plumage is, in fact, a double moult combining the spring and autumn moults, so that the briefly worn eclipse plumage is equivalent to the winter plumage of other birds. This ensures that the males are adorned in their bright colours throughout winter and spring, when they need them to display to mates and rivals.

Some large birds, such as many birds of prey, have long-lasting, overlapping moults which do not fit neatly into the scheme outlined above.

Feathers fade and wear with age, especially wing and tail feathers, which are moulted only once a year. In gulls, for instance, black areas fade to brown, and the white 'mirrors' on the wingtips can wear away completely.

Birds part way through a moult can look very odd, even to experienced birdwatchers. Examples you are likely to encounter include the varied appearance of young Eiders, and the blotchy plumage of waders such as the Ruff or Spotted Redshank, moulting from summer to winter plumage.

Although each species has a distinctive range of plumage patterns (adult, young, and sometimes different male and female plumages) many have colour variations too. Buzzards, for instance, come in a bewildering range of pale, dark and intermediate forms. Skuas have a similar but more predictable range of colour forms (called phases).

Occasionally, abnormally pigmented birds turn up; partial albino Blackbirds with patches of white, where the pigment is absent, are relatively common, and can be confused with Ring Ouzels; all-white Blackbirds are very rare, as are leucistic (lightly pigmented), melanistic (heavily pigmented) and erythristic (abnormally red) birds.

female

male winter

male summer

By spring, the male Linnet's drab female-like winter plumage becomes brighter, not by moulting but by the paler feather edges wearing away to reveal the colours beneath

BEHAVIOUR

The behaviour of birds may be as distinctive as their field characters, in a variety of ways. How species move over the ground, perch, fly, swim or dive can help identify them. Other behavioural traits – such as their sociability or lack of it – may also be important.

Walking, running and climbing

Look at different species or groups of species and see how they move. Pipits and sparrows, for example, are mostly small streaked brown birds, but a vital clue to separating them is that pipits walk while sparrows hop.

On the coast, different groups of waders feed in different ways. Plovers, for instance, run rapidly, then stop to peck off a worm from the surface of the mud, quite unlike the deep probing of a godwit or Curlew.

Or take the example of a small bird seen climbing a tree. The Nuthatch can move just as easily downwards as upwards, while woodpeckers, though jerkily ascending a trunk or branch with great efficiency, do not have this dual ability. Like the woodpeckers (and unlike the Nuthatch), the Treecreeper uses its stiffened tail feathers as a prop for climbing, but, unlike the others, it always spirals round the trunk before flying down to the base of the next tree.

Perching

The way in which a bird stands or perches, too, can help narrow down the field. Dabbling ducks, for instance, when out of the water hold their bodies horizontally, whereas diving ducks hold their bodies more upright. A male Sparrowhawk, like most other birds of prey, usually perches upright with its tail pointing downwards, while the similarly plumaged, though completely unrelated, Cuckoo perches horizontally, frequently swaying, and usually holds its tail horizontally too, often waving it from side to side.

Flight actions

Many birds have distinctive flight actions. Swifts race along high in the sky in search of flying insects, with long glides and flickering beats of their sickle-shaped wings – quite different from feeding Swallows, sweeping low over fields or lakes with an effortless-looking, fluid wing action. The purposive flight of a Grey Heron, with ponderous beats of its large, broad, bowed wings, the zigzag escape flight of a Snipe as it 'towers' up into the air, the deeply undulating flight of

---

THE SECRET OF JIZZ

Each species is distinguished by what is known as its 'jizz' – a particular subtle combination of its overall size, shape, proportions, posture, movements, flight-style and behaviour.

Knowledge of a bird's jizz is invaluable, particularly when only a fleeting glimpse is possible or when a bird is seen at a distance, on a dull day, at dusk, or silhouetted against the light – when plumage details cannot be made out. An experienced birdwatcher can put a name to a bird (or at least to its family) from just such a brief view, having become familiar with what makes each group of birds and species different from others.

Anyone interested in birds can acquire this skill. Over time, you will become familiar with the jizz of a bird, just as you have learnt to distinguish close friends and relatives from a distance: you recognise them by their body shape, posture, manner of walking, the way they put their hands in their pockets and other idiosyncrasies.

---

woodpeckers, and the straight, fast flight of a flock of Starlings, like living arrowheads – all these are characteristic.

Swimming and diving

On the water as well as in the air, birds behave distinctively. Cormorants, Shags and divers sit low in the water, their backs often almost awash, while Moorhens and Coots ride high. The first three all dive frequently, but only the Shag usually leaps forward before submerging; the others simply slip under the surface. Coots, too, are accomplished at diving, while Moorhens rarely dive. Furthermore, Moorhens nod their heads nervously (and often simultaneously jerk up their tails) with each stroke of their legs, unlike their larger relatives. Dabbling ducks take off from the water almost vertically, while diving ducks patter furiously across the surface before becoming airborne.

Sociability

Birds also differ in their sociability. Among the waders, Knots, for instance, are usually seen in large flocks, while Woodcock are almost always encountered singly or occasionally in pairs. Rooks nest in noisy colonies, while their close relatives, Carrion Crows, are solitary breeders. You are as unlikely to see a flock of Robins as to come across a solitary Long-tailed Tit.

SOUNDS

Experienced birdwatchers can pick out many bird species by sound alone. It is always a good idea to use your ears as well as your eyes. Apart from the usefulness of calls and song in revealing the position of a bird whose presence you were unaware of, they are of immense help in identification. Indeed, in some habitats, such as dense woodland, where birds are hard to see, it can be the best means of putting a name to the bird.

Voice can also help distinguish very similar-looking closely related birds, such as these two warblers: a Chiffchaff's monotonous repetition of the two notes that spell out its name instantly distinguishes it from the Willow Warbler, whose song is a beautiful, wistful series of silvery notes.

It is usually only males that sing, but there are some exceptions. Female Robins, for example, which look the same as males and, like them, defend a feeding territory in winter, also sing in autumn.

In this book I have used the term 'song' in its wider sense, to include not just the songs of thrushes, warblers and the other small perching birds, but also the territorial or courtship display sounds made by other species such as waders or owls.

Song flights

Birds living in open country lack tall perches from which to proclaim their presence by song. Instead, they may use song flights to achieve the same end. These are often distinctive, like the prolonged, high fluttering ascent of a singing Skylark, followed by a silent plummet to earth.

The Meadow Pipit usually sings during a climbing-and-parachuting song flight above its territory in open country

Calls

Most bird species utter a variety of calls – such as contact calls for keeping in touch with other members of the species, alarm calls warning the others of danger, or calls used during courtship displays. Call notes as well as song are often of great help in identification. For example, the Marsh Tit and Willow Tit, which look so similar that they were thought to be the same species until the turn of the century, are best distinguished by their different calls.

Non-vocal sounds

These, too, can provide vital clues. Like song, these are often associated with male breeding displays. Examples are the drumming of woodpeckers with their bills on tree trunks and branches, and the curious bleating sound made by the stiff outer tail feathers of a displaying Snipe as it dives earthwards.

HOW TO LEARN BIRD SOUNDS

When I started watching birds many years ago, there were few field guides or sound recordings. I found that by listening to a bird song or call and then locating the bird making it, I soon learned the characteristic sounds made by different species and was able to identify an increasing range of birds from their voices alone. As I joined my local birdwatching society, I met more experienced birdwatchers who could help me distinguish the sounds of less familiar species.

These may still be the ideal methods of learning the sounds that birds make, but it is much harder to find scarcer species. You can of course pick up a lot of knowledge by listening to the wide range of CDs and tapes now available.

In the field guide I have included verbal descriptions of the song and most of the usual calls of each species in the Key Facts boxes.

It is always worth bearing in mind that some birds are excellent mimics – like Starlings, which often fool the unwary with perfect renditions of the sounds of Curlews or Tawny Owls, among other birds (not to mention cats and even telephones and other artificial sounds!). These 'stolen' sounds, though, are usually incorporated into the male's regular song.

It is worth taking into account the time of year and time of day, too. You will not hear the familiar song of a Cuckoo in winter nor the soft growling chorus of a flock of Brent Geese in summer. Few birds sing at night, but Nightingales are renowned for doing so (though they also sing during the day). Some reported 'Nightingales' turn out to be Robins, which also sing loudly at night, especially under street lights in towns.

WHERE TO FIND BIRDS
Understanding bird habitats
If you know where a particular bird is likely to be found – its preferred habitat – then naturally you have a much better chance of first locating, then identifying, the species. To find out the habitats preferred by each species (which may be different in the breeding and non-breeding seasons), look under 'Habitat' in the Key Facts boxes in the field guide.

THE IMPORTANCE OF HABITAT

Although some highly adaptable birds, such as the Wren, Starling and Carrion Crow, are found in a wide variety of habitats, many species are intimately tied to a particular habitat – for example, Red Grouse to moorland or Bitterns to reedbeds. Kingfishers are never seen far from water, while Treecreepers are almost entirely restricted to trees. In some cases, a species' occurrence is further restricted by its distribution. Thus you are most unlikely to see a Crested Tit anywhere in the British Isles but in the Caledonian pine forests of Scotland.

Such precise preferences are largely connected with the need to find food and nest sites; other needs, such as cover in which to hide and available song perches, may also play a part. Tree Pipits, for example, are birds of open country with scattered trees or tall bushes, which provide the males with high enough song posts from which to claim territory and attract a mate. But the species also needs sparsely vegetated areas of ground on which to find its insect food, and banks or grass tussocks where it can nest. The birds find this particular combination of landscape features in different habitats – on heaths, scrubby downland, woodland clearings, coppiced woodland and young conifer plantations in the south and east, and in open, mature oak, birch and native pine woods in the north and west. Once you learn what that particular combination is, you know the right kind of place to look for a Tree Pipit and, equally, that you are unlikely to see one on bare moorland or grassland or in dense woodland.

Some birds occupy different habitats at different seasons; for instance, Curlews breed mainly on moorland and upland farmland, where they can find suitable nesting sites and food for their young. However, they forsake these habitats after the breeding season, when they become bleak places with little food, to spend the winter months chiefly on estuary mudflats and nearby grassland, joining together in flocks to seek out the rich bounty of worms, crabs and molluscs.

Becoming familiar with a bird's particular needs, which are outlined in this book, will help you understand why you need to look for it in a particular habitat or even locality. In general, the more varied the habitat, the greater the diversity of the birdlife it contains. Thus a patch of mixed woodland with a shrub layer and ground vegetation will contain far more species than a huge monotonous block of mature conifer trees in a plantation.

The 'edge effect'

You are most likely to see the greatest variety of birds at the edges of a habitat, where it meets one or more other habitats. The margins of a wood, for example, are likely to produce more species than its interior. You are also more likely to see the birds there, as they come out into the open. If there is a river, a lake or a patch of marshy ground next to a wood, then you may be able to see another range of species.

The importance of water

Water attracts a wide range of species such as Swallows, martins, warblers and finches that visit the waterside to drink, bathe or feed, as well as obviously wetland birds such as Grey Herons, ducks and waders. It is much easier to see shy woodland species, such as Hawfinches, by concealing yourself and remaining quietly near a woodland pool or stream in summer than searching among trees or dense vegetation.

Birds in the wrong places

While knowledge of habitats is crucial, you should always bear in mind the fact that birds are highly mobile and can sometimes turn up anywhere. Thus, although Leach's Petrels and Puffins spend most of their lives far out at sea, visiting remote islands and coastal cliffs only to breed, they may occasionally be blown far inland by severe storms, and turn up on an urban reservoir; indeed, a Puffin was once encountered walking up the Strand, in the heart of London!

Migrants often find themselves in atypical habitats, and you should be prepared, for example, for the initial surprise of seeing a Long-eared Owl winging its way in across the sea from Scandinavia on an autumn afternoon at a treeless east coast observatory.

TOWNS, PARKS AND GARDENS

The best place to begin birdwatching is close to home. If you have a garden, you can watch through a window, using the house as a hide.

Most garden birds were originally woodland birds. Nationwide, gardens and allotments form a huge habitat mosaic of great importance to birds, as they provide cover, food, nesting and roosting sites. The larger and more varied the plot, and the nearer it is to other habitats such as woods and rivers, the more species it will attract – but even a small city garden will have birds worth watching. You can encourage a greater range by providing bird tables and nut feeders, nestboxes and water in the form of a bird bath or pond. Planting shrubs that provide cover, nest sites and/or food (insects or berries) also brings in the birds.

It is surprising how much you can see if you watch regularly. Looking out of my study window in the heart of north London, I may see a Sparrowhawk or Kestrel fly past, or a Grey Heron, Cormorant, or flock of Mallards or Canada Geese on their way to and from the local canal and park lake, as well as the more predictable Blue Tits, Great Tits, Robins, Blackbirds and other typical garden birds. Swifts and House Martins hunt for insects overhead in summer, and on an autumn night I can hear the thin lisping calls of a passing flock of Redwings newly arrived from northern Europe. A short trip to a nearby reservoir adds a variety of ducks, gulls and waders, as well as the chance of a Kingfisher or a scarce migrant such as a Black Tern in autumn.

Parks are excellent places to get to know a wider variety of birds. A lake is likely to contain Mute Swans, Canada Geese, Mallard, Moorhens and Coots, and perhaps also other ducks. Diving ducks, such as Tufted Ducks and Pochards, favour deeper water, and other species may turn up in winter, like the small parties of Shovelers that have visited my local London park lake.

Although they may not be the most pleasant places to spend a day's birdwatching, refuse dumps are often teeming with Starlings, Carrion Crows, Rooks and especially gulls, squabbling over the rich pickings of our throwaway society or the insects attracted by the rotting rubbish. In winter, you may see rarer species such as a Glaucous or Iceland Gull among the common Black-headed, Herring and Lesser Black-backed Gulls, or a Short-eared Owl hunting for voles above an overgrown area.

Filled-in gravel extraction pits, derelict industrial sites and other urban wastelands can also be great places for birds, including such scarce species as Little Ringed Plovers and Black Redstarts as well as the more familiar Robins, Wrens and so on.

A large suburban garden like this could attract 30 or even more species of birds

FARMLAND

Over 70 per cent of the land area of the British Isles is farmland. It can be divided into two chief types of habitat: arable land where crops are raised, and pasture, for grazing livestock. Although the birds are often harder to find and less approachable, the range of species is usually much wider than you will find in your garden or local park.

Within the two main types, there is a great variety of farmland habitats, from lowland cereal growing areas to remote upland sheep farms. The best for birds are the more traditional farms, with a mix of crops and livestock and a variety of features including hedges, woods and ponds. Here, a wide range of birds may breed, from Swallows, Pied Wagtails, Stock Doves and Barn Owls among farm buildings to Skylarks, Grey and Red-legged Partridges and Lapwings in the fields, and many species, such as Yellowhammers and Whitethroats, in the hedgerows, while winter brings different birds, including Golden Plovers, Redwings and Fieldfares.

Increasingly, however, intensive methods of farming threaten many birds, common species as well as rarer ones. Skylarks, for instance, could once be heard throughout open farmland, but have declined dramatically in many places, as grassland is ploughed and the trend to sowing cereals in autumn rather than spring reduces their food supply. Many

FARMS ON THE FRINGES

Upland and western farms contain exciting birds such as Buzzards, Ravens, Stonechats and Wheatears. Even more local are Choughs, almost entirely confined to traditionally close-cropped pasture or heath above coastal cliffs in some parts of west Wales, a few western isles of Scotland and south and west Ireland, and Cirl Buntings, nowadays restricted almost entirely to farmland in south Devon.

species are damaged by pesticides and herbicides, too. The destruction of thousands of miles of ancient hedgerows to accommodate combine harvesters and other large machinery has led to major declines of some of our most familiar farmland birds, from Turtle Doves to Yellowhammers and Tree Sparrows. Where hedgerows remain, the older, wider, taller hedgerows with a greater mix of different bushes and trees contain the greatest variety of birds, but even here mechanized hedge cutters can reduce numbers.

The advent of 'set-aside' schemes and the encouragement towards planting hedges, trees and wild flowers, as well as leaving strips of land around the margins of fields free of pesticides and herbicides, have helped to some extent, but the problem of disappearing habitats is still a major one.

Mixed farms, with crops and livestock as well as plenty of hedges, are best for birds

WOODLAND BIRDWATCHING

Only about 8 per cent of Britain's land surface is now wooded, with even less (5 per cent) in Ireland, but woods can still be good places for birds. However, you should bear in mind that it can often be difficult to see birds in woods; a knowledge of their calls and songs is essential if you want to identify many of them.

Spring is the season when birds are most noticeable, as the woods burst into life, and residents and newly arrived summer visitors find mates and nest sites and then busy themselves seeking food for their young. The birds tend to be most widespread then, as each pair defends an exclusive territory.

Summer, too, is a good time, though the birds are more likely to be hidden among the dense foliage. The 'edge effect' described on page 20 is particularly important in woodland birdwatching; you are much more likely to see birds if you watch the margins or clearings, or at the side of a pond or lake. It is usually easier to watch bigger birds such as Buzzards, Sparrowhawks or rare Goshawks, Red Kites and Honey Buzzards, which breed in woods, from outside the wood, as they soar above it in spring display flights or search for food in surrounding open habitats.

By autumn, when the young have flown, most species flock together and roam the woods in search of food. You can spend long periods without seeing anything and then

WOODLAND MANAGEMENT

The best woods for birds are those where there is just the right amount of human management, allowing trees to die and decay. This provides more places for insects to live, opens up clearings where trees have fallen, and enables woodpeckers to bore holes that after a year or two are often abandoned and taken over by other hole-nesting birds such as tits, Nuthatches and Pied Flycatchers. Where there is a shortage of natural sites for hole-nesters, the provision of nestboxes has helped to increase populations.

Coppicing can also help woodland birds. This is the practice of cutting trees such as hornbeam, hazel and sweet chestnut right down to ground level every 10 years or so, and then allowing a dense growth of slim shoots to grow out of the stump, which can be used for fence posts, hurdles, firewood and so on. This dense growth and the layer of tangled shrubs and ground vegetation that develops in the early stages suits birds such as Wrens and Garden Warblers, which like skulking in the undergrowth, and in particular the Nightingale in some parts of southern England.

suddenly encounter a mixed flock of tits, Goldcrests and other small birds bustling past you, or a flock of Siskins, Redpolls or other finches flying overhead or feeding in the trees. This is a good time to practise your identification skills on a good variety of familiar and not so familiar species.

Winter can be a rather unproductive time for the woodland birdwatcher, since many birds have migrated south to the Mediterranean and Africa, and numbers of those that remain feed outside the woods and return only to roost in the warmer, more sheltered conditions there.

You are likely to see most birds by adopting a 'sit-and-wait' technique or, especially in autumn and winter, by walking slowly and quietly through the wood, pausing to look, and, especially, listen. As soon as you hear or see something, stop and wait until the feeding flock reaches you; you will often be rewarded with very close views as the birds are preoccupied with finding food.

Generally speaking, woods in the south and east of the country contain more bird species than those in the north and west. Also, the larger the wood, the more species it will tend to contain, since it can offer them a wider range of habitat diversity and more food.

Beechwoods include some special birds

OAKWOODS

The most widespread type of woodland in Britain is oak woodland. Oakwoods are of two main kinds: pedunculate oak, found mainly on the deeper, richer soils of the southern and eastern lowlands, and sessile oak, restricted chiefly to the shallower, poorer, more acid soils of the northern and western uplands.

Pedunculate oakwoods usually have a complex structure, with ash, beech, sycamore, holly and other trees mixed with the oaks, hawthorn, elder, ivy and other shrubs, as well as brambles and a rich ground layer of dog's mercury, wood anemones and other wildflowers. They are particularly rich in birdlife, because they provide a living for a great variety of huge numbers of insects and other invertebrates, on which many birds feed, from tits, warblers, thrushes and woodpeckers to that remarkable woodland wader, the Woodcock.

Sessile oakwoods are very different. They often grow along the sides of river valleys and on hill slopes. In rocky areas at higher altitudes, the old trees are stunted and gnarled, but they grow tall and slender at lower levels. Birches and rowan trees may grow beneath the oaks, but the shrub and ground vegetation layers are often sparse, and may be further reduced by sheep grazing. A trio of beautiful birds is characteristic of the sessile oakwoods: Wood Warbler, Redstart and Pied Flycatcher. The first two are shared with beechwoods, but the latter is more confined to sessile oaks. Buzzards and Sparrowhawks are common breeders, and in parts of Central Wales they are joined by the rare Red Kite.

BEECH AND OTHER WOODLANDS

Beechwoods, found mainly in southern England, especially in the Chilterns, North and South Downs, and Hampshire, contain relatively few species, since the big, high-crowned, dense-canopied trees cut off most of the sunlight from the ground below. The dense shade results in little undergrowth, so that birds that rely on shrubs or ground vegetation for nest sites or feeding cannot find a home there. However, two of the special birds that can live in these conditions are the Wood Warbler and Redstart, and others, like Marsh Tits and Nuthatches, are particularly numerous here. If there is a lake or river, you may even see Mandarin Ducks, exotic introductions from the Far East.

In winter, you may be lucky to chance upon a roving flock of Bramblings, visitors from Scandinavia, Finland and Russia, searching for beechmast (the fruit of the tree), often with their more familiar relatives the Chaffinches. Even more exciting is the sight of a flock of Hawfinches. These are

Oakwoods contain huge numbers of insects, providing food for rich bird populations

extremely elusive birds, rarely seen in spring and summer when they remain high in the trees, but slightly easier to find when they feed on the ground in autumn and winter; they are most likely where hornbeam is mixed with the beech or other trees.

Birch trees, often mixed with clumps of Scots pine, grow on the edges of moorland in the north and west and also around heaths in the south. Breeding birds may include Tree Pipits as well as the more widespread and common Chaffinches, Willow Warblers, Wrens and Robins; in parts of the Highlands, Redwings, common here as winter visitors, breed in tiny numbers in birchwoods.

Alders, often mixed with willows, may replace oakwoods in damp valleys and the waterlogged edges of rivers and lakes. These stands of alder and willow can be very rich in birdlife throughout the year, with a good chance of Lesser Spotted Woodpeckers, as well as finches (especially Redpolls and Siskins) and commoner species such as Wrens, Robins and Willow Warblers.

MIXED WOODLAND

Mixed woodland, where a scattering of conifers adds different species such as Goldcrests, Coal Tits and Crossbills, is often very productive. Sparrowhawks, though hunting over a wide range of woodlands and hedgerows, prefer conifers for nesting.

Plantations hold a good variety of birds

CONIFEROUS WOODLAND

Coniferous woodland, too, is of several types. Large tracts of mature plantation can be very monotonous, with the dense, dark foliage of the regularly spaced trees creating an underlying gloom in which little undergrowth can survive. Here there may be few birds apart from Goldcrests, Coal Tits, Chaffinches and Woodpigeons, but clearings and rides attract a wider range of species, especially where a mixture of natural and artificial clearings occur among blocks of trees of varying ages.

Such varied plantations can contain a wealth of species such as Redpolls, Siskins, Crossbills and, very locally, Goshawks. As well as Tawny Owls, you may be lucky enough to find Long-eared Owls, especially in Ireland, where Tawny Owls do not occur.

Young plantations

With their mixture of small trees, heath and grassland, young plantations often contain a rich variety of birds in summer, including Tree Pipits, Whinchats, Grasshopper Warblers, Redpolls and Yellowhammers.

Locally, very young plantations are home to Hen Harriers and Short-eared Owls in the north, and Nightjars and Woodlarks in the south. Where young conifers border moorland in the north, dwindling numbers of Black Grouse breed.

SCOTS PINE FOREST

Our prime coniferous habitat for birds is the ancient Caledonian forest of the Scottish Highlands. Although a mere remnant of its former area, these magnificent stands of native Scots pine contain an exciting range of rare birds. Often far more open than forestry plantations, they may also contain birch, rowan, juniper or alder scrub, and a ground layer of heather, bilberry and bracken.

As well as the commoner tit species, they are home to Crested Tits, which although widespread on the Continent, are confined here to old pinewoods in the central Highlands, especially the native ones. As well as Black Grouse along the margins, the Caledonian forests hold their giant relative the Capercaillie. Instead of the widespread Crossbill, you should seek out the stouter-billed Scottish Crossbill – the only species unique to the British Isles. There are many Buzzards, Sparrowhawks and Kestrels, and scattered pairs of Goshawks, Golden Eagles, and, where there are lakes, Ospreys.

HEATHLANDS

Sadly, although once occupying large areas, heathland is an increasingly rare and threatened habitat in the British Isles, as in the rest of Europe; much of what remains is found in these islands.

Heaths tend to consist of flat or gently rolling expanses of sand or gravel overlying a layer of acid peat. Although usually poor habitats for birds in winter, because their impoverished soils support few berry-bearing shrubs or insects, they come into their own in summer, when they are home to a select group of exciting birds.

As its name suggests, heathland is usually dominated by heather. Often there is gorse too, and scattered Scots pines, birches or other trees, providing shelter and food for birds. As well as the large area of grass heathland, or breck, in Breckland, East Anglia, extensive heaths are found in a narrow belt extending from Surrey through the New Forest in Hampshire to Dorset and east Devon.

Afforestation and development for housing, industrial development, roads and so on all present threats to what is left of our heathlands, but protection in nature reserves and the creation of new heathlands is helping to ensure that the special birds of this habitat continue to delight birdwatchers.

A real heathland speciality is the Dartford Warbler. This jaunty little bird is restricted to lowland heaths in the southernmost counties of England, especially Hampshire, Dorset and Devon, though with the help of conservation programmes, it is slowly spreading and increasing. As it is a year-round resident, on the edge of its range, numbers can drop rapidly in severe winters.

That handsome, dashing falcon the Hobby is also on the up, and still holds its own on many heaths. Linnets, Yellowhammers and Meadow and Tree Pipits are much more widespread, the pipits attracting Cuckoos to lay their eggs in their nests. On warm, still summer nights the strange churring song of the Nightjar can still be heard on some of our heaths, but numbers have decreased greatly, and it is now more often found in young or recently felled conifer plantations. One of very few birds to have become effectively extinct as a breeding bird in Britain is the Red-backed Shrike, once a regular heathland breeder.

One of its last strongholds was Breckland, which still contains its own special mix of other interesting birds. As well as the common heathland species, there are still a few Stone Curlews, although their numbers are falling as the stony heaths are fragmented by forestry plantations and increasing development and human disturbance. The rare Woodlark still pours out its passionately lovely song among barer areas.

Heathland contains exciting breeding birds, but is increasingly under threat

MOORLANDS AND MOUNTAINS

Some of our most exciting birds live on moors and mountains – amid breathtaking scenery. These habitats are mainly in north and southwest England, Wales, Scotland and parts of Ireland.

Birdlife here is generally sparse, because the poor, acid soil, low temperatures and high rainfall and snowfall mean that relatively few plants grow, and there is less insect and other prey. The higher you climb, the harsher the conditions and the fewer the birds, especially in winter. Moorlands are also found down to sea level in the far north of Scotland.

On the lower hills, the greater variety of birds includes Hen Harriers, Merlins and Short-eared Owls, as well as the more widespread Buzzards, Kestrels, Skylarks, Linnets and, especially, Meadow Pipits. Extensive areas of heather are home to Red Grouse, while a mixture of rocks and close-cropped grass brings Wheatears. Another mountain and moorland speciality, found among rocky outcrops, gullies and scree slopes, is the Ring Ouzel, while Ravens and Peregrines, too, find a stronghold. In Mid-Wales, Red Kites may range up from rough farmland on the upland fringes onto the moorland proper.

Moorlands also provide safe nesting sites for some of the waders familiar to us on lowland coasts and estuaries in winter.

Golden Plovers, Dunlin, Curlews and Snipe are more widespread, while Lapwings and Redshank favour grassy moors and blanket bogs (deep peat bogs carpeting large areas of northern uplands in areas of high rainfall), and Oystercatchers, Ringed Plovers and Common Sandpipers breed on shingle along upland streams and rivers. Herring, Great and Lesser Black-backed, and Common Gulls breed locally on boggy moorland, while Black-headed Gulls and Common Terns favour rushy pools. In Scotland, the Greenshank breeds on the remote, wet moors of the far west and north. The extraordinary Flow Country of Sutherland and Caithness – a unique mosaic of blanket bog and small shallow pools, one of the last great wilderness areas in Europe – contains breeding wader and bird of prey populations of international importance. Sadly, this wonderful area is threatened by development of peatlands for commercial forestry.

The remote mountains and moorlands of the Highlands are also the domain of Golden Eagles and Ptarmigan, along with small numbers of Dotterel and a handful of Snow Buntings. When searching for these birds, remember that remote mountain areas can be dangerous places, with difficult terrain and sudden changes of weather. Also, make sure you keep disturbance of these rare and vulnerable birds to a minimum.

Though quite empty in winter, mountains and moors hold scarce breeding birds

RIVERS AND STREAMS

These long, linear habitats pass through a wide range of landscapes, from upland to lowland, so their birdlife varies accordingly.

The clear, shallow, fast-flowing rocky streams of our northern and western uplands have two special birds of their own, the Dipper and the Grey Wagtail, although they also breed in smaller numbers on lower, slower rivers that have weirs and waterfalls producing fast-flowing water, and they may visit lowland rivers and lakes in winter. In the north and west, Common Sandpipers also nest by upland streams, and, where woodlands fringe stretches of upland rivers, so do small numbers of Red-breasted Mergansers and Goosanders. Even fewer Goldeneyes breed in similar sites, their numbers increased by RSPB provision of nestboxes. Ringed Plovers, Oystercatchers and Common Terns breed on shingle banks in upland streams in Scotland.

When rivers reach the lowlands, they become deeper and wider, meandering slowly across the landscape, and gathering increasing amounts of sediment. The lush vegetation this encourages provides cover, nest sites and food for a wide range of species, from Mute Swans and Moorhens to Sedge Warblers. Kingfishers and Sand Martins breed in soft river banks, while Grey Herons often visit rivers to search for fish or frogs. Riverside trees may hold Willow Tits, Chiffchaffs and other small birds, while dense fringing vegetation is often home to Sedge Warblers.

The chief threats to lowland rivers come from the replacement of natural banks with barren concrete sides, and from the nitrates and phosphates from agricultural fertilizers and sewage effluent, which overload the water with nutrients and deplete oxygen. Another problem facing rivers, especially in the uplands, is the acidification of the water along stretches bordered by large new conifer plantations. This kills off the insect prey for birds such as Dippers.

LAKES AND PONDS

Most of these freshwater habitats in the uplands of England and Wales, together with the lochs of Scotland and the loughs of Ireland, contain deep, acid water with few nutrients. Supporting few plants and invertebrates, they provide little in the way of food and cover for birds. Nonetheless, upland lakes are home to some of our rarest breeding birds, the Black-throated and Red-throated

An unspoilt lowland stream like this one can support a wide variety of birds

Divers of the lochs of the Scottish Highlands and islands (though the Red-throated flies to the sea to fish).

Other fish-eating birds you may find breeding in tree holes or holes in rocks and banks by wooded upland lakes and lochs in spring and summer are Red-breasted Merganser and Goosander, while Teal and Mallard and much smaller numbers of Wigeon are the only dabbling ducks that breed on upland waters. In winter, there is usually little to see, though some northern lakes contain small numbers of Goldeneyes or a family of Whooper Swans from the far north of Europe. Those at lower altitudes may have Common Sandpipers at their edges.

In lowland Britain, there are relatively few natural lakes left, with nutrient-rich, alkaline water. But where they provide shelter and nesting sites in the form of a dense fringe of reeds or sedges, they support rich bird populations, including Great Crested and Little Grebes, Coots, Moorhens and perhaps Water Rails. There may also be wildfowl such as Mute Swans, Mallards and, locally, Gadwalls and Shovelers; if the water is deep enough, it may attract diving ducks such as Tufted Ducks and Pochards. If there are trees, there may be a colony of Grey Herons, and Kingfishers sometimes fish in secluded, well-vegetated bays at the mouths of streams.

In winter, a good lake will act like a magnet in attracting a great variety of waterbirds, including up to a dozen species of wildfowl and, if you are lucky, a Black-necked or Slavonian Grebe, while a variety of migrant gulls, terns and waders – or even an Osprey – may turn up and linger for a while in spring or autumn. In Scotland, well-vegetated lowland lochs may provide nesting sites for Common Gulls as well as the more usual Black-headed Gulls, and Black-necked and Slavonian Grebes breed at a few favoured sites. Winter brings many wildfowl, not just ducks and swans but also grey geese, sometimes in spectacular numbers.

At some lowland lakes, drainage and disturbance from boats and water-skiers, along with pollution, pose serious threats to the birds. The loss of many farmland ponds, too, through drainage or neglect, reduces numbers of birds such as Moorhens, Mallards and Sedge Warblers.

RESERVOIRS AND FLOODED GRAVEL PITS

The creation of lowland reservoirs has helped to make up for the loss of natural lakes and they can be very rich habitats for birds (upland reservoirs, like their natural counterparts, tend to be poor in birdlife).

Cormorants are increasingly common inland on reservoirs, while the odd diver may pause to rest and feed on its way to the coast; a variety of waders, as well as other birds such as Little Gulls and Black Terns, may pass through briefly on spring or autumn passage. A good crop of seeding weeds on the banks in late summer and autumn is likely to bring in large flocks of Linnets and other finches. As the water level rises in winter, the seeds are washed into the reservoir, providing food for Canada Geese and such dabbling ducks as Mallards, Teals and Shovelers.

Gravel pits that have been flooded after extraction has finished can also be great places for birds. Although their steep-sided banks of gravel or sandy soil attract few waders, they can be meccas for huge flocks of wildfowl in winter, especially diving ducks, including the occasional Scaup or Common Scoter, or (in southern England) the chance of seeing a small party of Smews.

Islands of gravel or purpose-built artificial rafts on some pits, as well as reservoirs, may persuade migrant Common Terns to stop and nest, along with the more usual Great Crested and Little Grebes, Mallards and Canada Geese, while the vertical sandy banks may hold a colony of Sand Martins. Little Ringed Plovers nest in increasing numbers where there are flat areas of disturbed ground, especially where work is still in progress. Ruddy Ducks breed in increasing numbers on reed-fringed flooded gravel pits and pools, especially in parts of the Midlands and Cheshire.

With careful management, reservoirs can be great places for birds

FRESHWATER MARSHES AND REEDBEDS

Waterlogged land attracts a range of exciting birds to breed and feed. Sadly, wetlands are becoming increasingly scarce and local, and many have already been drained for farmland or other development. If they are not kept wet, they will dry out and become covered with shrubs and trees. Careful management schemes are necessary to prevent this.

Marshes are formed when rushes and other waterside plants 'take over' a bend of a slow-moving river, say, and grow into a narrow belt of vegetation. They also form more extensive areas at the margins of shallow lakes.

Such wetlands add variety to the birdlife of the area, with species like Sedge Warblers and Reed Buntings breeding. Larger marshes, with a mosaic of rushes, grasses, reeds, and aquatic plants interspersed with patches of shallow water, are great bird habitats. The soil consists of deep layers of organic peat derived from slow accumulation of decaying plants over thousands of years. There are two basic sorts: bogs and fens.

Bogs

The acid, nutrient-poor conditions in bogs favour the growth of spongy sphagnum moss and sedges. There are four types of bog.

Valley bogs occupy small valleys or channels where drainage is poor. They are found in some heathlands in southern England, particularly in Surrey, Hampshire and Dorset. Special breeding birds include Lapwings, Snipes and Redshanks, as well as the more widespread wetland species such as Moorhens, Mallards and Reed Buntings.

Basin bogs are much smaller, occurring where stagnant water collects in hollows, and attract fewer birds. Most are in lowland areas of the Midlands, northern England and southern Scotland.

Raised bogs develop on the flood plains of rivers and estuaries. They usually have gently undulating surfaces with little open water. The relatively few birds that breed on them include Mallards, Curlews, Snipes, Common Gulls, Cuckoos and Meadow Pipits.

Blanket bogs develop in uplands in areas of high rainfall; see page 27.

Fens

Fens contain nutrient-rich, rather alkaline water. They form in continually waterlogged depressions, and many contain a rich variety of vegetation, from water lilies and other aquatic plants to reeds and sedges where the peat accumulates. If the fenland vegetation is not cut and kept free from encroaching bushes, it gradually develops into scrub, known as carr, in which buckthorn, alder, willows and other shrubs and trees form a dense, low tangle.

The few big reedbeds that remain contain specialities such as Bearded Tits and Bitterns

These different stages in fenland vegetation produce varied habitats for birds: for example, the wetter swamps attract ducks, Moorhens and Water Rails; marshy scrub suits Grasshopper Warblers and, locally in southern England, Cetti's Warbler; and the drier carrs are home to Redpolls, Lesser Spotted Woodpeckers, Willow Warblers and many other warblers on migration.

Once spread over the flood plains of many of our lowland river valleys, most natural fens are now long gone, drained and developed for agriculture. But not all interference has been damaging; ironically, almost all the fens we see today are a by-product of human activity. The most famous is the Norfolk Broads, which resulted from peat extraction in medieval times; other smaller but still important sites include Stodmarsh, in the Stour Valley, Kent, created by subsidence from coal mining. There are still notable areas of fen in north-east Ireland.

Reedbeds

Most large reedbeds have been drained or become overgrown as a result of drying out, choked with dead reeds. Those few that have escaped such a fate are precious places for some of our rarest and most specialized birds as well as a wealth of other wetland species. The most important remnants are in the Norfolk and Suffolk Broads and coasts, along the River Humber, at Leighton Moss in Lancashire, in Anglesey in North Wales and in places along the south coast of England such as Radipole Lake, Dorset. These rare and fragile habitats need careful management of water levels and regular cutting to prevent drying out and the invasion of scrub.

The fast-declining Bittern still just hangs on as a breeder only in the largest reedbeds, though the odd individual may wander to smaller areas of reeds in winter. Marsh Harriers are also reedbed breeders, able to colonize smaller areas of reed as long as they are not disturbed, though they also need large areas of unimproved open land nearby for hunting. Bearded Tits are another reedbed speciality. Even scarcer is Savi's Warbler; birds from the Continent have recolonized reedbeds in eastern and southern Britain in recent decades.

Water Rails thrive in large reedbeds but, like many reedbed birds, are usually hard to see, though frost and ice in winter forces them out to search for food on the open mud and in the shallows. In winter, too, Hen

Strumpshaw Fen, in the Norfolk Broads, is protected as an RSPB reserve

Harriers often hunt over the reeds, replacing the Marsh Harriers, most of which move south as far as Africa; Barn and Short-eared Owls also quarter the reedbeds in search of prey, the latter by day as well as at dusk.

Surprisingly, reedbeds are also often occupied by Pheasants – though their original habitat in Asia was mainly reedswamps – and Blue Tits and Wrens are frequent visitors, too, in search of insects and spiders. Reedbeds are also important to migrants: huge numbers of Swallows and Sand Martins roost in them in autumn, as do Pied and Yellow Wagtails, Starlings, Reed Buntings and, locally, Corn Buntings. In turn, these often attract Hobbies and Sparrowhawks searching for prey.

Wet grasslands

Another dwindling habitat of great importance for birds is wet grassland. The most significant areas that have escaped drainage are the Somerset Levels, the North Kent Marshes and the winter-flooded Ouse Washes on the borders of Cambridgeshire and Norfolk. Nesting wildfowl include scarce breeders such as Shovelers, Garganeys, Pintails and Pochards, and these areas are strongholds for breeding waders, too, such as Snipes, Redshanks and Curlews, and small numbers of Black-tailed Godwits and Ruffs at the Ouse Washes. This wonderful site is thronged with wildfowl in winter, including huge numbers of ducks, and is a major wintering site for Bewick's Swans.

COASTAL HABITATS

The varied coastline of the British Isles, lengthened immensely by its masses of convolutions, provides food, shelter and breeding sites for huge numbers of a wide range of birds. The different types of coastline have their own special mixture of birds, discussed here and on pages 34-7.

Rocky shores occur mainly in the north and west, many of them with towering sea-cliffs that attract breeding seabirds which are absent from flatter rocky shores with their rock pools, heaps of seaweed and mussel beds. Low-lying softer coasts predominate in the south and east, and are very varied, including sandy beaches, dunes, shingle banks, brackish coastal lagoons and shallow estuaries and broad, sheltered bays with extensive mudflats and fringing saltmarshes.

ESTUARIES AND SALTMARSHES

Estuaries, while home to few breeding birds, are crucially important to migrant and wintering waders and wildfowl. Mudflats exposed by the tide often teem with worms, crabs, molluscs and other invertebrates,

providing a rich source of food for the birds. As many as 1.5 million waders visit our estuaries each winter to find food and shelter – about 40 per cent of the total visiting northwest Europe. Of the 200 or so estuaries in the British Isles, over 30 are sites of major international importance. Some, such as the Wash between Norfolk and Lincolnshire, Morecambe Bay, between Lancashire and Cumbria, and the Solway Firth, between Cumbria and southeast Scotland, are vast complexes including several estuaries.

Large estuaries make for superb birdwatching, but getting near the birds can be difficult. When the tide is out, waders will be scattered over a great expanse of mud, and may be difficult to see well, even with a telescope, but, as the tide comes in, they become concentrated closer to shore. At high tide, the birds fly to roost on the few higher sand or mud banks that are left exposed, or onto a stretch of shoreline, often in huge, densely packed flocks. Consult tide tables and time your visit accordingly for the best views.

Different parts of the estuary contain different groups of species, their distribution

Our estuaries are home to over 2 million waders and wildfowl each winter

governed primarily by the tide. Dunlins, Redshanks and Grey Plovers, for instance, prefer to spread out over the inner areas, while Knots are found in the more open regions further out, forming larger, more concentrated feeding flocks. These can be huge at favoured sites such as the Wash and Morecambe Bay, gathering into vast, densely packed roosts at high tide, and flying around in swirling flocks when disturbed. Curlews and Bar-tailed Godwits may join the other waders of the inner flats, but feed particularly nearer the mouth of the estuary, where the mud is mixed with sand and there are many lugworms for them to extract with their long bills. Oystercatchers, too, occur there.

On many estuaries, the mudflats are backed by saltmarsh, also a major habitat for birds. There is often a maze of larger creeks and smaller channels (or runnels), whose muddy sides provide feeding and resting sites. Snipes and Jack Snipes are particularly fond of these sheltered places, as are Redshanks, and Curlews visit them to feed on crabs.

A few species breed on the saltmarsh, including Redshanks, Lapwings, Black-

THREATS TO ESTUARIES

With such a wealth of birds, including huge numbers of wintering waders and wildfowl from as far away as Scandinavia, Siberia, Canada and Greenland, it is vital that our estuaries and saltmarshes are allowed to flourish. Sadly, however, of all the endangered habitats in these islands, they are among the most vulnerable. They are under constant threat from land reclamation for agriculture, industrial sites, marinas and other development, as well as from pollution and plans for tidal barriers. The RSPB and other conservation bodies have a difficult but crucial task ahead of them.

headed Gulls, Meadow Pipits, Reed Buntings and, more locally, terns. But it is at migration times and in winter that saltmarshes and estuaries attract most birds. Shallow saltmarsh pools attract migrating waders in spring and autumn, and are a good place to look for such species as Spotted Redshanks, Ruffs and Little Stints, especially in autumn. Gulls may include the odd rarity, and terns often pass through in good numbers.

Shelducks are common and widespread, while many other wildfowl from northern Europe spend the winter on our estuaries. Like the Shelducks, Brent Geese feed on the mudflats, grazing on eelgrass and algae, as well as on saltmarsh creeks and, increasingly, on arable fields bordering the estuary; other geese are scarcer and more local. Wigeons are grazing ducks that feed on the lower reaches of saltmarsh, while deeper creeks may contain Pintails, Shovelers or Teals as well as Mallards, searching for seeds or invertebrates.

The rich crop of seeds produced by the saltmarsh plants also attracts flocks of finches. Many of these will be commoner species such as Linnets and Greenfinches, but you may come across a flock of Twites, which winter almost exclusively on saltmarshes.

Such concentrations of birds in winter attract birds of prey, such as Sparrowhawks, Merlins and Peregrines. Short-eared Owls quarter the saltmarsh in search of voles, and along the east coast Rough-legged Buzzards do the same – although in most years they are very scarce, irregular and unpredictable.

Out on the estuary, Cormorants are a common sight. Other birds may include the odd Slavonian Grebe, Great Crested Grebes, divers, and sea ducks such as Goldeneyes, Scaups or Red-breasted Mergansers.

MUDDY, SANDY AND SHINGLY SHORES

Soft coasts may contain areas of mud, sand or shingle. Muddy shores have similar birds to those on estuaries (page 32), but sandy and shingly ones are much less hospitable places, with far fewer species. Gulls are usually to be seen, flying overhead or offshore or resting on the beach. Small numbers of waders such as Curlews, Grey Plovers, Dunlin and Turnstones may feed or rest there.

One wader in particular, the Sanderling, really favours sandy shores. Small flocks scurry like clockwork toys along the edge of the waves to snap up morsels of food; they are most numerous on passage and in winter, but a few non-breeders remain here in summer.

Two waders, the Oystercatcher and Ringed Plover, nest on shingle beaches, and, more locally, there are breeding colonies of gulls and terns. Little Terns are almost entirely restricted to this habitat for breeding. Winter brings Snow Buntings, Lapland Buntings and Shorelarks to favoured sites along eastern coasts, where they can also feed on nearby saltmarshes and rough farmland. It is always worth looking out to sea, where there may be divers, grebes, skuas, auks and sea ducks, including flocks of scoters, Eiders and, especially in Scotland, Long-tailed Ducks.

Shingle beaches include the huge area of Dungeness, in Kent, a real mecca for birdwatchers, with a wide range of habitats. Protected by an RSPB reserve and with a thriving bird observatory, it boasts an impressive list of birds. Like other places on the east and south coasts, it is a great place to see migrants, such exciting birds as Hoopoes and Firecrests as well as the commoner species, and it has plenty of interest in summer and winter, too. Other good shingle beaches are on the coasts of East Anglia, Dorset, Wales, Cumbria and parts of Scotland.

Coastal lagoons

Behind some beaches lie large lagoons of fresh or brackish water. Most of the natural ones have been drained, but new ones are created in nature reserves. They can be great places for birdwatching at all seasons. Some waders, such as Ringed Plovers, Snipes and Redshanks, breed around their edges. At some coastal lagoons in East Anglia and Kent, especially on the RSPB reserves at Minsmere and Havergate in Suffolk and at Titchwell in Norfolk, there are increasing numbers of one of our most beautiful waders, the Avocet. Spring and autumn bring a superb selection of migrant waders, rarities as well as the more usual species, and other exciting birds such as Black Terns and Little Gulls. Wintering wildfowl such as Wigeons, Gadwalls and Shovelers are easier to see on a lagoon than on a large saltmarsh.

Shingle beaches hold major colonies of breeding birds such as Ringed Plovers

Sand dunes

In some places, such as Norfolk, Devon, Wales, Cumbria, Northumberland and many parts of Scotland, there are large areas of sand dunes. Stabilized by marram grass, they contain a small but select group of breeding birds. For example, Shelducks nest in abandoned rabbit holes, and Eiders breed in large numbers on northern dunes. Black-headed, Herring and Lesser Black-backed Gulls and, more locally, Sandwich Terns, gather in big, noisy colonies; other species breeding on dunes include Grey Partridges, Ringed Plovers, Skylarks, Meadow Pipits, Wheatears, Stonechats and Reed Buntings.

Where the dunes are extensive and permanent, heath or grassland can develop behind them, and this is often invaded by scrub or planted with conifers. This succession of different zones of vegetation makes for a greater variety of birds. Small birds such as Wrens, Dunnocks, Willow Warblers, Whitethroats, Linnets and Yellowhammers breed among the scrub, which also attracts many migrants, especially in autumn. Large numbers of newly arrived thrushes gorge themselves on berries, and warblers also take advantage of this ready source of food before embarking on their long migrations. On a good day, the dunes and scrub may be full of Redstarts, Pied Flycatchers, Wheatears and other small birds,

MACHAIR

Machair is a very special habitat found on the Atlantic coasts of some of the Western Isles of Scotland, Orkney and Shetland, and in a few places in Ireland. Above the beach and a narrow zone of dunes, there is a flat plain of white shell-sand, carpeted with grass and wildflowers. Further back, there is often a loch, and then a zone of grassland and marshes. This rich and complex habitat contains higher concentrations of breeding waders than anywhere else in the British Isles, including much of our entire breeding population of Ringed Plovers, as well as many Oystercatchers, Lapwings, Dunlins, Snipes and Redshanks. Other birds breed there too, including Little Terns, Common Gulls and Corn Buntings, and almost all of the British Isles' tiny, threatened population of Corncrakes.

The machair is best developed in the Outer Hebrides, still cultivated by crofters on a strip rotation system. This preserves nesting and feeding places for a wide range of birds. Often, though, modern farming has caused declines, especially of Corncrakes.

and there is always the chance of a Red-breasted Flycatcher or even a rarer migrant.

Wet areas, called dune slacks, often form in the hollows between dunes. These may be visited by wintering waders and wildfowl.

Sand dunes provide nest sites and a haven for tired migrants

ROCKY SHORES

Low-level rocky shores have few breeding birds, apart from Rock Pipits and Wrens, and Eiders in the north, but a good variety of species, especially waders, feed and rest on them in winter and on spring and autumn migration. The waders include Curlews, Oystercatchers, Knots, Dunlins and Redshanks, and two rocky shore specialists, the Purple Sandpiper and Turnstone.

Other birds that can be seen foraging on rocky shores are a wide variety of gulls, as well as crows and Grey Herons; the strandline at the top of the shore is also visited by feeding Starlings, pipits, wagtails, finches, buntings and even the occasional Song Thrush, Kingfisher or Dipper in severe winters when the ground and water elsewhere are frozen.

SEA-CLIFFS

The magnificent cliffs that fringe many coastlines and islands, especially in north and west Britain and many parts of Ireland, contain some of the largest concentrations of seabirds in Europe. A visit to a big breeding colony in spring or early summer is an unforgettable experience, as you are surrounded by the constant comings and goings of thousands of birds and their tumultuous chorus of calls.

Each species has distinct preferences as to choice of nest site. Colonies of Puffins often nest in burrows on the grassy slopes of the cliff top, while Lesser Black-backed and Herring Gulls occupy grassy ledges, the latter generally near or just below the cliff edge, where Fulmars also nest. The more solitary Great Black-backed Gulls select the highest sites, often on top of a tall sea stack that has been isolated from the cliff by erosion.

Cormorants like to nest on broad ledges, often high up. Narrow ledges on the cliff face provide breeding sites for dense colonies of Guillemots and Kittiwakes, while Razorbills, often in ones and twos, prefer the darkness of deep clefts and cavities. Shags, too, often choose such secluded sites, sometimes low down, though they also nest on open ledges or among the tumble of boulders at the base of a cliff. Black Guillemots nest among the boulders too.

Other birds breed on the cliffs. Among birds of prey, Peregrines are found on many western and northern sea-cliffs, as well as Buzzards and Kestrels, a few Golden Eagles and a tiny reintroduced population of White-tailed Eagles in the west of Scotland. Ravens and, much more locally, Choughs also use sea-cliffs for breeding, as do the much more widespread Jackdaws and Carrion or Hooded Crows. Stock Doves sometimes colonize cavities in the cliff face, as do Rock Doves in the far north and west.

Sea-cliffs, especially in the north and west, contain magnificent seabird colonies

ISLANDS

Although many of the seabirds breed in greatest numbers on islands, some are island specialities. Most of our 188 000 pairs of Gannets (almost three-quarters of the entire world population) breed in big, noisy colonies on a handful of islands, although there are a few mainland sites, notably at Bempton Cliffs, Yorkshire. They usually choose ledges on sheer cliffs or huge stacks on which to nest, but at some sites up the tops as well. Manx Shearwaters, Storm Petrels and Leach's Petrels are burrow nesters. Over 90 per cent of the world population of Manx Shearwaters breeds on a number of islands off the west coasts of Britain and Ireland, with the largest colonies on the Inner Hebrides, the islands off south-west Wales, the North Wales island of Bardsey, and islands off the coast of Kerry in southwest Ireland. Storm Petrels have their strongholds on the northern islands of Scotland and on islands off the west coast of Ireland, while Leach's Petrels are much scarcer, restricted almost entirely to a few remote islands off the north and northwest coasts of Scotland.

Islands are great places for other birds, too. In Shetland, for instance, moorland holds almost the entire British breeding population of Whimbrel, along with many Arctic and Great Skuas and Arctic Terns. Many islands attract huge numbers of migrants, including many rarities, and there is a chain of island bird observatories, any of them well worth a visit, such as Fair Isle, to the south of Shetland, or Cape Clear, off the Cork coast. The Scilly Isles are justly famed for the huge numbers and great variety of migrant birds in spring and autumn, including rare wanderers from North America, Europe and Asia; they also have many other birds, including colonies of breeding seabirds such as Razorbills and Puffins.

THE OPEN SEA

Many seabirds, including those mentioned above, spend most of their lives out in the open sea, riding the waves in all weathers, and visit the coast only to breed. One way of seeing them is from a boat; special sea-going birdwatching trips on small boats are available, but are not to everyone's taste – though they may provide views of a wide range of seabirds, conditions are usually basic and the water often rough. Ferry trips across the Irish Sea or the English Channel are a more comfortable if less exciting alternative.

SEAWATCHING

The alternative to going out in search of the birds is to wait on a headland until they fly past. Seawatching, as this is known, has developed into quite an art. Most of the birds you will see may be well out to sea, often in conditions of poor visibility, so you will need a telescope and tripod as well as binoculars (see pages 38-9). To identify them, you will need to become familiar with the 'jizz' of each species (see page 18) as your views will often be fleeting and plumage details elusive. It is a good idea to get help from an experienced seawatcher.

The best seawatching sites are those on headlands that extend furthest into the sea, such as St Ives in Cornwall, Portland Bill in Dorset, Beachy Head in Sussex, Flamborough Head in Humberside, Fife Ness in Fife, or Brandon Point in Kerry. However, it is possible at the right time of year to see many seabirds from lesser promontories and even straight coasts. Ensure your watchpoint is at a good height above the sea (if you watch from low down you will miss birds further out) and provides reasonable comfort and protection, otherwise wind and rain will make it hard to find and watch the birds. If possible, keep the sun behind you; if it is in your eyes you will see only silhouettes.

How much seabird movement you will see and what species are involved depends on the geographical position, the time of year and, in particular, the wind. Peak times are the spring and autumn migrations, with concentrations of species at different times. Inshore gales blow seabirds closer to land – often close enough for you to get good views – and sometimes right inshore. A particularly productive time is after a storm has forced large numbers of migrating seabirds off course; in the lull that follows, you can see them returning to their usual routes.

Gannets and Fulmars can be seen offshore all year, especially near their breeding cliffs, where they stay for months. Manx Shearwaters are particularly abundant along some coasts, mainly between March and October, and, if you are lucky and in the right place, you may see a Great, Sooty or Cory's Shearwater in autumn. Storm and Leach's Petrels are harder to find, as they are small and usually low over the water; auks, too, skim the waves and can be hard to make out at a distance. Gulls and terns may be accompanied by skuas, especially in autumn – the best time for seawatching.

OBSERVING AND RECORDING

This last section of the book before the field guide itself goes beyond identifying birds and knowing where to find them, to techniques of actually observing species in the field and recording your findings. Knowing how best to use the various optical aids maximizes your chances of successful birdwatching, while an awareness of practical fieldcraft is the bedrock of good practice. Making notes of what you see, and when and where, can reinforce your knowledge as well as building into a permanent record of great value.

Finally, I have given information on societies and publications for those readers who may wish to take their birdwatching beyond the fledgling stage.

BINOCULARS

You can of course see common and easily approachable birds close up at a bird table or in a park but, for most birdwatching, a pair of binoculars is essential.

Choosing binoculars

The huge range available need not be daunting if you follow some basic rules and buy only from a specialist dealer.

● Price: between the extremes of too cheap and wildly expensive, there is a choice of reasonably priced models on the market that will serve you well for a lifetime. Their prices range from about £80 to £400.

● Magnification: binoculars are rated by two numbers, such as 7x50, 8x30, 9x40. The first is the magnification, the second the diameter in millimetres of the object lenses (the large lenses at the ends). Go for a magnification of between 7 and 10 times. A magnification of 6x will be inadequate for distant birds while at high magnifications such as 12x, the field of view will be small and the binoculars big, heavy and tiring to hold. Avoid zoom binoculars – they are rarely of good enough optical quality.

● Object lenses: best sizes for birdwatching are between 30mm and 50mm. Wider ones let in more light, so should give brighter images. But image brightness also depends on the quality, so a cheap pair of 8x50s will not produce such a clear image as a good quality pair of 8x30s. For all-round birdwatching, 8x30s or 8x40s are best.

● Weight and shape: ensure the binoculars are not too small and light, or too heavy – you may be carrying them all day (for this reason alone they should feel comfortable to hold).

FOCUSING BINOCULARS

Before using your binoculars, you must adjust the setting of the individual focusing wheel, located on one eyepiece, usually the right-hand one. This compensates for any difference between your eyes.

1 Point the binoculars at a handy object with fine detail, such as a car number plate.
2 Close your right eye or cover the right-hand lens and look through the left eyepiece.
3 Focus on your chosen object with the central focusing wheel until it is sharp.
4 Close your left eye or cover the left-hand lens and look at the same object with the right eye; do not touch the central focus, but turn the eyepiece focusing wheel until the image is blurred, then turn it back slowly until it is as sharp as possible.
5 Now, looking with both eyes, the stereoscopic image should appear precisely in focus. Memorize the eyepiece setting. From now on, you should move the eyepiece adjustment again only if it happens to have been changed somehow. Otherwise, leave it alone and use only the central focusing wheel.

Rubber armour protects binoculars from damage

● Eyecups: deep eyecups can be pushed up against the eyes, excluding unwanted light from the sides. Fold-down eyecups allow for spectacle wearers.

8x40 binoculars   *10x50 binoculars*

20x75 telescope

Generally, the higher the magnification, the smaller the field of view and the dimmer the image, as these images of a juvenile Knot show

Using binoculars

● Carry binoculars round your neck, never in one hand or by the strap – not only will it take you longer to get them to your eyes, but you might drop them. Shorten the straps, if necessary, so the binoculars are ready for instant action, sitting snugly on your chest, and not thumping painfully against your stomach each time you move.

● You must focus to the bird's distance from you. If the bird moves, you will need to make constant adjustments to keep it in focus, unless it is a long way away.

● To make out detail, you must hold your binoculars as steady as possible. It helps to support them near the far end, though this makes reaching the focusing wheel slow. You could also tuck your elbows into your sides or steady yourself against a tree.

● When you see a bird, do not look down at your binoculars before bringing them up to your eyes – it will be hard to find the bird, especially if it is flying. Keeping your eyes on the bird, raise the binoculars without looking at them. Focus as quickly as possible. Practise until your aim is accurate and your focusing almost automatic.

● Do not keep binoculars in their case except when storing or transporting them. If you have to fumble to get them out when a bird appears, you will miss it.

● **Never, ever,** look at the sun with binoculars or a telescope – it will blind you.

TELESCOPES

Telescopes are not essential, and are little use in a wood with their narrow field of view and lack of close focus. In open country, however, their high magnifications can transform birdwatching, giving good views of distant waders out on a mudflat or a group of auks out to sea. At closer ranges, telescopes allow you to see a bird with stunning clarity – useful for picking out the fine details of plumage.

Choosing telescopes

As with binoculars, buy only from a specialist dealer. Suitable telescopes have eyepieces that magnify in the range 20x to 60x, with object lenses of 60mm to 80mm. They are heavy and unwieldy to hold, so they need the support of a tripod (see box, right).

Zoom eyepieces change magnification; locate a distant bird on low power, then zoom to a higher magnification to get a closer view. The alternative is interchangeable eyepieces. An advantage of these, especially the wide-

With a telescope, you can easily show others a bird you have already 'locked onto', provided it does not move

angle types, is that they give a wider field of view and let in more light than a zoom lens at the same magnification. Telescopes come with either straight-through or angled eyepieces. With the angled type, you have to look down when the telescope is level or pointing upwards and finding the bird takes more practice, but they are less tiring to use once you are accustomed to them, since you can easily stand or sit, rather than stooping as with the 'straight-through' type.

Using telescopes

Aiming at the bird is the same for telescopes as binoculars, though it is trickier to master. The major difference is that you have to get used to viewing one-eyed; keeping the other eye closed can be tiring – it is better to learn to keep both eyes open, and let the one that is not doing the viewing go out of focus. This also enables you to draw what you see.

USING TRIPODS

● A good tripod is essential to keep the telescope steady. Aim for a sensible compromise between firmness and lightness; if it is too lightweight and flimsy, it will not form a firm enough support and can be more easily knocked over, but if too heavy, it will be a burden to carry.

● The pan-and-tilt head allows you to swing the telescope smoothly from side to side or up and down to locate a bird precisely or follow it when it is moving, though this takes some practice, especially with birds in flight. It can also be locked firmly in one position, so that you can watch a static bird for long periods without fatigue or shaking.

FIELDCRAFT

Part of the challenge of birdwatching is that wild birds are wary creatures, with keen eyes and ears ready to pick up the slightest movement or sound that might mean danger. For this reason, you should remain as inconspicuous as possible.

● Dress to suit the weather, but avoid brightly coloured clothes and material that makes a rustling sound. Patterned clothing can help break up your outline.

● Keep as still and quiet as you can. Spend time waiting and watching; while you need to actively search for birds in large spaces such as mountainsides, often it is better to wait for the birds to come to you. This can work especially at such spots as a woodland edge, or a small pool where birds come to drink and bathe. Keeping still and quiet also allows you to hear songs and calls more clearly.

● Camouflage yourself against your background; stand in the shadows or among foliage, or peer from behind a wall, etc.

● When you do have to move, do so slowly and smoothly, with frequent pauses. Take care to avoid snapping twigs, etc. Talk to others only when necessary; loud whispers carry farther than low, subdued speech.

● Always try to keep below the skyline; even distant birds will see you easily if you walk along the top of a seawall, clearly silhouetted against the sky.

● Make the best use of any available cover when stalking birds; before moving closer, work out a route that keeps you hidden at all times. Check the birds regularly with your binoculars to make sure they are not becoming nervous and ready to fly off.

● In open habitats such as moorlands, crouch down and move extra stealthily, using whatever cover there may be.

● Make use of the hides provided at many nature reserves. Approach and leave them as quietly and unobtrusively as possible; do not shout or point out of the windows. Cars make excellent hides, giving you remarkably close views – birds generally ignore them unless they stop or start suddenly.

Other points to bear in mind:

● When planning a trip, listen to weather forecasts: apart from indicating suitable clothes, they may point to opportunities for seeing birds. For example, a severe cold spell in winter may attract many ducks to deep lakes where the water remains unfrozen.

● Start early if you can – birds are generally most active early in the morning.

● Consult tide tables before a trip to coast or estuary – waders gather to feed on the mud exposed as the tide goes out, and roost on mud and sand banks at high tide.

● When searching for birds, look all round, behind you and up into the sky. Always remain alert to the slightest clue that will betray a bird's presence, such as an oddly moving leaf among hundreds of others that may turn out to be a warbler.

● When pointing out a bird to other birdwatchers, use the clock system (see illustration below) or refer to prominent landmarks such as a cliff. You can combine both methods; for example, to pinpoint a bird as being 'At eight o'clock from the top of the blue boat in the middle of the estuary'.

● Be patient; nothing will be gained by rushing about, and a long wait or stalk is often rewarded by memorable views.

Birdwatchers' code of conduct

This can be summarized thus:

● Always put the birds' welfare first. Do not disturb them, particularly on the nest. Rare birds, especially when breeding, need special consideration both in terms of their welfare and the consequences of publicity. Write to the RSPB (address on page 42) for information on bird protection laws.

● Respect the birds' habitat. Follow the Country Code (obtainable from the Countryside Commission).

● Be considerate of other birdwatchers.

● Help to increase knowledge about birds by keeping accurate notes and sending records to your county bird recorder (details in latest edition of *The Birdwatcher's Yearbook and Diary* – see page 42).

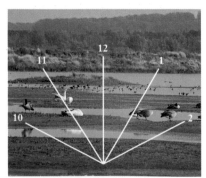

Using the 'clock system', you can point out a bird to others by saying it is at 10 o'clock, 11 o'clock and so on

FIELD NOTES AND SKETCHES

Recording what you see will greatly enhance the satisfaction you get from birdwatching. As well as evoking memories of great days and exciting birds, it is the best way of developing identification skills.

Use a pocket-sized notebook and a pencil to record your observations in the field. A miniature tape-recorder leaves your hands free to use binoculars, but your voice may annoy other birdwatchers or disturb the birds, and you will still need a notebook for making sketches (see below).

Make your notes on an unfamiliar bird at the time you see it – never rely on your memory until you take a break or go home; you will be bound to forget details, and it will be tempting to try and make your vague recollections fit one of the pictures and descriptions in the field guide.

Of course, your bird may disappear, and you will be able to record a brief impression only of the most noticeable features, but if you can watch it for some time, note down everything that will help you make an identification. This includes plumage details, using the precise names for the different areas (see pages 12-13); the bird's shape; its structure; the length and colour of bill and legs; size, if possible; the way it feeds and flies, and other details of behaviour. Try to summarize the bird's 'jizz' (see page 18) and note your impression of any calls or song.

Make drawings, too: these are a quick and effective way of recording information. They can substitute for detailed notes when you have little time, and add to your written record when the bird is more obliging. Draw a simple outline of the bird. You don't need to be a great artist: you can use egg shapes for the head and body, adding neck, wings, tail, bill and legs. Sketch in the details of plumage patterns, and label them with brief notes on colours, tone and shape; include as many other details as possible, as outlined above. Add small sketches of the bird's appearance in different postures, in flight and so on.

For every trip, record details of date, time, location, habitat and weather (including wind strength and direction).

Permanent records

When you get home, transfer your field notes to a permanent bird journal, possibly in the form of a diary – loose-leaf files are best, so

Keeping notes will greatly increase your pleasure and skill; transfer field notes (foreground) into a permanent log

you can insert pages with photographs, maps and so on. You could index your diary, but it is easier to keep a separate loose-leaf or card-index system, with records extracted from the diary and arranged by species or site.

Computer software programmes have recently become commercially available for recording notes and lists. Though not without teething problems, they make it easier to extract information on species, locations and so on from a single set of notes. They are not suited to recording drawings.

Lists

Making lists is great fun and can provide useful information. Printed checklists of British species (available from the BTO; details overleaf) make it easy to tick off what you have seen. You can keep such 'tick lists' of birds seen at a particular site, on a particular day, from the kitchen window, or on a regular journey. Most birdwatchers also like to keep a 'life list' of every species they have seen.

More ambitious, but very rewarding, is to keep a regular tally of birds seen at a good birdwatching area near your home. For each visit, record the numbers of each species and, if possible, their sex and age. Over the years, this can help you build up a picture of how the birdlife of your 'local patch' changes with the seasons, with damage or improvements to habitat, and so on. Such lists can also provide the basis for records sent in to the county recorder, which can then by published in an annual report.

41

SOCIETIES AND PUBLICATIONS

Although solo birdwatching has much to commend it, it is good to meet other birdwatchers, and you can learn a lot from experts. A great way of doing this is by joining your local bird group. You will find all the details listed in the current edition of *The Birdwatcher's Yearbook and Diary* (see below).

National societies
Royal Society for the Protection of Birds
Every birdwatcher should join the RSPB or its junior 'wing', the YOC (Young Ornithologists' Club). It is Europe's largest voluntary conservation body, protecting wild birds and their habitats. Membership brings free entry to reserves throughout the UK, the option of joining a local members' group, with a varied programme of field trips, lectures and previews of RSPB films, and the magazines *Birds* (RSPB) and *Bird Life* (YOC).

British Trust for Ornithology
The BTO provides amateur members with the chance of taking part in censuses and surveys, providing the information its scientists need to help monitor populations and provide sound evidence for conservation. It has a national network of regional representatives. The BTO also administers the national bird-ringing scheme and most of the major bird observatories. Members receive *BTO News* six times a year.

Wildfowl and Wetlands Trust
The trust carries out research on wildfowl and their habitats, and promotes their conservation. It also manages wildfowl refuges.

Scottish Ornithologists' Club
Welsh Ornithological Society
Irish Wildbird Conservancy
These are well worth joining if you live in or regularly visit Scotland, Wales or Ireland. Each promotes the study, conservation and enjoyment of birds in its region.

Magazines
British Birds
Indispensable to the serious birdwatcher, this is an excellent monthly journal. Available only on subscription, it includes identification articles, bird reports, recent news, book and equipment reviews, short notes, letters and detailed scientific papers. A free sample copy is available from British Birds, Fountains, Park Lane, Blunham, Bedford MK44 3NJ.

Bird Watching and *Birdwatch*
These are more popular monthly magazines. Both contain a lively mix of up-to-date news and regional reports, information features and other articles, and are packed with colour photographs. *Birdwatch* is generally pitched at a slightly more advanced level. *Bird Watching* is available on subscription from EMAP, Tower House, Sovereign Park, Market Harborough, Leics LE16 9EF, and *Birdwatch* from Fulham House, Goldsworth Road, Woking, Surrey GU21 1LY; both are also available from many newsagents.

Books
Enjoying Wildlife: a Guide to RSPB Nature Reserves
Full details of over 100 reserves.

Where to Watch Birds in Britain
By Redman and Harrop, published by Christopher Helm.

Where to Watch Birds in ...
A series of regional guides, published by Christopher Helm.

The Birdwatcher's Yearbook and Diary
This invaluable reference book has details of local and national societies, county bird recorders, projects, bird reserves and observatories, tide tables, a diary for bird notes, a log for listing, and much else besides. It is available from Buckingham Press, 25 Manor Park, Maids Moreton, Buckinghamshire MK18 1QX.

USEFUL ADDRESSES

Royal Society for the Protection of Birds
The Lodge, Sandy, Bedfordshire SG19 2DL
Tel: 01767 680 551

British Trust for Ornithology
The Nunnery, Thetford, Norfolk IP24 2PU
Tel: 01842 750 050

Wildfowl and Wetlands Trust
Slimbridge, Gloucestershire GL2 7BT
Tel: 01453 890 333

Scottish Ornithologists' Club
21 Regent Terrace
Edinburgh EH7 5BT
Tel: 0131 556 6042

Welsh Ornithological Society
Crud yr Awel, Bowls Road, Blaenporth, Cardigan SA43 2AR
Tel: 01239 811561

Irish Wildbird Conservancy
Ruttledge House, 8 Longford Place, Monkstown, Co Dublin
Tel: (01) 280 4322

THE FIELD GUIDE
How the pages work

The information for each species is set out in a standardized way. A typical page is reproduced below, with numbered areas keyed into the explanatory text.

❶ Introductory panel
A summary of each order (dark green panel) or family and any further subgroups (paler green panel) of birds.

❷ Text
Descriptions of the bird's general appearance and plumage details, plus details of flight, feeding action, courtship display and other behavioural features.

❸ Key Facts box
The first three headings refer to both male and female, unless otherwise specified.
Length: bird in fully stretched posture, from bill tip to tail tip. **Wingspan:** distance from wingtip to wingtip when wings are fully spread. **Weight:** varies greatly with season, food supply etc; a normal range is given. **Habitat:** all the typical habitats (though birds may turn up in unlikely places, on migration or if they have gone astray). **Movements:** typical migration patterns and other movements (e.g. irregular immigration). Otherwise 'sedentary' (moving little or not at all). **Population:** figures refer to both Britain and Ireland, unless otherwise stated. Breeding figures refer to pairs, except for a few species where, e.g., each bird may have more than one mate; then, numbers of individuals are given. Winter figures refer to individuals. **Diet:** typical food, which may vary with time and habitat. **Voice:** main call notes, as well as song (latter usually heard in breeding season). **Nest:** typical site, structure, material etc; also whether colonial. **Eggs:** typical number in a clutch, and their

colour. **Incubation:** typical time from egg-laying to hatching; whether both parents involved, or just the female (rarely male).
Fledging: time taken from hatching to acquiring first full set of feathers and ability to fly (at least to some extent).
Broods: number raised each year (not including second broods raised after destruction of first nest/eggs). **Maturity:** typical age of sexual maturity. **Confusion species:** refers to similar-looking species.

❹ Calendar bar
At base of Key Facts box; indicates in which months a species may be seen here. Odd individuals may be present at other times.

Key to calendar bars
■ *breeds during this period*
□ *occurs but does not breed*

❺ Illustrations
● Both adult males and females, where these have plumage differences.
● Winter and summer plumages, where different,

plus other seasonal variations where relevant.
● Distinctive subspecies (geographical races), and also major colour variations.
● Appearance in flight, from both above and below where this aids identification.
● Courtship displays, song flights, feeding/hunting methods and other behaviour, where distinctive.
● Juveniles, or later immature stages, unless indistinguishable from adults.
● If it is not labelled, an illustration shows a bird in adult plumage.

❻ Map
Showing where the bird occurs in the British Isles at different times. Each species has its own map, except most of the scarcer ones that do not merit full-page treatment. The small scale of the maps can exaggerate the range of species, especially those with specialized habitats, e.g. Kingfishers. Ranges of a few rare, localized species have been deliberately exaggerated to ensure they show up on the maps. For many wintering birds, ranges can vary depending on weather and food availability.

Key to maps
□ *breeds, but migrates to winter elsewhere*
■ *breeds, and is present throughout the year*
■ *winters, but does not breed*
□ *seen as a passage migrant only*
● The number in the top left-hand corner of the map box refers to the species number on the video that accompanies this book.

DIVERS
Order Gaviiformes, Family Gaviidae

Largish aquatic birds, superb swimmers and divers. Powerful legs with webbed feet, set at rear of cigar-shaped body, are efficient paddles in water, but on land allow only a clumsy walk; divers rarely visit land except to nest. Dive from swimming position, submerging quickly and smoothly. Fly with fast wingbeats on slender, pointed wings; over long distances, may fly high, unlike grebes. In flight, hunchbacked shape with head and neck outstretched and often held slightly lower than body; feet project beyond tiny tail. Downy chicks leave nest soon after hatching; shelter on parents' backs. Sexes alike.

● Note: in winter, pattern of light and dark on head, neck and flanks, back plumage and size and shape of bill; more distinctive in summer. In flight, plain upperwings, without white patches, distinguish them from larger grebes.

RED-THROATED DIVER *Gavia stellata*

134

KEY FACTS

Length: 50-60cm.
Wingspan: 106-116cm.
Weight: 1.2-1.6kg. **Habitat:** breeds chiefly by small lochs in hilly country, often flying long distances to larger lochs or the sea to fish. Winters mainly off coasts; a few on inland lakes and reservoirs, especially after gales.
Movements: British breeders leave nest sites in autumn to disperse around coasts, plus many moving S from breeding grounds in N Europe and Greenland. **Population:** 1200-1500 breeding pairs, probably increasing; most in Scotland, very few N Ireland. 12 000-15 000 birds winter.
Diet: mainly fish, also frogs and invertebrates. **Voice:** noisy in breeding season; repeated harsh cackling 'kwuk' in flight; on water utters high wails, barking croaks and harsh, throaty, cooing song.
Nest: as Black-throated (opposite); on islets or loch-sides. **Eggs:** 2, yellowish-olive to dark brown, usually with dark spots. **Incubation:** 26-28 days, mainly by female.
Fledging: 43 days.
Broods: 1. **Maturity:** 2-3 years. **Confusion species:** in winter, Black-throated Diver (opposite), Great Northern Diver (p46), Great Crested Grebe (p48).

| J | F | M | A | M | J | J | A | S | O | N | D |

Smallest of the divers (Mallard-sized) and the most widespread in Britain. In winter, generally the commonest diver, especially in E. Slightly smaller than Black-throated, with smaller head, more flattened forehead, more angular nape and thinner, straighter neck. Best identification feature is the slender, uptilted bill.

adult summer

juvenile

△ Juvenile as adult winter, but browner above, forehead darker, speckled sides of neck, paler grey bill, less spotted upperparts; may have small dark chestnut patch on upper foreneck.

adult winter

◁ In winter, back pale, finely speckled with white, paler above than Black-throated; paler overall than other divers. Head mostly white, with white extending above eyes. Often in small, loose flocks.

▷ In summer, grey head and neck with black and white stripes on hindneck and brick-red throat patch (looks black at distance). Back grey-brown, unpatterned. Bill black.

adult summer

Gavia arctica BLACK-THROATED DIVER

135

More heavily built than Red-throated, with thicker neck and straighter, slightly heavier bill; head, neck and bill much less massive than Great Northern Diver, which has a steep forehead, but head may look large and bulbous, especially in summer. Back darker than neck in winter (back of Great Northern paler than neck). Often shows distinctive white flank patch.

adult summer

△ In summer, grey crown and hindneck, throat patch black with black and white stripes on sides of neck and breast. Bill dark grey. Upperparts black with squarish white spots in two distinct patches on either side.

adult winter   *juvenile*

KEY FACTS

Length: 60-70cm.
Wingspan: 110-130cm.
Weight: 2-3kg. **Habitat:** breeds on larger freshwater lochs; winters at sea around coasts, occasionally on inland lakes and reservoirs.
Movements: Scottish breeders disperse to coasts in autumn, mainly in W, along with breeders from N Europe.
Population: *c*150 breeding pairs, *c*1300 birds winter.
Diet: mainly fish, also some frogs and invertebrates.
Voice: usually silent in flight, but may give deep, barking 'kwow'; on water, in breeding season, has a loud, rhythmic wailing song, also a variety of shorter wailing calls and croaks. **Nest:** on islets; shallow scrape on ground near water, lined with varying amounts of vegetation; occasionally raised heap of vegetation in shallow water.
Eggs: 2, olive to dark brown, with dark spots. **Incubation:** 28-30 days, mainly by female.
Fledging: 60-65 days. **Broods:** 1. **Maturity:** 2-3 years. **Confusion species:** in winter, Red-throated (opposite) paler and more slightly built, with uptilted bill; Great Northern (p46) larger, with thicker neck, bigger head and bill, and steep, not sloping, forehead. In winter, at distance on sea, may look similar to Guillemot (p194); latter much smaller, with dark line running back from eye.

△ In winter, darker than other divers, dark head and upperparts contrasting strongly with white underparts. Lacks Red-throated's fine white speckles on back; shows prominent white patch at rear of flanks, lacking in other divers. Pale grey bill with dark upper edge and tip.

summer

△ As with other divers, breeding Black-throated Divers are very vulnerable to disturbance from boats, tourists, fishermen and birdwatchers. On no account should one approach anywhere near a nest, or the birds may desert, leaving the eggs to be taken by predators. The other main cause of breeding failure is flooding of the nest.

△ Juvenile resembles adult winter, but has browner upperparts with pale scaling. May be confused with juvenile Red-throated; look for white flank patch and straight bill; very similar in flight.

Black-throated   *Great Northern*

△ Seen from behind, head looks club-shaped and body narrow; head of Great Northern of even width, more angular, and body broader.

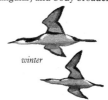

winter

△ In flight, compared with Red-throated, longer feet project further behind tail and head held horizontally; wings long and narrow, wingbeats stiff and shallow.

GREAT NORTHERN DIVER *Gavia immer*

summer

△ Larger than Black-throated and, especially, Red-throated (size of Cormorant). In summer, has black head and neck with small striped patch above striped collar, chequered black and white back. Bill blackish, heavy, dagger-shaped.

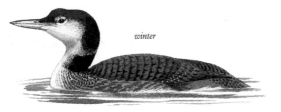

winter

juvenile

△ In winter, darker above than Red-throated, but paler than Black-throated, due to pale patches on back. Pale eyering. Wedge-shaped white area above dark half collar (Black-throated lacks this collar). Has longer head, steeper forehead and more massive bill than Red-throated or Black-throated.

△ Juveniles paler and browner above than winter adults, with distinct pale scaling, and have less contrasting neck markings. May be confused with juvenile Black-throated, especially in flight.

KEY FACTS

Length: 70-80cm.
Wingspan: 127-147cm.
Weight: 3-4kg. **Habitat:** winters mainly at sea, a few on inland waters; breeds on large lakes in Iceland, Greenland and N America. **Movements:** mainly winter visitor from Iceland; some seen in summer, especially along N and W coasts. **Population:** has bred in Scotland; up to several hundred winter, chiefly off N and W coasts. **Diet:** mainly fish, also molluscs, crabs and shrimps. **Voice:** during breeding season, eerie, wolf-like wails and vibrating tremolo call; also occasionally heard from migrating groups. **Maturity:** 2-3 years. **Confusion species:** larger, stouter-billed than Red-throated (p44) and Black-throated (p45); rare White-billed Diver (see right) has pale upturned bill without dark upper edge.

▷ Bulkier in flight than Red-throated or Black-throated, with longer, broader wings, longer, larger feet and larger head/bill. Flight action a bit slower, more goose-like.

winter

winter

△ Like other divers (and grebes), often rolls over in water to preen, when white underparts clearly visible. Sometimes, when doing this, a diver will wave one foot in the air.

winter

Great Northern

White-billed

◁ **White-billed Diver** *(Gavia adamsii)* is a rare vagrant (Oct-Jun) from Arctic Russia, mainly to N and E coasts. In late winter may be confused with Great Northern, which can then have pale tip to bill. Best distinction is White-billed's yellowish-white (not greyish-white) bill, which looks slightly more uptilted, also hindneck usually paler.

GREBES

Order Podicipediformes, Family Podicipedidae

Small to medium aquatic birds, expert swimmers and divers. Feet lobed, not webbed; position near rear of body makes walking very difficult, but allows grebes to propel themselves powerfully through water. Not often seen in flight, which is low over water, with neck outstretched and just below level of body, wings beating rapidly. White eggs stained brown by damp vegetation with which adults cover them when leaving nest. Downy chicks leave nest soon after hatching, shelter on parents' backs. Sexes alike.

● Note: head and neck pattern, shape of head, length of neck, bill shape and colour; in winter, shape of dark crown patch. Smaller than divers, with slimmer necks, shorter, deeper-flanked, tailless bodies; all except much smaller Little Grebe show white upperwing patches in flight (divers have plain wings).

163

Podiceps grisegena RED-NECKED GREBE

Great Crested

winter

Red-necked

△ Smaller and stockier than Great Crested, in winter with smudgy dark crown extending below eye, shorter, thicker, dusky neck and dusky cheeks, thicker, shorter, dagger-like bill, dark grey with a yellow base. May look as small and squat as Slavonian (p50) or as big as Great Crested, though not as slim.

winter

△ Often very active, diving frequently and on surface only briefly. Usually seen in winter on coastal waters and estuaries. Sometimes in small flocks or with other grebes or diving ducks, e.g. those illustrated above: Little Grebes (foreground), Great Crested Grebe (right) and (at rear, left to right), Red-breasted Merganser, Tufted Ducks and Pochards.

▷ Distinctive combination of white cheeks, chestnut neck and black crown makes for easy recognition in summer plumage. Eyes brown; bill black with bright yellow base.

summer

juvenile

◁ Juvenile resembles adult summer but shows traces of dark head stripes until winter moult, has paler bill, yellow eyes and a paler chestnut-buff foreneck.

KEY FACTS

Length: 40-46cm.
Wingspan: 77-85cm.
Weight: 700-900g. **Habitat:** in winter on estuaries, coastal waters and sometimes freshwaters. **Movements:** mainly winter visitor, chiefly from Baltic region and Netherlands. **Population:** scarce winter visitor (typically 80-100 birds), most appearing after harsh weather in N and E Europe; seen increasingly in summer (up to 10 birds) and has attempted to breed. **Diet:** fish, crustaceans, mainly aquatic insects in summer. **Voice:** generally silent outside breeding season. **Maturity:** probably 2 years. **Confusion species:** Great Crested (p48) larger, more elegant, slimmer, with longer, thinner neck; other grebes smaller with different head patterns.

J F M A M J J A S O N D

GREAT CRESTED GREBE *Podiceps cristatus*

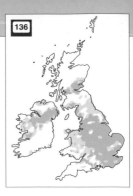

136

summer

△ Summer adults unmistakable, with black cap and striking chestnut and black head plumes ('tippets'), erected in dramatic courtship displays. The largest and most often seen British grebe.

courtship displays

△ Various stages in courtship rituals, seen in early spring, include 'penguin dance' in which pair rise out of water, breast to breast, paddling furiously, and shake heads from side to side, their beaks full of waterweed.

winter

Red-necked Grebe winter

△ Always looks paler than Red-necked, with more angular head, longer, slimmer neck. In winter, gleaming white foreneck and cheeks; neat dark crown does not extend down to red eyes. Slender pointed bill is pink, and longer relative to head than Red-necked's. May form quite large flocks in winter.

winter

Red-breasted Merganser female

juvenile

△ Juvenile resembles adult winter but shows traces of chick's dark head stripes until winter moult; bill paler.

△ Like other grebes, needs lengthy take-off, with feet pattering across water; like all but Little Grebe, brown and white plumage produces a flickering effect. Looks very elongated compared to other grebes, with larger white areas on upperwings; Red-breasted Merganser (p98) and Goosander (p99) also have long bills and white patches on wings but lack trailing feet.

J F M A M J J A S O N D

Tachybaptus ruficollis **LITTLE GREBE**

summer

△ In summer, dark-looking, almost black above with rich chestnut sides to face and neck; bright yellow patch at base of bill; flanks brown. Wary and often hard to follow as it dives frequently or hides among aquatic vegetation, but loud trilling song often draws attention to breeding pairs.

KEY FACTS

Length: 25-29cm.
Wingspan: 40-45cm.
Weight: 100-200g. **Habitat:** breeds on well-vegetated ponds, lakes, reservoirs and rivers; winters mainly on freshwaters, also sheltered estuaries. **Movements:** after breeding, British breeders disperse to more open waters, Aug-Apr. **Population:** difficult to census; 8000-16 000 pairs breed; rough estimate of 20 000-30 000 birds winter. **Diet:** small fish, aquatic insects, molluscs. **Voice:** high whistling 'whit'; song a loud, whinnying trill. **Nest:** floating heap of vegetation anchored to reeds or other vegetation. **Eggs:** 4-6, white, becoming stained brown. **Incubation:** 20 days, by both sexes. **Fledging:** 44-48 days. **Broods:** 2, occasionally 3. **Maturity:** 1 year. **Confusion species:** darker plumage and 'sawn-off' tail help distinguish it from Slavonian (p50) and Black-necked (p51); different bill and head shape from Black-necked.

| J | F | M | A | M | J | J | A | S | O | N | D |

winter

△ In winter, duller brown above, pale yellowish-brown on sides, neck and cheeks, with whitish throat. Seen more often on open water in winter. 'Ball-shaped' body.

summer

△ Does not often fly; flight, on whirring wings, usually weak, brief and pattering over water surface. In contrast to all other British grebes, lacks any white markings on wings.

winter

alert

diving

◁ The smallest British grebe, with a stubby bill and a steep forehead. Small round head; neck can look very short and thick or long, thin and erect. Dumpy little body, looks tailless; bobs about on water like a cork. Pale feathers at rear end often fluffed out, accentuating broad stern.

juvenile

△ Juvenile darker above, with reddish-brown tinge to neck and breast, head striped.

SLAVONIAN GREBE *Podiceps auritus*

KEY FACTS

Length: 31-38cm.
Wingspan: 59-65cm.
Weight: 375-450g. **Habitat:**
breeds on shallow, well-
vegetated lakes and ponds;
winters mainly on sheltered
coasts and estuaries.
Movements: winter visitor
(Sep-May, especially Nov-
Feb), mainly from Iceland and
Scandinavia. **Population:**
60-70 pairs breed in the
Scottish Highlands; *c*400 birds
winter. **Diet:** crustaceans and
aquatic insects in summer,
mainly fish in winter. **Voice:**
rarely heard outside breeding
season, when utters shrill,
rolling trills and long nasal
screams. **Nest:** as Little Grebe
(p49). **Eggs:** 4-5, white,
becoming stained brown.
Incubation: 20-22 days, by
both sexes. **Fledging:** 55-60
days. **Broods:** 1, occasionally
2. **Maturity:** probably
2 years. **Confusion species:**
Black-necked (opposite) has
different head and bill shape,
black, not red, neck in
summer, and less clear-cut
cap in winter; also tends to sit
higher in water, often with
'sawn-off' tail. Female and
immature Smew (p97) have
bigger, rounder heads,
chestnut crowns and duck
bills; winter male Ruddy Duck
(p85) has brown upperparts,
large bluish duck bill, long tail
and is dumpier.

| J | F | M | A | M | J | J | A | S | O | N | D |

winter

△ Small grebe, usually seen
here in winter plumage,
when easily confusable with
Black-necked Grebe. In
flight, shows broad white
wingbar on rear edge of wing
and small white patch where
forewing meets body.

summer

△ In summer, glossy black head with broad golden stripe from
bill back to expanded 'horns' at nape; upperparts almost
black; neck and flanks dark chestnut-red. Eyes red.

winter

△ In winter, clear-cut black cap, ending sharply at eye-level,
contrasts strongly with pure white lower face and foreneck.
More white on neck and head than Black-necked, white
extending further onto nape. Bill stubbier and straight.
Winters on coasts and estuaries, unlike most Black-necked.

Black-
necked

winter

Slavonian

△ Has proportionately larger,
flatter head and usually
thicker, snakier neck than
Black-necked. As well as
difference in bill shape,
Slavonian's bill has pale tip
(visible only at close range).

juvenile

△ Juvenile similar to adult winter; very similar to juvenile
Black-necked, but without smudgy band at neck base.

Podiceps nigricollis BLACK-NECKED GREBE

164

winter

▷ Small grebe, usually seen here in winter plumage, when easily confusable with similar-sized Slavonian Grebe. In flight, shows single white wingbar on trailing edge of wing only, and at best very faint forewing mark. White on trailing edge of wing extends to inner primaries, unlike Slavonian's.

KEY FACTS

Length: 28-34cm.
Wingspan: 56-60cm.
Weight: 250-350g. **Habitat:** breeds on shallow lakes and ponds with fringing vegetation; winters mainly on large freshwaters, especially reservoirs and gravel pits, mainly near coast, less often on estuaries or coastal waters.
Movements: winter visitor, mainly from E Europe.
Population: *c*25-40 pairs breed in England, Scottish lowlands and W Ireland; *c*120 birds winter. **Diet:** insects, crustaceans, molluscs, few fish. **Voice:** harsh chattering and soft fluting or whistling calls at breeding sites.
Nest: floating heap of vegetation anchored to reeds or other vegetation. **Eggs:** 3-4, white, becoming stained brown. **Incubation:** 20-22 days, by both sexes.
Fledging: unknown.
Broods: 1, occasionally 2.
Maturity: probably 2 years.
Confusion species: Slavonian Grebe (opposite) has differently shaped head and bill; very similar in winter but Black-necked is duskier, without sharp black/white contrast. Black-necked often looks more buoyant on water, showing more of flanks and even more abrupt, 'sawn-off' tail, almost like Little Grebe's (p49). Confusion also possible with female or immature Smew and winter male Ruddy Duck: see end of Key Facts opposite.

| J | F | M | A | M | J | J | A | S | O | N | D |

summer

△ In summer, distinguished from Slavonian by black neck with high black forehead and smaller, fan-shaped tuft of golden feathers behind red eye. Upperparts black, flanks rusty-red.

winter

△ In winter, cheeks and foreneck greyer than Slavonian, larger dark cap extends below eye and is duskier and less sharply separated from white at bottom of face; obscure pale patch on rear cheek. Head shape different, with high rounded crown, and black bill more slender and slightly uptilted.

juvenile

△ Juvenile similar to adult winter, but upperparts browner, cheeks duskier, sides of upper neck buffish and smudgy band across base of neck. Bill often less uptilted, making separation from juvenile Slavonian difficult.

PETRELS AND SHEARWATERS
Order Procellariiformes, Family Procellariidae

Ocean-going birds that normally visit land only to breed, typically laying their eggs in burrows or under rocks; clumsy walkers, with webbed feet set near rear of body, they are vulnerable to predators at the breeding colonies, so most are nocturnal on land (cliff-nesting Fulmar is an exception). Relatives of albatrosses and, like them, have hooked bills topped with two prominent tube-shaped external nostrils. Superbly adapted to soaring on stiff wings over waves for long periods. As their name suggests, shearwaters generally skim waves with a series of wingbeats followed by a long bank or glide; Fulmars often seen soaring along cliffs. All swim buoyantly. Shearwaters have cigar-shaped bodies, longer than plumper, more gull-like Fulmar, which has a stubby bill compared with longer, slimmer bills of shearwaters. Sexes alike.

● Note: head and rump patterns, amount of white on underwings.

FULMAR *Fulmarus glacialis*

223

KEY FACTS

Length: 45-50cm.
Wingspan: 102-112cm.
Weight: 700-900g. **Habitat:** in breeding season on sea cliffs (locally on dunes, scree, ruins); winters at sea.
Movements: some British breeders stay inshore all year, visiting breeding cliffs at all seasons except autumn, others disperse as far as Greenland; non-breeders stay at sea. **Population:** c570 000 pairs breed. **Diet:** crustaceans, squid, fish, offal.
Voice: feeding flocks cackle and grunt; soft croon in flight; chuckling, crooning and cackling at nest. **Nest:** lays eggs on bare ledge or recess. **Eggs:** 1, white.
Incubation: 52-53 days, by both sexes. **Fledging:** 46-50 days. **Broods:** 1. **Maturity:** 7-10 years. **Confusion species:** gulls (pp174-85) can look similar, but Fulmar has 'bull neck', dark eye and thick bill with tubenose visible at close range; unlike gulls, stiff-winged in flight. No British gull has an all-grey upper tail. Larger shearwaters all much darker and flap wings even less, though Cory's Shearwater (p54, bottom) can look quite similar in poor light when size and colours difficult to distinguish.

J F M A M J J A S O N D

△ Despite superficial gull-like appearance, wings held stiffly and much straighter in flight, which is mainly by gliding and soaring, with short bouts of flapping. Wings, back and tail grey, with pale patch at base of primary wing feathers; head and underparts white; very distinctive thick 'bull neck', short, thick yellow hooked bill made of separate plates, often with bluish base, tubenose on top; legs bluish-green to pinkish.

△ Fulmars spend much of the day resting on the water; buoyant swimmers, they feed from the surface. Occasionally they make shallow plunges beneath the water.

▽ A breeding colony of Fulmars is a noisy place, with birds cackling loudly as they wave their heads and bow at their mates or rivals. A pair vigorously defend their nest site, remaining faithful to each other and returning to the same ledge year after year.

Puffinus puffinus MANX SHEARWATER

224

KEY FACTS

Length: 30-38cm.
Wingspan: 76-82cm.
Weight: 350-450g. **Habitat:** breeds on grassy tops of islands, remote headlands and scree; winters at sea.
Movements: adults abandon young in nest burrow and make long journeys over the ocean to winter as far away as the South American coast; young make their own way about 2 weeks later.
Population: *c* 250 000-300 000 pairs breed. **Diet:** mainly small fish, also squid.
Voice: very noisy when visiting breeding colonies at night, giving loud cackling, chuckling and mewing calls.
Nest: in burrows dug out by both sexes, usually over 1m long; sometimes lined with plants and feathers.
Eggs: 1, white. **Incubation:** 51-54 days, by both sexes.
Fledging: 70 days. **Broods:** 1.
Maturity: 5-7 years.
Confusion species: Great Shearwater and Cory's Shearwater (p54) larger with different head/tail patterns; Mediterranean Shearwater (right) is darker; Sooty Shearwater (p55) much darker, with more flapping flight.

J F M A M J J A S O N D

△ The commonest shearwater in British waters, and the only one to breed here. Black above, white below. Typical shearwater flight, with series of rapid stiff-winged flaps followed by long glide on stiff straight wings, near surface of sea, lower wingtip almost shearing the water. In strong winds, the wings are angled back and the birds fly in high bounding arcs, using greater lift generated by stronger updraughts from wave crests.

◁ **Mediterranean Shearwater** (*Puffinus yelkouan*), W race *mauretanicus*, seen in small numbers off our coasts in late summer. Formerly regarded as a race of Manx; browner above and duskier below, without sharp black/white contrast; pale belly. Can look all-dark in poor light, when confusable with Sooty Shearwater though latter larger, with slower wingbeats.

Mediterranean Shearwater

▷ Breeding Manx may travel several hundred kilometres from nesting colony to feed, picking fish and squid off surface or making shallow dives from surface.

▽ Small flocks usually seen as birds pass near coasts on migration in spring and autumn. Distinctive cross-shaped appearance as they fly low over sea, flashing alternately black and white as they tilt from side to side.

GREAT SHEARWATER *Puffinus gravis*

KEY FACTS

Length: 43-51cm.
Wingspan: 100-118cm.
Weight: 800-900g. **Habitat:** breeds on S Atlantic islands, winters in open oceans.
Movements: after breeding in southern hemisphere summer, migrates N up coasts of the Americas, spending summer off E coasts of N America and S Greenland; in late summer passes through E Atlantic on return migration south, occurring annually off Ireland and SW England; only rarely in North Sea.
Population: up to 2000 birds. **Diet:** mainly squid and fish. **Voice:** may give harsh, barking, gull-like calls when feeding. **Maturity:** probably 6-7 years. **Confusion species:** flight similar to Manx (p53), but much bigger, browner, with different head and tail pattern; Cory's (below) similar size but lacks dark cap, white collar, white patch at tail base, dusky smudge on belly.

| J | F | M | A | M | J | J | A | S | O | N | D |

◁ A large shearwater, almost as big as Cory's; distinguished by dark cap, separated from grey-brown upperparts by white collar, and contrasting with white cheeks; also has much clearer white horseshoe-shaped band at base of tail. Slender black bill. From below, distinctive features, lacking in Cory's, are small dark smudges on breast sides, large dark smudge on lower belly and more extensive pattern of dark markings on underwings. Flight like Manx but more powerful.

CORY'S SHEARWATER *Calonectris diomedea*

KEY FACTS

Length: 45-56cm.
Wingspan: 100-125cm.
Weight: 700-800g. **Habitat:** breeds on Mediterranean islands, winters at sea.
Movements: after breeding, moves N and W, occurring regularly off SW Ireland and SW England. **Population:** from tens to (rarely) thousands in late summer. **Diet:** fish, shrimps, squid, offal from fishing boats. **Voice:** silent away from breeding areas. **Maturity:** probably 6-7 years. **Confusion species:** Great Shearwater (above); Fulmar, immature gulls, Gannet (see opposite, top).

| J | F | M | A | M | J | J | A | S | O | N | D |

▷ A little bigger than Great Shearwater, with larger head and more 'front-heavy' appearance. Paler upperparts, often with darker diagonal band across upperwings, and narrower, indistinct pale area at base of dark brown tail. Cap pale grey-brown, with dark smudge around eyes. Bill larger than other shearwaters', yellow with dark tip visible at close range.

Wings look longer and relatively broader than Great's; usually held gently arched and slightly forward, especially in strong winds. Flaps and soars more than Great, flight action more like Fulmar's. Wingbeats deep, slow and loose. Pure white underparts, without Great's dark smudges on flanks and belly, though may show faint grey mottling on lower flanks; underwing pattern plainer than Great's, dark edges surrounding much whiter inner area, and with proportionately more dark at tips.

Calonectris diomedea CORY'S SHEARWATER

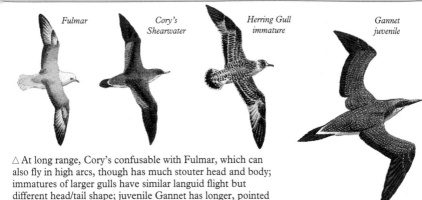

Fulmar *Cory's Shearwater* *Herring Gull immature* *Gannet juvenile*

△ At long range, Cory's confusable with Fulmar, which can also fly in high arcs, though has much stouter head and body; immatures of larger gulls have similar languid flight but different head/tail shape; juvenile Gannet has longer, pointed wings, long, pointed head/bill and tail.

Puffinus griseus SOOTY SHEARWATER

Arctic Skua, dark phase

Sooty Shearwaters

Mediterranean Shearwater

Sooty Shearwater

▽ Body as dark below as above; darker than other shearwaters, appearing dark brown to black depending on light. Close views reveal pale band along underwings. Wings set far back on rather heavy cigar-shaped body; long, thin black bill on small head. Purposeful flight on narrow, slightly swept-back wings; flaps more often than other shearwaters. Dark phase Arctic Skua (left and p172) has longer tail, pale 'flash' on outer wings and agile, dashing flight.

KEY FACTS

Length: 40-51cm.
Wingspan: 94-109cm.
Weight: 400-800g. **Habitat:** breeds on S hemisphere islands; on migration off coasts. **Movements:** makes huge clockwise migration up W side of Atlantic in spring, then across to E side as far N as Iceland and in summer/autumn down into British waters on return journey to southern breeding grounds. **Population:** 500-5000 birds; most in N and W, few off NW and SE English coasts. **Diet:** squid, shrimps, small fish. **Voice:** silent away from breeding grounds. **Maturity:** probably 5-7 years. **Confusion species:** flight action and dark plumage help to distinguish from other shearwaters, but beware confusion with rather smaller, more compact Mediterranean Shearwater (p53 and below), or at long range with juvenile Gannet (pp58-9 and above).

| J | F | M | A | M | J | J | A | S | O | N | D |

◁ Can be confused with dark Mediterranean Shearwater on water when latter's pale belly not visible.

STORM PETRELS
Order Procellariiformes, Family Hydrobatidae

Although related to albatrosses, these include the world's smallest seabirds: Storm Petrel is no larger than a sparrow. However, like albatrosses and their closer relatives, the fulmars, shearwaters and petrels, they normally visit land only to breed, spending the rest of their lives out at sea, coping with the roughest weather. Like their relatives, they are 'tubenoses': that is, they have tube-shaped nostrils atop their bills, but their bills are much smaller and shorter. Storm petrels visit the breeding colonies by night, to escape predators, shuffling along awkwardly or fluttering across the ground. Not often seen from land by day, and then usually at long range, when hard to identify because of small size, but severe gales force them closer to shore. Best seen during a long sea crossing. Sexes alike.

● Note: wing and tail shape, flight action, rump and wing patterns.

LEACH'S PETREL *Oceanodroma leucorhoa*

△ A bit paler, more brownish-black than smaller Storm Petrel. Wings relatively long and pointed, with pale diagonal bar across inner part of upperwing, but no pale underwing bar. Wings often held angled at 'wrists' (carpals) with inner half slightly raised and outer pointing down, like flattened 'M'. Wingbeats deep, slower than Storm's; flight more graceful but more powerful. White rump less obvious than Storm's, more V-shaped and divided above by dark central stripe. Tail forked, rear body longer.

△ Flight buoyant, one moment hanging motionless on the wind, the next bounding off with sudden changes of speed and direction; alternates between hovering, gliding and flapping. Dangles legs when feeding, but only occasionally patters across water, in contrast to Storm Petrel. Like latter, takes food with bill and sometimes settles on sea.

KEY FACTS

Length: 19-22cm. **Wingspan:** 45-48cm. **Weight:** 40-50g. **Habitat:** breeds on remote offshore islands; winters at sea, more often blown inshore (even inland) in autumn than Storm Petrel. **Movements:** migrates S in Sep-Nov to Gulf of Guinea and sea off Brazil, returns Apr-May. **Population:** difficult to census; *c*10 000-100 000 pairs breed on islands in far N of Scotland and NW Ireland. **Diet:** plankton, tiny fish. **Voice:** at breeding colonies at night, chattering, cackling and screeching, also purring from nest, interspersed with short whistle. **Nest:** as Storm Petrel. **Eggs:** 1, white. **Incubation:** 41-42 days, by both sexes. **Fledging:** 63-70 days. **Broods:** 1. **Maturity:** 4 years. **Confusion species:** Storm Petrel (see opposite).

| J | F | M | A | M | J | J | A | S | O | N | D |

Hydrobates pelagicus **STORM PETREL**

225

KEY FACTS

Length: 14-17cm.
Wingspan: 36-39cm.
Weight: 23-29g. **Habitat:**
breeds on offshore islands or
headlands; winters at sea,
though gales occasionally
force it inshore or even, rarely,
inland. **Movements:** spring
or autumn westerly gales may
blow large numbers off
course; migrates to S African
waters Sep-Nov. **Population:**
difficult to census; c70 000-
250 000 pairs breed. **Diet:**
plankton, tiny fish, scraps of
offal from ships. **Voice:**
repeated purring sounds, each
ending in a loud hiccup, and
high-pitched squeaking calls
from breeding colonies at
night. **Nest:** colonial breeders,
laying eggs among boulders
on rocky beaches or scree,
sometimes in stone walls or
rabbit burrows. No nest
material. **Eggs:** 1, white.
Incubation: 38-50 days, by
both sexes. **Fledging:** 56-73
days. **Broods:** 1. **Maturity:**
4 years. **Confusion species:**
Leach's Petrel (opposite) is
larger (Starling sized rather
than sparrow sized), with
longer, more pointed, more
angled wings, buoyant darting
flight, forked tail, pale diagonal
band on upperwings, all-dark
underwings. Third species,
Wilson's Petrel (*Oceanites
oceanicus*), occurs Jul-Sep well
out to sea off S Ireland and
Cornwall; has grey upperwing
panel, white rump, rounded
wings, longer legs and wings
raised in high 'V' when feeding.

J F M A M J J A S O N D

△ Wings shorter, less angled and more rounded than Leach's
and held more stiffly. Looks black at a distance except for
striking white rump which, unlike Leach's, extends further
down onto sides. Tail shorter, square-ended. Very narrow
pale diagonal bar on inner upperwings sometimes visible at
close range, especially on juveniles. White bar on underwing
separates this species from Leach's, but it is often difficult to
get a good view, especially at long range, and it is a variable
feature (see below).

*House
Martin*

△ The white underwing bar varies in size and prominence
between individuals, but it is always present and should be
looked for carefully. At a distance, Storm Petrel may resemble
House Martin (p225), which is only a little smaller; House
Martins migrate over sea and Storm Petrels are very occasionally
blown inland. However, House Martin has forked tail, white
underparts, blue-black upper body and tiny, very short bill.

*feeding
action*

△ Flight, just above surface of sea, is deceptively weak-looking,
resembling that of bat or martin, with rapid, fluttering
wingbeats alternating with short glides. When feeding, patters
across surface, long legs dangling onto water and wings raised.
Feeds by dipping head down to water and taking food with
bill. Often follows ships.

GANNETS
Order Pelecaniformes, Family Sulidae

Like the cormorants (pp60-1), the gannets belong to the order Pelecaniformes, whose four other families, of mainly fish-eating marine and freshwater birds, including the pelicans, are not found in Britain. Only one species of gannet occurs here; it shares with the other members of the order the unique feature of having all four toes connected by webs. Sexes alike.

GANNET *Sula bassana*

226

◁ Our largest seabird, much larger than any gull, its long, slender wings spanning nearly 2m. Cigar-shaped body, with pointed head ending in dagger-like bill, and pointed tail. Adults dazzling white, with extensive black tips to wings. At close range, yellow-buff on back of head visible. Away from breeding colonies, usually seen in flight, though will rest on sea briefly after feeding, before flapping awkwardly across the water to take off again.

Herring Gull, flight comparison

▷ Flight often low over waves, with short glides on stiff, angled wings alternating with deep, steady, powerful wingbeats, but also soars to considerable heights. Often flies singly at sea but also in straggling lines on migration.

▽ Juveniles are blackish-brown speckled white, with paler underparts and a whitish 'V' above the tail; they gradually acquire more white over the next four to six years.

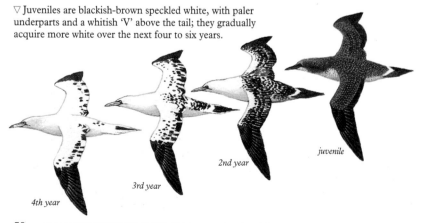

4th year

3rd year

2nd year

juvenile

Sula bassana GANNET

KEY FACTS

Length: 86-96cm.
Wingspan: 165-180cm.
Weight: 2.8-3.2kg. **Habitat:**
breeds on sea cliffs and stacks,
mostly on offshore islands, but
some on mainland; occurs off
all coasts and open ocean
outside breeding season,
especially during spring and
autumn. **Movements:** many
adults, especially non-breeders,
move S in winter to Bay of
Biscay and Mediterranean;
young winter mainly off
W Africa, but also as far as
Gulf of Mexico and
Greenland. **Population:**
c 188 000 pairs breed. **Diet:**
fish, especially herrings, sprats,
mackerel, cod and sand-eels,
mostly 2.5-30cm long. Often
scavenges for fish and offal
discarded by fishing boats.
Voice: normally silent except
when feeding in numbers and
at breeding colonies, when
gives loud, harsh, rhythmic
barks, groans and croaks;
young have yapping calls. All
these sounds from big colony
produce curiously mechanical
effect. **Nest:** large mound of
seaweed and other flotsam;
colonial breeder, on cliff ledge
or sloping ground. **Eggs:** 1,
pale chalky blue, turning
white, becoming stained
darker. **Incubation:** 44 days,
by both sexes. **Fledging:** 90
days. **Broods:** 1. **Maturity:**
5-6 years. **Confusion
species:** at long range,
juveniles and 1st-summers
may be mistaken for large
shearwaters, e.g.Cory's (p54);
adults possibly confusable
with large gulls, but shape and
flight action very different.

| J | F | M | A | M | J | J | A | S | O | N | D |

▷ About 70 per cent of the
world's breeding population
of approximately 265 000
pairs breeds in British Isles;
the world's biggest breeding
colony, with over 50 000
breeding pairs, is on
St Kilda off the west coast
of Scotland.

◁ Gannets often feed
communally at good feeding
sites, wheeling round above
the sea and suddenly plunging
headfirst from a height of 9-
30m like great gleaming white
arrowheads, half folding back
their wings and then closing
them as they hit the water at
100 km per hour or more with
a big splash. They are
submerged usually 5-7
seconds, reaching a depth of
about 3.5m, and often swallow
their fish prey underwater.

△ At their crowded, noisy colonies, Gannets, which usually
stay faithful to both mate and nest site, perform complex
bowing and 'sky-pointing' displays aimed at strengthening pair
bonds and proclaiming nest-site ownership.

CORMORANTS
Order Pelecaniformes, Family Phalacrocoracidae

Large, dark-plumaged aquatic birds that catch fish by diving from the surface. 'Prehistoric' appearance. Long necks and long bills; all four toes connected by webs. The two British species are larger than any duck. Superficially similar to divers, but distinguished by hooked tip to bill and longer wings and tail; on water, hold necks more erect and usually point head/bill at distinct upward angle. In flight, hold neck just above horizontal (whereas divers' necks droop slightly). Perch upright on land, often with wings held open. Breed colonially on cliffs or among rocks (Cormorant also in trees inland). Sexes alike.

● Note: bill size, size and shape of head and neck, and, in breeding season, crest and amount of white patches. Habitat difference also useful clue; Cormorant regularly occurs on inland freshwaters and flies over land, while Shag generally exclusively marine.

SHAG *Phalacrocorax aristotelis*

▷ Adult has all-blackish plumage with green gloss visible in good light and bright yellow patches at base of bill. In spring sports a tufted, forward-curving crest at front of crown. Immatures are brown, generally uniformly buff beneath, with little, if any, white (though throat usually pale). Bill even finer than adult's and much finer than most young Cormorants'. 1st-winter birds in worn plumage have large pale panel on upperwings, lacking in Cormorant.

immature   adult summer

adult summer

△ Wings broader than Cormorant's; wingbeats faster, with fewer glides, neck stretched out, not crooked; usually low over water.

△ Like Cormorants, Shags often rest with wings outstretched, but usually hold them wider open.

▽ In winter, more easily confused with Cormorant, but has slimmer, shorter neck, smaller rounder head with steeper forehead, and finer bill. No white on side of face, and very small pale throat patch hard to see. Size deceptive unless both species seen together for comparison. Shag tends to feed in more open water, in rougher seas, staying underwater longer. Typically dives with more distinct leap clear of water than Cormorant, often entering water almost vertically.

adult winter

KEY FACTS

Length: 65-80cm.
Wingspan: 90-105cm.
Weight: 1.75-2.25kg.
Habitat: breeds along rocky coasts and islands; winters mainly along rocky coasts; rare inland, after gales, mainly immatures. **Movements:** after breeding, disperse to all coasts, immature birds moving further. **Population:** *c*47 000 pairs breed; 100 000-150 000 birds winter. **Diet:** fish, mainly sand-eels and herrings.
Voice: grunts, clicks and hisses when nesting. **Nest:** bulky, made of seaweed and twigs; colonial, on sea cliffs, in sea caves or under boulders.
Eggs: 3-4, pale blue, overlaid with chalky white.
Incubation: 28-31 days, by both sexes. **Fledging:** 53 days.
Broods: 1. **Maturity:** 4-5 years. **Confusion species:** larger Cormorant (opposite).

J F M A M J J A S O N D

Phalacrocorax carbo CORMORANT

227

adult summer　　　*adult winter*

immature

KEY FACTS

Length: 80-100cm.
Wingspan: 130-160cm.
Weight: 2-2.5kg. **Habitat:**
breeds mainly on sea cliffs and
rocky islets, with small
numbers by freshwaters;
winters chiefly along coasts
and estuaries, also on tidal
rivers, large lakes and
reservoirs. **Movements:** after
breeding, disperse to all coasts,
locally inland, Sep-Mar, some
S as far as Iberia; some
immigrants from Continent.
Population: *c* 11 700 pairs
breed; 25 000 birds winter.
Diet: fish, especially bottom-
dwelling flatfish and eels.
Voice: guttural croaks when
nesting. **Nest:** colonial, on
cliffs or rocks, made of
seaweed and twigs; some
inland in trees using twigs etc.
Eggs: as Shag. **Incubation:**
30-31 days, by both sexes.
Fledging: 50 days. **Broods:**
1. **Maturity:** 4-5 years.
Confusion species: Shag
(opposite) slighter, with
smaller head, steeper forehead,
finer, proportionately shorter,
bill and thinner neck, has crest
and no white thigh patch in
breeding season. Immatures
trickier to distinguish.

J	F	M	A	M	J	J	A	S	O	N	D

△ Adults are bulkier than Shag, with much heavier bill, and
cheeks white as well as throat. Plumage blackish, with blue
gloss to head and underparts and bronze gloss on upperparts
(duller in winter); may show slightly ragged feathers on back
of head. Breeding adults always have large white face patches
and thigh patches (Shag has only tiny pale area on throat in
winter and never has white on thighs). Older adults may have
many white feathers on head in breeding season, some with
almost all white heads like immigrants from Continent.
Immatures browner, generally with variable amounts of white
on belly as well as neck. Bill heavier than immature Shag's,
head larger, crown flatter, never has pale wing panel.

adults summer

△ Cormorants often fly in lines or in V-formation, from a few
metres above water (Shag usually hugs water closely) to high
up over land, when they may also soar. Steady goose-like wingbeats, slower than Shag's, with occasional short glides. Neck
shows a distinct kink compared with straight neck of Shag.

adult winter

◁ Like Shag, swims low in
water with neck erect and
head/bill pointing upwards,
but is generally more solitary
when fishing. They avoid
competition for food as
Cormorants eat mainly
seabed fish, especially flatfish
in shallow waters, while
Shags prefer free-swimming
fish in deeper waters.

◁ Cormorants rest on rocks,
sandbanks, groynes, buoys
etc, often in long lines, and
frequently with wings held
half open.

HERONS AND BITTERNS
Order Ciconiiformes, Family Ardeidae

Medium to very large, mainly freshwater birds with long legs, long necks and long dagger-like bills. Wade in shallows. Large, broad wings; fly with head/neck retracted and legs trailing behind tail. Nest among reeds or in trees. Sexes alike in both British breeding species. Little Egret *(Egretta garzetta)* scarce but increasing migrant to S and SW coasts. Much smaller (53-58cm) than Grey Heron, all white, with black bill and legs; yellow feet. Spoonbill *(Platalea leucorodia)* scarce migrant to S and E coasts; large (80-90cm), heron-like (but in family Threskiornithidae), all-white, with long spatula-shaped bill.

Spoonbill

Little Egret

BITTERN *Botaurus stellaris*

115

△ Smaller than Grey Heron, generally looks plumper and more ungainly. Neck often retracted, but sometimes extended; never as long and thin as Grey Heron's. Golden-brown plumage is richly mottled and barred darker. Large green legs. Rarely seen as it spends much of day skulking solitarily in dense reedbeds, emerging only at dusk to feed. Clambers about, clutching bunches of reed stems with feet. Often only clue to presence is remarkable booming song of male in spring and early summer, similar to sound made by blowing over the mouth of an empty bottle.

KEY FACTS

Length: 70-80cm.
Wingspan: 125-135cm.
Weight: 900-1100g.
Habitat: breeds only in large, wet reedbeds; in winter also visits reedy margins of lakes and rivers. **Movements:** some British breeders disperse in winter, when small numbers of immigrants also arrive from Continent. **Population:** fewer than 20 breeding pairs after long-term decline; *c*50-100 birds winter here. **Diet:** fish, frogs, insects. **Voice:** short, harsh 'kaurr-kaurr' flight call; male's spring song sounds like short blast of distant foghorn. **Nest:** mound of reeds and other vegetation among tall reeds. **Eggs:** 4-6, olive-brown, sometimes with fine dark spots. **Incubation:** 25-26 days, by female. **Fledging:** 50-55 days. **Broods:** 1. **Maturity:** 1 year.

△ When alarmed, stretches out neck and points head and bill skywards, the striped plumage camouflaging it superbly against reed stems. It even sways gently, mimicking the movement of the reeds in the breeze.

△ Best chance of seeing a Bittern is early on a summer morning, when it flies to and from feeding sites. Flies on broad, rounded wings with head drawn back onto shoulders; wingbeats quicker than Grey Heron's; very large feet on trailing legs. Can look owl-like in flight, especially in poor light.

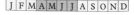

J F M A M J J A S O N D

Ardea cinerea **GREY HERON**

single bird,
stages in feeding

KEY FACTS

Length: 90-98cm.
Wingspan: 175-195cm.
Weight: 1.6-2kg.
Habitat: rivers, lakes, marshes, estuaries; may rest and nest well away from water. **Movements:** disperses after breeding, some immigration from Continent in winter.
Population: *c*14 000 pairs breed; *c*43 000 birds winter.
Diet: fish, frogs, small mammals and birds, insects.
Voice: harsh 'frarnk' in flight, various squawks and croaks and bill-snapping at nest colonies. **Nest:** usually colonial, bulky platform of twigs in trees; locally in reeds, bushes, long heather or on cliff ledges or rocks, rarely on ground. **Eggs:** 4-5, pale blue. **Incubation:** 25-26 days, by both sexes.
Fledging: 50 days.
Broods: 1. **Maturity:** 2 years.

J F M A M J J A S O N D

△ Herons are patient solitary feeders, standing motionless for long periods, or carefully stalking, then darting out head to seize prey in dagger-like bill. Distinctive features are large size, grey upperparts with white head, neck and underparts, black streak through eye extending into long, wispy black crest and black streaks on long, thin neck. Long bill is yellowish, long legs yellow-brown, both becoming reddish in early spring.

▽ Flight direct, ponderous, with slow, deep beats of distinctively bowed wings; neck retracted, head hunched between 'shoulders'; long legs and big, ungainly feet project far behind tail. Steep take-off with powerful flaps; descends in glide or with twisting aerobatics.

△ When not feeding, Grey Herons often rest together at traditional sites, frequently hunched up on one leg.

▷ These large birds are surprisingly agile as they move around in the treetops at their nesting colonies (heronries). Eggs may be laid as early as Feb, with young leaving nests by May, but the latest broods may not fledge until early Sep. The large stick nests, which are added to each year, are usually easy to see from a distance, but the occasional single nest and those in evergreen trees are easily missed.

▽ Juvenile and 1st-winter birds have smaller, greyer crest, all-dark crown and darker neck.

juvenile

WILDFOWL (SWANS, GEESE AND DUCKS)
Order Anseriformes, Family Anatidae

All birds in this large group are aquatic, with feet webbed between the three front toes. Most swim well and some dive. They have long necks and flattened bills with comb-like plates (lamellae) for filtering food; narrow, relatively pointed wings; bodies well insulated with a layer of down beneath the outer feathers. Almost all have an annual moult in which the flight feathers are shed simultaneously, so that they are flightless for a brief period until they grow a new set. Most build simple nests of vegetation lined with down from female's body, on ground; some nest on cliff ledges or in tree holes. Downy young can walk, swim and feed shortly after hatching. Wildfowl are divided into several distinct groups (see below).

swans (pp64-7)
geese (pp68-74)
shelducks (p75)
dabbling ducks (pp76-83)
sawbills (pp97-9)
diving ducks (pp86-96)
stifftails (p85)
perching ducks (p84)

SWANS

The largest wildfowl, with the longest necks. Feet set relatively far back on body, giving ungainly waddling walk. Plant-eaters, swans often up-end, immersing head/neck below water, to browse on aquatic plants on bottom; they also graze on land. Build bulky nests. All three British species have all-white bodies and wings as adults; young (cygnets) are grey-brown. Include some of the world's heaviest flying birds; need to run across water for long distance before they become airborne. Sexes similar (males bigger).

● Note: bill colours/pattern, shape of head, length of neck; also listen for calls/wing noise.

MUTE SWAN *Cygnus olor*

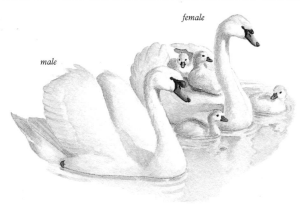

female

male

◁ Generally curved neck is distinctive, even at long range, as is the relatively long, pointed tail (usually held elevated) and the orange bill with prominent black knob (larger in males). Bill generally angled downwards when swimming. Newly hatched cygnets often climb aboard their mother's broad back for shelter. The parents pull up food from under water and pass it to cygnets; also stir up food for them with their feet.

Cygnus olor MUTE SWAN

138

male chasing rival

KEY FACTS

Length: 145-160cm.
Wingspan: 208-238cm.
Weight: female 10kg; male 12kg. **Habitat:** shallow lakes, rivers, marshes, nearby fields; also (especially winter) on sheltered coasts and estuaries.
Movements: considerable local movement within British Isles. Longer-distance movements occur, chiefly associated with summer moult period. **Population:** *c*46 000-47 000 birds. **Diet:** chiefly aquatic plants; also grasses from meadows and salt marshes. **Voice:** despite name, gives various snorts, grunts and hisses, especially at nest. Wings make distinctive loud throbbing sound, distinguishing it from other 2 swan species. **Nest:** large mound of reeds and other vegetation on bank or in reedbed. **Eggs:** 5-8, pale greenish-white. **Incubation:** 34-38 days, by female.
Fledging: 120-150 days.
Broods: 1. **Maturity:** 3-4 years. **Confusion species:** Bewick's and Whooper Swans (pp66-7) are winter visitors that have differently patterned yellow and black (not orange and black) bills and loud calls.

| J | F | M | A | M | J | J | A | S | O | N | D |

male 'busking'

△ Breeding birds, especially males, very aggressive towards rivals and territorial disputes involve chases across the water, with the pursuer half splashing, half flying; in the distinctive 'busking' threat posture, the breast is thrust forwards and the neck curved back so the head rests between the arched wings. Breeding birds are bold in defence of their nests, eggs and young, driving off intruders, including dogs and humans.

1st winter　　　　　*juvenile*

△ Juvenile has uneven dingy grey-brown markings (rare 'Polish' form all white); bill is grey with black base and no knob. The plumage gradually whitens, but some grey-brown markings until 2nd winter; bill of 1st-year bird turns pink, then dull orange, and knob develops.

▷ As with all swans, take-off from water is laborious, the feet pattering noisily on the surface. Unlike other species, wings make loud rhythmic throbbing sound in flight that enables instant identification.

BEWICK'S SWAN *Cygnus columbianus*

140

△ Winter visitor, like Whooper and unlike Mute. Smallest of the three British swans, with most goose-like proportions. Neck may be held erect or curved. Tail short, square and held flat. Walks less clumsily than Mute.

Whooper

Bewick's

△ Crown of Bewick's more rounded than Whooper's, and forehead and smaller bill have a concave, not straight, profile. Neck shorter and proportionately thicker than Whooper's.

Bewick's juvenile

Whooper juvenile

Bewick's juvenile

Whooper juvenile

Whooper adult

△ Juvenile and 1st-winter Bewick's and Whoopers more difficult to distinguish than adults, but identification helped by fact that young usually stay with their own parents throughout 1st winter. Both are much paler and more uniformly dingy grey-fawn than immature Mute. Juvenile Bewick's usually have bill creamy-pink at base, shading into deeper pink towards tip, while Whoopers have dirty pink bills with a dark tip. Bills gain more black at tip during 1st-winter and Whoopers often have bill more like adult by spring; best distinctions are size and structure.

KEY FACTS

Length: 115-127cm.
Wingspan: 180-211cm.
Weight: female 5.7kg; male 6.5kg. **Habitat:** winters mainly at traditional sites on flooded fields and lakes.
Movements: winter visitor from breeding grounds on marshy tundra of N Russia/ Siberia. Migrates S Oct-Nov, N Mar-Apr. **Population:** up to 17 000 birds; distribution dependent on weather. **Diet:** aquatic plants, grass, grain, potatoes and rootcrops.
Voice: goose-like honking or bugling, higher-pitched, more abrupt than Whooper, like baying of hounds in chorus; flocks make musical babble.
Maturity: 3-4 years.
Confusion species: Whooper Swan (opposite) is larger, with pointed yellow area on bill, straight crown/bill profile. See also Mute Swan (pp64-5).

| J | F | M | A | M | J | J | A | S | O | N | D |

Bewick's, variations

△ Extent and shape of yellow base on bills of Bewick's vary considerably between individuals, but it is always smaller than Whooper's (at least half the bill is black) and is typically rounder or squarer. In Whooper, yellow area extends forwards in a point towards tip.

KEY FACTS

Length: 145-160cm.
Wingspan: 208-238cm.
Weight: female up to 9kg;
male up to 11kg. **Habitat:**
winters on large lakes, rivers
and estuaries and nearby
stubble fields and wet
meadows; shallow sea bays.
Movements: winter visitor
from breeding grounds on
marshy tundra and swamps,
mainly from Iceland. Migrates
S Oct-Nov, N Mar-Apr.
Population: up to 17 000 or
more birds winter, depending
on weather; a few summer,
with up to 5 pairs breeding,
some probably feral. **Diet:**
aquatic plants, grass, grain,
potatoes. **Voice:** loud 'whoop-
whoop' calls, trumpet-like
from flocks; especially noisy in
flight. **Maturity:** 1 year.
Confusion species: Mute
Swan (pp64-5) is same size,
but neck usually held in S-
shaped curve, bill orange and
black, not yellow and black,
and tail longer and more
pointed. Smaller Bewick's
Swan (opposite) has concave
crown/bill profile, and smaller
bill with different pattern of
black/yellow. Juveniles of all
three species more similar, best
separated by head/bill profile.

| J | F | M | A | M | J | J | A | S | O | N | D |

△ Whooper has a long slim neck, usually held very erect,
and a straight crown/bill profile; the bill is larger than
Bewick's. Breast usually bulges more. Tail short and square.
Like Bewick's, walks less clumsily than Mute.

*Whooper
juvenile*

*Mute
juvenile*

△ Juvenile/1st-winter Whoopers have much paler, greyer,
neater, more uniform plumage than juvenile/1st-winter
Mutes. Plumage of Mute becomes patchy brown/white as it
matures. Bill of young Mute grey with black base; that of
young Whooper dull pink with black tip.

◁ All swans, but especially
Whooper, may have rust-
coloured stains on heads and
necks from feeding in water
rich in iron oxides or algae;
can also become discoloured
by feeding in ordinary soil.

▽ In flight, Whooper's neck looks particularly long and slim;
Bewick's more goose-like, with shorter, thicker neck and faster
wingbeats; Mute heavy-bodied, wings make unique far-carrying,
loud rhythmic throbbing sound (Bewick's and Whooper
produce only swishing sound audible at close range).

Bewick's

Whooper

Mute

'GREY' GEESE
Anser species

Plumage generally grey-brown, with bold white undertail coverts. Both 'grey' geese and 'black' geese (pp72-4) are smaller than swans, but larger, bulkier and longer-necked than ducks; good walkers, feed mainly on land, grazing on coastal saltmarshes, mudflats or fields. Highly gregarious; usually fly in chevrons (sometimes lines or Vs) especially over long distances. Sexes identical in appearance; males slightly larger.

● Note: bill and leg colours, bill shape, general proportions, plumage features, especially colour of head/neck and pattern on wings in flight. Thorough knowledge of calls is also very useful, as is knowing traditional wintering areas, though small flocks or single birds may turn up in odd places and various species escape from captivity.

PINK-FOOTED GOOSE *Anser brachyrhynchus*

variations in head pattern

△ Looks short-necked compared to other grey geese, with small, round, very dark head contrasting sharply with pale pinkish-buff breast and pinkish-grey or blue-grey mantle; relatively small stout body; obscure dark bands on belly and flanks. Stubby triangular bill dark with pink band; legs pink. Some individuals show traces of white patch at base of bill. Walks and feeds quickly. Often in large flocks.

juvenile

▽ In flight, neck looks very short and head small, round and dark; upper forewings form pale grey panel (as in larger Greylag but less striking). Flight faster, more buoyant than Bean or Greylag, with aerobatic tumbling and twisting corkscrew descents.

△ Juvenile/1st-winter darker, browner; scruffier upperparts than adult, with less clear pattern of pale bars; mottled underparts. Legs may be dull yellow rather than pink in autumn. Assumes adult plumage with moult Oct-Feb.

KEY FACTS

Length: 60-75cm.
Wingspan: 135-170cm.
Weight: male 2.5-2.7kg; female 2.2-2.5kg. **Habitat:** winters on stubble, crop fields, pastures, locally on coastal saltmarshes; roosts on estuaries, sandbanks, lakes.
Movements: winter visitors from N breeding grounds, mainly Iceland (also Greenland). **Population:** over 150 000 winter, chiefly in S and C Scotland, N England (especially Lancs), the Wash and N Norfolk.
Diet: grass, grain, cereals, potatoes. **Voice:** flocks very noisy, with highest-pitched calls of all geese; yelping 'wink-wink' distinctive; also deep, cackling 'unk-unk'.
Maturity: 3 years.
Confusion species: other 'grey' geese (pp69-71), especially Bean (see Key Facts, opposite).

| J | F | M | A | M | J | J | A | S | O | N | D |

Anser fabalis BEAN GOOSE

forest race
fabalis

tundra race
rossicus

KEY FACTS

Length: 66-88cm.
Wingspan: 147-175cm.
Weight: male 2.6-3.2kg;
female 2.3-2.8kg. **Habitat:**
winters on wet pastures.
Movements: winter visitors
from N Europe. **Population:**
up to 350 birds winter each
year in Yare Valley, Norfolk;
smaller numbers less regularly
in Stirling and Kirkcudbright,
Scotland; a few elsewhere,
especially during periods of
severe freezing. **Diet:** grass,
grain, other crops. **Voice:**
generally quieter than other
geese; rich nasal cackling
'kayak' or 'kayakak', lower-
pitched and more braying
than Pink-footed. **Maturity:**
3 years. **Confusion species:**
closely related Pink-footed
(opposite) smaller, with
shorter neck and more
compact head profile; more
contrast between dark neck
and pale body; in flight shows
pale upper forewings, mantle
and back; and has higher,
shriller calls. See also other
'grey' geese (pp70-1).

J	F	M	A	M	J	J	A	S	O	N	D

△ Generally darker and browner than other grey geese, with
darker head and neck. Large, tall, elegant, with long body.
Neck long and slender, head/bill profile long, wedge-shaped.
Pale feather tips on upperparts give brighter, more lined
appearance. Breast pale buff-brown. Legs bright orange. Race
fabalis (breeds northern forests and makes up most of British
wintering population) has larger bill with more orange;
tundra-breeding race *rossicus* often has just small orange band
near tip of shorter, otherwise black, bill and longer neck. Some
individuals have very narrow white patch at base of bill (never
as much as on adult White-fronted).

juvenile

◁ Juvenile duller than adult,
with less distinct scaly
appearance on back and flanks;
bill and legs greyish-orange.
Assumes adult plumage after
moulting Oct-Apr.

▷ In flight, Bean looks long-
necked and long-headed;
has dullest and most
uniform-looking forewings
of all grey geese, without
obviously contrasting wing
coverts; darker lower back
than Pink-footed and,
especially, Greylag; calls like
those of Pink-footed but
distinctly lower-pitched and
not so frequent.

WHITE-FRONTED GOOSE *Anser albifrons*

169

race
albifrons
adults

race
albifrons
juvenile

light-barred
individual

dark-barred
individual

△ Distinguished from other regularly seen grey geese by striking large white patch at front of head and bold black irregular bars on grey-brown belly. Some more heavily barred than others. Similar size to Pink-footed, smaller than Greylag. Legs orange. Bill of adult Siberian race pink, slightly shorter and more slender than on Greenland race. Dark grey-brown above with pale bars on back (less distinct than on Bean); chest pale buff-brown, head darker brown. Juvenile/1st-winter lacks white forehead patch and black bars on belly; browner, more mottled below, with duller pink bill and orange legs.

race flavirostris

adult

juvenile

△ Adults of Greenland race slightly larger/darker than Siberian race, with less white on forehead, less contrasting chest, bill longer, heavier and orange. Juvenile/1st-winter duller than Siberian race, bill dull orange-yellow. Juveniles of both races have dark tip to bill; 1st-winters may have white front to face.

◁ In flight, lacks contrasting upper forewings of Pink-footed and Greylag and, when white forehead and belly bars not visible, may look like larger Bean, but wings longer and narrower and head and neck shorter. Wingbeats relatively fast, more agile in take-off; rises and turns more sharply than other grey geese. Frequently in large flocks. Makes twisting descents.

KEY FACTS

Length: 65-78cm.
Wingspan: 130-165cm.
Weight: male 2.1-2.5kg; female 1.9-2.2kg. **Habitat:** winters on wet grassland and other fields, peat bogs, less often on saltmarshes; roosts on estuaries and floodwaters.
Movements: Siberian race *albifrons* winters mainly S England (especially Slimbridge on Severn estuary and Kent), mainly Dec-Mar; Greenland race *flavirostris* winters mainly Ireland and W Scotland, mainly Oct-Apr; odd birds seen at other sites.
Population: 4000-5000 Siberian race in most winters, though may be considerably more in hard winters; *c*20 000 Greenland race winter. **Diet:** grass, clover, grain, winter wheat, potatoes. **Voice:** musical 'kow-yow', sounds like yelping of pack of dogs when heard from flock; also loud, buzzing calls and high yodelling 'lyo-lyok' in flight.
Maturity: 3 years.
Confusion species: may be confused with larger Bean Goose (p69) in flight when its distinctive black belly markings and white face patch are hidden (and juveniles lack both these features anyway); shares Bean's absence of pale upper forewing, but look for distinctive structural features: shorter head and neck and proportionately narrower, longer wings. Faster wingbeats than those of larger Greylag (opposite).

| J | F | M | A | M | J | J | A | S | O | N | D |

Anser anser **GREYLAG GOOSE**

race
rubirostris

race anser

race anser

race anser
juvenile

KEY FACTS

Length: 76-89cm.
Wingspan: 147-180cm.
Weight: male 3.4-3.7kg;
female 2.9-3.1kg. **Habitat:**
breeds by moorland lochs and
on coastal islets in N Britain;
introduced birds also breed
beside lakes and gravel pits;
winters on flooded grassland,
crops, stubble, saltmarshes.
Movements: winter visitors,
Oct-Apr, mainly from Iceland.
Population: only grey goose
to breed here; c1500 wild
pairs in N Scotland, c22 000
feral breeders in many areas.
About 100 000 winter visitors.
Diet: green plants in summer,
grass, grain and roots in
winter. **Voice:** like farmyard
goose; usual flight call loud,
deep, cackling 'aahng-ung-
ung'. **Nest:** scrape on ground,
with sparse lining, among
heather or rushes near water;
sometimes in colonies. **Eggs:**
4-6, cream. **Incubation:**
27-28 days, by female.
Fledging: 50-60 days.
Broods: 1. **Maturity:**
3 years. **Confusion species:**
other grey geese smaller, with
smaller heads and bills,
slimmer necks and darker
plumage; juvenile White-
fronted (opposite) similar, but
smaller, slighter, darker, with
smaller head and bill. In flight
from above, pale blue-grey
upper forewings distinguish
from all but smaller Pink-
footed (p68), which has darker
blue-grey forewings; from
below, bicoloured pale/dark
grey underwings striking.

J F M A M J J A S O N D

△ Largest and heaviest of the grey geese, with larger head,
longer, heavier bill and thicker neck. Plumage pale brownish-
grey, with head and neck only slightly darker than underparts.
Legs pink (more rarely orange in feral breeders). Many have
white at base of bill and black mottling on belly, but never as
marked as on White-fronted. Almost all birds seen here
belong to W race *anser*, with orange bill. A few belong to
E race *rubirostris* (which also occasionally escapes from
captivity); this is paler, with longer, pink bill. Juvenile and
1st-winter birds have less clearly marked back and flanks, no
dark belly marks and duller pink legs.

◁ In flight, from above,
shows very pale blue-grey
area on forewing; from
below, wings have similar
pale/dark pattern. Needs
longer take-off than other
grey geese; flight heavier,
more powerful, with slower
beats of broader wings,
bigger head, thicker, more
'pinched-in' neck. Flocks
more often straggling.

△ Greylag is ancestor of most farmyard geese. Many feral
birds are derived from introduced stock; these may be quite
tame and breed on small freshwaters, even in wooded areas;
truly wild pairs breed by remote lochs. Female does all work
of incubation and usually broods goslings alone, while male
stands guard nearby. As with other geese, they pair for life,
remaining together year round, and families stay together all
winter, even in the largest flocks.

71

'BLACK' GEESE
Branta species

Plumage is a combination of grey or brown, black and white. Distribution and habitat help in identification, but 'black' geese are in any case much easier to identify than 'grey' geese (pp68-71); each has a distinctive black-and-white head pattern. All three regular British species have a black neck, black bill and black legs, and combination of white rump and white undertail coverts surrounding black tail. Sexes look identical; males slightly larger.

BARNACLE GOOSE *Branta leucopsis*

171

juvenile

adult

adult

△ Unique combination of black, white and grey, with entire face creamy-white, apart from thin black stripe from bill to eye. Very small black bill. Crown, back of head, neck and breast black, back grey, strongly barred black and white. Underparts white; flanks barred very pale grey. Legs look relatively long. Juvenile/1st-winter has duller, brownish or greyish tinge to black areas of plumage, white (not cream) face mottled greyish, wings duller with buff bars.

△ At a distance, may be confused with smaller Brent, but Barnacles have longer wings and slower wingbeats and are not so dark. All-white face unique among black geese. Appear black and white in flight, with grey wings showing black trailing edge. Flocks fly in straggling lines or close-packed ragged groups. Gregarious, grazing at night; more terrestrial than other geese, rarely settling on sea; usually less wary than other geese.

KEY FACTS

Length: 58-70cm.
Wingspan: 132-145cm.
Weight: male 1.6-2kg; female 1.5-1.8kg.
Habitat: winters on coastal grasslands and saltmarshes.
Movements: Greenland breeders winter Ireland and W Scotland, mostly island of Islay; Spitsbergen breeders winter Solway Firth, SW Scotland; Russian breeders winter mainly in Netherlands, but some visit England, especially Kent and Norfolk. Often escape from captivity, associating with Canada Geese. **Population:** over 30 000 Greenland breeders and over 10 000 Spitsbergen breeders winter here. **Diet:** grass, clover, seeds. **Voice:** rapidly repeated shrill, single barking calls, like yapping dogs; muffled growls when feeding.
Maturity: 3 years.
Confusion species: Canada Goose (opposite) larger, longer-necked, with less white on face and brown upperparts; also smaller Brent Goose (p74 and see left).

| J | F | M | A | M | J | J | A | S | O | N | D |

72

Branta canadensis CANADA GOOSE

141

juvenile

adult

adult, small
N American race

KEY FACTS

Length: 90-110cm.
Wingspan: 150-180cm.
Weight: male 4.7-5kg; female
4.3-4.5kg. **Habitat:** lakes,
flooded gravel pits, rivers,
marshes, grazing on nearby
farmland; also in town parks
and other urban habitats; some
on estuaries. **Movements:**
some local dispersion and
migration to moulting
grounds; a few individuals of
small races from N America
reach Ireland and W Scotland
most winters; usually seen
among flocks of White-fronted
and Barnacle Geese.
Population: over 60 000
individuals, including non-
breeders; increasing in
numbers and range. **Diet:**
grass, aquatic plants, cereals,
grain, clover. **Voice:** loud,
trumpeting, nasal 'a-honk',
rising on second syllable,
especially in flight.
Nest: scrape on ground, lined
with female's down feathers;
colonial. **Eggs:** 5-6, cream.
Incubation: 28-30 days, by
female. **Fledging:** 40-48 days.
Broods: 1. **Maturity:** 3 years.
Confusion species: Barnacle
Goose (opposite) has all-white
face and grey (not brown)
back and is much smaller.

| J | F | M | A | M | J | J | A | S | O | N | D |

△ Introduced to Britain from N America in 17th century,
Canada Goose now firmly established here as widespread
breeder. Descendants of original escaped birds have thrived on
lakes, reservoirs and other freshwaters, even in largest cities.
Easily identified by large size (longer, though less bulky, than
Greylag), long slender black neck with white 'chinstrap', black
head and large black bill. Back barred brown, chest strikingly
pale creamy-buff and underparts buff. Occasional individuals
of smaller races escape from captivity; very rarely the odd wild
one turns up, blown off-course from N America. Juveniles
duller than adults, more lightly built.

△ Nest often built beneath tree or bush. Female incubates
eggs, lowering her head and neck to hide the conspicuous
white throat patch. As with other species of geese, goslings
leave nest soon after hatching. Tended by both parents, but
driven away from breeding waters during following spring. In
contrast to N American ancestors, British Canada Geese not
migratory, but some have developed a pattern of regular flights
in late summer to moult in large flocks on sheltered estuaries.

▷ Flies fast, with powerful
beats of large wings. Neck
long and slender, giving
swan-like appearance.
Pale chest. Flocks usually
assume V-formation or
long lines.

BRENT GOOSE *Branta bernicla*

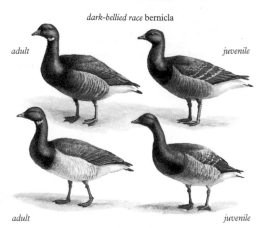

dark-bellied race bernicla

adult

juvenile

adult

juvenile

pale-bellied race hrota

△ Darkest of all black geese, and smallest – only as long as Mallard, though looks larger and heavier, especially in flight. White 'flash' on short, thick black neck distinctive. Adults of dark-bellied race show little contrast between black head, neck and breast and very dark brown belly. Adults of pale-bellied race have much paler underparts, contrasting strikingly with upperparts. Juveniles of both races lack white neck patches (start appearing by 1st winter) and have pale bars on wings. Juvenile pale-bellied has darker underparts than adult; sometimes as dark as adult/juvenile dark-bellied, but usually less dark above.

dark-bellied race
bernicla

△ Flight fast and agile, with more rapid wingbeats than other geese; dark-bellied race, especially, looks very dark except for striking white stern bordered by tiny black tail, showing only as a thin black line (unlike broad dark tails of all other geese). Wings of juvenile/ 1st-winter show pale stripes above.

KEY FACTS

Length: 56-61cm.
Wingspan: 110-121cm.
Weight: male 1.4-1.6kg; female 1.3-1.5kg. **Habitat:** muddy estuaries, saltmarshes and short grass or cereal fields near sea. **Movements:** dark-bellied race *bernicla* (breeds USSR) winters E and S Britain; pale-bellied race *hrota* (breeds Greenland and Spitsbergen) winters Ireland and Northumberland (Lindisfarne). **Population:** dark-bellied race: over 80 000 birds, but varies greatly with breeding success; pale-bellied race: *c*20 000 Ireland and 3000 Northumberland. **Diet:** eelgrass (*Zostera*), green algae, saltmarsh plants. **Voice:** deep, soft, throaty, nasal 'rronk' or 'rruk', producing distinctive growling sound in flock (low murmur in distance; roar when alarmed). **Maturity:** 2-3 years. **Confusion species:** Barnacle Goose (p72) larger, with contrasting black/grey/ white plumage and white face; Canada Goose (p73) much larger, with mainly brown plumage, white throat patch on black neck and pale chest.

| J | F | M | A | M | J | J | A | S | O | N | D |

◁ Brent Geese fly, feed and roost in large, tight-packed flocks, forming shapeless masses or long undulating lines and flying fast and low. Lean forward when feeding. Often swim on estuary or sea, with stern and tail angled upwards.

SHELDUCKS

Shelducks are large, goose-like ducks that spend a good deal of time on land and nest in holes. One species (Shelduck) is widespread; two others far less often seen. The similarly sized Ruddy Shelduck (*Tadorna ferruginea*) may occur as a genuinely wild vagrant from N Africa or SW Asia, but most seen here have escaped from wildfowl collections. Egyptian Goose (*Alopochen aegyptiacus*) is rather larger and longer-legged; introduced from tropical Africa to Norfolk and one or two other areas in S England, where it breeds in the wild; also escapes from captivity. Sexes similar.

female — *males* — **Ruddy Shelduck** — *rufous type* — *grey type* — **Egyptian Goose**

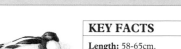

male

adult, asleep

female

male eclipse

juvenile

△ Mainly dazzling white with areas of black, chestnut and dark green; appears black and white at distance. Male has large knob above bright red bill. Legs pink. Female usually has small white marks around eye and base of duller bill. Feeds mainly by pushing bill through wet mud. Swims well.

△ Adults in duller eclipse plumage (late Jun-early Dec) have dull blackish heads with white on face, and only traces of chestnut breast band and black belly stripe; females even drabber than males. During wing-moult (Jul-mid-Oct), when flightless for about a month, loses black flight feathers. Juveniles duller, with white face and throat, all-white underparts, pinkish-white legs and bill; 1st-winter males similar to adult eclipse.

male

juvenile

△ Striking pattern in flight. Much duller juvenile shows white band along rear edge of wings. Flight steady, on arched wings, heavier, slower, more goose-like than other ducks, though with more rapid wingbeats than geese.

KEY FACTS

Length: 58-65cm.
Wingspan: 110-133cm.
Weight: male 1.1-1.45kg; female 850-1250g. **Habitat:** muddy estuaries, sandy shores, locally on inland waters; breeds some distance inland among farmland in places. **Movements:** most adults migrate Jul-Nov to moult in Waddenzee area, N Germany; much smaller numbers, mostly from Ireland, moult on Bridgwater Bay (Somerset), Wash and Forth. **Population:** c12 000 breeding pairs; c26 000 non-breeders. **Diet:** mainly small snails, also crustaceans and other invertebrates. **Voice:** mostly heard during breeding season; male makes variety of melodious whistling calls, female long growling 'aaark-aaark' and loud, cackling 'ga-ga-ga-ga-gak'. **Nest:** in holes, especially rabbit burrows, also tree holes, cavities in old buildings or among rocks or even in haystacks. **Eggs:** 8-10, cream. **Incubation:** 29-31 days, by female. **Fledging:** 45-50 days. **Broods:** 1. **Maturity:** 2 years (female); up to 4-5 years (male). **Confusion species:** male Shoveler (p82) smaller, sits low in water, has much larger chestnut area on belly/flanks, and huge bill.

| J | F | M | A | M | J | J | A | S | O | N | D |

DABBLING DUCKS

Dabbling (or surface-feeding) ducks feed by dabbling with bills (a 'nibbling' action) at surface of water, or in damp places on land, or by up-ending with heads and necks below water surface to reach bottom. On land, hold bodies horizontal and walk quite easily. When taking wing, they spring rapidly up almost vertically. Have a brightly coloured, often metallic rectangular patch (speculum) on secondary feathers of upperwing, often bordered at front and rear by pale bands; this is different in each species, providing a useful identification mark, and is particularly noticeable in flight. Sexes differ – males much easier to distinguish than drabber females – but during post-breeding eclipse plumage in late summer, when (like other ducks and geese) they lose all their flight feathers simultaneously and become flightless, males closely resemble females. Usually nest on ground.

● Note: size, proportions, facial markings, wing markings; females often stay close to males of their own species. Strictly speaking, Mandarin and Ruddy Duck (pp84-5) belong to separate groups (perching ducks and stifftails); they do not fit easily elsewhere and are included here for convenience.

Mallard

female

male

male, dabbling

female, up-ending

WIGEON *Anas penelope*

male eclipse

male

female, rufous type

juvenile

female, grey type

△ Rather dumpy, short-necked appearance compared to other dabbling ducks, with steep forehead and small bill. Male has chestnut head with striking yellowish-cream forehead and crown, mainly grey body; brilliant white forewings form a flash along flanks; rear flanks white, ending in black undertail coverts. Whistling calls of males useful identification feature. Females much drabber, though share male's white belly; some are more rufous, others greyer. They have a darker area around eyes and, like males, a short grey bill and grey legs. In eclipse plumage (Jun-Oct) males resemble females, but have more rufous head, breast and flanks, and white forewings often visible. Juveniles have more spotted head and neck, darker upperparts, sometimes a mottled belly and paler, greyer forewings, usually with some white.

Anas penelope **WIGEON**

174

males

females

△ In flight, wings look long and narrow, head small and rounded and tail quite short and pointed. Noticeably white belly. Males show striking white patch on inner forewings; females and immatures have greyish-brown forewings. Speculum dark green in males, duller and blackish in females and juveniles.

1st-winter male

◁ 1st-winter birds resemble adults after moult (Oct-Apr), but male's forewings not white until 2nd autumn, though they may show paler area that increases with wear.

female

male

male

△ More terrestrial than other British ducks, Wigeon walk easily and feed frequently on land, grazing in dense packs on pastures like geese, cropping the grass with their short bills. They also graze saltmarsh plants, eelgrass and other vegetation on muddy estuaries, as well as taking food on the water. They swim high in the water, with upward-pointing tails. Only small numbers breed in freshwater habitats in N Britain; large numbers winter, mainly on coast (though many visit inland Ouse Washes).

KEY FACTS

Length: 45-51cm.
Wingspan: 75-86cm.
Weight: male 700-900g; female 500-850g. **Habitat:** breeds by moorland lochs, pools and rivers and on marshes; winters on muddy estuaries and coasts and on inland marshes; visits nearby fields. **Movements:** British breeders make only local movements; large-scale immigration from N Europe Sep-Mar. **Population:** *c*500 breeding pairs; up to 250 000 birds winter. **Diet:** aquatic plants, grasses, roots; eelgrass on coasts in winter. **Voice:** male has loud whistling emphatic '*whee*-oo'; female deep rhythmic growling calls. **Nest:** on ground among dense cover near fresh water, lined with vegetation and female's down. **Eggs:** 8-9, cream. **Incubation:** 24-25 days, by female. **Fledging:** 40-45 days. **Broods:** 1. **Maturity:** 1 year. **Confusion species:** male Teal (p80) smaller, with green eyepatch and much less white on wings. Female Wigeon generally more rufous than other female dabbling ducks.

| J | F | M | A | M | J | J | A | S | O | N | D |

▷ Wigeon are very gregarious, flying in tight flocks or long irregular lines, often containing many hundreds of birds. Wingbeats are shallow and flickering and they fly fast and often high up. When landing, they make an abrupt, twisting descent.

MALLARD *Anas platyrhynchos*

male

female

142

△ Our largest and bulkiest dabbling duck, as well as the commonest and most widespread. Urban birds are tame. Large, long bill forms a smooth, continuous curve with the rounded head. Male easily identified by dark green head with white neck ring, chocolate-brown breast, pale body and uniquely curled black central feathers on white tail. Bill usually yellow, in some cases olive-green. Female mottled brown with paler head, usually with a narrow, dark eyestripe and pale stripe above eye. Tail whitish. Bill dark greyish with dull orange or greenish-brown near tip and at base; some have orange sides to bill (rarely as much as Gadwall).

juvenile   *male eclipse*

△ Juvenile resembles adult female, but often looks smaller and slighter, with neater, darker, more orange-brown plumage, black crown and eyestripe (like eclipse male). Neatly streaked underparts (coarsely mottled on eclipse male, spotted or mottled on female). Bill dull reddish-grey, soon darkening; gains adult colours during winter. In eclipse plumage (Jun–Sep), adult male distinguished from adult female by all-yellow (or all-olive) bill, darker crown and eyestripe, redder underparts and all-dark rump and upper tail coverts.

males

females

△ In flight, which is fast and direct, appears solid and heavy. Speculum bright purple-blue, with narrow black and white borders to front and rear; forewings greyish in male. Creamy underwing coverts contrast with darker flight feathers and, in female and juvenile, with brown body.

◁ Mallard frequently up-end to reach submerged food, revealing bright orange legs. Belly of female largely brown (whitish in Gadwall).

KEY FACTS

Length: 51-62cm.
Wingspan: 81-98cm.
Weight: male 850-1500g; female 750-1300g. **Habitat:** from remote sea lochs and coastal marshes to village ponds and city lakes or rivers; often in grassland away from water; also on sea near coast in winter. **Movements:** passage migrants and winter visitors from N Europe, Sep-Apr, especially E Britain. **Population:** *c*125 000 pairs breed; over 700 000 birds winter. **Diet:** very wide, including seeds, acorns and berries, plants, insects, shellfish and other small aquatic animals; also feeds far from water, e.g. on stubble fields for grain. **Voice:** female has familiar loud quacking; male has much quieter, high-pitched whistles and grunts during late autumn courtship, and nasal, froglike calls, mainly in spring. **Nest:** usually on ground, in vegetation; sometimes in bush or tree or on building; lined with vegetation and female's down. **Eggs:** 9-13, cream to greenish. **Incubation:** 27-28 days, by female. **Fledging:** 50-60 days. **Broods:** 1. **Maturity:** 1 year. **Confusion species:** female/ eclipse male/juvenile similar to Gadwall (opposite). Female/ eclipse male/juvenile Pintail (p83) slimmer, more elegant, with longer, more slender bill, uniformly pale head, longer, slimmer neck and longer, pointed tail.

J	F	M	A	M	J	J	A	S	O	N	D

Anas strepera **GADWALL**

143

△ Rather drab; males may be mistaken for females of other dabbling ducks. Mainly white speculum may be visible when on water or land. At closer range, greyer male shows mottled grey-brown head with dark eyestripe, neck peppered with black, finely barred grey back and flanks, black crescents on grey breast, buff scapulars, dark grey primaries and dark grey tail with strikingly black stern. Bill black, finer than Mallard's. Female has browner, more closely spotted head; resembles other female dabbling ducks but greyer; grey-brown tail, bill with prominent orange-yellow sides. Much less white on speculum than male. Distinctive head profile, with steep forehead and high curved nape. Swims high on water.

female *male*

juvenile *male eclipse*

△ In eclipse plumage (Jun-Aug), male resembles female (including orange-yellow sides to bill), but is darker and less strongly patterned above, with slightly less distinct, greyer crown and eyestripe, sometimes with black spots on belly. Juvenile differs from female in having darker, neater, less mottled, more uniform plumage, with bolder, blacker crown and eyestripe, paler, more contrasting face, orange-tinged breast, with even black lines of streaks on breast (mottled in female) and heavily spotted belly (female's is plain white).

males

females

△ In flight, which is fast and agile, with rapid beats of pointed wings, white underwings and clear-cut white belly are good identification features. Upperwings on male show large black and white speculum with chestnut panel in front; on female, white of speculum smaller, with duller blackish borders and no chestnut; looks smaller, slighter than Mallard.

▷ When up-ending, both sexes show white belly (brown in female Mallard) and orange-yellow legs; males can easily be distinguished by their black sterns.

male *female*

KEY FACTS

Length: 46-56cm.
Wingspan: 84-95cm.
Weight: male 700-900g; female 650-850g. **Habitat:** breeds by inland lakes, ponds, flooded gravel pits, reservoirs and marshes, with dense vegetation; winters on more open waters and locally on estuaries. **Movements:** many Scottish breeders winter in Ireland; N and E European breeders winter Aug-Apr. **Population:** over 800 pairs breed; up to 7500 birds winter. **Diet:** mainly freshwater plants, also seeds and insects. **Voice:** male utters deep nasal croaks and high-pitched, wheezy whistles; female's quacks quieter, higher pitched than female Mallard's; alarm call at breeding site a repeated 'ehk'. **Nest:** on ground by water's edge, among dense vegetation, lined with leaves and down from female. **Eggs:** 8-12, cream. **Incubation:** 24-26 days, by female. **Fledging:** 45-50 days. **Broods:** 1. **Maturity:** 1 year. **Confusion species:** female, eclipse male and juvenile Mallard (opposite) most similar, but larger, bulkier and less elegant in shape, and lack Gadwall's mainly white speculum. Adult male Wigeon (pp76-7) has white upperwing patches at front, not rear, and has different proportions and flight action. Female Pintail (p83) paler, with longer, slimmer neck, longer pointed tail, blackish bill.

TEAL *Anas crecca*

male

female

△ Smallest of all our ducks. Male has colourful striped head pattern, but looks simply dark-headed at long range. Noticeable at considerable range are long horizontal black and white stripe along scapulars separating grey back and flanks, and bold cream-yellow patches surrounded by black undertail. Female has similar plumage to Mallard (p78) but much smaller, with much more featureless face (indistinct dark eyestripe), buff-white streak along sides of undertail, and green, not blue, speculum. Bill slender and grey, in female yellowish-orange with darker spots. Legs dark grey.

male eclipse

juvenile

△ In eclipse plumage (Jun-Oct) males hard to distinguish from females unless they open one of their wings, when dull grey forewing visible (female's forewing is brown); head often shows dark cap/pale face contrast. Juvenile resembles female, but darker with much neater streaks or spots on breast, less contrasting belly and mainly pinkish bill.

males

females

△ In flight, from above, look for green and black speculum bordered by broad buff-white wingbar in front and narrow white one behind. From below, dark head and cream-yellow/black undertail distinctive.

male

female

▷ Leap almost vertically from water in take-off and dash off very quickly (wildfowlers' name for a flock is a 'spring' of Teal). Compact flocks fly fast with rapid beats of narrow, pointed wings and may resemble waders as they twist and turn in unison.

144

KEY FACTS

Length: 34-38cm.
Wingspan: 58-64cm.
Weight: 250-400g.
Habitat: breeds in marshes, also by moorland pools, streams, vegetated lakes and pools; winters on shallow freshwaters and estuaries.
Movements: many N European breeders winter here. **Population:** 3000-4500 pairs breed, up to 200 000 birds winter. **Diet:** aquatic plants, seeds, some invertebrates. **Voice:** male has short, piping, almost insect-like whistle, female a harsh, high-pitched 'quack' and low growl on take-off.
Nest: hollow among vegetation near water, lined with vegetation and female's down. **Eggs:** 8-11, cream to pale olive-buff. **Incubation:** 21-23 days, by female.
Fledging: 25-30 days.
Broods: 1. **Maturity:** 1 year.
Confusion species: Garganey (females, eclipse males and juveniles): see opposite.

| J | F | M | A | M | J | J | A | S | O | N | D |

female   *male*

△ Very active when feeding, filtering seeds from shallow water/mud. Large numbers winter at favoured sites.

female   male

△ Scarcely larger than Teal, with longer bill and less rounded crown. Male has rich brown head with a dazzlingly white stripe extending from above eye to nape, pinkish-brown breast with blackish markings, drooping black and white scapulars, and grey underparts. Female similar to female Teal, but paler and more coarsely patterned; different head pattern, with bolder white stripe above eye, accentuated by dark crown and stripe through eye, and whitish patch behind bill and whitish throat patch, usually separated by dark bar across cheeks.

KEY FACTS

Length: 37-41cm.
Wingspan: 63-69cm.
Weight: male 300-500g; female 250-450g. **Habitat:** shallow reedy pools, rushy marshes, fens, water meadows. **Movements:** summer visitor to British Isles and much of Europe, wintering in W Africa. **Population:** 40-50 pairs breed most years; occasionally 90 or more pairs. Long-term decline due to habitat loss. **Diet:** aquatic invertebrates and plants. **Voice:** generally silent; male has a dry, crackling rattle; female utters short sharp quacks. **Nest:** hollow among vegetation near water, lined with plant material and female's down. **Eggs:** 8-11, creamy buff. **Incubation:** 21-23 days, by female. **Fledging:** 35-40 days. **Broods:** 1. **Maturity:** 1 year. **Confusion species:** Teal (opposite). Females, eclipse males and juveniles slightly smaller, with shorter, narrower bill with yellow-orange base, no pale spot behind bill, less well-marked head and pale patch at tail base.

male eclipse   juvenile

△ Eclipse male (Jun-Feb) very like female, but crown generally darker, sides of head streaked; easily distinguished if opens wing, when pale grey forewing visible. Juvenile differs from adult female in being darker, with neater patterning, especially on breast and flanks and duller, streaked belly, and often with an orange-brown tint to underparts.

males

females

△ Most distinctive feature in flight is blue-grey upper forewing (paler, brighter and more noticeable in males), larger than that of much bigger, heavy-billed Shoveler (p82). Speculum dull (green), edged on both sides with bold white bars; in female, front bar often smaller and duller (in Teal, both sexes have narrower and duller hindbar). Looks longer-bodied than Teal; flight somewhat slower, less dashing.

| J | F | M | A | M | J | J | A | S | O | N | D |

▷ Unique among ducks in visiting British Isles/Europe only in summer, to breed in very small numbers; more often seen on migration in early spring/autumn. Usually seen in pairs or small groups; unobtrusive. Feeds mainly by dabbling, rarely up-ends.

male   female

SHOVELER *Anas clypeata*

female

male

147

△ Males very distinctive, with green-black head, chestnut flanks, white breast, black back and stern, and staring yellow eyes. They have a dramatic head-bobbing courtship display from mid-winter to spring. Females have similar mottled brown pattern to female Mallard (p78), but huge bill usually distinguishes them immediately; also have plainer face pattern, more coarsely patterned upperparts, and often orange-brown underparts; eyes brown. Legs bright orange in both sexes.

juvenile

male 'supplementary'

male eclipse

△ Males in eclipse (Jun-Aug) quite distinct from females, with blackish head, bright yellow eyes, rich orange-buff flanks and belly, plain blackish upperparts. Later (Sep-Nov), with further moult, some males develop redder 'supplementary' plumage, becoming white on breast and rear flanks, with large whitish crescent between eye and bill. Juvenile darker and greyer than female, with more neatly patterned plumage, especially underparts. Bill smaller than adults' and legs duller orange.

male

males

female

△ This heavy-looking, short-necked medium-sized duck has a huge, broad, shovel-shaped bill, which it pushes through the water to filter seeds and invertebrates, trapping the food on rows of tiny spines. It swims with its front end low in the water, sometimes almost awash. Groups may feed in unison, swimming in lines or circles and stirring up the water to bring food to the surface. Also up-ends and dives.

▷ 'Front-heavy' in flight: big head, huge bill in front, short tail behind, small pointed wings set far back. Wings beat fast; often flies high. From above, pale blue-grey inner forewing, speculum green with white bar in front; both brighter in male. Whitish underwings.

males

females

KEY FACTS

Length: 44-52cm.
Wingspan: 70-84cm.
Weight: male 475-1000g; female 400-750g. **Habitat:** breeds in shallow marshy areas and wet meadows; more widespread in winter on lowland freshwaters, coastal lagoons and estuaries. **Movements:** most of British breeding population move S by Oct to winter in Mediterranean region; large numbers migrate from N and E Europe and Russia to winter here. **Population:** *c*1500 pairs breed; as many as 10 000 birds winter. **Diet:** small crustaceans, molluscs, insects, seeds, aquatic plants. **Voice:** male has a gruff, quiet 'took-took' call, female a 'quack', usually quieter than Mallard's. **Nest:** hollow among vegetation near water, lined with vegetation and female's down. **Eggs:** 8-12, pale buff to greenish. **Incubation:** 22-23 days, by female. **Fledging:** 40-45 days. **Broods:** 1. **Maturity:** 1 year. **Confusion species:** forewing of male Garganey (p81) also bluish, but less striking; Garganey much smaller and lacks huge bill.

| J | F | M | A | M | J | J | A | S | O | N | D |

Anas acuta PINTAIL

KEY FACTS

Length: male 63-70cm, including 10cm tail streamers; female 53-59cm. **Wingspan:** 80-95cm. **Weight:** male 750-1200g; female 550-1000g. **Habitat:** breeds by moorland pools and lakes, and in East Anglian marshes; winters mainly on flooded fens and on estuaries. **Movements:** breeders from Iceland, N Europe and Russia migrate to winter here. **Population:** fewer than 30 pairs breed, *c*26 000 birds winter. **Diet:** seeds, other vegetation, on estuaries in winter mainly tiny snails; can up-end deeper than other ducks and thus feed in deeper water; increasingly flies to farmland to feed at night on cereal stubble, waste potato and sugar-beet. **Voice:** male has low, quiet whistle and long, nasal 'whee' in display, female low, hoarse 'quack' and croaks. **Nest:** hollow among short vegetation near water lined with plant material and female's down. **Eggs:** 7-9, creamy to greenish. **Incubation:** 22-24 days, by female. **Fledging:** 40-45 days. **Broods:** 1. **Maturity:** 1-2 years. **Confusion species:** female differs from other similarly plumaged female dabbling ducks in paler, more graceful appearance, with longer bill and neck and longer, more pointed tail. Male Long-tailed Duck (pp92-3) also has long tail feathers, but is much more marine with different plumage.

| J | F | M | A | M | J | J | A | S | O | N | D |

female *male*

△ This slim, elegant, long-necked duck has long, blackish-grey bill on neat, round head, and dark grey legs. Males have gleaming white breast, noticeable at long range. The white extends in stripe up neck and onto chocolate-brown head. Grey body ends with distinctive cream-and-black undertail and long black central tail feathers. Females pale buffish with featureless head and often gingery tinge to head and neck; body strongly and coarsely patterned with cream and gold, flanks with large dark crescents; belly whitish.

male eclipse *juvenile*

△ Male eclipse (Jul-Sep) like female, but often greyer, more finely patterned. Best distinctions are grey mantle, long black rear scapulars, and especially paler grey sides to bill. Juveniles tend to look neater than adult females, with paler, duller bills, but some males resemble adult eclipse males.

male *female*

△ The long central tail feathers of males often raised, but lowered when birds are nervous or up-ending for food.

males *females*

△ In direct, fast, high flight looks long and slim, with small head on long thin neck and pointed tail. From above, male shows pale inner forewing and dull bronze-green speculum. Females and juveniles have even more inconspicuous brownish speculum. In both sexes, speculum has dull buff line in front and conspicuous white trailing edge behind. From below, both sexes show grey underwings and pale belly.

MANDARIN DUCK *Aix galericulata*

148

male

Wood Duck

female

male

Mandarin Duck *female*

△ Small, large-headed duck with short neck and long tail. Exotic-looking male sports striking multicoloured plumage with drooping metallic green and chestnut crest, bold white eyebrows, large chestnut and orange whiskers and bright orange 'sails' on back. Female drab by comparison, with narrow white 'spectacles' on grey head, smaller crest, brown upperparts and buff underparts with cream spots. Both sexes have white undertail coverts. **Wood Duck** (*Aix sponsa*): male darker-headed than male Mandarin, with buff belly and no 'sails'; female very like female Mandarin, but with smaller crest, slightly darker upperparts, smaller white flank spots, larger white patch around eye, dark (not white) tip to bill and less pointed tail.

male eclipse

juvenile

△ Male Mandarin in eclipse plumage (May–Sep) resembles female, but head paler grey, bill dull red, white 'spectacles' less distinct, no white behind bill, and breast and flanks streaked with buff. Juvenile more uniform above with very vague head markings and streaked/spotted brown below.

males

females

△ Mandarin flies fast and with great agility among trees; primary wing feathers edged with white, secondaries tipped with white; speculum green with black border on rear edge.

▷ Needs old trees with large holes for nesting. Member of the perching duck group, just as much at home perching on branches as swimming on water. Ducklings leap from nest within 24 hours of hatching.

female

chicks

KEY FACTS

Length: 41–49cm.
Wingspan: 68–74cm.
Weight: male 500–700g; female 400–600g. **Habitat:** lakes, ponds and slow rivers bordered by broadleaved woodland. **Movements:** local movements only.
Population: *c*7000 or more birds; continued increase in range and numbers since introduction from E Asia in 1930s and first breeding of feral escaped birds. **Diet:** seeds, acorns, chestnuts, beechmast, snails, insects.
Voice: usually silent, but male utters brief whistle during courtship, while female makes repeated plaintive 'aak' and sharp coot-like 'keek'; flight-call 'kwick'. **Nest:** in holes in old trees, lined with down from female. **Eggs:** 9–12, cream. **Incubation:** 28–30 days, by female.
Fledging: 40–45 days.
Broods: 1. **Maturity:** 1 year.
Confusion species: Wood Duck, N American relative introduced into Britain, frequently escapes from captivity: see above left. In flight, Wood Duck shows blue speculum, in contrast to green speculum of Mandarin.

| J | F | M | A | M | J | J | A | S | O | N | D |

Oxyura jamaicensis RUDDY DUCK

149

male

male, courtship display

female summer

△ Male in breeding plumage unmistakable: rich chestnut body, black and white head, large brilliant blue bill, bold white undertail coverts. In dramatic courtship display, cocks tail vertically, raises two tufts of feathers on head and inflates an air-sac in neck, then rapidly drums on swollen neck with bill, producing a hollow rattling and a raft of air bubbles on the water surface. Female brown, darker above than below, with peaked dark brown crown, dingy whitish cheeks divided by an indistinct dark line and a duller blue-grey bill. Both sexes have big head with bill sloping up into steep forehead, dumpy body and long stiff tail (Ruddy Duck belongs to the stifftail group), which may be held cocked up or horizontally along water.

KEY FACTS

Length: 35-43cm.
Wingspan: 53-62cm.
Weight: male 550-800g; female 350-650g. **Habitat:** lakes, ponds, reservoirs, flooded gravel pits with reedy edges in breeding season; also open waters in winter.
Movements: seasonal local movements only.
Population: *c*2800 birds; continued increase in range and numbers since feral breeding began 1960 after escapes from Wildfowl Trust collection at Slimbridge, Glos, in 1952 and 1957; most breed W Midlands, but increasingly widespread in winter. **Diet:** mainly insect larvae, seeds of water plants.
Voice: usually silent; during courtship male utters grunts and low belches; female makes hisses and high squeaks; both rattle bill.
Nest: floating platform of vegetation anchored to reeds or other aquatic vegetation.
Eggs: 6-10, buff-white.
Incubation: 25-26 days, by female. **Fledging:** 50-55 days. **Broods:** 1. **Maturity:** 2 years. **Confusion species:** female, winter male and juvenile may be confused with Slavonian and Black-necked grebes (pp50-1) and female and immature Smew (p97).

| J | F | M | A | M | J | J | A | S | O | N | D |

juvenile

male eclipse

female winter

△ In eclipse plumage (Aug-Mar), males resemble females but with much darker crown, pure white cheeks and usually some chestnut on back. Females in winter have browner back than in summer, with pale barring, no rufous tinge, greyer cheeks and even more indistinct face stripe. Juveniles resemble winter females, but duller and greyer with more scaled breast and more strongly barred back, flanks and undertail. May gather in large flocks in winter. Seldom leave water and walk only with difficulty; swim buoyantly and dive frequently (may simply slip under surface like grebes).

males

females

▷ Flight rapid, on short, rounded whirring wings. Looks very short-necked, big-headed and long-tailed. Ruddy Ducks are small (scarcely bigger than Teal, though much dumpier-bodied), with an odd 'weight-forward' appearance.

85

DIVING DUCKS

Diving ducks dive for food from water surface and swim underwater. Unlike dabbling ducks, patter heavily along water before taking off; shorter-necked and dumpier-bodied; less mobile on land, where they stand upright and walk very awkwardly. Most lack speculum, but wingbars and patches important identification features. Nest in boggy moorlands, on lake shores or islands. Divided into 2 groups: pochards mainly freshwater species; males boldly patterned, females mostly duller. Some mainly vegetarian; others take more invertebrate animals. Eiders and other sea-ducks (Long-tailed Duck, scoters and Goldeneye) feed almost entirely on invertebrates; normally marine outside breeding season except for Goldeneye.

Pochard male — Tufted Duck male — diving — Velvet Scoter male, taking off

POCHARD *Aythya ferina*

KEY FACTS

Length: 42-49cm.
Wingspan: 72-82cm.
Weight: 700-1100g.
Habitat: breeds by well-vegetated lakes, pools, flooded gravel-pits, marshes and rivers; winters on open freshwaters and estuaries.
Movements: British breeders disperse in winter, some moving to Continent; many passage migrants/winter visitors from N and C Europe.
Population: up to 400 pairs breed, mainly in SE England (especially Norfolk Broads and N Kent and Essex marshes); up to 80 000 birds winter. **Diet:** chiefly plant material, including many seeds; also some invertebrates.
Voice: largely silent, but male utters soft double wheeze (like bellows) in courtship and female harsh growling calls in flight. **Nest:** dense mat of vegetation and down from female; on ground near water, often among reeds.
Eggs: 8-10, pale greenish.
Incubation: 25 days, by female. **Fledging:** 50-55 days.
Broods: 1. **Maturity:** 1 year.
Confusion species: Red-crested Pochard (opposite); also hybrids between Ferruginous Duck and Tufted Duck with Pochard (see opposite and p88).

| J | F | M | A | M | J | J | A | S | O | N | D |

male

female eclipse

△ Stocky shape, with high-crowned, peaked head and long bill. Male has striking combination of chestnut-red head and neck, black breast and stern and pale grey body; bill pale grey, with darker base and tip; eyes red. Female in eclipse (Mar-Oct) has dark yellowish-brown head, neck and breast with distinctive pale face markings, paler greyish-brown body, dark brownish stern; bill as male but darker; eyes brown, reddish in spring.

male eclipse — female winter — juvenile

△ Male eclipse (Jun-Sep) has duller, browner head with mottling on throat and neck, duller blackish breast with pale spots and browner-grey back. In winter, female has greyer body, contrasting more with head/breast and stern. Juvenile resembles adult female, but has duller, greyer head/neck without pale 'spectacles' and greyer upperparts.

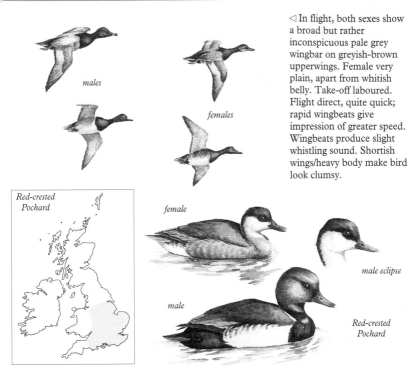

◁ In flight, both sexes show a broad but rather inconspicuous pale grey wingbar on greyish-brown upperwings. Female very plain, apart from whitish belly. Take-off laboured. Flight direct, quite quick; rapid wingbeats give impression of greater speed. Wingbeats produce slight whistling sound. Shortish wings/heavy body make bird look clumsy.

males

females

Red-crested Pochard

female

male eclipse

male

Red-crested Pochard

△ **Red-crested Pochard** (*Netta rufina*) larger than Pochard (length: 53-59cm), male with clearly distinct breeding plumage and bright red bill; female has dark cap contrasting with pale cheeks and mainly blackish bill (resembles female Common Scoter, p94, occasionally seen on freshwater, but larger, paler, with different head/bill shape, and sits higher on water). Eclipse male like female but retains red bill. In flight, shows broad white wingbar and white underwings. Most birds seen here have escaped from captivity; some breed in wild in S Britain. Found on freshwaters with reeds or other cover; on more open waters in winter.

Ferruginous Duck

female

male

male Ferruginous Duck x female Pochard hybrid

△ **Ferruginous Duck** (*Aythya nyroca*) small (length: 39-43cm) and dainty. Male distinctive: rich dark chestnut, blacker on back and tail, with striking white stern and white eyes. Female duller, more like female Tufted Duck (p88), but distinguished by much larger, gleaming white stern, smaller size and slimmer shape, and head profile: high crown, sloping forehead and long bill. In flight, broad white wingbar longer than on Tufted. Rare visitor to SE England from E/S Europe, mainly Sep-Apr, and occasionally escapes from captivity.

△ Hybrids between male Ferruginous Ducks and female Pochards resemble genuine Ferruginous Duck closely. Differences are faint grey crescents on upper back and typical Pochard wedge-shaped head and bill profile, with larger black tip to bill, sometimes with pale curved band behind, and greyer wingbar in flight.

TUFTED DUCK *Aythya fuligula*

151

female   *female 'Scaup-faced'*

male

△ Widespread and familiar duck, often found on urban freshwaters, where it is tame. Male all-black except for gleaming white flanks and belly; head has purple gloss in good light and bears a long drooping crest. Females are nondescript, unstreaked dark brown with paler barred brown flanks and belly and short crest; pale undertail, especially late summer; many have white on face, like female Scaup but never as extensive; also female Scaup have paler upperparts and head shape is different. Bills of both sexes have broader black tip than Scaup's, usually with whitish band behind tip.

male eclipse   *juvenile*

△ Male eclipse (Jun-Sep) has scruffier, shorter crest, duller, browner mantle/breast, pale grey-brown flanks barred darker; some have small white area at base of bill. Juveniles greyer than females, with buff feather edges, small buff patch at base of bill and dark-spotted pale grey undertail. 1st-winter males resemble adults but have shorter crests and grey-brown flanks.

male Tufted Duck x   *male Tufted Duck x*
female Scaup hybrid   *female Pochard hybrid*

△ Male Tufted Duck x female Scaup and x female Pochard hybrids are frequent. Tufted Duck x Scaup generally have less rounded heads than Scaup, often with slight crest, and slightly larger black tip to bill than Scaup. Tufted Duck x Pochard usually smaller than Scaup, often with slight crest, bill smaller and narrower, eye richer, darker yellow, back and flanks darker, greyer and larger black tip to bill.

males   *females*

△ Takes off more easily than many diving ducks; flight fast and direct on short wings; bold white wingbar on upper wings and white underwings; white flanks and belly very conspicuous.

KEY FACTS

Length: 40-47cm.
Wingspan: 67-73cm.
Weight: male 600-1000g; female 450-950g. **Habitat:** breeds on lakes, rivers and reservoirs, including those in cities, and flooded gravel-pits with fringing vegetation; winters on more open freshwaters, locally on sheltered estuaries.
Movements: mainly resident in British Isles, but Scottish breeders move to Ireland for winter; passage migrant and winter visitor from Iceland and N Europe (Sep-Apr).
Population: over 9000 pairs breed; up to 80 000 birds winter. **Diet:** mainly molluscs, insects and other invertebrates; also some plant matter. **Voice:** male generally silent apart from quiet, low, repeated whistles during courtship; female has gruff growling calls. **Nest:** hollow lined with vegetation and down from female; usually hidden in dense cover near water. **Eggs:** 8-11, pale grey-green. **Incubation:** 25 days, by female. **Fledging:** 45-50 days. **Broods:** 1. **Maturity:** 1 year. **Confusion species:** Scaup (opposite) and hybrids between the two species and with Pochard (see this page). Unlike Scaup, restricted mainly to fresh water. Some female Tufted Ducks have white undertails, but never as striking as on smaller, redder-brown Ferruginous Duck (p87).

| J | F | M | A | M | J | J | A | S | O | N | D |

female winter

female summer

male

KEY FACTS

Length: 42-51cm.
Wingspan: 72-84cm.
Weight: 800-1300g.
Habitat: breeds by moorland lakes, pools and rivers; winters along coasts and estuaries and occasionally visits freshwaters nearby; rare far inland.
Movements: passage migrant and winter visitor from Iceland/N Europe Oct-Mar; a few in summer. **Population:** a few pairs nest irregularly in N Scotland; up to 10 000 birds winter, chiefly in the Firth of Forth, Dornoch Firth, Islay, the Solway, the Cheshire Dee and Carlingford Lough.
Diet: mainly molluscs, also other invertebrates and some aquatic vegetation and waste grain. **Voice:** generally silent; males give deep whistles in courtship; females have similar growling call to Tufted Duck's but slightly lower pitched. **Maturity:** 1-2 years.
Confusion species: male Tufted (opposite) similar, but has distinct crest, purple, not green, gloss to head, and black, not pale grey, back; female Tufted more similar, but has small crest and never as much white on face as female Scaup; also Tufted slightly smaller and narrower (about size of Pochard) and with squarer head, less sloping hind crown and smaller, narrower bill. Habitat and season useful clues; almost all Scaup seen here are marine, and they are very rare in summer, unlike Tufted.

J F M A M J J A S O N D

△ Male easily distinguished from male Tufted Duck by very pale grey back with dense pattern of fine wavy grey lines (vermiculation) visible at close range. Head round, with steep forehead; has green gloss in good light. Female in summer is paler, richer brown than female Tufted Duck, particularly on flanks, with larger white area encircling base of bill than on any female Tufted, and an indistinct whitish patch on ear coverts. In winter, mantle and flanks have grey vermiculation and ear covert patch usually disappears.

male eclipse

juvenile

△ Male eclipse (Jun-Aug) has black parts of plumage much duller, with large whitish crescent on ear coverts and often some whitish at bill base and on breast; back and flanks greyer, blotchier. Juvenile (often seen on autumn passage) resembles eclipse female, but with smaller, duller buffish-white patch at bill base, greyer plumage and mottled belly. Bill darker and eyes duller than female's.

Scaup female

Tufted Duck female

◁ Larger, 'broader-beamed' than Tufted Duck; rear of head evenly rounded without any trace of a tuft (head of Tufted Duck squarer, rear crown more vertical); bill longer, broader, with smaller black tip than Tufted's.

males

females

△ Very similar to Tufted Duck in flight, though body and wings look broader; male's pale grey back good identification feature, and female's large white face patch also distinctive; females also look paler than female Tufted.

EIDER *Somateria mollissima*

male

male

female

198

△ Large, bulky, long-bodied, short-necked sea-duck with slope of forehead continuing down bill, eyes set far back, and feathers extending in point to below nostrils. Male is the only duck with combination of white upperparts and breast and black flanks and belly; also has black crown and much of wings black, pale green patches on rear of head, pink flush on breast, and white ovals in front of black stern. Female cinnamon-buff, mottled and barred black; pale line above eye visible at close range.

males eclipse

female eclipse

△ Male eclipse (Jul-Nov) almost all blackish-brown, mottled buff, apart from mottled whitish stripe above eye, narrow white line of wing coverts and some white feathering on mantle, scapulars and breast. Female eclipse (Aug-Mar) much darker, more sooty brown, than breeding female, with pale stripe above eye more conspicuous.

△ From autumn until spring, small groups of males gather round a female and court her, with much tossing of their heads and jerking of their necks, accompanied by their distinctive cooing calls. The chorus of sound from these assemblies of amorous males may be audible from a considerable distance.

KEY FACTS

Length: 50-71cm.
Wingspan: 80-108cm.
Weight: 1.2-2.8kg. **Habitat:** breeds mainly on offshore islands, rocky coasts, sandy shores, also locally on estuaries, sea lochs and even inland by freshwater rivers and lakes; winters out to sea, but also visits inshore waters, especially those with mussel beds. **Movements:** non-breeders move S; some winter visitors from Denmark and Netherlands. **Population:** *c*32 000 pairs breed; up to 72 000 birds in winter. **Diet:** mainly molluscs, especially mussels; also crabs, starfish and other invertebrates. **Voice:** very vocal, especially during courtship displays from late winter to spring, when males give loud, low, far-carrying cooing moans ('ah-haooh' with accent on second syllable); females respond with low chuckling guttural 'kok-kok-kok-kok' (like distant boat engine). **Nest:** hollow copiously lined with down from female; sometimes colonial; among rocks, under driftwood etc, often exposed, usually within a few hundred metres of sea. **Eggs:** 4-6, pale greenish-grey. **Incubation:** 25-28 days, by female. **Fledging:** 65-75 days. **Broods:** 1. **Maturity:** 2-3 years. **Confusion species:** female King Eider (rare but regular visitor to N Britain, especially Scotland), see opposite.

| J | F | M | A | M | J | J | A | S | O | N | D |

female

1st-winter male   *2nd-year male*

juvenile

△ As with other ducks, female Eiders line their nests with down plucked from their breasts, but it is particularly warm and copious in this species. (Eiders are 'farmed' in Iceland and Norway for their valuable 'eiderdown', used in quilted jackets, duvets etc.) The female sits tightly for her month-long incubation period, and, despite often nesting in remarkably exposed sites, is protected from predators by her superb camouflage.

△ Juveniles resemble adult females but upperparts dull blackish on males and very dark brown on females; mottled white streak above eyes, cheeks and throat pale buff streaked darker, underparts with whitish and buff barring, no white wingstripe. There follows a sequence of moults, through various piebald phases in the male, until the adult plumage is attained.

males   *females*

△ Long, laboured take-off; flight strong and direct, but appearing rather heavy on short, broad wings; flies low over water, flocks in long, irregular lines; male shows white back and inner wings, female narrow white wingbar.

female

King Eider males

King Eider eclipse male

King Eider female

△ Eider chicks make their way to the sea as soon as they have hatched and dried out their down. On land they are vulnerable to predators, particularly gulls, but once on the water they can escape by diving. Since they can feed only in shallow water, they gather in crèches guarded by a few females while the rest of the adults go off to feed in deeper water.

△ **King Eider** (*Somateria spectabilis*) generally smaller (53-60cm long) and neater-looking than Eider. Male unmistakable, with large orange bill shield (smaller in eclipse males and 1st-winter males, which are mainly dull black with whitish or grey-brown chest); females and juveniles distinguished from female and juvenile Eider by rounder head, shorter bill with less feathering on sides, more on top; paler throat and cheeks (and sometimes paler round eyes), and 'smiling' expression due to more distinct upcurved gape line. Often mixes with Eiders.

LONG-TAILED DUCK *Clangula hyemalis*

199

Small, neat, round-bodied, with very short neck, small square or domed head, high steep forehead and short bill. Adult male has very long central tail feathers, except in late summer (Jul-Sep) eclipse plumage. Females and immature birds have short pointed tails.

female winter

male winter

△ Male in winter (Nov-Apr) strikingly plumaged, mainly white, with boldly contrasting blackish-brown markings. Pale grey area around eyes and blackish-brown patch on side of neck; bill pink or orange-yellow with black base and blue-grey tip. Female in winter (Dec-Apr, though some remain in autumn plumage) much duller, with dark grey-brown head and large whitish patch around eyes. Underparts white except for brownish breast band. Bill dark grey.

male summer

female summer

△ Male in summer (May-Jun) has blackish-brown head and neck, with large greyish-white patch around eyes. Chest also blackish-brown; rest of underparts whitish. Elongated feathers on 'shoulders' black with chestnut and buff edges. Female in summer (May-Aug) has similar, though duller, head pattern to male, white neck band, darker upperparts than winter female, and similar underparts to winter female.

female eclipse

male eclipse

△ Male eclipse (Jul-Sep) dull version of summer male, without elongated central tail feathers. Female eclipse (Aug-Nov) has white head and neck except for blackish crown and cheek patch; otherwise like summer female, but with browner upperparts and more grey-brown on upper breast and flanks.

KEY FACTS

Length: male 58-60cm (including 13cm tail); female 38-41cm. **Wingspan:** 73-79cm. **Weight:** male 600-950g; female 520-850g. **Habitat:** breeds by Arctic tundra lakes in Iceland, Scandinavia, Russia, N America and Greenland; winters at sea, generally well offshore; rare on inland waters. Seldom seen on land. **Movements:** winter visitor and passage migrant to Britain, most common from Northumberland N to Shetlands and in Outer Hebrides. Seen in all months, but most in winter. Has nested in N Britain. **Population:** c20 000 winter, c75 per cent of them in the Moray Firth area of Scotland. **Diet:** chiefly molluscs and crustaceans in winter. **Voice:** male very vocal, uttering loud, musical, yodelling calls, typically 'a-ahulee'; female gives low barking quacks. **Maturity:** 2 years. **Confusion species:** only other duck with such a long tail as male is male Pintail (p83), but latter species is a larger, longer-necked, elegant coastal or inland surface-feeder, with a very different head pattern. Females/immatures may be confused with females/immatures of Harlequin Duck *(Histrionicus histrionicus)*, an extremely rare vagrant to Scottish waters, but latter have dark, not pale, underparts.

J F M A M J J A S O N D

female autumn　　　　　*male autumn*

△ Male in autumn plumage (Sep-Nov) like winter male, but head and neck white except for mottled greyish-brown patch on lower cheeks and upper neck. Female in autumn plumage (Nov-Dec/Feb) like winter female but with head and neck as eclipse female.

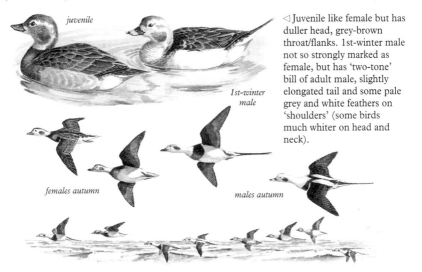

juvenile

1st-winter male

females autumn　　　　*males autumn*

◁ Juvenile like female but has duller head, grey-brown throat/flanks. 1st-winter male not so strongly marked as female, but has 'two-tone' bill of adult male, slightly elongated tail and some pale grey and white feathers on 'shoulders' (some birds much whiter on head and neck).

△ Only duck with combination of extensive white on body and unmarked blackish-brown wings. Dark breast band, in male extending up onto back to form 'Y', contrasts with white body. Rump black with white sides, like auks' (pp192-7). Flies very fast and usually low over water, swinging from side to side with distinctive 'rolling' action, to show alternately dark and white. Restless, often flying around together; small groups of males may be seen chasing a single female. Wings quite swept-back in flight, downcurved, and scarcely brought above horizontal on upstroke, but low on backward-flicking downstroke. Alights abruptly, breast first, with big splash.

autumn

◁ Swims buoyantly; long tail of male may not be apparent as often trailed on surface of water or even submerged, but it is raised when bird is alert. Dives frequently to depths of up to 20m, throwing back head, spreading tail and making distinct flick of wings before submerging. Can occur close inshore, but generally remains well out to sea, undeterred by the roughest waves.

COMMON SCOTER *Melanitta nigra*

200

Dark sea ducks, smaller than Mallard or Eider. Bulky body, thin neck and long head. Black legs. Swim very buoyantly, riding the waves like corks. Body often looks hunched-up on water, pointed tail frequently cocked. Usually seen well out to sea; rarely on land except when nesting or when sick or oiled. Very gregarious. Dive for food, usually with wings closed.

male

female

△ Male only duck with totally black plumage. Quite short, tapering black bill has bright orange-yellow patch on upper surface, and large black knob at its base. Female dark brown with mottled brownish-white underparts; pale greyish cheeks and throat, contrasting with dark crown and back of neck, are conspicuous. In late summer, some females have pale feathers on back. Greenish-black bill (often with yellow line on ridge of upper surface) has small knob at base. Legs blackish-grey.

juvenile

◁ Juvenile resembles adult female, but greyer above and paler below and on crown. May have very dull cheeks. Bill olive-green, yellowish-pink near base; no knob.

△ Fly very low over waves in long wavering lines or ragged bunches. A migrating group flying past in the distance resembles a kite in shape, the birds bunched up at front of group, with long 'string' snaking behind.

△ Often seen on water offshore in close-packed groups, or 'rafts'; may occur in favoured sites in large numbers. Frequently shake heads, stretch necks in 'S' shape and flap wings, and raise fanned tails vertically.

males

females

△ Flight strong, with rapid wingbeats. Wings of males make whistling sound on take-off. Look for female's pale cheeks and throat (though distant birds look all-dark). Underside of primary wing feathers looks pale in good light.

KEY FACTS

Length: 45-54cm.
Wingspan: 79-90cm.
Weight: male 1.3-1.45kg; female 1.2-1.3kg. **Habitat:** breeds by freshwater moorland or tundra lakes; winters at sea a few visit fresh waters inland.
Movements: British breeders at nesting sites Apr-Sep; winter visitors from Iceland and N Europe Sep-Apr; non-breeders all year. Migrants inland especially Mar-Apr/Jul-Aug. **Population:** over 100 pairs breed Scotland and Ireland; 25 000-30 000 winter Britain and Ireland. **Diet:** mussels, also cockles and other molluscs, crustaceans, fish eggs, worms, larvae, seeds. **Voice:** males give short, mellow piping whistles; females have louder, deep, harsh growling calls. **Nest:** hollow lined with down and plant material, on lake shore or island. **Eggs:** 6-8, cream or buff. **Incubation:** 30-31 days, by female. **Fledging:** 45-50 days. **Broods:** 1. **Maturity:** 2-3 years. **Confusion species:** Velvet Scoter (opposite) larger, with more wedge-shaped head/bill profile and striking white wing patches. Female/immature Ruddy Duck (p85) and Red-crested Pochard (p87) have similar plumage pattern; former much smaller/dumpier; latter bigger, paler, with pink bill tip; both have different head/bill shapes and found on fresh waters.

| J | F | M | A | M | J | J | A | S | O | N | D |

Melanitta fusca VELVET SCOTER

Velvet Scoters

male *female* *male*

Common Scoters

male *female* *male*

KEY FACTS

Length: 52-59cm.
Wingspan: 90-99cm.
Weight: male 1.2-2kg; female 1.1-1.25kg. **Habitat:** winters at sea; rare inland, usually after hard weather.
Movements: winter visitor (Oct-May) from breeding areas in Scandinavia and Russia; small numbers seen in other months. **Population:** 2500-5000 (occasionally up to 10 000) winter. Most frequent and numerous along E coasts England and Scotland; usually only individuals or small groups, except at favoured sites. Suspected of breeding in Scotland in the past. **Diet:** dives for mussels and cockles, also shrimps, crabs, worms and starfish. **Voice:** much less vocal in British Isles than Common Scoter; males may give a whistling 'whur-er' and female a harsh, croaking growl. **Maturity:** 2-3 years.
Confusion species: Common Scoter (opposite) smaller, with different head/bill profile and no white wing patches. Immature Eider (pp90-1) has somewhat similar head/bill profile, though with much flatter forehead, and strongly barred plumage. Juvenile Scaup (p89) sits higher on water, and has different head/bill shape and even shorter tail. Black Guillemot (p193) has white wing patches (though these cover much of inner wing) and red legs, but is much smaller, with very different bill.

△ Larger and bulkier than Common Scoter (males almost as big as Eider), and usually looks longer-backed and shorter-tailed. Long wedge-shaped forehead/bill profile, more like Eider than Common Scoter, head more triangular in profile; feathering extends almost to nostrils on top and sides of bill. May be difficult to distinguish from Common Scoter, especially at long range in rough seas, but white wing patches identify both sexes immediately – striking as birds fly or flap wings when on water. Also distinguished by red legs, if visible (as when bird diving or resting on sandbank). Generally scarcer than Common Scoter; usually in mixed groups with Common Scoters and/or Eiders. Often less wary than Common Scoter.

male

female, worn plumage

female

△ Male glossy black with small white crescent below eye, difficult to see except at close range. Bill orange-yellow with black knob at base and reddish tip. Female dark brown, usually with two distinct pale patches on face. In some females, these patches very faint; in older birds, front one especially may be absent. In both sexes, when swimming, white wing patch (secondary feathers) sometimes visible as small white triangle.

juvenile

1st-winter male

△ Juvenile paler than adult female, with larger, more prominent pale face patches; juvenile female with whiter belly than adult female. 1st-winter males develop blacker heads; by Jan-Mar, appear uniformly dull black, but yellow on bill much duller than in adult male and lacks latter's white eye-crescent.

males

females

△ Looks bulkier in flight than Common Scoter, with thicker neck and heavier head, usually held lower. Adults and immature birds show large brilliant white wing patch and, from below, red legs.

GOLDENEYE *Bucephala clangula*

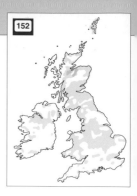

152

Dumpy, short-necked, with large, oddly shaped, high-peaked triangular head. Bill short. Tail quite long, held flat on water or cocked when resting. Yellow eyes (brighter in males) that give the species its name noticeable only at close range. Legs orange. Swims buoyantly, often with head sunk on shoulders, exaggerating humped back. Dives continually. Rarely seen on land except when breeding, but walks with ease and stands upright. Wary, readily flies off when approached, after long, pattering take-off. Usually gregarious, seen in small groups.

female   *male*

△ Male has boldly pied plumage and prominent circular white patch between bill and eye. Head has green gloss in good light. Upperparts show angled black lines across white of closed wing. Looks gleaming white at distance. Female smaller and squatter, with chocolate-brown head, mottled greyish upperparts, white collar (not visible when head retracted) and white patches usually visible on closed wing. Looks very dark at distance.

male eclipse   *juvenile*

△ Male eclipse (Jul-Oct) resembles female, but larger, with blackish-brown head, no white collar and browner mantle and flanks. Juvenile has duller, grey-brown head and mainly brown chest and upperparts.

males, displaying

female

◁ In late winter and early spring, groups of males display to females. They throw back their heads and point them skywards, showing off their gleaming white breasts, and splash with their feet. They may utter harsh piercing double notes and soft rattles.

males

females

△ In flight looks large-headed, short-necked. Flight very fast, usually low, with rapid wingbeats making loud whistling noise (loudest in adult male). Male flickers black and white. White wing patches extend almost to front of wing.

▷ Nest usually sited in tree hole 10-15m above ground. Provision of nest-boxes by the RSPB and the Forestry Commission has enabled Goldeneye to colonize Scotland over the last 25 years.

KEY FACTS

Length: 42-50cm.
Wingspan: 65-80cm.
Weight: male 820-1200g; female 600-900g. **Habitat:** breeds around wooded lakes and along river banks; winters in coastal waters and estuaries, and inland on reservoirs, lakes, large rivers.
Movements: passage migrant and winter visitor from N Europe, Oct-Apr.
Population: c100 pairs breed, almost entirely in Scotland; 10 000-20 000 birds winter. **Diet:** dives for molluscs, crustaceans and insect larvae. **Voice:** usually silent; during courtship display, male gives loud, harsh, nasal 'ze-zeee' call, followed by a low, hollow, quiet rattle, female a grating 'berr-berr'. **Nest:** usually in tree holes, sometimes in rabbit burrows and regularly and increasingly in nest-boxes; lined with down from female. **Eggs:** 8-11, bluish-green. **Incubation:** 29-30 days, by female. **Fledging:** 57-66 days. **Broods:** 1.
Maturity: 2 years.

| J | F | M | A | M | J | J | A | S | O | N | D |

female

SAWBILLS

Sawbills have slender, hook-tipped bills with saw-toothed edges, used for gripping fish which they catch by diving underwater. Long, slender bodies with proportions more like divers or cormorants than other ducks. Head with crest or shaggy feathers at rear. Look long and slim in flight, with head, neck and body horizontal, and have large white patches on upperwings. Nest in holes or on ground.

● Note: size; shape of crest, bill. See also differences between female/immature/eclipse male Red-breasted Merganser and Goosander (pp98-9).

Mergus albellus **SMEW**

female

male

△ Smallest sawbill: neat, with steep forehead, slight crest, small bill. Dives frequently. Male largely white with bold black eyepatch and black stripe on back. At close range, white crest with black streak, narrow black lines on body and pale grey flanks visible. Female smaller, darker, with grey back and pale grey breast and flanks, and slightly crested chestnut-brown cap contrasting with white cheeks and throat; blackish eyepatch.

juvenile

1st-winter male

△ Juvenile has paler orange-buff cap than female, browner mantle and dingy white wing patches. 1st-winter male has white flecks on orange-brown cap and on shoulders, and beginnings of black eyepatch and black lines on breast.

females

males

△ Smew can take off abruptly from water. Flight very fast and agile, with sudden swerves – birds do not bunch together closely. Looks more elongated, larger and heavier-bodied than on water, small head stretched forward. Male's largely white body contrasts with bold pied upperwings and back, and with dark underwings. Chestnut-brown cap and white cheeks of females and immatures distinctive. Adults have brilliant white patches at front of upperwings; smaller, duller in immatures.

KEY FACTS

Length: 36-44cm.
Wingspan: 55-69cm.
Weight: male 600-800g; female 500-650g. **Habitat:** winters on reservoirs, lakes, gravel pits, small pools; few on estuaries. **Movements:** winter visitor from breeding grounds in Scandinavia and Russia, Nov-Apr.
Population: up to *c*150 in normal winters, up to *c*350 in hard winters, when birds forced to leave major Dutch wintering grounds. **Diet:** chiefly fish, also some insect larvae and other invertebrates. **Voice:** usually silent in winter. **Maturity:** probably 2 years. **Confusion species:** females and immatures could be confused at distance with Slavonian Grebe (see p50).

J F M A M J J A S O N D

> Smew occur at favoured sites in small groups usually of adult females and immature birds (collectively known as 'redheads'), which tend to winter further S and W than adult males. Males may sometimes be seen displaying, raising crests and drawing heads back into 'shoulders'.

females

males, displaying

RED-BREASTED MERGANSER *Mergus serrator*

154

Long, slim body with long, thin, very slightly upcurved bill and wispy crest. Thin neck. As with Goosander, often searches for fish by submerging bill and eyes below surface. Often rises up in water, with or without wing flapping. Less buoyant on water than Goosander; usually swims with to-and-fro head motion, unlike Goosander. Walks easily, body held horizontal. Winters mainly along coasts and estuaries, unlike Goosander.

male   *female*

△ Male very distinctive, with glossy dark green head, orange-brown breast with black spots, black back separated from pale grey flanks by creamy-white streak along wing, and pattern of large white spots on black background separating breast and flanks. Bill bright red. Smaller female has rusty-brown head, brown and red bill, whitish throat and neck and brownish-grey body; similar to female Goosander, but smaller and slighter, with thinner neck, darker, browner body, wispier crest and more uniformly narrow, upcurved bill, and (especially) lack of clear-cut division between head, throat and neck. Variable amount of black around eyes, and thin white streak between bill and eyes (also present on juvenile Goosander). 'Smiling' facial expression compared with 'stern' Goosander. Legs red.

male eclipse   *juvenile*

△ Male eclipse (Jun-Nov) resembles female, but with blacker back, redder bill and male wing pattern, broad white streak showing along sides when on water. Juvenile similar, but with shorter crest, duller bill and greyer upper back. As with Goosander, immature male gradually acquires adult plumage during 1st winter and early spring; in early winter, may still have female-like head but other plumage as adult male.

males   *females*

△ Flies fast and usually low with strong wingbeats, thin neck and slender head stretched out straight. Wing pattern similar to Goosander's, with large white patch on upperwing; in male extends almost across whole wing, with two distinct black lines across it (none on male Goosander). Female's white wing patch divided by more distinct black line than female Goosander's.

KEY FACTS

Length: 51-62cm.
Wingspan: 70-85cm.
Weight: male 1-1.25kg; female 850-950g.
Habitat: breeds on islets in sea lochs and by open or forested lakes and rivers; winters mainly at sea, along sheltered coasts and estuaries. **Movements:** British breeders mainly resident, moving to coasts in winter; winter visitors from Iceland and Scandinavia, Sep-May. **Population:** *c*3000 pairs breed, chiefly in Scotland and Ireland, with smaller numbers in NW England and N Wales; up to 11 000 birds winter. **Diet:** chiefly fish, also invertebrates. **Voice:** male sometimes utters rattling purr in courtship; female gives muffled croaks or harsh 'krrr'. **Nest:** usually concealed among vegetation or in hollow among rocks or tree-roots. **Eggs:** 8-11, greenish or buffish. **Incubation:** 31-32 days, by female. **Fledging:** 60-65 days. **Broods:** 1. **Maturity:** 2 years. **Confusion species:** female/juvenile similar to female/juvenile Goosander (see left and opposite).

| J | F | M | A | M | J | J | A | S | O | N | D |

In late winter and early spring, small groups of males display, making strange mechanical-looking movements, jerking head and body up and down and raising wings slightly.

Mergus merganser **GOOSANDER**

KEY FACTS

Length: 57-69cm.
Wingspan: 82-98cm.
Weight: male 1.55-1.65kg;
female 1-1.25kg. **Habitat:**
breeds by large lakes and
rivers, especially with wooded
banks; winters mainly on
lakes and reservoirs, locally
on sheltered coasts and
estuaries. **Movements:**
British breeders resident all
year; winter visitors in hard
weather from N Europe.
Population: *c*3000 pairs
breed, mainly in Scotland,
with smaller numbers in
N England and a few in
Wales; 7000-8000 winter.
Diet: fish. **Voice:** generally
silent; during courtship, male
utters double frog-like croaks,
also bell-like or twanging
notes; female has harsh 'karrr'
and cackling calls. **Nest:**
often in tree holes, though in
some areas many nest in
heather or in holes in banks
or among rocks; also in nestboxes. **Eggs:** 8-11, cream.
Incubation: 30-34 days, by
female. **Fledging:** 60-70
days. **Broods:** 1. **Maturity:**
2 years. **Confusion species:**
female/juvenile similar to
female/juvenile Red-breasted
Merganser (see right and
opposite).

J F M A M J J A S O N D

▷ Large white patch on male's
upperwing lacks crossbars of
male Merganser; smaller white
patch on female's upperwing
has only hint of crossbar seen
in female Merganser.

Larger, bulkier than Red-breasted Merganser, with relatively
shorter, thicker-based, straighter, more strongly hooked bill,
steeper forehead, and neater, larger, drooping crest. Walks
easily, body held horizontal. In winter, far more on fresh
waters than in coastal waters, unlike Red-breasted Merganser.

male   *female*

△ Male much whiter than male Red-breasted Merganser; mainly
white body, with cream or salmon-pink tint to underparts
(fading in late winter), black back and glossy greenish-black
head. Bill deeper, more purple-red. Smaller female similar to
female Red-breasted Merganser, but paler bluish-grey body
and dark rufous head clearly separated from white throat and
breast; white areas have orange or pinkish tint. Legs red.

male eclipse   *juvenile*

△ Male eclipse (Jun-Nov) resembles female, but has redder
bill, blacker back, whiter flanks and male wing pattern, with
broad white streak showing along sides when on water.
Juvenile similar, but with yellow-brown bill, much shorter,
thinner crest, greyer head, less clearly defined white throat and
browner upperparts; has white line between bill and eyes, like
female Red-breasted Merganser.

Goosander   *Red-breasted*
female   *Merganser*
                       female

△ Female, eclipse male and immature Goosanders and Red-
breasted Mergansers are best distinguished by looking at head
and neck: in Goosander reddish-brown of head is sharply
demarcated from whitish breast, and throat patch clearer and
whiter; in Red-breasted Merganser head colour merges into
ill-defined whitish throat and chin. Also, Goosander has a
fuller, shaggy, drooping crest; that of Red-breasted Merganser
is wispy and usually forms two distinct tufts.

males   *females*

BIRDS OF PREY
Order Falconiformes

The day-active (diurnal) birds of prey (or raptors) are a big group of medium to huge long-winged birds with sharply hooked bills and strong talons for killing, holding and eating prey, which ranges from mammals and birds to fish and insects; many also eat carrion. Bare fleshy area at base of bill (cere) contains openings of nostrils. Typical active flight a series of wingbeats followed by a glide. The larger species, in particular, spend much time gliding, or soaring in upward spirals, while the smaller species, especially the falcons, are often seen in active flight, a few wingbeats alternating with a glide. Several species hover. Many also spend hours on end perched. In most species, females larger than males; otherwise, sexes usually alike. Identification may be difficult, especially as often seen in flight at distance, and immature plumages very confusing. Details of proportions, wing and tail shape, flight action and position of wings during gliding and soaring help identification even at long range. Divided into several distinct groups, classified in three families: Pandionidae (Osprey), Accipitridae (kites, harriers, eagles, hawks and buzzards) and Falconidae (falcons).

Osprey (below)   *harriers (pp103-5)*   *buzzards (pp110-13)*   *falcons (pp114-19)*   *hawks (accipiters) (pp108-9)*   *kites (p102)*   *eagles (pp106-7)*

OSPREY
Family Pandionidae

The Osprey, the single species in its family, is a specialist fish hunter. Adaptations are waterproof plumage, nostrils that can be closed as bird plunges into water, bare legs to avoid soiling with fish scales and slime, a long hook to the bill for eating fish, and, for grasping this slippery prey, a reversible outer toe, long curving talons and tiny spines on the undersurface of the toes. One of the most widespread of all birds, breeding throughout much of world. Most northern breeders are long-distance migrants, wintering in the south. Sexes very similar.

OSPREY *Pandion haliaetus*

juvenile

adult male

118

◁ Spends much of day at rest perched upright on favourite branch high in tree, or on rock or post. Almost always seen near water. Large, pale bird of prey, about size of Buzzard (pp110-11), but with longer, narrower wings. Upperparts dark brown and blackish, head white with slight brown-streaked crest and bold dark bands through eyes; underparts white with variable breast band of rusty to brown streaks, usually more prominent in female; male may even lack breast band altogether. Bill black, with blue-grey cere, legs blue-grey. Juvenile has pale cream edges to feathers of upperparts, more heavily streaked crown and nape, and less distinct breast band.

KEY FACTS

Length: 55-65cm.
Wingspan: 145-170cm.
Weight: male 1.2-1.75kg;
female 1.2-2kg. **Habitat:**
lakes, reservoirs, large rivers,
estuaries, coasts.
Movements: summer visitor
Apr-Sep, wintering in
Mediterranean and Africa;
also passage migrants from
Scandinavia pass through
Apr-May and Aug-Oct.
Population: extinct as a
British breeder from 1916
until 1955, when started to
nest again in Scottish
Highlands; now *c*100 pairs.
Diet: wide variety of fish,
averaging 300g in weight.
Voice: loud yelping contact
call, plaintive cheeping display
call of male above territory
and repeated short shrill
whistling 'pyew pyew pyew' at
nest. **Nest:** large structure of
sticks, lined with grass, moss
and finer material,
replenished annually until
massive size; usually at top of
tall conifer near water, also on
ruined buildings on islands
and on artificial platforms.
Eggs: 2-3, white or cream,
with brown blotches.
Incubation: 37 days, mainly
by female. **Fledging:** 44-59
days. **Broods:** 1. **Maturity:**
2-3 years. **Confusion
species:** confusable in flight
at distance with large gulls
(see below). Female and
immature Marsh Harrier
(p103) similar from above,
but smaller, with dark
underparts and yellow legs,
and usually seen gliding with
wings held in marked 'V'.

J F M A M J J A S O N D

▷ Osprey's habit of gliding
and soaring with upwardly
kinked, bowed wings means
that it may be confused at a
distance with large gulls.
Gulls have bigger, longer
heads, narrower, pointed
wings, flapped more often
with more languid beats; also
lack black 'wrist' patches.

*fish-catching
technique*

△ An Osprey catches fish in spectacular fashion, pausing in
flight to hover *c*10-40m above water, legs dangling and head
bent downwards to search for prey. May descend in stages,
hovering in between, to pinpoint position of prey. Dives
headlong, but enters water feet-first with loud splash, partially
or completely submerging except for open wings, and sinks its
talons deep into fish's body. On emerging, shakes plumage
vigorously before flying off. Carries fish head-first in talons,
usually with one foot behind the other. Sometimes hunts from
perch, or plucks fish from surface without hovering.

◁ A pair of Ospreys soar
and chase one another in
courtship display, male
making series of dramatic
roller-coaster dives and
ascents while dangling feet.

▽ Flight powerful, with shallow, stiff wingbeats. Head small
and stubby; sometimes protrudes in upward curve. Wings long
and narrow and distinctly angled, with projecting 'wrists' and
slender 'hands'. Appears dark above and white below. From
above, dark wings, back and tail contrast with white of head.
Underwings whitish with black trailing edge and tips, black
patches at 'wrists', and broken, dark, diagonal bar and rows of
small dark spots between.

above

below

Osprey

Herring Gull immatures

Both sexes build large nest of
sticks. Despite its size, it can
be inconspicuous among
foliage at top of conifer.
While female incubates, male
brings fish to her on the nest.
The easiest way to see
Ospreys in Britain is at the
RSPB reserve at Loch
Garten, Scotland, where
there is a special observation
hide used by almost 80 000
visitors per year.

101

KITES
Family Accipitridae

Kites are medium-sized, with long wings and long forked tails. Glide and soar with great agility, using tail as rudder. Diet includes much carrion as well as live prey. Sexes alike. Only 1 species breeds in British Isles.

RED KITE *Milvus milvus*

KEY FACTS

Length: 60-65cm.
Wingspan: 145-165cm.
Weight: male 750-1000g;
female 950-1300g. **Habitat:**
in Wales breeds in mature oakwoods in steep valleys, hunting over high sheep-grazed moorlands; in winter also over bogs, meadows and other open country.
Movements: Welsh breeders mostly remain in breeding area, but some young birds wander as far as Scotland and Kent, staying away from home for 1st winter or even longer.
Population: widespread in British Isles, even in towns, until late 18th century, but persecution reduced it to near-extinction by end 19th century; rescued from this fate by conservationists aided by local farmers; now rare breeder in central Wales, with up to 150 pairs nesting; also recent programme of reintroduction of Swedish and Spanish birds to Scotland and England, where over 50 pairs breed. Still suffers from illegal poisoning. **Diet:** chiefly carrion, also birds, small mammals and invertebrates, especially earthworms. **Voice:** thin, shrill mewing 'wee-oo', also quavering, piping whistle 'weeè-wee-wee'. **Nest:** of sticks and mud, often decorated with rags, pieces of polythene and other rubbish; built high in tree on top of old nest of Buzzard, Raven or other large bird. **Eggs:** 2-4, whitish, with reddish-brown blotches. **Incubation:** 31-32 days, by female. **Fledging:** 48-60 days. **Broods:** 1. **Maturity:** 2-4 years.

J F M A M J J A S O N D

△ Whitish head, with blackish streaks; upperparts reddish-brown with pale edges to feathers, blackish wingtips; chestnut-red underparts with dark streaks; tail glowing reddish-orange, with blackish corners, deeply forked. Feeds on ground, where it hops rather clumsily and holds body horizontal; perches upright in trees.

below

adults

juveniles

above

△ From below, large, prominent whitish patches on outer wings, black primaries and grey-brown inner wings. Tail almost translucent, with blackish corners. From above, broad, pale creamy-brown diagonal bar across inner wings. Tail bright reddish with blackish corners. Juvenile has pale brown, not white, head and paler, more sandy, underparts. Tail less deeply forked, browner above. Wings show narrow whitish line along centre both above and below, and from above larger, paler diagonal bar.

△ Has exceptionally graceful, agile and buoyant flight, with wings held flat or slightly bowed and angled backwards at 'wrists'; long, forked tail constantly moved from side to side, twisted and fanned. Wingbeats slow and deep. Wings appear set far forward, due to long rear body and tail. In profile, often looks bowed, head and tail hanging down slightly. Like tail forks, wings constantly flexed independently. Fully spread tail less forked, but corners always look pointed.

HARRIERS
Family Accipitridae

Medium-sized, with rather owl-like heads, slender bodies, long slender wings and longish tails. Flight light and buoyant, usually low over moorland, fields, reedbeds and other open habitats. Slow wingbeats alternate with glides on raised wings, held in shallow 'V'. (Buzzards, which soar on raised wings, have broader wings and shorter, more fully spread tail; also, they glide on flat, not raised, wings.) Drop to ground to seize small mammals, birds and other prey with their long legs. Walk easily on ground and stand, often with bodies held horizontal, on rocks, posts and other low perches. Do not require trees or cliffs for breeding like most other birds of prey, but nest on ground. Sexes differ.

● Note: size, presence or absence of white rump, underwing and upperwing markings. Males quite easy to identify with reasonable views, but female and immature Hen and Montagu's Harriers very hard to distinguish, and often grouped together as 'ringtails'.

MARSH HARRIER *Circus aeruginosus*

117

female

male

KEY FACTS

Length: 48-55cm.
Wingspan: 110-125cm.
Weight: male 400-650g; female 550-800g. **Habitat:** breeds in large reedbeds; hunts over saltmarshes, fields and other open habitats.
Movements: most British breeders winter in Mediterranean and NW Africa; scarce passage migrant from Continent, mainly Sep-Nov/Mar-May. **Population:** over 100 pairs breed. **Diet:** small mammals, birds, eggs and chicks, frogs, carrion.
Voice: male utters shrill 'kee-oo', rather like Lapwing's (p143), in display flight, and hoarse chattering 'kyek-ek-ek-ek' when attacking an intruder; female gives long, mewing, high whistles, and pair have 'kye-ki-ki-ki' and 'keesh' calls in courtship flight. **Nest:** bulky mound of reeds and twigs, lined with aquatic plants, on ground or over shallow water among dense reeds. **Eggs:** 4-5, very pale blue, often stained darker. **Incubation:** 31-38 days, by female. **Fledging:** 35-40 days. **Broods:** 1. **Maturity:** 2-3 years. **Confusion species:** other harriers (pp104-5) at distance, though Marsh Harrier bulkier and broader-winged.

| J | F | M | A | M | J | J | A | S | O | N | D |

△ Largest harrier (almost size of Buzzard), with bulkiest body and broadest wings. Darker than other harriers. Nests only in large reedbeds; also hunts over marshes and fields; seen elsewhere in open country on migration. In spring, male displays high up, swooping and climbing.

adult male   *adult female*   *adult male*

above

juvenile   *adult female*

△ Flies low over reeds. From above, slimmer male has whitish head; large grey areas on inner wings and grey tail contrast with brown wing coverts and dark wingtips. From below, male has streaked reddish-brown body, whitish underwings with reddish-brown to creamy coverts; dark trailing edges, dark wingtips and grey tail. Individual males differ considerably; may be much duller than example illustrated. Bulkier female dark chocolate-brown, with creamy-buff 'shoulders' and distinctive dark mask/pale crown. Juvenile resembles adult female, but without pale shoulders; some all-dark.

HEN HARRIER *Circus cyaneus*

Intermediate in size between Montagu's Harrier (opposite) and Marsh Harrier (p103). Wings look 'ragged-fingered' at tips. Wingbeats faster, glides usually briefer than Marsh Harrier's. More likely to glide on flat (as opposed to raised) wings than other harriers. Male has dramatic 'roller coaster' display flight, including backward flying, rolls, spins and somersaults.

male   *above*   *female*

△ From above, male pale bluish-grey with black wingtips, white rump; tail unbarred. Female dark brown, with prominent white rump and broad dark brown bands on paler tail.

▷ Male's white underparts contrast with grey head and breast, black wingtips and dark trailing edges to white underwings; tail unbarred. Female buff-brown below, with blackish streaks, whitish flight feathers with broad dark bars and broad dark bands on whitish tail.

male

below

female

female

male

△ Bluish-grey male smaller than female, which has streaky-brown head with indistinct face pattern; slightly darker crescent on rear cheeks. Immatures hard to distinguish from adult female, except for paler edges of upperwing coverts and secondaries, visible only at close range; often more contrasting face markings. Most juveniles have slight orange tint below; some more strongly coloured. Cere and legs of juveniles yellow, like adults', but eyes dark brown rather than yellow.

▷ From time nest built until chicks well grown, male delivers prey to female in a spectacular 'food pass'. He calls to attract female's attention; she flies up towards him, making loud begging calls. As she approaches, he drops the prey, and female turns on her back in mid-air and seizes prey with her talons, then flies back to nest.

male

food pass

female

KEY FACTS

Length: 43-50cm.
Wingspan: 100-120cm.
Weight: male 300-400g; female 400-700g. **Habitat:** breeds in uplands, mainly on moorland and young conifer plantations; winters in wide range of open habitats, especially coastal marshes.
Movements: British breeders mainly resident, but some, especially young birds, winter as far away as Norway and S France. Passage migrants (Apr-May, Aug-Oct) and winter visitors from Continent, mainly females or immatures. **Population:** *c*650 pairs breed. Up to *c*1000 birds in winter. **Diet:** small birds and chicks, small mammals.
Voice: noisy during breeding season. Male utters thin, high-pitched plaintive 'pee-yoo' or hoarse chattering calls in display flight; female gives staccato 'yek-kek-kek-kek-kek' calls of alarm near nest, and piping 'psee-oo' during food pass (see left). **Nest:** platform of sticks and twigs on ground, lined with rushes and grasses, in dense vegetation. **Eggs:** 4-6, very pale blue, often stained on damp sites, rarely with reddish marks. **Incubation:** 29-39 days, by female.
Fledging: 35-42 days.
Broods: 1. **Maturity:** 1-3 years. **Confusion species:** Montagu's Harrier (opposite). Males fairly distinct; females and immatures so similar that many are noted simply as unidentified 'ringtails'.

J	F	M	A	M	J	J	A	S	O	N	D

Circus pygargus MONTAGU'S HARRIER

One of our rarest birds of prey, on the edge of its breeding range. Slimmer and with narrower wings than Hen Harrier; wings have very long tips, especially in male. Flight more graceful than other harriers', with slower, 'softer' wingbeats and slower, more wavering glides. Long supple wings always held in 'V', exaggerated when soaring. In active flight, wingbeats more powerful, lifting body and giving buoyant tern-like character. Display flight like Hen Harrier's.

male *above* *female*

KEY FACTS

Length: 40-45cm.
Wingspan: 100-120cm.
Weight: male 225-300g; female 300-450g. **Habitat:** breeds in arable farmland, especially cereal/rape fields (formerly on heaths, moors, reedbeds and young conifer plantations). Seen on passage in wider range of habitats, from heaths and moors to saltmarshes. **Movements:** summer visitor, Apr-Sep, wintering in Africa; also passage migrant, especially on S and E coasts England, Apr-May, Aug-Oct. **Population:** *c*10 pairs nest . **Diet:** mainly small birds, eggs and chicks and small mammals, also lizards and snakes. **Voice:** less vocal than other harriers and rarely heard away from nest area. In display flight, male utters shrill, staccato, high-pitched 'yek-yek-yek', clearer than Hen Harrier's; female has rapid harsh cackling 'chek-ek-ek-ek' alarm call and a clear whistling 'peee-ee' when begging food. **Nest:** platform of twigs lined with grasses and other vegetation, on ground among crops.
Eggs: 4-5, very pale blue with vague reddish markings.
Incubation: 27-30 days, by female. **Fledging:** 35-40 days.
Broods: 1. **Maturity:** 2-3 years. **Confusion species:** Hen Harrier (see Key Facts opposite – but Montagu's usually absent Nov-Mar, so 'ringtail' confusion does not apply then).

△ From above, male bluish-grey (slightly darker and 'dirtier' than male Hen Harrier), slightly darker on crown and wing coverts, with black wingtips and a narrow black bar along centre of each wing. Usually paler grey panel on inner primaries and outer secondaries. Outer tail shows slight barring; rump grey or, at most, narrow and whitish. Female very similar to female Hen Harrier: dark brown, with slightly paler, buffish-brown wing coverts, white rump, variable in size (usually less prominent than in Hen Harrier), and grey-brown tail with broad dark brown bands.

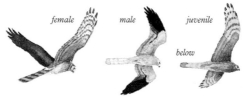

female *male* *juvenile*

below

△ Male has dark grey chin, throat and breast and faint rusty streaks on whitish underwing coverts, flanks and belly; black wingtips merge into whitish secondaries rather than forming clear-cut division; one or two black bars on secondaries and greyish trailing edge; wing coverts flecked blackish; lightly barred pale grey tail. Female very like female Hen Harrier, but facial pattern bolder; secondaries barred or dark brownish, contrasting with rest of wing. Juvenile resembles female but underbody and underwing coverts are rich unstreaked rufous.

Hen Harrier female   *Montagu's Harrier female*   *Montagu's Harrier juvenile*

△ Bolder facial pattern of female makes head appear darker at distance than Hen Harrier's, same colour as breast: prominent dark crescent on cheeks and dirty whitish area surrounding eye divided by indistinct dark streak; usually lacks distinct pale neck ring. Juvenile usually has darker cheeks extending further forwards towards bill, sometimes with pale rusty-toned neck ring and usually with pale spot on nape.

J F M A M J J A S O N D

EAGLES
Family Accipitridae

Very large birds of prey with powerful, strongly hooked bills, long, broad wings and shortish tails. Though not closely related, the two British species are treated together here as they have features in common and may be confused. White-tailed Eagle is a sea eagle, adapted for catching fish, while Golden Eagle is one of the true, or booted, eagles with feathered legs. Frequently seen soaring at a distance. Majestic flight, with powerful wingbeats. Take years to reach full adult plumage, which is in itself variable. Females larger than males.

WHITE-TAILED EAGLE *Haliaeetus albicilla*

KEY FACTS

Length: 70-92cm.
Wingspan: 200-245cm.
Weight: male 3.1-5.5kg; female 4.1-7kg. **Habitat:** rocky coasts, also on moorland, estuaries and inland waters. **Movements:** reintroduced birds, especially immatures, wander widely in Scotland. Rare winter visitor (Oct-Apr), chiefly to E and S England, from Continent. **Population:** fewer than 10 pairs breed. Formerly bred widely but extinct by 1916 through persecution. Successful reintroduction to Rhum since 1976, involving eaglets from Norway. **Diet:** mainly fish and carrion, also seabirds and mammals. **Voice:** noisy during breeding season, giving loud, repeated yelping, barking and screeching calls. **Nest:** huge structure of sticks in large tree or on cliff ledge, added to annually. **Eggs:** usually 2, white, becoming stained. **Incubation:** 36-42 days, chiefly by female. **Fledging:** 70-75 days. **Broods:** 1. **Maturity:** 5-6 years. **Confusion species:** may be confused with Golden Eagle (opposite), though structure of White-tailed different, with prominent head/huge bill and very short wedge-shaped tail giving front-heavy appearance in flight; has bigger, uniformly broad wings held flat or almost so when soaring and gliding.

| J | F | M | A | M | J | J | A | S | O | N | D |

△ Largest bird of prey in N Europe, even larger than Golden Eagle. Heavily built, with big head and massive bill. Likened in flight to 'flying barn-door'. No other British bird of prey has the all-white tail of an adult White-tailed Eagle. Long, very broad wings with almost parallel edges and blunt ends, with widespread primaries like fingers. Flight rather clumsy – heavy, shallow wingbeats alternating with short glides – but soars majestically, its great rectangular wings held flat or very slightly arched. Head extends far forward, more than in any other bird of prey – protrudes as far in front of wings as tail does behind them. Front-heavy appearance exaggerated further by huge bill and very short tail. Flies low over water to catch fish at surface; occasionally plunges deeper.

▷ From above, adult dark brown, with yellowish-brown wing coverts, pale buff to cream head, strikingly white tail. From below, greyer-brown. Juvenile blackish-brown with paler, rusty or yellowish flanks and undertail coverts, whitish marks on 'armpits', all-dark tail. Attains adult plumage in *c*5 years, becoming more mottled pale yellowish-brown or whitish, fronts of wings becoming paler, tail feathers acquiring whitish centres. Adult's head colour and yellow eyes take further 3-5 years.

above

adults

below

above

juveniles

below

Aquila chrysaetos GOLDEN EAGLE

Golden Eagle, soaring

Golden Eagle

Buzzard, for size comparison

Hooded Crow, for size comparison

KEY FACTS

Length: 75-85cm.
Wingspan: 190-220cm.
Weight: male 2.9-4.5kg;
female 3.8-6.7kg. **Habitat:**
chiefly wild mountains and
moorland, some in open pine
woods and along sea-cliffs.
Movements: almost all remain
on or near breeding grounds
year round; extremely rare
elsewhere (a few wandering
immatures). **Population:**
*c*420 pairs breed Scotland,
1 pair since 1969 in English
Lake District; *c*1200
individuals winter in Scotland.
Diet: mammals, birds and
carrion. **Voice:** generally silent,
even during breeding season,
though may give thin shrill
yelping 'kya' at nest and
whistling 'twee-oo' of alarm,
thinner and less ringing than
Buzzard's mewing. **Nest:**
massive structure of sticks on
cliff or in tree, added to
annually. **Eggs:** 1-3 (usually
2), whitish, usually blotched
reddish-brown. **Incubation:**
43-45 days, mainly by female.
Fledging: 63-70 days.
Broods: 1. **Maturity:** 4-5
years. **Confusion species:**
superficially similar to White-
tailed Eagle (see Key Facts
opposite); often confused with
much smaller Buzzard (pp110-
11), but structure and flight
action differ (see above right).

J F M A M J J A S O N D

△ Very large, but graceful and can look relatively lightly
proportioned. Head protrudes, but not as far as White-tailed
Eagle's. Wings long, broad, trailing edge with distinct 'S'
curve; when soaring, have more oval shape, with bulging
secondaries between narrower tips and base. Tail longer than
head/neck, as long as breadth of wings. Active flight powerful;
slow, deep wingbeats alternate with long glides on raised
wings. Soars with wings raised in more of a 'V' and held
slightly forwards, primaries upcurved. May look smaller than
it really is at a distance, when may be confused with Buzzard,
though actually twice its size, but proportions of head, wings
and tail and flight actions very different. Circles slowly and
majestically, in contrast to quickly wheeling Buzzard. Not seen
on roadside poles or fences like Buzzard; perches on crags and
trees and on ground. When hunting, usually flies quite low,
searching for prey on ground, then makes fast slanting dives to
drop on victim with half-closed wings.

adults

below

juveniles

above

△ From below, adult dark brown except for often paler grey-
brown bases of flight feathers and base of tail. Juvenile blackish-
brown with striking, variable white bands along mid-wings and
white tail base. From above, adult brown, with yellowish-
brown or greyish wing coverts, forming pale patch on
forewings, visible at long range. Juvenile dark brown with
smaller white patches than on underwings and white tail base.

juvenile

adult

△ Massive body, bulky folded wings and heavily feathered legs. Appears dark at any distance,
but with clear view in good light, yellowish-golden crown and nape visible (paler with age).
Often distinct greyish to yellowish oblong panel on upperwing coverts, and base of tail paler
than tip. Juvenile has paler 'trousers' and often white mottling on blacker body.

HAWKS (ACCIPITERS)
Family Accipitridae

Small to medium-sized birds of prey with rather short, rounded wings and relatively long tails. Active flight fast, with rapid wingbeats alternating with glides; manoeuvre among trees, hedges and other cover with great agility. Specialize in hunting birds in cover by combination of stealth and speed. Have long legs and long middle toes for snatching birds from cover. Prey ranges in size from small finches to pheasants. Nest in trees. Sexes differ dramatically in size (female much larger), and in some species sexes show marked plumage differences.

GOSHAWK *Accipiter gentilis*

KEY FACTS

Length: 48-61cm (female much larger than male).
Wingspan: 95-125cm.
Weight: male 500-1100g; female 800-1350g. **Habitat:** large tracts of mature coniferous or mixed woodland, especially pine or beech. **Movements:** British breeders almost entirely sedentary, but rare wanderers far from breeding sites may include juveniles, escaped falconers' birds or visitors from Continent. **Population:** possibly over 400 pairs breed. Extinct in Britain by *c*1880s; present population probably descended almost entirely from escaped falconers' birds. **Diet:** medium-sized birds such as Jays and Woodpigeons, also squirrels and other mammals. **Voice:** usually heard only at nest site; harsh chattering 'gek-gek-gek' of alarm, and short melancholy mewing 'pee-aa' when female begging food. **Nest:** very large, deep structure of twigs high in tree, lined by male with fresh, leafy twigs or conifer branches; occasionally uses old nest of crow or other bird of prey. **Eggs:** 2-4, very pale blue sometimes marked reddish-brown. **Incubation:** 35-41 days, by female. **Fledging:** 40-45 days. **Broods:** 1. **Maturity:** 2-3 years. **Confusion species:** smaller Sparrowhawk (opposite), Honey Buzzard (p113), Peregrine (p118) or even immature/female Hen Harrier (p104).

| J | F | M | A | M | J | J | A | S | O | N | D |

Male as big as large female Sparrowhawk; female very big, size of Buzzard. Structure differs from Sparrowhawk: relatively longer wings, shorter tail, much bulkier, deeper-chested body; head more protruding, wingtips less rounded (especially when gliding and, most of all, diving, when may even resemble very large falcon); trailing edge of wing more S-shaped; tail broader based, with broader, rounded tip.

female   *male*

△ Male and female show whitish underparts, with fine grey-brown barring visible only at close range, broadly barred grey-brown flight feathers and greyish tail with four or five dark bands. White undertail coverts especially prominent during courtship display flights, when birds soar over breeding area and raise undertail coverts like a white fan (also fly with extra slow wingbeats, and make dramatic dives and roller-coaster flights). Juveniles from below heavily marked with large dark brown teardrop-shaped streaks; lack white undertail coverts.

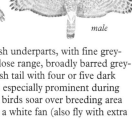

female   *male*

△ From above, male grey-brown; tail shows three or four dark bands and white tip. Female similar but browner. Crown and ear coverts blackish, giving hooded appearance, and forming strong contrast with whitish eyebrows and nape, more prominent in female. Juvenile has paler, browner plumage with rufous or buff tinge, and bolder tail bands.

56

Spends much time perched upright in dense woodland cover; most noticeable when hunting or during spring courtship display of male, when he soars, beats wings slowly or performs roller-coaster flights high over territory. Males small, only half weight of female. Both sexes have yellow cere and long yellow legs. Female has faint whitish eyebrow; both sexes lack strong head pattern of Goshawk. Male's eyes orange, female's yellow, giving fierce expression; juvenile's grey-green.

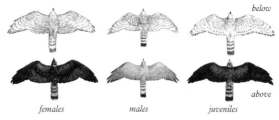

below

above

females *males* *juveniles*

△ Male has whitish underparts and underwing coverts with fine orange-red barring (looks uniform orange at distance), white chin, and dark bands on flight feathers and on greyish tail, which has narrow white tip. Female barred brown below, some have rufous-orange flanks. White undertail coverts usually less distinct than Goshawk's. Juveniles whitish to warm buff with ragged brown bars on underbody. From above, male dark slate-grey to paler blue-grey with rufous cheeks and often rufous forehead. Tail with 4-5 dark brown bands (last one broader) and narrow white tip. Female dark brown to grey. Juvenile brown with rufous tinge; looks warm orange-brown at distance.

Sparrowhawk male, soaring *Sparrowhawk male, gliding* *Kestrel male, soaring* *Kestrel male, gliding*

△ In active flight, bursts of few rapid wingbeats alternate with long glides. When soaring, wings held flat and tail not fanned, or only briefly so, unlike Goshawk. Tail square-ended rather than rounded as in Goshawk. Generally distinguished from other small birds of prey by combination of short, rounded wings and long tail but, when gliding or diving, wings may look more tapered. Soaring Kestrel or Merlin may also look quite round-winged. Hunts birds by surprise attack, weaving among branches with great agility. Often flies low along one side of hedge, before suddenly flicking over to other to seize prey.

male, plucking prey

◁ Takes prey to regular plucking post, typically stump or log; remains of prey usually obvious. When female on nest, male leaves food at nearby plucking post, noisily calling to her before he departs.

KEY FACTS

Length: 28-40cm (female much larger than male). **Wingspan:** 60-80cm. **Weight:** male 150g; female 280-320g. **Habitat:** woodland, farmland with hedgerows, upland scrub and heathland with scattered trees, urban parks and gardens. **Movements:** British breeders sedentary; some Scandinavian breeders pass through or winter here Sep-Apr. **Population:** *c*35 000 pairs breed, plus *c*45 000 non-breeders; *c*170 000 birds by late summer. Still increasing after devastating decline due to pesticides in late 1950s and 1960s. **Diet:** male takes smaller birds, such as tits and chaffinches, females mainly thrushes and starlings. **Voice:** loud, shrill, monotonously repeated 'kek-kek-kek-kek' at or near nest, ringing 'keeow' during aerial displays and 'peee-ee' food-begging call, thinner than Goshawk's. **Nest:** untidy mass of sticks lined with fresh leafy twigs high in conifer; sometimes uses old nest of crow or other bird. **Eggs:** 4-5, whitish, often blotched dark reddish-brown. **Incubation:** 32-35 days, by female. **Fledging:** 24-30 days. **Broods:** 1. **Maturity:** 1-2 years. **Confusion species:** Goshawk (opposite); Merlin and Kestrel (pp114, 115) have longer, more pointed wings and different plumage, and Kestrel frequently hovers (see right). See also Cuckoo (p205).

J F M A M J J A S O N D

BUZZARDS AND HONEY BUZZARD
Family Accipitridae

Large birds of prey resembling miniature eagles, but with relatively smaller heads and bills. Broad wings, with moderately 'fingered' tips, and broad tails. Buzzard widespread and common in W; Rough-legged Buzzard scarce winter visitor mainly to E coast. Honey Buzzard, rare summer-visiting breeder, more closely related to kites but easily confused with other two, true, buzzards. Most often seen soaring in broad circles. Rough-legged Buzzard habitually hovers, Buzzard sometimes does so. True buzzards eat mainly live prey, caught on the ground, but also feed on carrion; Honey Buzzard feeds mainly on bees, wasps and their larvae. Nest in trees or on cliffs. Sexes similar.

● Note: underwing and tail markings, shape of head, wings and tail, profile when soaring and gliding. Confusing, because of extreme individual variation in plumage.

BUZZARD *Buteo buteo*

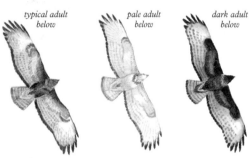

typical adult
below

pale adult
below

dark adult
below

23

typical
juvenile
below

typical
juvenile
above

△ Commonest bird of prey in much of W England, Wales and Scotland. Plumage very variable, especially from below: typical adults brown (dark grey-brown to warmer reddish-brown), often mixed with paler streaks or blotches, and paler throat, usually with pale 'U' on breast, pale bar on underwing coverts, inconspicuous dark patches at 'wrists', paler bases to flight feathers, obscurely barred greyish-brown tail. Pale adults mainly creamy-white below, often showing clear-cut dark patches at 'wrists' and dark belly or flanks; head may be pale or dark. Dark adults may be blackish-brown on much of underparts, with only bases of primaries distinctly paler. Flight feathers always have well-defined dark trailing edge.

▽ From above, rather less variable. Typically dark brown, often with paler patch at base of outer primaries; pale birds may have creamy-white heads and be mottled, blotched or streaked whitish on head, body, upperwing coverts, rump and base of tail. Others very dark with hardly any paler markings.

△ Juveniles very similar to adults; pale birds often indistinguishable. From below, terminal tail band not wider than others; also, band along rear of wing paler, more diffuse.

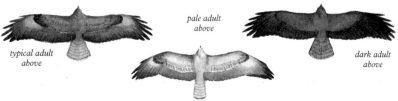

typical adult
above

pale adult
above

dark adult
above

110

KEY FACTS

Length: 50-57cm. **Wingspan:** 113-128cm. **Weight:** male 550-850g; female 700-1200g. **Habitat:** mountains, moors, heaths, wooded farmland, coastal cliffs. **Movements:** mainly sedentary; small numbers of passage migrants (Aug-Nov, Mar-Apr) and winter wanderers (Aug-Apr) outside breeding range. **Population:** 12 000-17 000 pairs breed. **Diet:** rabbits, voles and other small mammals, also young birds, frogs, earthworms, insects, carrion. **Voice:** loud, ringing 'pee-ow'. **Nest:** bulky structure of sticks and twigs, lined with green leafy twigs; in tree or on cliff ledge; occasionally on ground. **Eggs:** 2-4, white, blotched reddish-brown. **Incubation:** 33-38 days, mainly by female. **Fledging:** 40-45 days, sometimes up to 50. **Broods:** 1. **Maturity:** 2-3 years. **Confusion species:** Rough-legged Buzzard (p112) has less variable plumage, white tail with broad black band at tip, more prominent, darker underwing patch on 'wrists', more obvious, darker patch on belly/flanks, soars on only slightly raised wings, and often hovers. Honey Buzzard (p113) soars on flat wings, has small protruding head, differently shaped wings, deeper wingbeats and longer tail. At distance, Golden Eagle (p107) may be confused with Buzzard (nicknamed 'tourist's eagle' in Highlands), but flight action and proportions of head, wing and tail different, and Buzzard actually only about half size of Golden Eagle.

| J | F | M | A | M | J | J | A | S | O | N | D |

△ Buzzard has stocky body, broad head and short neck. Perches prominently for long periods on trees, telegraph poles, posts and rocks etc, with head hunched into 'shoulders'.

▽ After scanning landscape from perch or while soaring, Buzzard drops down onto prey. Walks awkwardly; sometimes searches for prey, especially earthworms, on ground. Many Buzzards, along with rarer birds of prey, die from eating illegally poisoned baits.

soaring

gliding

△ In flight, compact, with broad wings and quite short tail; short, broad, rounded head does not protrude much beyond wings. Seen most often soaring in circles (often several together), frequently giving loud, ringing mewing calls, with wings held forwards in distinct shallow 'V' and tail fanned (often so much so that sides reach trailing edge of wings). When gliding, wings held horizontally or slightly raised, with 'hand' pointing backwards, occasionally with 'hand' slightly drooping; wings of gliding bird can look quite pointed at tips. Active flight slow, heavy-looking, with rather jerky, stiff, quite shallow wingbeats alternating with glides. Some birds hover when searching for prey, but not as regularly or persistently as Rough-legged Buzzard.

▷ During courtship flights near nest site, pairs soar overhead and spiral upwards, the lighter male climbing faster and then diving on the female before shooting up again almost vertically.

courtship flight

ROUGH-LEGGED BUZZARD *Buteo lagopus*

adults below

dark

juvenile

pale

juvenile below

△ From below, lacks warm reddish-brown hues of many Buzzards. Tail has blackish band at tip and 2-3 narrower bands nearer pure white base. Dark birds have dark brown head streaked white, dark brown breast and underwing coverts, heavily barred secondaries. Pale birds have lightly streaked whitish head, breast and underwing coverts. Dark patches at 'wrists' larger and more prominent than on Buzzard, especially on pale birds. Often show whitish 'U' on upper breast, between dark throat and blackish belly; latter barred paler in older birds. Most seen here are juveniles, typically very pale below, with strongly contrasting blackish wingtips, blackish 'wrist' patches, solid blackish belly and single tail band. When perched, legs appear feathered right to base.

adult

above

juvenile

△ From above, adults look all-dark except for dark-streaked, whitish head and variable pale patch on primaries. Many have whitish leading edge to inner wings. White tail typically has broad band at end. Juveniles usually paler above, especially on head and wing coverts, with larger whitish patch on primaries and single, paler, broader band at tip of white tail; can look like young Golden Eagle (p107) at distance, but latter almost twice size, with different structure and flight.

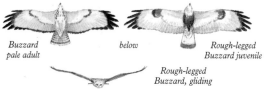

Buzzard
pale adult

below

Rough-legged
Buzzard juvenile

Rough-legged
Buzzard, gliding

△ Slightly larger and sturdier than Buzzard, with longer wings and more prominent broad tail; looks more like small eagle. Soars with wings raised in shallow V, glides on kinked wings with 'arms' raised and 'hands' level. Active flight with slower, deeper, more elastic wingbeats than Buzzard. Similar pale Buzzards lack broad dark band at end of white tail.

◁ Hovers frequently, regularly and more persistently than Buzzard, often twisting and turning its tail. White leading edge of wing often noticeable when seen head-on.

KEY FACTS

Length: 50-60cm.
Wingspan: 120-150cm.
Weight: male 600-950g; female 950-1300g. **Habitat:** moors, marshes, heaths, downs and dunes.
Movements: normally very scarce passage migrant and winter visitor (Oct-Apr) from Scandinavia, but periodically in greater numbers, associated with high breeding population after increase in numbers of rodent prey. **Population:** usually fewer than 20 birds each year, but up to 250 on passage and 100 wintering in major influx years (last one, 1994). **Diet:** rabbits, voles, other small mammals. **Voice:** migrants usually silent; occasionally gives similar call to Buzzard, but louder, lower, more mournful.
Maturity: 2-3 years.
Confusion species: Buzzard (pp110-11) smaller, with shorter wings and tail, stiffer, heavier wingbeats, but pale Buzzards may have very similar plumage; however, they lack clear-cut tail pattern of Rough-legged. Also, pale Buzzards rarely have pale patch at base of primaries on upperwing. Honey Buzzard (opposite) has even deeper, more elastic wingbeats and slower flight, small, weak-looking protruding head, different wing shape (narrow tips, broad centres and 'pinched in' where meets body), and longer, narrower tail, and soars on flat wings.

J F M A M J J A S O N D

Pernis apivorus **HONEY BUZZARD**

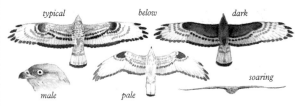

typical   below   dark

soaring

male   pale

KEY FACTS

Length: 52-60cm.
Wingspan: 135-150cm.
Weight: 600-1100g (sexes similar). **Habitat:** breeds in mature woodland, chiefly broadleaved or mixed (but occasionally coniferous), interspersed with clearings, heaths, farmland.
Movements: summer visitor (May-Sep), wintering in tropical Africa; few passage migrants seen in Britain, mainly May-Jun, Sep-Oct, along S and E coasts.
Population: fewer than 30 pairs breed. **Diet:** larvae, pupae, adults and honeycombs of wasps and bees, as well as ant pupae, all dug out with feet; also other insects, small mammals, young birds and eggs, lizards, frogs, earthworms. **Voice:** far less often heard than Buzzard; rather plaintive, clear whistling 'peee-ha', often trisyllabic in male. **Nest:** platform of sticks, lined with green leafy twigs, high up in tree; often uses old nest of Carrion Crow, Buzzard or other species as base. **Eggs:** 1-3 (usually 2), white or pale buff, heavily blotched reddish-brown. **Incubation:** 30-35 days, mainly by female. **Fledging:** 40-44 days. **Broods:** 1. **Maturity:** probably 2 years. **Confusion species:** Buzzard (pp110-11) and Rough-legged Buzzard (opposite); may also resemble huge accipiter (hawk) in flight; see Goshawk (p108).

J F M A M J J A S O N D

△ Weak-looking, almost pigeon- or cuckoo-like head and neck protrude well beyond wings. Wings broad at centre, with narrower bases ('pinched-in' effect where they meet body) and tips. Tail long and narrow (as long as maximum breadth of wing); sometimes bulging at sides with rounded tip. Soars on flat wings, tips sometimes slightly drooped. Glides with wings angled and slightly arched. Active flight often more sustained than true buzzards, with soft, deep, flexible wingbeats. Plumage very variable. From below, typical adults whitish with prominent dark barring across breast, belly and underwing coverts; palest birds have mainly cream or white underbody and inner underwing coverts; darkest birds have chocolate-brown underbody and wing coverts and dark grey secondaries; all gradations in between. All have broad black trailing edge to underwing and dark tips to flight feathers. Undertail of adults has 1 broad dark bar at tip and 1 or 2 narrower, paler bands towards base (difficult to see in dark birds).

dark   above   typical

△ From above, typically grey-brown, with 3 bands on tail similar to those on undertail and 3 similarly spaced bands on wings, but these much less prominent than underside markings and visible only at close range. Male usually greyer on crown and sides of head, female browner. Many paler birds have whitish head contrasting with rest of upperparts.

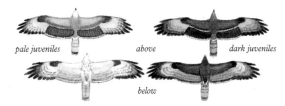

pale juveniles   above   dark juveniles

below

△ Juveniles even more variable than adults. Typically dark brown above, with pale patch on primaries and whitish band on uppertail coverts. Pale juveniles also have whitish upperwing coverts and white head with dark eyepatch. Above and below, tail (which often appears slightly forked) has 4 indistinct, quite evenly spaced bars, 1 at end broadest; tail tip usually white. From below, reddish-brown or brown body and underwing coverts. Pale birds have whitish body and underwing coverts, often with brown streaks, not bars. All juveniles have greyish secondaries and tail, larger dark area on wingtips and vague, narrow (not broad) dark band on trailing edge of wings.

FALCONS
Family Falconidae

Small to medium-sized birds of prey with long, pointed wings and fast, direct, often dashing flight. Found in open habitats. Females often distinctly larger than males; differ in plumage in Merlin, Kestrel and Red-footed Falcon, but little difference in Hobby and Peregrine. Do not build nest, but lay eggs directly on ledges or in holes in cliffs and buildings, or use old tree nests of other birds such as crows.

● Note: head pattern, presence/size of moustache streak, proportions of wings and tail.

MERLIN *Falco columbarius*

103

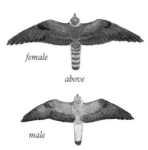

female

above

male

KEY FACTS

Length: 25-30cm.
Wingspan: 60-65cm.
Weight: male 140-180g; female 190-230g. **Habitat:** breeds in uplands, on moors, young conifer plantations, rough grazing; in winter in open habitats, from coastal marshes to farmland.
Movements: most British breeders move to lowlands in winter; passage migrants and winter visitors (Aug-May) from N Europe. **Population:** c1000-1200 pairs breed; c3000 birds in midwinter.
Diet: mainly small birds.
Voice: rapid, harsh chattering 'kik-ik-ik' or 'kee-kee-kee' near nest. **Nest:** scrape on ground in cover; some use old nests of crows etc in trees or on cliffs. **Eggs:** 3-6, creamy-buff, heavily spotted reddish-brown. **Incubation:** 28-32 days, mainly by female.
Fledging: 25-32 days.
Broods: 1. **Maturity:** 1 year.
Confusion species: female/juvenile confusable with female/juvenile Kestrel (opposite). Sparrowhawk (p109) barred, not streaked, beneath, with broader wings and longer tail. Hobby (pp116-17) larger, with longer, narrower wings and bold moustache stripe. Peregrine (pp118-19) much larger, with heavier body, shorter-looking tail and bold moustache stripe. Cuckoo (p205) has barred belly, stiff, shallow wingbeats and long graduated tail.

J F M A M J J A S O N D

△ Our smallest bird of prey (male only thrush-sized, female slightly smaller than male Kestrel). Quite short, broad-based wings taper abruptly to sharp point; medium-length tail. From above, male blue-grey, with darker wingtips, rufous nape and broad, dark band towards tip of tail (some have several narrower dark bars towards base). Female and juvenile dark brown above (sometimes with a little white on nape and rusty edges to mantle/'shoulders') and creamy bands on tail. Male has buff to rusty underbody with blackish streaks, buff underwing coverts streaked and spotted rufous, and whitish flight feathers with dark bars. Tail whitish with broad dark band near tip. Female and juvenile have whitish-buff underbody with heavy reddish-brown streaks; tail barred brown and whitish, with broad dark band near tip.

female   *male*

△ At close range, head pattern visible: male has rufous to greyish sides of face, female/juvenile have white throat, streaked cheeks and, often, whitish nape; all lack clear moustache stripe; look big-headed/large-eyed.

Meadow Pipit   *Merlin male*

△ When hunting, flight fast, agile and usually low, with shallow, flickering wingbeats and few, short glides. Closes in on prey with undulating flight, then seizes it in mid-air after final chase.

114

above

male

female

△ Britain's most widespread and abundant bird of prey. From above, male shows blue-grey head, chestnut mantle and upperwing coverts lightly spotted with black, and blue-grey tail ending in conspicuous black band and white tip. Female has much browner, duller upperparts, heavily barred blackish, and numerous dark bands on tail. Often has greyish tinge to head and tail; may be almost as pronounced as in males, but females always show multiple tail bands. Both sexes have only small, indistinct moustache stripe. Juveniles very similar to females, but never grey on head or tail.

male   *female*

below

△ From below, male pale to dark buff, lightly spotted with black on breast, flanks and underwing coverts; flight feathers whitish, barred pale grey. Tail pale grey with same pattern as above. Female creamy-buff below, more heavily streaked and spotted than male, and flight feathers more distinctly barred. Tail barred as above but with paler bands. Juveniles like females but with broader, paler streaks below.

▷ Active flight a short series of rapid, shallow wingbeats interspersed with glides. Sometimes flies obliquely or twists from side to side. Usually looks slender with long wings and tail. May soar, with quite rounded wingtips and fanned tail, when may resemble Sparrowhawk (p109). Often perches, looking for prey; takes to air by dropping sideways from perch.

soaring

gliding

active flight

KEY FACTS

Length: 34-39cm.
Wingspan: 65-80cm.
Weight: male 190-240g; female 220-300g. **Habitat:** farmland, open woodland, moors, heaths, marshes, waste ground, motorway verges, city centres. **Movements:** British adults mainly resident, though many upland breeders migrate to lowlands and some young birds move as far S as Spain. Immigrants from Europe winter mainly in E, Aug-May. **Population:** *c*50 000-53 000 pairs breed in Britain; *c*10 000 in Ireland; *c*100 000 birds in midwinter.
Diet: voles, other small mammals, birds (especially for urban Kestrels), insects, earthworms. **Voice:** shrill 'keee-keee-keee', especially in nesting area. **Nest:** on ledge or in hole on cliff, old nest of crow, in hollow tree, even on ground; urban Kestrels often nest on ledges of buildings.
Eggs: 4-6, whitish, heavily marked with reddish-brown.
Incubation: 27-29 days, mainly by female. **Fledging:** 27-32 days. **Broods:** 1.
Maturity: 1-2 years.
Confusion species: habit of hovering distinctive. Female/juvenile may be confused with female/juvenile Merlin (opposite), but latter smaller, with shorter, broader-based wings (lacking pale inner/dark outer contrast), shorter tail and brown, not rufous, upperparts. See also Hobby (pp116-17), Cuckoo (p205).

J F M A M J J A S O N D

◁ Frequently hovers to scan ground for prey, wingbeats rapid and shallow, head stationary, tail broadly fanned; wings almost motionless when facing into upcurrent. Often descends in stages with further hovering before finally dropping on half-closed wings to seize prey. Also catches birds by sudden dashes.

gliding

Swift

Hobbies

soaring

△ Lightly built, streamlined, with shortish tail and slender, scythe-like wings, Hobby often has silhouette like an anchor or like a Swift, which it is capable of catching. Look out for Hobbies in early autumn at reedbed roosts of Swallows, House Martins and Sand Martins, where they take many birds at dusk. When hunting birds, flight dashing, with rapid, stiff, regular wingbeats alternating with frequent, short, fast glides; capture prey by sudden dive, with wings almost closed, or by rapid chase, with wings pointing backwards. At other times, flight slower, with flatter, more relaxed wingbeats. Also soars high with wings flat and tail more or less spread. Rarely hovers. Larger female has broader-based wings.

above

▽ From below, striking whitish throat and cheeks with bold black moustache stripe, cream to pale buff underparts heavily marked with broad blackish streaks, and rufous thighs and rufous undertail coverts. Underwings densely spotted (underwing coverts) and barred (flight feathers); apart from pale throat, looks uniformly dark beneath at any distance. Tail narrowly barred beneath.

△ From above, entirely dark slate-grey except for slightly paler grey unbarred tail and whitish neck ring. Adults in worn plumage (especially females) slightly browner above. Bill greyish with yellow cere; legs yellow.

below

eating dragonfly

◁ Often seen hunting large insects, which it catches and holds in talons, tears apart with bill, and eats in mid-air. Usually takes birds to perch to pluck and eat.

KEY FACTS

Length: 28-35cm.
Wingspan: 70-84cm.
Weight: male 130-230g; female 140-340g. **Habitat:** heaths and downs with scattered pine trees, farmland with mature hedgerow trees, edges of woods. **Movements:** summer visitor (late Apr-Sep) and passage migrant from Continent (Apr-Jun, Aug-Oct); winters Africa.
Population: over 500 pairs and maybe as many as 900 pairs breed. **Diet:** small birds, especially martins, Swallows, Swifts and Starlings, large insects, especially dragonflies, moths and beetles, also flying ants; occasionally bats; prey almost always caught in air.
Voice: often noisy, mainly during courtship and at or near nest; variable, clear 'kyu-kyu-kyu-kyu-kyu' and rapidly repeated 'ki-ki-ki-ki'.
Nest: in old nest of crow or other bird in tree. **Eggs:** 2-3, yellowish, heavily blotched reddish-brown. **Incubation:** 28-31 days, mainly by female.
Fledging: 28-34 days.
Broods: 1. **Maturity:** 2 years. **Confusion species:** Merlin (p114) smaller, but lacks prominent white sides to neck and has only hint of moustache stripe; wings shorter and broader; usually hunts low over ground, but may fly and soar higher. Kestrel (p115), like Hobby, sometimes feeds on flying insects, but wings broader, tail longer, lacks clear white neck/bold moustache stripe pattern. Peregrine (pp118-19) larger, less streamlined, with much bulkier body and broader wings; flight heavier. Adult Peregrine has barred, not streaked, underparts; juvenile Peregrine has dark streaks below like Hobby, but has broader moustache stripe and barred upper tail. Hobby summer visitor and passage migrant only; others resident.

| J | F | M | A | M | J | J | A | S | O | N | D |

Falco subbuteo **HOBBY**

90

▷ Juveniles darker and browner above with buff edges to feathers; front of head paler. From below, more heavily streaked, with buff, not rufous, thighs and undertail coverts. Bill greyish but with blue-green cere; legs pale yellowish.

Hobby juveniles   *above*

below

◁ **Red-footed Falcon** *(Falco vespertinus)* rare but annual visitor from SE Europe, mainly to S and E England, May-Jun. Similar shape to Hobby, but smaller (length 28-31cm), less powerful-looking, with longer tail. May look like short-tailed Kestrel; has smaller bill and, when perched, wings extend just beyond tail tip, not well short of it as in Kestrel. Catches insects in mid-air like Hobby, but unlike Hobby (and like Kestrel) sometimes hovers (when wingbeats deeper than Kestrel's). Often perches across wires and fence posts, tilting tail to balance. May be very tame.

Red-footed Falcon juvenile

Red-footed Falcon male

Kestrel male below

Red-footed Falcon male below

Red-footed Falcon 1st-summer male, hovering

▽ 1st-summer male Red-footed Falcon has whitish on face, orange to rufous sides of neck and upper breast, strongly barred tail and underwings, and orange-yellow eyering, cere and legs. Adult female similar to female Kestrel, with crown and underparts orange-buff, but these brighter and lack strong streaking; also has bolder dark eyestripe, greyer mantle and upperwings, bright orange-buff underwing coverts and orange eyering, cere and legs. 1st-summer female has darker crown. Juvenile like adult female but with browner mantle and upperwings and paler feather edgings; crown and underparts streaked brown; paler forehead than juvenile Hobby. Adult male (least likely to be seen here) unmistakable, all dark grey except for bright chestnut 'trousers' and red eyering, cere and legs. Pale wingtips in flight.

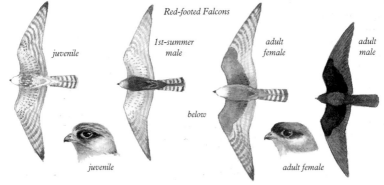

Red-footed Falcons

juvenile

1st-summer male

adult female

adult male

below

juvenile

adult female

PEREGRINE *Falco peregrinus*

above

below

229

△ Bluish-slate above, with faint dark barring and darker wingtips. Head blackish and pattern of broad moustache/pale cheeks prominent. Tail grey above, with narrow blackish bands. From below, whitish to pinkish-buff, densely barred with black except for unmarked chin. Females often more heavily barred below, with bigger drop-like markings on chest. Underwings lightly barred, with little contrast between coverts and flight feathers.

▷ Juveniles buff-grey to blackish-brown above and yellow-buff to off-white below with heavy brown streaks (especially on female) except on chin and throat. Underwings resemble adults' but bolder markings on duller background make them look darker.

above

below

juveniles

juvenile

◁ Adults have spotted upper breast merging into barred underparts. Eyering, cere and legs yellow. Juveniles browner above and darker below than adults, with streaked, not barred, underparts. Head pattern less clear-cut than adults', with often narrower, blackish-brown moustache stripe and duller, yellowish-cream cheeks with fine brown streaks; some have pale stripe above eye curving backwards towards nape. Some buff feathers on nape. Cere and eyering pale greyish-blue or bluish-green; legs usually blue-grey to blue-green, occasionally yellow.

adult male

KEY FACTS

Length: 39-50cm.
Wingspan: 95-115cm.
Weight: male 600-750g;
female 900-1300g. **Habitat:**
breeds on cliffs in moorlands
and mountains and along
coasts, locally on crags in
wooded areas; in winter also
seen on estuaries, saltmarshes
and other open habitats.
Movements: many British
breeders winter near nesting
sites; others, mainly non-
breeders and immatures,
wander widely in winter,
including to E. **Population:**
*c*1500 pairs breed; *c*4000 birds
in early winter. **Diet:** mainly
medium-sized birds, especially
pigeons, seabirds, crows,
waders, grouse; also some
mammals. **Voice:** range of
harsh calls, especially at
breeding sites, including high-
pitched 'kek-kek-kek-kek' of
alarm, shrill whining 'kee-
arrrk' and creaking 'wee-
chew'. **Nest:** on ledge or
crevice of cliff or quarry, or,
very occasionally, church or
other building; no nest
material; occasionally uses old
nest of Raven. **Eggs:** 3-4,
whitish, heavily blotched
reddish-brown. **Incubation:**
28-32 days, mainly by female.
Fledging: 35-42 days.
Broods: 1. **Maturity:** 2-3
years. **Confusion species:**
large female, in particular,
usually distinctive, but smaller
male may be confused with
Merlin (p114) or Hobby
(pp116-17), particularly when
at distance when size difficult
to judge. Merlin smaller, with
only vague moustache stripe.
Hobby slimmer, more elegant,
with longer, narrower wings,
relatively shorter tail and more
graceful flight; darker,
especially below, moustache
stripe thinner. Adult Peregrine
has pale breast, unlike Hobby
and Merlin; flight action
usually stiffer-winged than
both these species; wingbeats
shallow, with only tips of
wings appearing to move.

| J | F | M | A | M | J | J | A | S | O | N | D |

Redshank

△ Usually attacks prey in mid-air. After spotting victim from a
distance during a circling flight or from a high vantage point, it
'stoops' in a steep power dive on nearly closed wings; it may
reach speeds of 180km/hr or more. Prey usually struck on
head with rear talon, force of blow either killing the bird
outright or knocking it unconscious, and it drops to ground.
Peregrine then lands and retrieves its meal. Sometimes, prey
seized in mid-air after a level chase or an upward swoop, and
occasionally from a perch.

male

female

△ Pairs perform dramatic aerial displays at their breeding sites
in spring, soaring together in spirals high in air, plummeting
down to earth and then suddenly shooting up again, rolling
over on back and sometimes clasping talons in mid-air. Often
these displays accompanied by harsh chattering and other calls.

GAMEBIRDS
Order Galliformes

Plump-bodied, ground-dwelling birds with strong feet and toes. Bill short, strong and slightly downcurved. Often have coloured wattles, combs or other areas of bare skin on head. Run quickly, and may be reluctant to take to air, relying instead on camouflage to escape predators. If disturbed, rocket up into air at last minute with explosive noise, and fly off with series of rapid, whirring beats of short, rounded wings, alternating with long glides in which wings are distinctly bowed. Feed mainly on plant matter, though chicks need diet of insects. Chicks leave nest on hatching; able to fly long before fully grown. In many species, sexes differ markedly, with males much larger and more brightly coloured; females have camouflaged plumage. Nests simple scrapes on ground, among cover; incubation and care of young entirely by females.

grouse (pp120-5) *partridges* (pp126-7) *quail* (p128) *pheasants* (pp128-9)

GROUSE
Family Tetraonidae

Mainly northern or mountain-dwelling family. Medium to large, stout-bodied and short-tailed; legs, and often toes, thickly feathered, helping them survive snow and cold; together with rows of horny pads on undersides of toes, feathered feet also act as snowshoes. Coloured combs (patches of bare skin) above eyes larger in males. Have elaborate courtship displays. Seldom fly long distances and generally very sedentary, though some living on high ground make local movements to lower altitudes in winter. Some roost on ground, others in trees. Sexes very similar in some species, very different in others.

● Note: size, colour/pattern of plumage, presence/absence of white on wings, tail shape, calls.

PTARMIGAN *Lagopus mutus*

males winter

males winter

female winter

male winter

Shy though inquisitive. Often crouches instead of flying at approach of predator or human, 'freezing' motionless and relying on superb camouflage; often amazingly approachable. Uses boulders as look-out perches. Walks or runs over stones and boulders on steep slopes with great agility. Will also take to air to escape danger, flying strongly and quickly up and down steep slopes and suddenly disappearing over ridges. Roosts on ground.

104

Restricted to Scottish Highlands, chiefly on stony high-mountain slopes above heather line, except when driven lower by severe winter weather. At all seasons, has all-white or almost all-white wings. Only British bird to turn white in winter. Black tail, really distinctive only in flight. Legs and feet covered with white feathers at all seasons. 4 distinct seasonal plumages in male, 3 in female. Birds in intermediate stages of moult may look very patchy. Crackling call distinctive. Occur in large flocks (packs) of up to 100 or more birds in late autumn and winter.

male summer

female summer

KEY FACTS

Length: 34-36cm.
Wingspan: 54-60cm.
Weight: 400-600g. **Habitat:** rocky and stony areas of high mountains, only in Scotland, chiefly above 700m (lower in far NW). **Movements:** sedentary, apart from some local movements in hard winters. **Population:** numbers fluctuate considerably, with natural cycle of abundance having period of *c*10 years; at least 10 000 pairs are thought to breed. **Diet:** shoots, leaves, leaf buds, berries, insects; chicks feed on insects. **Voice:** alarm call as birds fly off 'kuk-uk-uk, hurr-hurr-kakarr', hoarse and crackling in male, higher-pitched and yapping in female; female also has low 'kuk'; song 'err-ook-kakakkaka ... kwa-kwa-kwa', belching at first, then cackling, softer at end. **Nest:** shallow scrape on ground, sparsely lined with grass. **Eggs:** 5-9, cream with many dark brown blotches. **Incubation:** 21-26 days, by female. **Fledging:** young can fly weakly at 10-15 days; independent at 70-84 days. **Broods:** 1. **Maturity:** 1 year. **Confusion species:** unmistakable in winter when plumage all-white; in summer may be confused with larger Red Grouse (pp122-3), but latter darker, and reddish-brown rather than greyish-brown, with little/no white on belly and all-dark upperwings.

△ In summer (after moult May-Jun) male dark grey-brown, barred/mottled blackish, buff and white except for white wings, belly and legs. Comb above eye bright red. Female paler, more strongly barred blackish/golden-buff, with big irregular black spots, and much less white below; comb smaller, orange-red.

male autumn

female autumn

△ After further moult Jul-Sep male becomes paler, greyer, with finer barring; comb smaller, duller. Female in autumn similar but yellower grey, still with some boldly dark-barred golden feathers. Juvenile resembles autumn female, but smaller, without white on wings and black on tail; lacks comb.

▷ In winter (after moult Sep-Dec), male all-white except for black sides to tail, black line between bill and eye, and red comb. Female lacks red comb, and rarely has black line between bill and eye.

male winter

female winter

▽ In display flight, male rises steeply, then stalls before returning to ground after a long glide.

▽ In spring, male looks very patchy above with large blackish areas contrasting with white, and white below.

male spring

J F M A M J J A S O N D

RED GROUSE *Lagopus lagopus scoticus*

KEY FACTS

Length: 37-42cm.
Wingspan: 55-66cm.
Weight: 650-750g. **Habitat:** heather moorland, damp cottongrass and sedge bogs; nearby stubblefields; from sea-level up to 600m (900m in C and E Scottish Highlands).
Movements: sedentary.
Population: *c*250 000 pairs breed. Numbers fluctuate in quite regular cycles, though complicated by artificial management of grouse moors for shooting. Very small populations on Exmoor and Dartmoor derived from birds introduced 1915-16. Low breeding density in Ireland since decline in 1920s.
Diet: heather, seeds, berries, insects; chicks feed on insects.
Voice: rapid, explosive 'go-back-go-back-back-back-back' call often given on alighting; other calls include crowing 'raa ka-ka-ka', rapid, cackling 'ko-ko-ko' and (in female) soft 'vehk'.
Nest: shallow scrape on ground among heather, lined with some vegetation.
Eggs: 6-9, cream, blotched brown. **Incubation:** 19-25 days, by female. **Fledging:** young can fly at 12-13 days; independent at *c*8 weeks in years with good food supply, but may be abandoned at *c*6 weeks in poor years.
Broods: 1. **Maturity:** 1 year.
Confusion species: slightly smaller Ptarmigan (pp120-1) greyer, not reddish, in summer, and plumage all-white in winter; much scarcer and restricted to high stony mountain sides and tops in Scottish Highlands. Female Black Grouse (p124) larger, with greyer plumage, slightly forked, paler tail and faint pale wingbars on paler wings; unlike Red Grouse, essentially a bird of woodland edge rather than open moor. Partridges (pp126-7) paler, with rufous outer tail feathers and paler, more heavily patterned, wings.

△ Once thought to be unique British species, now considered race of Willow Grouse (found mainly in willow and birch scrub in N Eurasia, from Scandinavia to Siberia, and N America). A bird of upland heather moors, chiefly in N; most found where habitat managed to provide large numbers for shooting. Larger than Grey Partridge. Dark red-brown, with even darker wings, it may look almost all-black at distance. Most often seen when disturbed from heather; suddenly rockets up noisily to fly off with fast-whirring wingbeats alternating with long glides on bowed wings. Birds often look back in flight and tilt from side to side before landing.

Golden Eagle

△ Spend much time crouching, camouflaged against heather, to avoid predators such as Golden Eagles, but will stretch up to peer warily over vegetation. Roost on ground. Plumage colour very varied, especially males'. Irish birds generally paler, perhaps camouflaging them on moorland where sedges and grasses mixed with heather. Family parties (coveys) often join to form large flocks in autumn/winter.

intermediate male summer

female summer

typical male summer

dark male summer

△ In summer (after moult Apr-Jun) males rufous to almost purplish-black, heavily barred black. Red comb above eye prominent. Smaller females paler-bodied, buffish-yellow, and more contrastingly barred and spotted blackish; red comb less prominent. Wings in both sexes blackish-brown. Legs and feet covered with white feathers.

J	F	M	A	M	J	J	A	S	O	N	D

typical male winter   *female winter*

△ In winter (with continuing moult Jul-Nov) males even darker, more finely barred; females redder, more like summer males. In both sexes, variable white tips to feathers of belly and flanks, sometimes forming small white patches.

juvenile

males displaying

△ Juveniles resemble females, but smaller, with duller buff ground colour, browner barring on underparts and no comb above eye; same as adults after moult Jul-Nov.

△ In early spring, territory-holding males display, bowing, extending neck, erecting red comb above eye, flicking and drooping wings, fanning tail over back and jumping about wildly. Frequent chases and fights between rivals. Red combs largest in highest-ranking males.

male summer

male songflight

△ White underwings visible when birds fly, especially when males alight in display, giving their loud 'go-back-back-back' calls.

△ In songflight display, male takes off and flies towards edge of territory, climbs steeply as he nears boundary, briefly glides ahead and then slowly parachutes down to earth on fast-beating wings with tail fanned and head/neck extended, calling as he does so.

▷ Chicks as young as 12 days old ('cheepers'), no larger than thrushes and still partly clad in mottled and streaked golden and chestnut down, can fly for a few metres with their parents.

male summer

chicks

BLACK GROUSE *Tetrao tetrix*

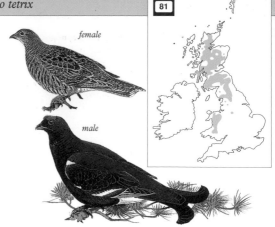

female

male

KEY FACTS

Length: females *c*40cm; males *c*55cm. **Wingspan:** females *c*65cm; males *c*80cm. **Weight:** males 1-1.4kg; females 750-1100g. **Habitat:** among trees and in open along wooded edges of moorland and heathland; birch scrub, young conifer plantations, rough pasture, boggy ground.
Movements: sedentary.
Population: serious decline since last century; now numerous only in Scotland, where no reliable estimates; recent surveys suggest fewer than 1000 males in England/Wales. Total population *c*23 000-34 000 birds. **Diet:** succession of buds, shoots, leaves, catkins and berries of various plants, including heather, bilberry, sedges, birch, pine and hazel. Chicks feed mainly on insects. **Voice:** at communal display ground (lek), males give strange surging dove-like cooing (known as 'rookooing'), interspersed with explosive hissing 'tshew-eesh'; females utter loud, barking 'chuk-chuk' from perch, pheasant-like crowing calls in flight.
Nest: hollow on ground among heather, bracken or other cover; little or no lining.
Eggs: 6-10, buff with brown spots. **Incubation:** 23-27 days, by female. **Fledging:** can fly at 10-14 days; independent at *c*3 months.
Broods: 1. **Maturity:** females 1 year; males 2-3 years.
Confusion species: female rather like Red Grouse (pp122-3) and female Capercaillie (opposite). Red Grouse much more common, smaller, shorter-necked, with redder or yellower plumage, no fork in much darker tail, no pale upperwing bar. Female Capercaillie larger, paler, with plain rufous breast and longer, more rounded, rufous-brown tail. Black Grouse occasionally interbreed with Capercaillies, Red Grouse and Pheasants, resulting in confusing hybrids.

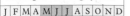

J F M A M J J A S O N D

△ Male (Blackcock) unmistakable; mainly glossy blue-black, contrasting with white on wings and undertail and bright red comb above eye (largest in spring); black tail long and lyre-shaped; wings brownish-black. In eclipse plumage, after partial moult Jun-Jul, head and throat of male mottled white, and nape and neck barred rufous. Smaller female (Greyhen) mainly rufous-grey with longish, slightly notched tail. Bill black or dark blue-grey in male, brown-black in female; legs/feet dark grey-brown in both sexes. Unlike Red Grouse, often among trees, perching with ease, even on slender twigs, especially when feeding (though usually roosts on ground).

female

males

△ Fly fast, usually higher than Red Grouse, with longer glides; neck and tail longer. When flying between trees, tilt from side to side, like Capercaillie. Male shows striking white wingbar on upperwing and distinctive lyre-shaped tail, female short, faint, narrow, pale wingbar on upperwing and slight fork to tail. Large area of white on underwings in both sexes.

males

female

△ Communal display ground (lek) used year after year, where cocks gather to display to females. Display most intense in spring but occurs throughout year except late summer, when birds are moulting. Takes place chiefly at dawn and dusk in spring, and in autumn only at dawn. In spectacular courtship display, males spread and raise tails, fluffing out the white undertail feathers, droop wings, inflate neck feathers, distend red combs and utter bubbling, cooing song.

82

Largest grouse, huge male almost size of turkey, but often elusive, flying off noisily or creeping quietly away. Surprisingly nimble when climbing branches of pine trees to feed on needles in winter. Roost in trees. Most visible when males display (see below) or when birds feed in clearings on berries in summer and autumn.

KEY FACTS

Length: females *c*60cm; males *c*85cm. **Wingspan:** females *c*87cm; males *c*125cm. **Weight:** females 1.5-2.5kg; males 3.4-4.4kg. **Habitat:** restricted to Scotland, mainly in old, mature coniferous forests in E central area; also found in mature oakwoods in summer. **Movements:** essentially sedentary. **Population:** reintroduced 1830s after extinction as British bird in late 18th century, due to overhunting and deforestation; now probably 1000-2000 birds. **Diet:** buds, shoots, seeds, berries; pine needles in winter. **Voice:** male utters variety of harsh retching and croaking notes and hisses; extraordinary song a series of accelerating 'plops', like water dripping, then a loud pop like cork coming out of bottle, ending with a rhythmic wheezing gurgle. Female has loud, harsh, rather pheasant-like crowing, 'kok-kok', a soft nasal braying and a loud crooning call. **Nest:** scrape on ground, often at base of tree, lined with grass/pine needles. **Eggs:** 5-8, buff, speckled brown. **Incubation:** 24-26 days, by female. **Fledging:** can fly after 14 days; independent at 70-90 days. **Broods:** 1. **Maturity:** females 1 year; males 2-3 years. **Confusion species:** female may be confused with Black Grouse (opposite), also seen in woodland (though Capercaillie has much more restricted distribution); Black Grouse smaller, with duller plumage lacking contrasting pattern and orange breast.

male   *female*

△ Male distinguished from all other gamebirds by great size. Mainly slate-grey and brown; breast glossed metallic blue-green in sunlight. Big pale bill and small white shoulder patches often noticeable. Performs dramatic courtship display during early morning in spring. One or more males fly to traditional display ground (lek) on branches of tree, rocks or ground, and attract females by remarkable vocal performances. As he sings, male stretches up neck and head, sticks out bristly throat feathers, droops wings and fans tail; may also leap into air, flapping wings noisily. Very aggressive, displaying and attacking not only rival males but even dogs, people and cars!

female

immature male

△ Goose-sized female best distinguished from other gamebirds by large size and broad tail, often fanned. Richly coloured back and white flanks/belly have strong black barring; orange-rufous breast almost plain. Juveniles resemble adult females, though males greyer above and on throat. As they moult, immature males show mixture of young and adult plumage.

J	F	M	A	M	J	J	A	S	O	N	D

◁ Flap wings noisily on take-off, but otherwise silent in fast flight, a series of powerful flaps followed by a glide. Fly with great agility between trees, tilting from side to side; may fly quite high above canopy. Striking white underwing coverts.

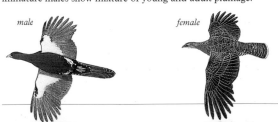

male   *female*

PARTRIDGES, PHEASANTS AND QUAIL
Family Phasianidae

Unfeathered legs often bear pair of sharp spurs at rear. Wings short, rounded, though Quail (p128), long-distance migrant, has longer wings. Pheasants (pp128-9) largest, with long tails and more elongated bodies. Sexes differ. Partridges medium-sized, with more rotund bodies and short tails. Quail similar in shape to partridges but much smaller. Both partridges and Quail roost on ground; sexes very similar. Pheasants found mainly in woodland, partridges and Quail in open country. All nest on ground; lay large clutches.

● Note: length of tail; markings on head, flanks and belly; calls.

GREY PARTRIDGE *Perdix perdix*

25

KEY FACTS

Length: 29-31cm.
Wingspan: 45-48cm.
Weight: 350-450g. **Habitat:** open areas, mainly cultivated farmland; also locally on heaths, low moors, sand dunes. **Movements:** highly sedentary. **Population:** serious decline in numbers and contraction of range over last 40 years; now probably fewer than 150 000 pairs breed. **Diet:** mainly grass leaves, cereals, clovers, grain and weed seeds; chicks feed mainly on insects. **Voice:** usual call of male high-pitched, grating 'keerrr-ick'; also heard as alarm call in flight after harsh, rapid 'krrip-krrip...' **Nest:** shallow hollow, lined with grass and leaves, on ground among thick vegetation. **Eggs:** olive-brown, 10-20, average 15, sometimes as many as 24 or more. **Incubation:** 23-25 days, by female. **Fledging:** can flutter off ground at *c*10 days and fly at *c*15 days, but not fully grown until *c*14 weeks. **Broods:** 1. **Maturity:** 1 year. **Confusion species:** juvenile confusing: very like juvenile Red-legged (opposite), but has dark spots and pale streaks above, and pale longitudinal streaks below; and Red-legged has traces of adult face pattern, necklace, flank stripes. Juvenile Grey also similar in size to Quail (see right and p128), but latter has much bolder head pattern.

J F M A M J J A S O N D

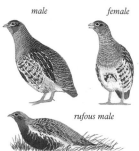

male   *female*

rufous male

△ Quite small, dumpy-bodied. Shy, crouch like clods of earth; rarely perch. Distinctive calls sound like creaking rusty gate. Appear pale buff-grey at distance, but closer view reveals pale streaking on brown upperparts, orange-red face, grey neck and breast, bold chestnut bars on flanks and variable dark chocolate-brown inverted horseshoe marking on upper belly. Female has paler face, browner neck, breast and upperparts; horseshoe reduced or even absent. Bill pale bluish- or greenish-grey, legs bluish-grey. Some birds more orange above, much more chestnut below, with hardly any grey.

△ In autumn/winter found in flocks (coveys). As in Red-legged, rust-coloured outer feathers of short brown tail noticeable as birds fly away fast and low on whirring wings. Unlike Red-legged, readily takes wing; take-off more abrupt, flight lighter. White-streaked back/upperwings help distinguish in good light, if distinctive face cannot be seen or calls heard.

▷ Juvenile smaller, browner than adults; pale-streaked, darker head/upperparts, whitish throat, pale buff breast/flanks streaked whitish. Bill brown, legs yellowish-brown.

Quail   *juvenile Grey Partridge*

126

juvenile

adult

△ Larger, more upright and darker than Grey Partridge, with very different voice. Adults have plain (not streaked) chestnut or olive-brown upperparts, bold head pattern, with long white stripe above eye, and black 'necklace' surrounding white chin and throat; lower part of necklace broken up into small black spots. Lavender-blue flanks heavily barred vertically with black, chestnut and white. Female slightly smaller, with duller head and bib. In both sexes, bill and legs bright sealing-wax red. Juvenile similar to juvenile Grey Partridge but shows traces of adults' dark necklace and flank streaks. Bill dull pinkish-brown and legs pale rose-pink.

▷ Unlike Grey Partridge, often perches on walls, fences, haystacks and other places, even on farm buildings.

◁ More often seen out in open (away from cover of crops, grass, etc) than Grey Partridge, and, when disturbed, prefers to run rather than fly.

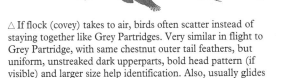

△ If flock (covey) takes to air, birds often scatter instead of staying together like Grey Partridges. Very similar in flight to Grey Partridge, with same chestnut outer tail feathers, but uniform, unstreaked dark upperparts, bold head pattern (if visible) and larger size help identification. Also, usually glides on flat, not bowed, wings.

Chukar *(Alectoris chukar)* very similar to Red-legged Partridge; Chukar and hybrids between the 2 species were introduced on a large scale for shooting, until ban at end of 1992. Chukar 'cleaner-cut', with no black spots on breast below necklace and broader flank stripes on creamy, not lavender-blue, background. Hybridization between the 2 species was not common in the wild, and released Chukars and hybrids have very low breeding success, so 'purity' of Red-legged now almost restored.

KEY FACTS

Length: 32-34cm.
Wingspan: 45-50cm.
Weight: males 500-550g; females 400-500g. **Habitat:** farmland, heaths, dunes, coastal shingle; found in drier habitats than Grey Partridge and, unlike it, in open woodland. **Movements:** sedentary. **Population:** native of SW Europe, introduced from France from 1790; still most abundant in S and E; 100 000-200 000 pairs breed, but accurate estimates of purebred wild birds difficult, as artificially reared birds still released on a large scale, and pre-1993 releases of hybrids with Chukar are still working their way out of the system. **Diet:** very similar to that of Grey Partridge, but also includes large seeds, such as those of beech and other trees, and sugar beet roots. **Voice:** harsh 'chuk ... chuk ... chuk-uk chuk-ar'; also short, sharp, barking 'tschregh, tschregh' of alarm. Male's song rhythmic, chuffing 'kok-chak-chak-kok-chak-kok-chak-chak', like sound of distant steam engine. **Nest:** shallow scrape on ground among thick cover, often sheltered by bush or grass tussock, lined with small amounts of vegetation. **Eggs:** 7-20, usually 10-16, cream or pale buff with reddish or grey speckles. **Incubation:** 23-24 days; by female if 1 clutch laid, but male incubates 2nd clutch. **Fledging:** can fly at *c*10 days; full size at 50-60 days. **Broods:** 1 or 2, 2nd laid only a few days after 1st. **Maturity:** 1 year. **Confusion species:** Grey Partridge (opposite) smaller and less bulky, without striking black/white face pattern and streaked upperparts. Red-legged reluctant to fly; looks heavier in air than Grey Partridge. Introduced Chukar and hybrids very difficult to distinguish (see left).

| J | F | M | A | M | J | J | A | S | O | N | D |

QUAIL *Coturnix coturnix*

KEY FACTS

Length: 16-18cm. **Wingspan:** 32-35cm. **Weight:** males 70-100g; females 85-135g. **Habitat:** cornfields, meadows, downs. **Movements:** summer visitor (May-Oct); winters S Europe, Africa. **Population:** huge year-to-year fluctuations; peak invasion years include 1964 (over 600 singing males), 1989 (*c*2700 singing males). **Diet:** mainly weed/cereal seeds, insects. **Voice:** male's song often repeated, liquid '*quic*-we-wik'. Also quiet trilling/rasping, and toy-doll-like 'mama', often preceding song. **Nest:** shallow scrape on ground among grass/crops, lined with vegetation. **Eggs:** usually 7-12, creamy-buff, heavily blotched dark brown. **Incubation:** 16-21 days, by female. **Fledging:** flutter off ground at *c*11 days, fully fledged *c*19 days, independent 30-50 days. **Broods:** 1, occasionally 2. **Maturity:** 1 year. **Confusion species:** juvenile partridges (pp126-7).

| J | F | M | A | M | J | J | A | S | O | N | D |

Usually heard but not seen. Males tend to arrive first, uttering far-carrying ventriloquial calls, both day and night but mainly at dusk. Once male has found a mate, usually stops singing. Normally very scarce breeder, but sometimes nest in larger numbers, especially on chalk hills of S England.

male, singing

female

◁ Resembles tiny neckless partridge: small neat head, very short tail. Combination of small plump body/longish pointed wings unique in gamebirds. Brown, streaked creamy-buff and blackish, above; sandy below with large blackish-edged pale streaks along flanks; no vertical barring. Head pattern distinctive. Female lacks central dark throat stripe; sides of breast spotted blackish. Juvenile as female, but narrower streaks above and smaller spots on breast.

◁ Britain's only migrant gamebird; smallest, most secretive. Usually seen only when almost underfoot, when may fly off low, soon dropping back into cover with flutter. Wingbeats shallow, very fast; few glides; action like Snipe (p154) but no zigzags and does not fly high. On migration, flight action powerful, like Starling (p297), but with continuous flapping.

PHEASANT *Phasianus colchicus*

male colchicus   *male* torquatus   *melanistic male*   *female*

Very long, spiky barred tail. Males colourful, with iridescent head and body. Plumage highly variable due to interbreeding between races. In every type, male has dark green head with bare red patch of skin (wattle) on face. *Colchicus* type has no white neck ring; *torquatus* has olive crown, prominent white neck ring and greyish rump. Melanistic male mainly glossy green above and glossy purple below, like occasionally released Green Pheasant (*P. versicolor*), but without bluish rump. Females sandy-brown to pinkish-buff or darker, rufous-brown, with brown, chestnut and blackish mottling; shorter but still lengthy tail.

28

▷ Explosive take-off and sharp climb. Flight strong and direct; rapid, noisy wingbeats alternating with long glides.

female

half-grown chick

juvenile Grey Partridge

male torquatus

KEY FACTS

Length: males 75-90cm, including tail 35-47cm; females 52-64cm, including tail 20-35cm. **Wingspan:** males 80-90cm; females 70-80cm. **Weight:** males 1.05-1.4kg; females 900-1050g. **Habitat:** mainly wooded lowland farmland and parkland, also forestry plantations; may feed in more open habitats such as fields; sometimes in marshes, reedbeds. **Movements:** sedentary. **Population:** introduced from S Asia since 11th century or earlier; just over 2 million males and *c*2.2 million females (only half of males territorial, each mating with up to 18 females). **Diet:** grain, seeds, berries, shoots, insects, worms and other invertebrates. **Voice:** male's territorial call loud, explosive, crowing 'korrk-kok', often followed by loud burst of wing flapping; alarm call similar but repeated. Also loud, hoarse clucking in flight, and husky 'kia kia' and purring from females. **Nest:** shallow scrape on ground among cover, unlined or sparsely lined with vegetation. **Eggs:** 8-15, usually olive-brown. **Incubation:** 23-28 days, by female. **Fledging:** can fly at *c*12 days; independent at 70-80 days. **Broods:** 1. **Maturity:** 1 year. **Confusion species:** females and juveniles very similar to those of Golden and Lady Amherst's Pheasants (see right).

J F M A M J J A S O N D

△ Half-grown chicks, capable of flight, have short reddish tails, and may be confused with partridges (pp126-7). Reared by gamekeepers in huge numbers, young remain together until spring, if they survive predators and shooting syndicates. Juvenile like small, short-tailed female, but usually duller, paler, more streaked buff above and more spotted on head.

male *female*

△ **Golden Pheasant** *(Chrysolophus pictus)* introduced from China; *c*1000-2000 breed in wild in dense, half-grown conifer plantations, mainly in Norfolk and Suffolk Brecklands, S Downs of Hants/W Sussex, Anglesey and Galloway. Male (80-115cm, including tail 45-75cm) unmistakable, with bright red underparts. Female (60-80cm, including tail 30-45cm) similar to female Pheasant but more slightly built, more rufous above, with more definite pattern of barring, especially on wings and tail, domed head and longer tail; very similar to female Lady Amherst's (see below). Both species very shy; rarely fly but slip away unobtrusively through dense cover.

male *female*

△ **Lady Amherst's Pheasant** *(Chrysolophus amherstiae)* also introduced from China. A few hundred breed in wild in conifer plantations and mixed/deciduous woods in Beds, Herts and Bucks (especially around Woburn). Male (105-150cm, including tail 73-95cm) unmistakable, with white underparts and very long black and white tail. Female (60-68cm, including tail 31-73cm) very similar to Golden Pheasant, but darker, with more rufous crown and paler tail with bolder black bars; bill, bare patch of skin around eyes, and legs blue-grey, not yellow. The 2 species interbreed.

RAILS AND CRAKES
Order Gruiformes, Family Rallidae

Compact, small to medium ground-dwelling birds, with short rounded wings and a short, often cocked, tail. In many species, body deep but narrow from side to side, so bird can slip through dense vegetation. Except on migration, flight usually low, weak and brief, with long legs and toes dangling. Most live in marshes, reedbeds and other densely vegetated wetland habitats; Moorhen and, especially, Coot spend much time on open water; Corncrake found in meadows away from water. Most species shy, though Moorhen and Coot may be very tame. Mostly omnivorous; some largely or exclusively herbivorous. Nest among aquatic vegetation or on ground. Sexes generally similar.

● Note: colours/patterns of bill, legs, flanks and undertail; calls (though often silent outside breeding season).

CORNCRAKE *Crex crex*

Active mainly at dusk and during night; usually very secretive and spends much of time hidden in dense vegetation, though may be seen peering out, head raised on slender neck, or walking about, usually with head/tail kept down. Readily identified by loud, rasping two-note song of male, monotonously repeated, mainly from dusk and through night, but also during day. Once a familiar sound throughout rural Britain, but now almost entirely restricted to W Isles of Scotland and W Ireland, where becoming increasingly rare. Decline in much of NW Europe over last 100 years due chiefly to agricultural changes, with earlier/repeated cuts of grass for silage by mechanical harvesters destroying eggs and chicks.

male summer

female summer

△ Slim, oval body; smaller than Moorhen. Breeding male yellowish-buff above with grey tinge and blackish centres to feathers, blue-grey eyebrows, throat sides and breast. Female very similar but with less grey. Flanks barred chestnut and wings chestnut, often visible when bird on ground.

▷ After rapid moult Aug-Sep, adults become more yellow-buff above, males with less grey on eyebrows and breast (none on breast in females). Juveniles similar to non-breeding females, but with less strongly barred flanks.

female autumn

juvenile

29

female

△ In flight, when legs are trailed behind as with other crakes and rails, rounded rufous wings a good identification feature. Despite their weak short-distance flight, Corncrakes fly more strongly, with legs drawn up, on migration. Because they fly low, they often collide with overhead wires.

male summer   *female winter*

Spotted Crakes

△ **Spotted Crake** *(Porzana porzana)* very scarce annual passage migrant, Mar-May and (especially) Sep-Nov, to dense aquatic vegetation; a few breed and a handful seen in winter. Similar to Water Rail (p132), but smaller (at 22-24cm, only about size of Starling), with much shorter bill, legs and tail. White-spotted underparts, pale orange-buff undertail and yellow bill with red base distinctive, otherwise plumage similar to Water Rail's, though dark/white bars on flanks less clear-cut. Winter plumage duller, head/breast browner with more white spots, especially in female. Even more reclusive than Water Rail, especially during spring and summer, though can be identified then by distinctive song, heard at night: far-carrying, rhythmically repeated 'hwit ... hwit ... hwit' like whipcracks or (at distance) water dripping into barrel. Male also has monotonous hard, throbbing, ticking call. May be glimpsed at dusk when it feeds at edge of thick cover.

◁ Juvenile Spotted Crake like winter female, but breast browner with fewer spots; lacks grey on face/neck; bill dark with yellowish base.

juvenile Spotted Crake

> **Little Crake** *(P. parva)* and **Baillon's Crake** *(P. pusilla)* much rarer visitors, even smaller (Little 20cm, Baillon's 18cm). Little has olive-brown upperparts with fewer white spots than Spotted Crake, faint barring on flanks and red base to bill; underparts pale grey in male, buff in female; sharp 'kwek kwek' call, accelerating into descending trill, more rolling in female. Baillon's has more rufous upperparts boldly marked white, strongly barred black/white flanks like Water Rail's and wholly olive bill; frog-like call and rapid trill.

KEY FACTS

Length: 27-30cm.
Wingspan: 46-53cm.
Weight: 135-200g. **Habitat:** hayfields, clover meadows, boggy pastures, nettle patches, iris beds. **Movements:** summer visitor mid-Apr to Sep, winters Africa; passage migrants mid-Apr and May, Aug-Oct. **Population:** huge long-term decline in range and numbers over last 100 years; today fewer than 750 calling males, all but a handful in Scotland (almost all on Inner Hebrides and Western Isles) and Ireland, where as recently as 1988 1494 calling males were counted. **Diet:** mainly insects; also other invertebrates, seeds, leaves and shoots of weeds and cereals. **Voice:** male's song, heard mostly at dusk and throughout night, loud, far-carrying, monotonously repeated rasping 'crake-crake' (or 'krrrx-krrrx'), imitated by grating teeth of a comb on striking edge of matchbox. **Nest:** shallow hollow in ground lined with dead grass stems and sometimes a few leaves, often with crossed living stems pulled over top to form loose roof. **Eggs:** 8-12, pale grey-green to brownish-cream, spotted red-brown, purple or grey. **Incubation:** 16-19 days, by female. **Fledging:** 34-38 days. **Broods:** 1, sometimes 2. **Maturity:** 1 year. **Confusion species:** other short-billed members of rail family, especially Spotted Crake (left), also rare Little and Baillon's Crakes (below), though no other rail so brightly coloured on upperparts/wings.

| J | F | M | A | M | J | J | A | S | O | N | D |

males summer

Little Crake

Baillon's Crake

WATER RAIL *Rallus aquaticus*

adult *1st winter* *juvenile*

△ Only rail with long bill, red and slightly downcurved. Small and dark; looks much smaller and slighter than Moorhen. Very secretive but readily identified by extraordinary calls. Upperparts olive-brown, with blackish centres to feathers; face, throat and breast dark blue-grey; distinctively and strikingly barred black/white flanks and whitish undertail coverts. Eyes glowing red. Legs pinkish-brown. Juvenile has buff face and whitish throat; more uniform underparts than adult, mottled or barred brown and buff; red on bill often duller and less distinct; brownish eyes.

△ Prefers to run from danger rather than fly. Very slim body, compressed from side to side, enables it to slip through densest cover, slowly with high-stepping gait or fast with crouching run. Can also climb rapidly and nimbly through dense tangled vegetation. Usually moves only when almost stepped on. Tail held cocked or lowered, constantly flicked when alarmed but held still at other times. Can swim well over short distances.

△ In hard winter, when water freezes, may become much bolder, even venturing out into open in search of food. May chase and kill small birds and mammals, stabbing them to death with bill; also feeds on carrion. Shape alters in cold as plumage fluffed up.

◁ When disturbed, may take to air, flying off weakly on quite long, loosely fluttering wings, with long legs and toes dangling. Soon lands in cover and conceals itself.

KEY FACTS

Length: 22-28cm. **Wingspan:** 38-45cm. **Weight:** males 100-190g; females 85-135g. **Habitat:** dense reedbeds, overgrown ditches and other aquatic vegetation. **Movements:** British breeders mainly sedentary; winter visitors from Continent Sep-Apr. **Population:** difficult to count as very secretive; probably at least 1300-2600 pairs breed, more in winter. **Diet:** from insects and molluscs to frogs and newts; in winter sometimes kills and eats small mammals and birds, and feeds on carrion and scraps; also tubers, rhizomes, berries, seeds, grasses and other plant matter. **Voice:** range of extraordinary noises; pig-like grunts and squeals, screams and whistles (known as 'sharming') given by both sexes from dense cover throughout year, but especially when breeding. In spring, male utters rhythmic, hammering 'kippkippkipp...' song. **Nest:** cup of dead leaves and stems in or near water among dense vegetation. **Eggs:** 6-11, cream, spotted and blotched red-brown. **Incubation:** 19-22 days, by both sexes. **Fledging:** 20-30 days. **Broods:** 2. **Maturity:** 1 year. **Confusion species:** distinguished from other crakes by long red bill, boldly black/white striped flanks, plain whitish undertail coverts and distinctive calls.

| J | F | M | A | M | J | J | A | S | O | N | D |

Gallinula chloropus **MOORHEN**

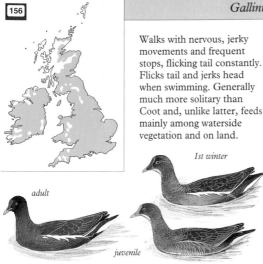

156

Walks with nervous, jerky movements and frequent stops, flicking tail constantly. Flicks tail and jerks head when swimming. Generally much more solitary than Coot and, unlike latter, feeds mainly among waterside vegetation and on land.

1st winter

adult

juvenile

KEY FACTS

Length: 32-35cm.
Wingspan: 50-55cm.
Weight: males 250-420g; females 260-375g. **Habitat:** from small pools, streams and ditches to large lakes, rivers, reservoirs, marshes; from remote rural areas to city centres; often feeds in fields. **Movements:** British breeders mainly sedentary; but some immigrants from NW Europe, Sep-Apr. **Population:** over 300 000 breeding territories (more than 1 female may lay in the same nest); over 1 million birds winter. **Diet:** water plants, seeds, fruit, grasses, insects and larvae, snails, earthworms, tadpoles, carrion, scraps, occasionally eggs of birds. **Voice:** loud, harsh, sudden 'kurrruk' or 'kittick' of alarm; brief, high-pitched squawking 'kik' or 'kek', stammering 'kik kikikik-kik-kik-kik'; nocturnal song, given in flight, repeated clucking 'krek-krek-krek ...' **Nest:** deep cup of twigs/coarse stems lined with grasses and finer vegetation, in reeds or other aquatic vegetation, on branches of overhanging bushes in water or just above it, sometimes among brambles, in hedges or even in trees (sometimes in old nest of other bird species) up to 8m above ground; also uses artificial rafts/platforms in water. **Eggs:** 5-11, buff with reddish-brown and dark grey blotches. **Incubation:** 21-22 days, by both sexes.
Fledging: 40-50 days.
Broods: 2, sometimes 3.
Maturity: 1 year. **Confusion species:** Coot (p134) larger, bulkier, all-black with prominent white frontal shield above white bill, and often in large flocks on water.

△ From a distance, adults look all-black, but at closer range dark olive-brown above and dark slate-grey below, with ragged white streak along flanks, prominent white undertail divided by black, bare red frontal shield above yellow-tipped red bill, red eyes and long yellow-green legs and feet, with small red 'garter' at top. Juveniles browner than adults, with whitish throat and belly, narrower buffish flank stripe, greenish-brown bill without frontal shield and dull green legs. During 1st winter become more like adults but still tinged brown, with pale throat and thinner flank stripe.

△ Down-covered chicks swim buoyantly soon after hatching and follow parents closely, shivering tiny wings and begging for food. Can easily be distinguished from Coot chicks by lack of ruff of orange-red down on sides of head and neck.

> Frequently venture away from water to feed in fields, hedgerows and other adjacent areas. At first hint of danger, run fast into cover or back to water, heads down and wings flapping. Good climbers, long thin toes enabling them to perch and clamber among branches with great agility, unlike clumsier Coots whose lobed toes are adapted for diving. Moorhens sometimes roost and even nest in trees and/or bushes.

▷ Though preferring to run or swim from danger, Moorhen will take to air to cross water when suddenly disturbed; after lengthy pattering, flies weakly with long legs dangling behind.

| J | F | M | A | M | J | J | A | S | O | N | D |

COOT *Fulica atra*

adult

juvenile

1st winter

157

KEY FACTS

Length: 36-38cm.
Wingspan: 70-80cm.
Weight: males 650-900g;
females 575-800g. **Habitat:**
breeds on vegetation-fringed
lakes, reservoirs and slow-
moving rivers; also feeds in
adjacent fields, etc; sometimes
on tidal waters (especially in
Ireland); in winter on any
large area of water, including
bare reservoirs, estuaries.
Movements: British breeders
mainly sedentary, but local
movements in winter result in
very large groups on big
freshwaters; many winter
visitors from Continent Oct-
Apr. **Population:** possibly
50 000 birds breed; *c*200 000
winter. **Diet:** mainly aquatic
plants, grass and seeds; also
insects, snails, leeches, small
fish, tadpoles, occasionally
eggs/young of birds. **Voice:**
loud, repeated, variable
squawk, 'kowk' or 'koot'
(hence name), higher-pitched
'teuk', disyllabic variants, e.g.
'kt-kowk', and various shrill,
metallic, resonant calls,
including very characteristic,
high-pitched, explosive 'pik'
or 'pfwitt'. **Nest:** bulky cup of
dead/living stems/leaves,
usually lined with slightly finer
vegetation, in shallow water,
usually concealed in aquatic
vegetation, sometimes in
open; also uses artificial
rafts/platforms. **Eggs:** 6-9,
buff, spotted dark brown.
Incubation: 21-24 days, by
both sexes. **Fledging:** 55-60
days. **Broods:** 1, often 2.
Maturity: 1 year. **Confusion
species:** Moorhen (p133) has
red frontal shield above red/
yellow bill, ragged white line
along flanks, dark brown (not
black) upperparts, prominent
white undertail coverts.

J	F	M	A	M	J	J	A	S	O	N	D

△ Larger than Moorhen, with much bulkier, broader body,
rounded head and back. Adults have all-black plumage with
striking white frontal shield above white bill, visible at long
range. Eyes glowing red, as in Moorhen. Gregarious, especially
in winter, when form large flocks many hundreds strong on
favoured waters; often associate with ducks. May become very
tame when used to humans, in contrast to more timid
Moorhen. Chicks make incessant hoarse, plaintive 'creer' calls
when begging food. Juveniles brownish, with white on face,
neck, breast and belly, small greyish frontal shield and greyish
bill. 1st-winter bird more like adult, but with brown tinge and
often a few white feathers on throat/neck. Coots obtain most of
food by diving briefly 1-7m below surface, flattening feathers to
expel air and often leaping forward out of water before
submerging. Sometimes reappear on surface tail first.

△ In breeding season, Coots engage in territorial disputes,
calling loudly and chasing one another across water with much
splashing. A Coot threatens rival by arching its bunched wings
high over its short tail and laying its head and neck almost flat
on the water to show off its white bill and shield. Disputes
may escalate to fights in which opponents face one another
upright and lash out with their long sharp claws.

△ On land, stands upright, the large, lobed, grey-green feet looking huge and ungainly. Patters
noisily along water surface with feet to get airborne. Flight heavy, with fast beats of broad,
rounded wings, usually low, with feet trailing (except in cold weather). On landing, splashes
down breast first with feet lowered. When hurrying to escape rival or some other threat, half-
runs, half-flies across water, splashing loudly. Although most food found beneath water, flocks
also feed on land, particularly in winter, and, unlike Moorhen, away from cover.

WADERS
Order Charadriiformes

Large group of birds found mostly along coasts or on marshes and other wetlands. Sexes generally identical. Two major families here: plovers (p138) and sandpipers and snipes (p144). Also three with only one representative here: avocets (family Recurvirostridae), long-legged birds with elegant pied plumage, and thin bills, upturned in Avocet. Oystercatchers (family Haematopodidae), stout-bodied, with boldly pied plumage and sturdy, brightly coloured bills and legs. Stone curlews (family Burhinidae), with relatively short, strong bills and sturdy legs; British species has streaked brown plumage, providing excellent camouflage; active mainly at twilight and at night; in open country inland; not on coasts or wetlands.

Burhinus oedicnemus STONE CURLEW

adult

juvenile

KEY FACTS

Length: 40-44cm.
Wingspan: 77-85cm.
Weight: 370-450g. **Habitat:** open, stony, chalky or sandy country and, increasingly, arable farmland; also open areas in forestry plantations.
Movements: summer visitor Mar-Oct, wintering S Europe and Africa. **Population:** rapid decline now slowed; currently fewer than 150 pairs breed. **Diet:** insects and larvae, especially beetles, earthworms; also snails, slugs, mice and other small mammals, young and eggs of ground-nesting birds, frogs and lizards. **Voice:** flight call a rippling, wailing 'krrrooor-lee', often repeated, shriller than Curlew's (p158) and with accent on 2nd, not 1st, syllable; at night, variety of wild, startling calls, including vibrating, piping 'puee-vee-vee' and high yelping 'tuee tuee', both like calls of Oystercatcher (p137).
Nest: scrape on bare ground, often with rabbit droppings, shells or stones added.
Eggs: 2, buff, blotched with brown/ purplish-grey.
Incubation: 25-27 days, by both sexes. **Fledging:** 36-42 days. **Broods:** 1 or 2.
Maturity: 2-3 years.
Confusion species: when seen well, unmistakable; calls from unseen bird could be confused with those of Curlew or Oystercatcher.

△ Strange-looking, like big, ungainly plover, with heavy body and large rounded head. Big staring yellow and black eyes give it an angry look. Short stout yellow bill with swollen black tip; long, thick, yellow legs. Plumage mainly sandy-brown with blackish streaks, white on face forming dark/light pattern, white belly, bright cinnamon undertail and black/white pattern of bars usually visible on closed wing. Juveniles paler than adults, with narrower streaks; wingbars much less distinct. Inactive for much of day, often squatting with lower part of legs held forward horizontally along ground or standing hunched up. Walks or trots, making frequent stops like plover to seize prey. Runs fast and furtively, hunched up with head lowered and stretched forward. Noisy at dusk and during night, giving loud wailing calls.

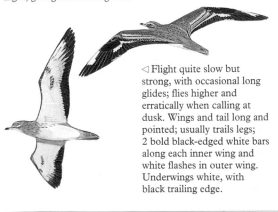

◁ Flight quite slow but strong, with occasional long glides; flies higher and erratically when calling at dusk. Wings and tail long and pointed; usually trails legs; 2 bold black-edged white bars along each inner wing and white flashes in outer wing. Underwings white, with black trailing edge.

| J | F | M | A | M | J | J | A | S | O | N | D |

AVOCET *Recurvirostra avosetta*

juvenile

adult summer

△ Tall, slim, extremely elegant snow-white and jet-black wader with distinctive upcurved black bill and long blue-grey legs. At distance, looks whiter than gulls. Walks briskly but gracefully, with neck curved, and makes short runs; often bobs head up and down when alert. Females have slightly shorter, more curved bills; some have pale brownish to white mottling on forehead and crown. In winter, both sexes usually show white mottling on forehead and in front of eye, and white of lower hindneck, mantle and part of 'shoulders' becomes pale grey. Juveniles resemble adults, but have dull dark brown markings with buff mottling in place of black; tail tipped pale brown.

summer, feeding

△ Frequently in small parties or larger flocks. Restless, noisy bird, often uttering loud fluty calls. In distinctive feeding action, sweeps bill sideways through shallow watery mud and seizes tiny shrimps or insect larvae. Long legs may be hidden as it wades in deeper water. In deep water, often swims (feet have small webs between toes), feeding by dipping head and up-ending like duck.

summer

△ Protruding neck, long bill, long body and long legs trailing far behind tail make Avocets look very elongated in flight; wings look relatively short. White appears dazzling in good light; from above, looks boldly pied, with all-white rump and tail; from below, mainly white, with flickering black wingtips. Flight quite rapid, direct, with fast stiff wingbeats.

KEY FACTS

Length: 42-46cm.
Wingspan: 77-80cm.
Weight: 250-400g. **Habitat:** breeds by shallow brackish coastal lagoons and estuaries; winters on muddy coasts and estuaries. **Movements:** some British breeders migrate as far S as Iberia, even N and W Africa for winter, but many stay here; major wintering sites on estuaries of rivers Alde (Suffolk), Exe (Devon) and Tamar (Devon/Cornwall), and at Hamford Water (Essex) and Poole Harbour (Dorset). Some wintering birds probably from Continent, also few passage migrants, late Mar-Jun, Jul-Sep. **Population:** recolonized Britain as regular breeder 1947, *c*100 years after becoming extinct here; *c*400-500 pairs breed, mainly at Minsmere and Havergate Island RSPB reserves, Suffolk, and N Norfolk reserves, notably Cley and Titchwell. **Diet:** insects, crustaceans, worms. **Voice:** loud, liquid, melodious, fluty 'kleep' or 'kloo-it'. **Nest:** scrape on ground near water, lined with a few bits of vegetation, often on low island. **Eggs:** 3-4, buff, spotted and blotched black. **Incubation:** 22-24 days, by both sexes. **Fledging:** 35-42 days. **Broods:** 1. **Maturity:** 2-3 years. **Confusion species:** Oystercatcher (opposite) far less white, with straight orange-red bill, pink legs.

| J | F | M | A | M | J | J | A | S | O | N | D |

Haematopus ostralegus OYSTERCATCHER

202

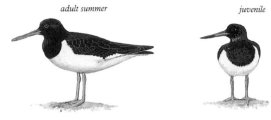

adult summer

juvenile

△ Large, portly, with long, stout, orange-red bill, flattened from side to side; red eyes ringed orange-red; sturdy pink legs. In breeding plumage, upperparts, head and breast glossy black, underparts white, bill tip often yellowish. In winter, duller black above, with white collar on foreneck; bill orange with dusky tip; legs duller pink. Juveniles duller, with brownish upperparts; eyes dark brown, no eyerings; bill more pointed, with extensive blackish tip; foreneck collar very indistinct or absent; legs greyish.

KEY FACTS

Length: 40-45cm.
Wingspan: 80-85cm.
Weight: 400-700g. **Habitat:** rocky, sandy and muddy coasts, estuaries; also feeds on nearby fields; in N Britain nests far inland, on shingle by rivers and on grass near lochs. **Movements:** some British breeders migrate to winter as far S as Iberia and N Africa; passage migrants/winter visitors from NW Europe, Jul-May. **Population:** *c*36 000-47 000 pairs breed; *c*300 000 birds winter. **Diet:** chiefly bivalve molluscs, especially mussels and cockles, and limpets; also ragworms; inland, earthworms. **Voice:** loud, shrill, penetrating 'kleep' and variants ('kleep-kleep', 'kleep-a-kleep' etc), also 'pic-pic-pic'; song during group gatherings consists of similar notes accelerating into excited piping trills. **Nest:** bare scrape, typically on shingle or sand. **Eggs:** 2-3, creamy-buff, spotted dark brown. **Incubation:** 24-27 days, by both sexes. **Fledging:** 34-37 days. **Broods:** 1. **Maturity:** 2 years. **Confusion species:** Avocet (opposite) more white, with upturned black bill and much longer blue-grey legs.

| J | F | M | A | M | J | J | A | S | O | N | D |

summer, threat display

adults winter, feeding

prober (juvenile)

chiseller (adult)

△ Gregarious, typically feeding in loose groups and resting in large, tightly packed flocks. Plodding walk, but can run fast with short steps. Extract mussels and cockles by hammering or stabbing at shells; rarely eat oysters; also pull marine worms out of sand/mud and shallowly probe soil for earthworms inland. Birds that feed by probing have pointed bills; those that feed mainly on shellfish have chisel-tipped bills.

summer

△ Large white bars on quite broad black wings make dazzling pattern in flight, which is strong with shallow, rather stiff wingbeats. Upper back black, contrasting with white rump extending in V up back; tail white with black band at tip. From below, black head contrasts with white underparts; wings white with black trailing edges.

◁ In spring, disputes over territory common, with one or both birds of a pair threatening an intruder by walking around, head pointing downwards and bill slightly open, with frenzied bursts of high-pitched piping calls. Males also perform song flights, with buoyant, slow, stiff wingbeats and wailing calls.

PLOVERS
Family Charadriidae

Small to medium short-legged waders, with stocky, compact bodies, rounded heads and large eyes. Short bill with slightly thickened tip, used for picking up food from surface or just below it, rather than for probing as with much longer bills of most other waders. Distinctive feeding action: stand stock still, then run a few steps, maybe tilting forward to take food from ground, then freeze again, and so on. Divided into 2 main groups: larger lapwings (1 species here) and smaller true plovers (3 species regular here). Lapwings have broad, rounded wings and generally slow flight; wings of true plovers pointed and flight faster. True plovers subdivided into 2 main groups; larger plovers and smaller ringed plovers.

● Note: in flight, presence/absence of wingbar in ringed plovers, colour of 'armpits' in larger plovers.

LITTLE RINGED PLOVER *Charadrius dubius*

204

KEY FACTS

Length: 14-15cm.
Wingspan: 42-48cm.
Weight: 30-50g. **Habitat:** breeds mainly on banks of flooded sand and gravel pits and reservoirs; some nest on shingle of dried-up river beds; on passage at coastal lagoons.
Movements: summer visitor late Mar-Oct, winters Africa.
Population: 1st recorded breeding 1938; now widespread but scarce over much of England; spreading into Wales and Scotland; *c*800-1000 pairs breed. **Diet:** insects, larvae; also spiders, molluscs, freshwater shrimps.
Voice: far-carrying '*pee*-u' flight call, descending in pitch but higher-pitched than Ringed Plover's; grating 'cree-ah'. **Nest:** similar to Ringed Plover's, often on small island.
Eggs: 4, buff, spotted dark brown. **Incubation:** 24-25 days, by both sexes.
Fledging: 25-27 days.
Broods: 1, sometimes 2.
Maturity: 1-2 years.
Confusion species: Ringed/Kentish Plovers (opposite)

J F M A M J J A S O N D

male summer

adult winter

adults summer

△ Smaller and slighter than Ringed Plover, with less rounded underbody and more tapering rear end; may look rather furtive. Also distinguished from Ringed Plover by thinner, black bill, bold yellow eyerings, longer, duller, pink/yellowish legs. Far less gregarious than Ringed, with very different voice In summer adults, black bands on head and breast often narrower than in Ringed; white line above eye extends onto crown; female's black markings often have brownish tinge, especially behind eyes. After moult Jul-Nov, face mask and breast band browner.

juvenile

◁ In contrast to juvenile Ringed Plover, juvenile Little Ringed has buff forehead, merging gradually with rest of crown; faint or almost invisible buff eyebrow and ear coverts little darker, almost same shade as crown, giving hooded effect; eyering present, though duller and narrower than in adults. Upperparts have paler feathered edges, giving scaly appearance; breast band brown and often incomplete.

◁ Plain wings, with no wingbar, distinguish it from Ringed. Flight fast, with wings fluttered on take-off, often rapidly ascending; wingbeats jerkier than in Ringed. Wings and tail look shorter and narrower.

Charadrius hiaticula **RINGED PLOVER**

Dumpy, neckless little plover; hunched posture. Stubby, black-tipped orange bill; orange or yellow legs; much less conspicuous eyering than Little Ringed. Brownish-grey above, white below, with black/white head/breast pattern. Runs rapidly like clockwork toy. Bobs head when nervous; often in flocks.

KEY FACTS

Length: 18-20cm.
Wingspan: 48-57cm.
Weight: 55-75g. **Habitat:** breeds mainly on shingly and sandy coasts; locally inland. Winters mainly on coasts, especially mudflats; passage migrants often inland.
Movements: mainly sedentary; some move W as far as Ireland; others winter as far S as N Spain. Winter visitors Aug-May, chiefly from Waddensee and Baltic coasts.
Population: *c*10 000 pairs breed, *c*35 000 birds winter.
Diet: when breeding, mainly flies, spiders, sandhoppers; otherwise chiefly marine worms, crustaceans, molluscs.
Voice: soft, mellow, fluty 'too-lee', rising in pitch on 2nd syllable; sharper, more piping 'queep'; song a hoarse 'too-wee-er', often repeated in long trills, in display flight with slowly flapped stiff wings.
Nest: shallow scrape on ground, near water, sparsely lined with tiny pebbles, vegetation, etc. **Eggs:** 3-4, greyish or yellowish-buff, speckled darker. **Incubation:** 23-25 days, by both sexes.
Fledging: 24 days. **Broods:** usually 2, occasionally 3.
Maturity: 1 year. **Confusion species:** Little Ringed Plover (opposite) smaller, slimmer, without wingbar; calls very different. Kentish Plover much rarer (see below).

| J | F | M | A | M | J | J | A | S | O | N | D |

male summer

juvenile

△ Summer males have clear black/white head pattern; white and black collars, latter enlarged to form breast band. In females, black markings mixed with brown. In winter plumage, black areas browner; bill all-black or with dull yellow base. Juveniles have brownish head markings, often incomplete, brown breast band; clearer whitish forehead/ eyebrow than juvenile Little Ringed; initially, upperparts have pale feather edges, creating scaly pattern, but by autumn have more uniform appearance. Bill black; legs dull yellowish.

adults summer

◁ Flight fast, usually low, with regular flicking action of rather straight wings, landing after glide and brief run with wings raised. Distinguished from Little Ringed by broad white wingbar; white patches on sides of rump; dark tail with white on sides and at tip; underwings white.

> **Kentish Plover** *(Charadrius alexandrinus)* formerly bred here, now scarce passage migrant to S and E English coasts; very rare elsewhere. Smaller (length 15-17cm) and much paler than Ringed Plover; usually looks large-headed and short-tailed. Sandy upperparts extending into narrow patches on either side of breast, snowy-white underparts, fine blackish/dark grey bill and blackish/dark grey legs, which look longer than Ringed Plover's. Male acquires breeding plumage as early as Jan, with thick black eyestripe, black bar on forecrown, part or all of the hindcrown bright cinnamon-orange, and neat black breast patches. Female has brown crown, eyestripe and breast patches. After moult Jul-Sep, sexes look very similar, though male has slightly darker breast patches and eyestripes. Juveniles even paler, with scaly upperparts, faint, mottled breast patches, and less well-defined head pattern. In flight, narrower white wingbar and more white at sides of tail than Ringed. Call: repeated short 'whit'.

male winter

male summer

female summer

GREY PLOVER *Pluvialis squatarola*

178

Grey Plover winter

Golden Plovers winter

△ Larger, stouter than Golden Plover, with thicker, rather swollen-looking bill, bigger head, bigger eyes and slightly longer legs. Paler and much greyer in winter than Golden Plover, without golden-yellow spangling on upperparts. Often appears hunched up, neckless and 'dejected-looking' at rest; wades in shallows more readily than Golden Plover; unlike latter, usually singly or in small groups.

male summer

adult winter

△ Male in summer plumage (Apr-Aug) has striking black/white/silver and grey pattern. Face and most of underparts jet-black; white 'frame' to black face; grey speckling on crown; white extends down hind neck into patch on side of breast; rear belly and undertail also white. Upperparts coarsely speckled silver and grey. Female browner black with whitish mottling, undertail with more brown barring. In winter, grey with whitish fringes to feathers above, largely white below (though some black may be retained as late as Oct-Dec); prominent dark eyes.

Grey Plover juvenile

Golden Plover juvenile

△ Juveniles more confusable with juvenile Golden, with pale yellowish-buff spangling on upperparts and extensive dusky streaking on pale greyish-buff breast/flanks, though never as golden-yellow above as Golden; structure, bill shape and 'armpits' in flight help distinguish. 1st-years often stay here through summer; plumage may be very worn and bleached.

Grey Plover

Golden Plover

KEY FACTS

Length: 27-30cm.
Wingspan: 71-83cm.
Weight: 200-250g. **Habitat:** in winter and on passage mainly on large muddy estuaries; some on muddy and sandy shores; very few inland on passage and in winter. Breeds in Arctic tundra.
Movements: non-breeding visitor (end Jul-May) and passage migrant (mainly May and Jul-Sep, adults, and Sep-Nov, juveniles) from W Siberian breeding population; some, especially 1st-year birds, stay through summer.
Population: up to *c*40 000 birds winter. **Diet:** burrowing invertebrates, especially marine worms, molluscs and crustaceans, in winter; mainly insects on breeding grounds.
Voice: plaintive 3-syllabled whistle 'tlee-oo-wee'.
Maturity: 2-3 years.
Confusion species: Golden Plover (opposite) similar in winter, but smaller, with slimmer bill, slightly less prominent eyes, yellower upperparts, and less white breast. Easily distinguished in flight by black 'armpits' (Golden Plover's are white), more noticeable white wingbar and white rump.

| J | F | M | A | M | J | J | A | S | O | N | D |

◁ In flight, readily identified by black 'armpits' contrasting with white underwing coverts (Golden Plover has white 'armpits'); also has bolder wingbar than Golden Plover and white rump.

Pluvialis apricaria **GOLDEN PLOVER**

male
summer

male
summer

S race

N race

female
summer

female
summer

KEY FACTS

Length: 26-29cm.
Wingspan: 67-76cm.
Weight: 140-250g. **Habitat:** breeds on moorland, bogs and upland pastures (and on Arctic tundra); winters on lowland grassland and arable land, often near coasts, also on saltmarshes, estuaries, but generally avoids larger expanses of mud/sand.
Movements: British/Irish breeders probably mainly resident, leaving breeding grounds from early Jul and returning from Feb. Winter visitors (Sep-Apr) and passage migrants (Oct-Nov and Mar-Apr) from Scandinavian and Russian breeding populations; also many Icelandic breeders winter W Britain and Ireland.
Population: *c*23 000 pairs breed, *c*600 000 birds winter.
Diet: mainly earthworms, beetles, other invertebrates; also some plant material, including seeds, berries and grasses. **Voice:** liquid whistle 'tleee'; at breeding sites, also gives shorter, higher 'tlee' and harsh 'a-treeolee' of alarm, and plaintive, wailing 'per-phee-oo-per-phee-oo' in 'butterfly' display flight with shallow wingbeats. **Nest:** shallow scrape lined with lichens or a few twigs of heather. **Eggs:** 4, yellowish-buff, heavily blotched brown. **Incubation:** 28-31 days, by both sexes. **Fledging:** 25-33 days. **Broods:** 1. **Maturity:** 1 year. **Confusion species:** Grey Plover (opposite).

J F M A M J J A S O N D

△ In summer plumage (Feb/Mar to Jul/Oct), amount of black on underside and especially on face varies between N and S populations. S populations, to which our breeders belong, tend to have less black than N birds (see below). Face and throat mottled grey and gold, black only in centre of breast and belly, with indistinct whitish or yellowish border. S females generally duller below, with brownish or whitish flecks on belly. Some N breeders turn up here as late passage migrants. Males have black on face to above bill, and much more black on underparts, with broader, pure white border. Females rather like S males, though more strongly marked.

Golden Plovers

Lapwings

△ Very gregarious in winter, forming flocks which may be large at favoured traditional sites. These often hard to spot, as well camouflaged when on ground. Often associate with Lapwings and Black-headed Gulls. In flight, which is fast and direct, reveals distinctive white 'armpits', whitish underwings and wingbar and no white rump or obvious tail markings (cf Grey Plover). Flocks generally bunch together closely and fly quite high; in mixed flocks with Lapwings, fly a bit faster and often soon separate and perform larger circuits before landing.

▽ In winter, loses black on head/underparts and may be confused with Grey Plover, but retains richly spotted gold and black upperparts (may look greenish or yellow-brown at distance). Has slimmer, less bulbous bill than Grey Plover's. Face and underparts flecked with golden-brown on crown, ear coverts and breast; white belly. Juvenile Golden similar to adult, but gold speckling paler, duller and more spotted; flanks with fine dark barring. Dull juveniles may look very like juvenile Grey Plover (see opposite).

adult winter

DOTTEREL *Charadrius morinellus*

106

KEY FACTS

Length: 20-22cm.
Wingspan: 57-64cm.
Weight: 90-145g. **Habitat:** breeds on mountain tops in N at 800-1300m, with sparse vegetation and bare stony areas; on passage, wide variety of open habitats, including upland moors and lowland fields, heaths and marshes.
Movements: summer visitor, May-Aug, wintering N Africa; passage migrants from N Europe Apr-May, Sep-Oct, mainly through E England, especially E Anglia, often stopping at traditional sites.
Population: 840-950 pairs breed, almost all in Scottish Highlands, especially central E Highlands; a few pairs nest S Scotland and N England.
Diet: mainly small flies and beetles; also other insects, spiders, snails, earthworms, occasionally seeds and other plant matter. **Voice:** often silent outside breeding season; soft 'peep-peep' in flight, quiet, sweet 'wit-ee-wee' alarm call, often developing into a trill. **Nest:** shallow scrape on open ground among sparse vegetation. **Eggs:** 3, buffish to yellowish with large dark blotches and spots.
Incubation: 24-28 days, usually by male. **Fledging:** 25-30 days. **Broods:** 1; sometimes female lays 2 clutches for different males.
Maturity: 1 year. **Confusion species:** in autumn, Grey or Golden Plovers (pp140-1), but Dotterel smaller, with shorter bill and shorter, less pointed wings; most important, has prominent pale eyebrows (all plumages).

J	F	M	A	M	J	J	A	S	O	N	D

▷ Flight rapid with fast wingbeats. No wingbar, but pale leading edge to outer primary; white edge to tail. Rear body and tail look broad. Migrants often travel in small, tightly knit flocks ('trips'), which circle round before skimming ground and settling.

Small, compact, with short fine bill. Looks very rounded at rest but slimmer and more upright when running. Despite bright colours, may be very elusive, as bold plumage pattern breaks up outline and camouflages it superbly against broken background of rocks, lichens and mosses. May be remarkably tame.

male summer

female summer

△ Summer adults have striking broad white eyebrows meeting on nape in 'V' (best identification feature), blackish crown, whitish throat and grey and brown upperparts. Grey breast separated from rich chestnut below by white line. Black belly and white undertail coverts. Legs yellowish. Unusually among birds, female larger and brighter-plumaged sex, and the dominant partner, taking lead in courtship and mating, and leaving male to incubate eggs and rear young while she joins other females.

adult autumn

juvenile

△ Autumn adults and immatures much duller, basically buff and brown, darker above, though still show distinctive whitish eyebrows and indistinct breast band. Juveniles have darker brown crown and upperparts with more contrasting buff fringes to feathers, more strongly streaked breast.

moulting from summer plumage

female summer

adult autumn

Vanellus vanellus LAPWING

Our largest plover, with unique wispy crest. Appears black and white at distance; closer views reveal mainly green upperparts. Cinnamon undertail contrasts with white underparts. Short black bill; dull reddish-pink legs.

adult female summer

juvenile

adult male summer

KEY FACTS

Length: 28-31cm.
Wingspan: 70-76cm.
Weight: 150-300g. **Habitat:** mainly farmland, breeding chiefly on arable land, especially when newly ploughed or fallow; also on freshwater marshes, saltmarshes and other open country; in winter few remain in uplands and most found on farmland, estuaries and coasts.
Movements: many British breeders make only short, localized movements, especially in C and S Britain, but some move to Continent and many northern breeders winter in Ireland. Many N European breeders are winter visitors/passage migrants to British Isles (Jun-May, with main influx Nov-Dec and main departure Feb-mid Mar). **Population:** 205 000-260 000 pairs breed, well over a million birds winter. **Diet:** mainly small invertebrates, including insects and larvae, spiders, earthworms and molluscs; also occasionally frogs, small fish. **Voice:** shrill, hoarse, wheezy 'peewit', rising in pitch (hence alternative popular name), also 'peeerst'; male's song in spring is repeated 'chair-owee-a-vip-a-vip'; alarm/threat call on breeding grounds when diving on intruders a shrill 'weew-ee weew-ee'. **Nest:** scrape in open, lining varying from scanty to substantial saucer of grass in wet sites. **Eggs:** 3-5, pale brown, heavily blotched blackish. **Incubation:** 21-28 days, mainly by female. **Fledging:** 35-40 days. **Broods:** 1. **Maturity:** 1 year.

△ In summer, male has largely black face, black crown/crest, throat and breast band and mainly iridescent bronze-green upperparts, with iridescent blue band on 'shoulders'. Female has slightly shorter crest, more white on black face and throat, and less glossy upperparts, lacking male's 'shoulder' band. Juveniles resemble winter adults but have only very short crest and even deeper buff, less patterned heads; duller green above, with yellow-buff fringes to feathers producing scaly or spotted effect; browner breast band.

winter

△ In winter plumage, face has much less black, upper part of head buff, throat and foreneck white; broad rusty-buff tips to feathers of back and wing coverts show as crescents. Very gregarious outside breeding season, forming large loose flocks on pastures, ploughed fields and other farmland, spending much of time standing still, occasionally running forward to seize food from ground by tilting forward.

winter

male

females

◁ Looks black and white in flight, with broad, very rounded wings (tips bulge most on males); large flocks fly in loose, straggling formations, with slow, rhythmic wingbeats producing 'twinkling' effect.

▷ In spectacular springtime display flight, male makes sudden swerves, tumbles, ascents and headlong dives, calling loudly, wingbeats producing loud humming.

| J | F | M | A | M | J | J | A | S | O | N | D |

Family Scolopacidae

Largest family of waders, ranging from the small, shorter-billed *Calidris* sandpipers, including the tiny stints, and the longish-billed, long-legged, larger sandpipers and `shanks' (*Tringa*), to the large, long-billed godwits and curlews and the secretive, long-billed snipes and woodcocks. Most have mottled, streaked or spotted upperparts and paler underparts; some have much brighter plumage in summer.

● Note: lower back/rump/tail pattern, wingbars.

SANDERLING *Calidris alba*

205

adult winter

juvenile

adult male summer

KEY FACTS

Length: 20-21cm.
Wingspan: 36-39cm.
Weight: 50-60g. **Habitat:** winters mainly on extensive sandy shores, also on mudflats and outer parts of estuaries; passage migrants more widespread, though scarce inland; breeds on Arctic tundra. **Movements:** winter visitor (Oct-Mar) and passage migrant, mainly Apr-Jun and Jul-Sep (adults), Sep-Oct (juveniles). **Population:** *c*12 000-14 000 birds winter Britain and Ireland.
Diet: feeds mainly near edge of water, chiefly on small marine worms, crustaceans and molluscs; also feeds on sandhoppers and flies along strand line at high tide.
Voice: high, liquid 'plit' or 'tyik tyik', heard as loud twittering from flocks.
Maturity: probably 2 years.
Confusion species: in winter plumage looks paler than any other small sandpiper and may show distinctive black smudge at bend of wing; habit of running along edge of waves highly characteristic. Larger than Dunlin (p146), with shorter, straight bill, much broader white wingbar and longer legs. Little Stint (p148) has similar plumage pattern, but is much smaller. In flight, Sanderling may be confused with winter-plumage Grey Phalarope (p168) but latter has very different habits, longer body and dark eyepatch.

J F M A M J J A S O N D

△ Moults Jul-Nov into very pale winter plumage. Pale grey crown, back and wing coverts (latter fringed white); blackish leading edge to closed wing sometimes shows as dark 'shoulders'. Face and underparts white. Juveniles have darker, blackish-streaked crown, forming narrow cap, bolder, more chequered black/cream/white pattern on upperparts, buff wash to breast. In summer, adult head/breast bright rufous spotted black, sharply demarcated from pure white belly and undertail. (Spring birds have paler 'frosted' upperparts.) Rest of upperparts blackish, fringed rufous (males) or greyish-buff (females); wing coverts grey with pale buff edges. Legs black at all times; at close range can be seen to lack hind toes, unlike other sandpipers. Late-summer adults have reddish necks, spotted upperparts.

winter

△ Slightly bigger than Dunlin, plumper, with shorter, straight black bill. Small loose groups twinkle along at great speed on sandy shores next to sea like clockwork toys, heads darting from side to side, chasing after retreating waves to snap up morsels left by tide. No other wader moves so fast or with such energy. Also feed less frenetically at edges of pools etc. Form larger, denser flocks at roost sites.

▷ In flight, reveals striking white wingbar, much bolder than in any other small wader, and white outer tail feathers.

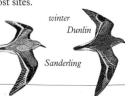

winter
Dunlin

Sanderling

Calidris canutus KNOT

180

KEY FACTS

Length: 23-27cm.
Wingspan: 47-54cm.
Weight: 125-215g. **Habitat:** chiefly on sandy and muddy estuaries; few on rocky coasts and inland (mainly juveniles) on passage; breeds in Arctic wastes. **Movements:** winter visitor (end Jul-May); also passage migrant, chiefly autumn, Jul-Aug (adults) and Sep (juveniles); fewer spring (most in May); few non-breeders remain in summer. **Population:** *c*250 000 winter. **Diet:** in winter mainly molluscs, also marine worms, crustaceans, seeds; in breeding season feeds mainly on insects and plant material. **Voice:** low, hoarse, quiet 'knut', heard as twittering from flocks; also a higher, more whistling 'twit-twit'. **Maturity:** 2-3 years. **Confusion species:** in winter plumage, may be confused with Dunlin (p146), but latter smaller, less portly, with less attenuated rear end, longer, slightly downcurved bill and longer legs. Plumage pattern very similar to that of Curlew Sandpiper (p147) but latter smaller, slighter, more elegant, with much longer, downcurved bill.

J F M A M J J A S O N D

winter

△ After moult Jul-Oct, upperparts pale dull grey with narrow white fringes to feathers, underparts whitish with streaks on greyer breast.

▷ In summer plumage, crown/upper back boldly mottled chestnut and black; head/underparts rich brick-red except for some whitish feathers on belly and mainly white undertail; females have greyer fringes to feathers of upperparts, white feathers mixed with chestnut of underparts; belly whiter.

juvenile

Medium-sized wader, stocky, short-necked, though with long body tapering towards rear; straight shortish bill, short legs. Actions slower, more deliberate, than those of smaller waders.

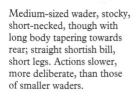

male summer

female summer

◁ Juveniles generally look a little slimmer than adults. Similar to winter adult, but upperparts browner, cream and blackish edges to feathers producing neatly scaled effect; white eyebrow curves down behind eye; underparts washed pale salmon-pink (soon fades as winter approaches).

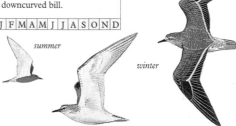

△ Often form huge densely packed flocks when feeding or roosting on mudflats; when they take wing, resemble drifting smoke cloud as they perform dramatic manoeuvres.

summer

winter

◁ In flight, which is stronger than that of smaller sandpipers, wings look long and tapered and body portly; shows narrow white wingbar and distinctive barred rump and all-grey tail (look uniform at distance); other small sandpipers have strongly patterned rumps and tails.

DUNLIN *Calidris alpina*

181

Most abundant of all our coastal waders in winter, occurring almost anywhere, especially on muddy estuaries. Size, plumage and bill length variable; may be confused with other small waders. If in doubt, it is likely to be a Dunlin! Usually in flocks, sometimes huge, outside breeding season. Stay close together in flight, twisting and turning and flashing alternately grey and white as they fly fast over an estuary.

summer

moulting

◁ Lively feeders, probing with bills into mud with rapid, 'sewing-machine' action before running rapidly to next feeding area. May wade or even swim in water. Mixes with other waders. Often quite tame, especially immatures.

▷ Winter adults grey-brown above; indistinct pale stripe above eye, grey-streaked breast and rest of underparts white. Dull and dark in poor light; brighter, browner in sunshine. Dumpy, hunch-backed, round-shouldered posture and longish bill with slight downcurve towards tip.

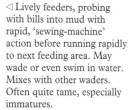

winter

juvenile

arctica moulting autumn

◁ Juveniles browner than winter adults; upperparts blackish, fringed chestnut and buff; often pale 'V' on mantle; breast suffused buff, with dark streaks/spots that extend onto sides of belly/flanks.

schinzii summer

alpina moulting autumn

△ Adults in summer plumage unmistakable: no other small wader has striking black lower breast and belly. Rich chestnut and black pattern on crown and back. Many adults still have partial black belly in autumn. Race *arctica* (breeding N Greenland), common passage migrant, paler/greyer above with small belly patch and short, almost straight bill. Race *schinzii* (breeding SE Greenland, Iceland, British Isles and S Scandinavia) has longer bill than *arctica*, richer upperparts and medium-sized, mottled belly patch. Race *alpina* (breeding N Scandinavia and NW Russia), common here in winter, has longest, most downcurved bill, and largest black belly patch.

winter

◁ In flight, from above, shows narrow white wingbar and dark line down centre of rump and grey tail.

KEY FACTS

Length: 16-20cm.
Wingspan: 35-40cm.
Weight: 40-50g. **Habitat:** breeds on damp moorlands and grassy saltmarshes; on passage/in winter on coastal mudflats, saltmarshes, some on inland marshes and reservoir or lake edges.
Movements: some British breeders winter as far S as W Africa; Russian and N Scandinavian breeders winter here. Icelandic and Greenland breeders pass through in spring/autumn. **Population:** *c*10 000 pairs breed, *c*430 000 birds winter. **Diet:** molluscs, worms, crustaceans, insects.
Voice: wheezy, rasping 'treerrr'; quiet, high 'beep-beep' when feeding; breeders give 'kwoi-kwoi' and 'wot-wot' alarm calls and a rich purring trilling song in flight. **Nest:** hollow on ground in grass tussock, lined with grass or leaves. **Eggs:** 4, pale greenish, with dark brown spots. **Incubation:** 21-22 days, by both sexes.
Fledging: 19-21 days.
Broods: 1. **Maturity:** 1-2 years. **Confusion species:** various small sandpipers in winter and juvenile plumages: Curlew Sandpiper (opposite) more elegant, with longer bill; Sanderling (p144) much paler, with straight, shorter bill; Knot (p145) larger, stockier, with straight shorter bill; also stints (pp148-9) much smaller, with straight, much shorter bills.

J F M A M J J A S O N D

Calidris ferruginea **CURLEW SANDPIPER**

Curlew Sandpiper winter   Dunlin winter   Curlew Sandpipers winter

△ Slightly larger, more elegant, longer-legged than Dunlin. Bill longer, though difference from long-billed Dunlin slight; Curlew Sandpiper's bill more evenly curved. Often feeds with Dunlin, usually singly or in small groups. Feeds more often than Dunlin in deep water, thrusting head/bill below surface.

autumn moulting   *summer*   *winter*

△ Most adults here are moulting and show only partial breeding plumage. Spring passage migrants usually have rich brick-red underparts partly obscured by whitish fringes; autumn adults have greyish-buff head and neck, and red mainly on breast and belly, often broken up into blotches. Full winter plumage not often seen here: very similar to Dunlin, but underparts usually whiter and pale stripe above eye more distinct.

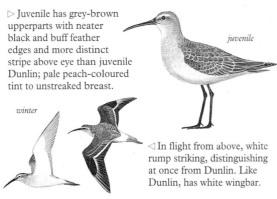

▷ Juvenile has grey-brown upperparts with neater black and buff feather edges and more distinct stripe above eye than juvenile Dunlin; pale peach-coloured tint to unstreaked breast.

juvenile

winter

◁ In flight from above, white rump striking, distinguishing at once from Dunlin. Like Dunlin, has white wingbar.

KEY FACTS

Length: 18-23cm.
Wingspan: 38-41cm.
Weight: 45-90g. **Habitat:** on passage on coastal mudflats and lagoons, also at inland marshes and freshwaters; breeds on Siberian tundra.
Movements: passes through chiefly late summer/autumn (mid Jul-mid Oct) on southward migration to Africa; northward route in spring usually far to E.
Population: scarce passage migrant, more abundant in some years; from 100 or so to several thousand in autumn, much scarcer in spring and very few in winter. **Diet:** similar to Dunlin. **Voice:** soft, twittering 'chirrip'. **Maturity:** 1 year. **Confusion species:** winter Dunlin (opposite) slightly smaller, shorter-necked, usually more hunched-up, less elegant, without white rump in flight. Also Knot (p145).

| J | F | M | A | M | J | J | A | S | O | N | D |

adult

juvenile

adults

◁ **Pectoral Sandpiper** *(Calidris melanotos)* rare but annual visitor from N America, chiefly in autumn, to marshes and wet grassland with shallow pools inland and on coast in W Britain and Ireland. Larger (19-23cm long) than Dunlin, with shorter bill, only slightly downcurved; usually yellowish legs. May resemble small version of female and juvenile Ruff (pp160-1). Upperparts with brown, buff and blackish scalloped pattern like Ruff but with double white 'V'. Throat and breast pale grey-brown, streaked black all over, with sharp demarcation from white belly. Head small with clear pale stripe above eye. In flight, long wings show only faint white bar and rump has black centre and white sides. When disturbed, often zigzags in flight like Snipe (p154). Flight call a loud, croaky 'chreep'.

LITTLE STINT *Calidris minuta*

183

Tiny plump sandpiper with short, straight fine black bill on neat, rounded head; slender, medium-length black legs. White throat; underparts very white, breast streaked more at sides. Often adopts crouching stance and remains in same area for long periods.

adult summer

juvenile

△ In summer, crown and upperparts blackish with rich rufous fringes to feathers, cream 'V' on back, breast pale rufous with brown speckles, otherwise white below.

△ Juveniles (most numerous visitors here) blackish-brown above with bright chestnut and whitish fringes, clear white double 'V' on back, greyish nape, buff sides of breast with a few darker streaks, and gleaming white underparts.

Little Stints winter, feeding

Little Stint winter

Dunlin winter

△ After moult Aug-Dec, grey above with pale fringes to wing coverts, slightly streaked greyish sides of breast, and white underparts. Often seen singly or in small numbers in mixed flocks with Dunlins and other small sandpipers. Generally very active in comparison, scampering about with non-stop, energetic, jerky feeding action, picking small invertebrates from surface of mud with rapid, nervous jabs. Rarely wades. Usually very tame.

Little Stint juvenile

Little Stints adults winter

Dunlin adult winter

△ In flight, which is faster than Dunlin's, with rapid wingbeats and sudden changes of direction, shows narrow white wingbar and black centre to white rump and grey tail; looks very small.

KEY FACTS

Length: 12-14cm.
Wingspan: 34-37cm.
Weight: 20-40g. **Habitat:** on passage mainly muddy lagoons, especially next to shore; also estuaries and inland wetlands, including reservoirs, with exposed mud.
Movements: almost entirely passage migrant; most are juveniles seen in autumn (mainly Aug-Sep); much scarcer in spring (late Apr-early Jun), including small numbers of adults in breeding plumage; very few winter.
Population: usually in groups of 1 to 10, totalling a few hundred (in best years 1000 or more). Fewer than 30 winter most years. **Diet:** mainly insects, also crustaceans and molluscs. **Voice:** quiet, high, hard, dry 'tip', 'tit' or 'tit-tit', lower twittering 'tirri-tit-tit'. **Maturity:** 1 year.
Confusion species: Temminck's Stint (opposite) much greyer, more uniformly marked, with longer, more tapered body, shorter, greenish or brownish (not black) legs and white (not grey) outer tail feathers; also very different voice. Dunlin (p146) also has black legs and shows narrow white wingbar and white sides to tail in flight, but is much larger, with much longer, slightly downcurved bill and less white underparts. Summer and juvenile Sanderlings (p144) are larger, with different feeding habits.

J F M A M J J A S O N D

Calidris temminckii TEMMINCK'S STINT

Much scarcer than Little Stint and, by contrast, occurs almost entirely in freshwater habitats. Slightly longer, with much greyer, uniformly marked plumage and no white 'V' on back. Major distinguishing feature is yellowish, greenish or brownish, not black, legs, though mud stains may obscure this. Longer, more tapered rear end, shorter legs and habit of bobbing body at times make it look more like a miniature Common Sandpiper than Little Stint or Dunlin. Generally solitary, secretive, unobtrusive and easily overlooked; spends much of time creeping around with mouse-like actions. Distinctive call.

KEY FACTS

Length: 13-15cm.
Wingspan: 34-37cm.
Weight: 17-32g. **Habitat:** on passage, muddy patches, often with cover, in marshes, by lakes, and by small pools and creeks in estuaries. Breeds chiefly in Arctic tundra; in Scottish Highlands breeds near wooded lochs.
Movements: scarce but regular passage migrant from N Europe (May-mid Jun, end Jul-Oct). Winters Africa.
Population: tiny breeding population (maximum of only 5 birds over last few years) just survives in Scottish Highlands. **Diet:** on passage, mainly small worms, crustaceans and molluscs; when breeding, insects and larvae. **Voice:** ringing 'tirrr' flight call, often extended into short, twittering trill with rising inflection; male's song a long, tinkling trill, rising and falling, given from ground and in display flight. **Nest:** shallow scrape on ground in open or among low cover. **Eggs:** 4, greenish-grey to buff, with brown spots. Each female lays 1-3 clutches in different males' territories.
Incubation: 21-22 days, mainly by male. **Fledging:** 15-18 days. **Broods:** 1-3.
Maturity: males 1-3 years; females 1 year. **Confusion species:** Little Stint (opposite) plumper, more upright, with longer black legs; more rufous above in summer, paler in winter.

J F M A M J J A S O N D

adult summer

◁ In summer, greyish-buff or brownish-buff above, with black spots and pale edges to median wing coverts, sometimes with warmer brown or dull rufous fringes to feathers but never with bright chestnut hues of Little Stint; breast grey-brown with darker streaks.

▷ After moult Jul-Nov, plainer, greyer above, darker than Little Stint. Loses black spots on back and pale tips on median wing coverts; greyish-brown on breast, sometimes only at sides.

adult winter

juvenile

◁ Juveniles brownish-grey above with fine, neat, crescent-shaped blackish and buff fringes to feathers, visible at close range; breast buff-grey with slightly darker streaks and contrasting white throat patch.

▽ Flight fast and twisting, with flicking action of swept-back wings; often rises to considerable heights when disturbed. White wingbar shorter than on Little Stint, and sides of tail pure white, unlike any other small sandpiper; this feature particularly noticeable on take-off and landing.

winter

summer

Temminck's Stints

Little Stints winter

PURPLE SANDPIPER *Calidris maritima*

winter

△ Plump and often neckless, with short yellowish or orange legs; slightly downcurved, stout-based bill about same length as head, yellowish at base. In winter, head/breast brownish slate-grey, upperparts blackish with dark grey margins to feathers and whitish fringes on inner wing coverts; white eyering, small whitish spot in front of eye, and white flanks and belly with blackish streaks and spots. Name misleading: purplish sheen visible only at close range on some of back feathers.

summer

△ In summer, has more scaly upperparts and paler face: dark brown crown, dark-streaked head, pale stripe above eye, blackish upperparts with broad buff and rufous fringes; throat, breast and flanks heavily streaked and spotted blackish; legs and base of bill darker, more greenish or orange-brown.

juvenile

△ Juveniles' upperparts neatly fringed chestnut, buff and whitish; rusty tinge to crown, upper breast heavily streaked greyish; lower breast streaked and spotted.

Of all waders, most maritime outside breeding season. Feed busily among rocks and seaweed close to sea, sometimes swimming. Usually in small flocks, often accompanied by Turnstones. Snatch shrimps, small fish etc washed ashore, or deftly remove periwinkles and other invertebrates from seaweed. Often very tame and approachable, but easy to overlook as superbly camouflaged against wet, seaweed-covered rocks.

▽ Flight direct, low over water, landing with flutter. Very dark; narrow white wingbar extends onto inner secondaries; narrow white sides to dark-centred rump. 'Armpits' and underwing coverts, mainly white, contrast with very dark breast.

winter

landing

KEY FACTS

Length: 20-22cm.
Wingspan: 40-44cm.
Weight: 60-75g. **Habitat:** on passage/winter on rocky shores and islands and around jetties, piers and breakwaters; breeds on Arctic tundra, heaths and moors.
Movements: passage migrant/winter visitor end Jul-May (mainly Oct-Apr); few in summer. **Population:** c25 000 birds winter. First bred Scottish Highlands 1978; up to 3 or more pairs have bred each year since.
Diet: chiefly molluscs, especially periwinkles, on migration and in winter; insects, spiders, crustaceans and other invertebrates, also seeds and other plant matter, on breeding grounds. **Voice:** generally silent away from breeding grounds; calls variable, including low, liquid, rather nasal 'weet-wit' or 'weet' in flight. **Nest:** hollow lined with leaves.
Eggs: 4, pale buff, blotched and spotted brown.
Incubation: 21-22 days, mainly by male, which cares for young almost exclusively.
Fledging: c28 days. **Broods:** 1. **Maturity:** 1 year.
Confusion species: darker than any wader in winter; larger, more robust than Dunlin (p146), with short yellow/orange legs. Only other wader regularly seen on rocky shores is Turnstone (opposite), which has very different plumage.

| J | F | M | A | M | J | J | A | S | O | N | D |

230

winter

moulting

△ Stocky, neckless, round-shouldered wader, with short orange legs and short, stout, pointed bill. Found mainly on rocky areas of coast or mussel beds with stones and seaweed. Earns its name from characteristic habit of turning over stones (and seaweed and shells) with bill in search of insects and other invertebrates, taking advantage of a food supply hidden from most other waders. Also takes food from surface and probes furiously in sand or mud. Usually in small lively flocks; larger groups at high tide. Frequently utters staccato chattering.

KEY FACTS

Length: 21-24cm.
Wingspan: 44-49cm.
Weight: 80-110g. **Habitat:** on passage/winter, favours rocky and shingly shores, but also found on sandy and muddy coasts and estuaries; breeds coastal tundra and islands N Europe.
Movements: passage migrant/winter visitor from Scandinavia, Russia, Greenland and Canada, end Jul-May; some in summer.
Population: *c*50 000 birds winter. **Diet:** molluscs, barnacles, other crustaceans, other invertebrates, also carrion. **Voice:** staccato 'tukatuk' and metallic 'teuk'.
Confusion species: Purple Sandpiper (opposite) lacks distinctive plumage pattern and has longer yellow bill.

| J | F | M | A | M | J | J | A | S | O | N | D |

male summer

female summer

△ In summer, adults have tortoiseshell pattern. Male has white head and neck with a few dark streaks on crown and intricate black pattern on face and breast, with broad black breast band; rest of underparts white; upperparts rich chestnut marked with black and buff. Female duller, with streaked head, buffish nape, smaller breast markings and duller upperparts.

▽ Flight low, fast, on flickering wings, flock often heading out to sea then turning back and landing or embarking on another circuit. Shows unmistakable complex dark/white pattern, with white wingbar, white wing patch, white on back and rump, and white-tipped black tail.

juvenile

adult winter

△ After moult Jul-Oct, distinctive overall pattern retained but much duller and less clear-cut, in shades of grey and brownish-black, with some pale fringes to feathers of upperparts. Sexes similar. Juveniles resemble winter adults, but browner above, with warm buff edges to feathers giving upperparts a scaly appearance. Legs duller yellow-brown.

winter

WOODCOCK *Scolopax rusticola*

KEY FACTS

Length: 33-35cm.
Wingspan: 55-65cm.
Weight: 250-420g. **Habitat:**
breeds chiefly in large tracts of
moist woodland with open
glades and rides, dense
ground cover of bracken and
brambles and damp areas for
feeding; also feeds in marshes,
by streams and ditches and in
boggy fields. **Movements:**
mainly sedentary, but a few
British breeders winter S to
Iberia; passage migrants and
winter visitors from Continent
Oct-Apr. **Population:** hard to
count, as relationship between
displaying males and breeding
females unclear; an estimated
10 000-26 000 females nest.
Several hundred thousand
birds winter. **Diet:** mainly
earthworms, also insects and
larvae, especially beetles, and
some seeds, fruits and other
plant food. **Voice:** generally
silent except during 'roding'
display flight of male (see
opposite). Occasionally gives
harsh, high-pitched 'tsveet'
when disturbed. **Nest:** shallow
scrape on ground among
cover, lined with dead leaves,
dry grass, a few feathers.
Eggs: 4, pale buff, spotted
brown or chestnut.
Incubation: 22 days, by
female. **Fledging:** 15-20 days.
Broods: male several, female
1. **Maturity:** 1 year for
females; 2 for most males.
Confusion species: much
larger, plumper and broader-
winged than Snipe (p154),
with russet tones to plumage.
If bill not visible, may be
confused with owl in twilight.

| J | F | M | A | M | J | J | A | S | O | N | D |

△ Largely nocturnal, spending day in dense cover, resting on
woodland floor; its intricately barred and mottled plumage
gives beautiful 'dead leaf' camouflage. Woodcocks usually
very difficult to find. You would be very lucky to see one on
the ground, but you may inadvertently disturb an individual
from its nest or resting place, when it flies off on broad wings,
zigzagging between tree trunks and usually soon dropping
back into cover again as if it had collapsed. Wings make
distinctive swishing sound on take-off, but bird rarely utters
any call. On migration (rarely seen), flight much stronger and
more direct. Occasionally, a Woodcock will be driven into the
open by severe winter weather. But by far the best chance of
seeing one of these elusive birds is during twilight hours in
spring and early summer, when males perform their display
flight, known as 'roding' (see opposite). Solitary apart from
breeding period.

▽ In flight distinguished by large, bulky, barrel-shaped body,
long bill pointing downwards at angle, and broad wings; looks
neckless and short-tailed. Much bigger and more rounded
than Snipe or Jack Snipe; slower wing action.

Snipe

Woodcocks

feeding

△ When probing with long bill for food in loose, damp leaf-litter carpeting woodland floor, in mud of boggy glade or in puddle, often makes curious bobbing movements of body while keeping head still; this may disturb earthworms and other burrowing prey so they can be caught more easily. Woodcocks also have remarkable habit of removing chicks from danger by flying off with them held between their legs, making several trips to move entire brood. Young can fly short distances by themselves when only 10 days old.

juvenile

◁ Plump, round-bodied and short-legged compared with other waders; long bill with broad yellowish or pinkish base and darker tip, very short neck and large dark eyes set well back on wide head. Crown buff, with broad dark bars across it, dark stripe between bill and eye and vague dark lower stripe. Upperparts intricately marked rusty-brown and black, with buff fringes and tips to some feathers. Underparts buff, with greyish-brown barring. Legs grey to pinkish or reddish, very short. Juvenile extremely similar to adult, apart from having spotted rather than plain buff forehead.

males, roding display flight

male landing near female

△ During breeding season (Mar-Jul) males make display flights, known as 'roding', above trees at dawn and dusk. Main function of roding seems to be to attract and locate females on the ground that are ready to mate. Male repeatedly follows a regular circuit of an area of woodland (and maybe more open country adjacent), usually just above treetops but sometimes considerably higher, as when there is a full moon. He flies with slow, deliberate, owl-like wingbeats, bill angled downwards at *c*45 degrees, head occasionally turning from side to side. As he does so, he utters series of soft, croaking 'orrrt orrrt' calls, followed by loud, explosive, sneezing 'tsiwick'. Sometimes, 2 or 3 males may be seen engaged in excited, twisting chases, uttering frequent 'tsiwick' calls. Females on ground may respond with softer version of male's sneezing call. When he has located an interested female, male will drop steeply and land near her in preparation for courtship displays (including bill tapping) and mating.

SNIPE *Gallinago gallinago*

120

feeding

△ Smallish wader with very long bill (almost twice length of head); striped head and heavily streaked plumage provide excellent camouflage. Generally seen singly or in small groups ('wisps'). Often remain hidden in cover, but will feed in open where undisturbed. Feeding birds tend to stay in same place, and feed by probing rapidly with bill up to its base into small area of water and mud. Close view shows buff/blackish stripes on crown, buff stripe above eye and blackish stripe through it, together with dark edges to ear coverts, making distinctive head pattern. Upperparts mottled black/rufous-brown, with bold creamy-buff stripes (narrower, whiter in juveniles) forming 'V' pattern. Neck/breast buff, with dark brown spots and arrowheads; belly white with dark-barred flanks.

escape flight

△ Usually, Snipe sit tight and rely on superb camouflage to escape danger. If approached too closely, however, will suddenly fly up, usually with distinctive call like tearing cloth. As they fly off, creamy-buff lines on back show up well; narrow white trailing edge to wings may also be visible; white band at tip of tail distinguishes from Jack Snipe. Distinctive escape flight, contrasting with Jack Snipe's, with sudden zigzagging, often 'towering' high into air, and travelling good distance before landing again with glide then sudden flutter. In longer flights, action appears jerky, with rapid, flickering beats of triangular wings; tail looks short.

male singing

◁ At breeding site, displaying birds perch on hummocks or posts (even overhead wires) when giving distinctive 'chipp-er chipp-er' song.

▷ Males display over breeding territory on spring and summer evenings by 'drumming': each bird rises, circles, then dives earthwards, air vibrating the stiffened outspread outer tail feathers to produce bleating sound.

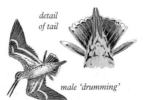

detail of tail

male 'drumming'

KEY FACTS

Length: 25-28cm.
Wingspan: 37-43cm.
Weight: 80-120g. **Habitat:** breeds on moorland bogs, marshy rough pastures, fens, coastal grazing marshes and other wetland areas with low vegetation; outside breeding season in even wider range of damp habitats with cover, from banks of streams and pools to saltmarshes on the coast. **Movements:** mainly resident, though some N British breeders winter in Ireland, and N and E birds move to SW of Britain or as far as France. Many passage migrants/winter visitors from N Europe, Aug-Apr.
Population: possibly as many as 53 000 pairs breed. Many hundreds of thousands winter.
Diet: earthworms, insects and larvae, molluscs, crustaceans and some seeds and other plant food. **Voice:** hoarse 'scaaap' of alarm in flight; during courtship, male dives over territory, spread outer tail feathers making remarkable throbbing ('drumming') sound; both sexes give rapid, loud, hollow, rhythmic, repeated 'chipp-er chipp-er' song. **Nest:** shallow scrape among cover, lined with grass. **Eggs:** 4, pale green to olive, blotched reddish-brown.
Incubation: 18-20 days, by female. **Fledging:** 19-20 days.
Broods: 1, sometimes 2.
Maturity: 1-2 years.
Confusion species: Jack Snipe (opposite).

| J | F | M | A | M | J | J | A | S | O | N | D |

feeding

△ Jack Snipe often feed in company with Snipe. Have peculiar feeding action, body bobbing up and down rhythmically as if on springs like strange clockwork toy (in contrast to Snipe's more vigorous 'sewing-machine' feeding style). Jack Snipe also pick food items from surface of mud with much shorter bill and probe less than Snipe. Much less gregarious than Snipe, usually seen singly or in twos or threes. Rarely encountered away from densely vegetated damp habitats such as coastal marshes and overgrown ditches.

Jack Snipe   *Snipe*

△ Compared with Snipe, Jack Snipe considerably smaller, with bill only a little longer than head. Has different pattern of stripes on head; crown all-dark, lacking central buff stripe of Snipe, but has short, slender stripe between dark crown and eyestripe; also eyestripe curves round behind eye to join up with lowermost dark stripe. Creamy stripes on back brighter and more prominent than Snipe's, and flanks striped, not barred. Tail more wedge-shaped and lacks white margin.

KEY FACTS

Length: 17-19cm.
Wingspan: 30-36cm.
Weight: 35-70g. **Habitat:** on passage/winter, overgrown ditches, edges of reedbeds, inland and coastal marshes and other well-vegetated damp places; avoids open mud. Breeds in open forest bogs in N Europe.
Movements: passage migrant/winter visitor from N Europe Sep-May.
Population: possibly as many as 100 000 birds winter. **Diet:** insects and larvae, molluscs, worms; eats more seeds and other plant matter than Snipe.
Voice: usually silent outside breeding season; occasionally utters barely audible, weak version of Snipe's hoarse alarm call. **Maturity:** 1 year.
Confusion species: smaller, shorter-billed than Snipe (opposite), with low, fluttering, direct flight, and usually silent when disturbed (Snipe zigzags upwards quickly and gives hoarse rasping call); Jack Snipe also lacks Snipe's buff centre stripe to crown, white on tail and barred flanks, and has more prominent golden back stripes and more rounded wings.

| J | F | M | A | M | J | J | A | S | O | N | D |

escape flight

△ Although quite widespread in winter, scarcer than Snipe and very difficult to observe. Unlike Snipe, avoids open ground and generally keeps well hidden among cover when resting and feeding. Usually, only seen when suddenly flies up as you are literally just about to tread on it. Unlike Snipe, generally flies up low and straight, with slower, weaker, more fluttering action, and soon drops back into cover with half-closed wings. Has shorter, more rounded wings than Snipe. Normally silent, unlike Snipe, though occasionally utters very weak version of the latter's alarm call. When several together, typically fly up 1 or 2 at a time.

BLACK-TAILED GODWIT *Limosa limosa*

185

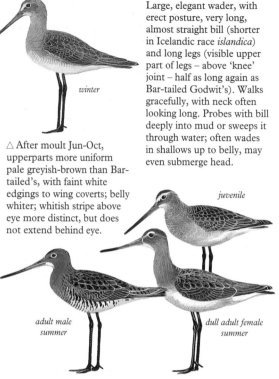

winter

juvenile

adult male summer

dull adult female summer

Large, elegant wader, with erect posture, very long, almost straight bill (shorter in Icelandic race *islandica*) and long legs (visible upper part of legs – above 'knee' joint – half as long again as Bar-tailed Godwit's). Walks gracefully, with neck often looking long. Probes with bill deeply into mud or sweeps it through water; often wades in shallows up to belly, may even submerge head.

△ After moult Jun-Oct, upperparts more uniform pale greyish-brown than Bar-tailed's, with faint white edgings to wing coverts; belly whiter; whitish stripe above eye more distinct, but does not extend behind eye.

△ In summer plumage, head, neck and upper breast chestnut (redder, more intense on Icelandic race *islandica*, seen here on passage/in winter). Mantle and scapulars grey, with variable amounts of black and chestnut feathers; wing coverts plain grey with whitish fringes. Pale stripe above eye, if present, does not extend behind it. Flanks barred; lower breast/belly white with some barring. Males usually brighter than females. Juveniles more like summer adults than winter adults, with rufous tinge to neck and upper breast (may be very bright on *islandica* birds); neat, orange-buff feather edgings (thicker, brighter and more prominent in *islandica*) on upperparts produce tortoiseshell pattern; flanks unbarred.

winter

◁ Easily identified in flight by striking, broad white wingbar and combination of square white rump and tail ending in broad black band. Legs trail far behind tail in flight. Flight fast, with rapid wingbeats; bill, body and legs held in same plane, giving 'flying cross' appearance. Often performs twisting dive as it loses height to land.

KEY FACTS

Length: 36-44cm.
Wingspan: 62-70cm.
Weight: 280-500g. **Habitat:** breeds mainly on lowland wet grasslands; also on coastal grazing marshes; in winter and on passage on sheltered muddy estuaries, saltmarshes, flooded grasslands inland.
Movements: British breeders winter W Africa; passage migrant/winter visitor from Iceland mainly to Ireland and N and W Britain, and from N and E Europe mainly to S and E Britain Jul-May; some non-breeders in summer.
Population: ceased breeding here 1830s; bred regularly again from 1952, with peak of *c*70 pairs in mid 1970s; now only 35-40 pairs breed, chiefly on Ouse and Nene Washes (Cambs/Norfolk) and N Norfolk coast. **Diet:** worms, molluscs, other invertebrates; seeds and other plant matter.
Voice: noisy when nesting, with loud, clear 'weeka-weeka-weeka'; otherwise occasional brief 'tuk'. **Nest:** scrape amid lush vegetation; nests in loose colonies. **Eggs:** 3-4, olive-green to dark brown, blotched darker brown. **Incubation:** 22-24 days, by male and female. **Fledging:** 25-30 days. **Broods:** 1. **Maturity:** 2 years or more. **Confusion species:** Bar-tailed Godwit (opposite), shorter, less elegant; less erect posture; shorter, slightly upturned bill, shorter legs; no wingbar, barred tail; streaked upperparts in winter.

J F M A M J J A S O N D

Limosa lapponica **BAR-TAILED GODWIT**

Much shorter-legged, slightly smaller and somewhat stockier than Black-tailed, with shorter neck generally held less erect and forehead slightly steeper. Bill very long and, in contrast to Black-tailed's, appears slightly more upcurved. Sometimes chases after prey in brief, awkward dashes, with bill thrust forwards. Much more abundant and widespread than Black-tailed; in large, dense flocks on favoured estuaries.

adult winter

adult female summer

adult male summer

juvenile

◁ After moult Jul-Nov, adult in winter plumage looks far more streaked above, with larger pale fringes and darker centres to feathers, than winter Black-tailed; whiter below, with faint streaks across buffish breast; pale stripe above eye more distinct.

KEY FACTS

Length: 33-42cm.
Wingspan: 61-68cm.
Weight: 280-450g. **Habitat:** on passage and in winter on estuaries and shores, preferring sandier areas; breeds on tundra and open boggy woodland in N Europe and Russia. **Movements:** passage migrant and winter visitor from breeding range in N (Aug-May). **Population:** up to 100 000 winter; numbers fluctuate considerably with severity of winter in major resting place, Wadden Sea, Netherlands, and perhaps also with variations in breeding success. **Diet:** chiefly worms, bivalve molluscs in winter; mostly flies, beetles and worms, plus some plant matter, when breeding. **Voice:** silent away from breeding grounds, apart from rapid, low, barking 'kirruk kirruk' flight call. **Maturity:** 2 years. **Confusion species:** Black-tailed Godwit (opposite). In winter and, especially, juvenile plumage (see centre right) upperparts very like those of Curlew (p158) and Whimbrel (p159); could be confused in flight, if slightly upcurved bill (downcurved in Whimbrel and Curlew) cannot be seen. Much smaller than Curlew, slimmer than Whimbrel, and paler above and much paler below than both, without strong streaking on underparts. (See also right.)

△ Adults, especially males, differ more strikingly in summer than Black-tailed. Males have bright brick-red head, neck and entire underparts, with dark brown streaks on crown and nape; lack white belly and strongly barred flanks of Black-tailed. Upperparts similar to those of Black-tailed, but browner, boldly marked with chestnut, brown and black, producing more variegated pattern. Females much duller and browner than males, some keeping winter-like plumage throughout summer. Juveniles browner, more streaked than juvenile Black-tailed, upper breast uniformly streaked or washed with buff; upperparts have more variegated pattern, like that of Curlew and Whimbrel.

winter

△ Very different from Black-tailed in flight, without wingbars and with bold white inverted 'V' on rump and barred tail; shorter legs only just extend beyond tail. Flight fast, with rapid wingbeats; flocks perform impressive manoeuvres in unison. Sometimes makes burst of more powerful wingbeats with head and bill appearing to drop below line of body; glides with wings held out straight; twists and tilts from side to side and makes dramatic, steep plunges when landing.

J F M A M J J A S O N D

CURLEW *Numenius arquata*

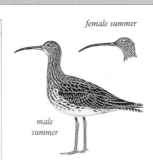

female summer

male summer

KEY FACTS

Length: 50-60cm.
Wingspan: 80-100cm.
Weight: 575-950g. **Habitat:** breeds mainly on moors, upland pastures, locally on farmland, heaths, water meadows and sand dunes; in Britain winters mainly on coastal and estuarine mudflats and nearby grassland; in Ireland winters inland as well, especially along river valleys and by loughs. **Movements:** many breeders remain here, with major SW movements to W British and Irish estuaries, though some migrate as far as France and Iberia; passage migrants/winter visitors from N Europe Jul-May.
Population: 45 000-50 000 pairs breed; up to *c*200 000 birds winter. **Diet:** on breeding grounds, insects and larvae, earthworms, some plant matter; on passage and in winter, earthworms and marine worms, crabs and small bivalve molluscs. **Voice:** loud, ringing 'coour-li' and more melancholy 'whaup', rapid, harsh 'kvi-kvi-kvi' of alarm; song, heard almost all year, begins with slow, low-pitched 'coour-li' notes, then accelerates and rises in pitch in ecstatic crescendo of liquid notes and bubbling trill.
Nest: scrape among moss hummocks, grass tussocks or crops, lined with dry grass and few feathers. **Eggs:** 4, greenish to brownish, spotted darker.
Incubation: 27-29 days, by both sexes. **Fledging:** 32-38 days. **Broods:** 1.
Maturity: 2 years.
Confusion species: juvenile in particular confusable with Whimbrel (opposite).

| J | F | M | A | M | J | J | A | S | O | N | D |

△ Biggest of all European waders, with very long, downcurved bill. Plumage basically brown and buff, streaked darker. Looks uniform grey-brown at distance but, at closer range, dark bars and blotches on upperparts, which have buffish edges to feathers, and dark streaks on head, neck and breast. Lacks any clear stripes above eye. Dark-streaked cheeks contrast with pale chin and upper throat. Lower breast and flanks heavily streaked; belly much whiter, less streaked. Winter plumage very similar, but drabber, greyer, losing buff tones; considerable individual variation on basic plumage. Female larger than male, usually with longer bill. Juvenile similar to adult, but with shorter bill than male.

male, display flight

△ Beautiful, wild, sad, bubbling song, heard throughout year but most intensely on breeding grounds, given in display flight, in which male rises steeply, hovers momentarily, then glides down with wings held in shallow 'V'.

Whimbrel

Curlew

◁ Curlew larger, paler and longer-legged than Whimbrel, with longer, more evenly downcurved bill (Whimbrel's looks abruptly `bent' towards tip); lacks Whimbrel's diagnostic striped crown. Curlew typically walks slowly and deliberately, probing deeply in mud for food or picking it from surface (though may run to catch prey and when taking off). Whimbrel more active on ground, often running quickly; takes far more food from surface. Curlew often in large flocks, which disperse when feeding; Whimbrel usually seen singly or in small groups.

summer

◁ Quite slow, gull-like action. Whitish triangular rump extends up onto lower back. Looks paler than Whimbrel, with more contrasting pattern formed by dark outer wings. Large flocks often fly high in straggling lines or chevrons.

*alert
posture*

KEY FACTS

Length: 40-46cm.
Wingspan: 71-81cm.
Weight: 270-450g. **Habitat:**
in Scotland breeds on exposed
heathland and moorland. On
passage on estuaries,
saltmarshes, coastal lagoons,
muddy and rocky shores,
nearby fields; some seen
inland. **Movements:** breeding
birds summer visitors May-
Aug, probably, like other
European breeders, wintering
Africa; on passage from
Iceland/N Europe mid
Apr-late May and Jul-Oct.
Population: 430-500 pairs
breed, with c95 per cent in
Shetland. **Diet:** on breeding
grounds, chiefly insects, snails
and slugs, also insect larvae
and earthworms; on passage,
crabs, shrimps, sandhoppers,
molluscs, marine worms.
Voice: usual call rapid, far-
carrying, tittering whistle
'tititititititi', often of 7 notes
(rarely gives rather Curlew-
like 'coor-ew' as well); song
liquid rippling similar to call
but longer, more liquid and
interspersed with repeated
shrill 'tsoo-eeeep'.
Nest: shallow scrape on
hummock among heather or
other low vegetation, sparsely
lined with vegetation.
Eggs: 4, olive-green to buff,
blotched and spotted dark
brown. **Incubation:**
27-28 days, by both sexes.
Fledging: 35-40 days.
Broods: 1. **Maturity:**
2 years. **Confusion species:**
Curlew, especially juvenile
(see opposite); distant Bar-
tailed Godwits in flight may
be confused with Whimbrel
when bill not visible (see left).

△ Smaller, dumpier than Curlew, with shorter legs, shorter
bill, abruptly downcurved near tip, and boldly striped crown –
two dark bands on crown separated by pale buff central band.
Distinct whitish stripe above eye, narrow dark stripe through
eye and uniformly pale throat (whiter than on Curlew) give
quite different facial 'expression' from Curlew. However, head
pattern often difficult to distinguish unless bird at close range.
Darker, browner upperparts than Curlew. Much more active
than Curlew, and generally far less wary. Look out – and listen
– for migrating Whimbrels on brief spring and longer autumn
passage, inland as well as on coast.

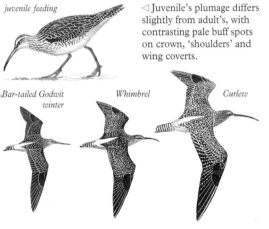

juvenile feeding

◁ Juvenile's plumage differs
slightly from adult's, with
contrasting pale buff spots
on crown, 'shoulders' and
wing coverts.

*Bar-tailed Godwit
winter*   *Whimbrel*   *Curlew*

| J | F | M | A | M | J | J | A | S | O | N | D |

△ In flight, wings shorter, more triangular than Curlew's,
producing lighter, faster wingbeats. Carries head high, level
with line of back; looks pigeon-chested. Takes off much more
easily than Curlew, without preliminary run, can turn more
tightly and lands with rapid fluttering of wings. Wing pattern
more uniform than Curlew's. As with latter species, prominent
white 'V'-shaped rump extends up onto lower back. Flying
birds often give distinctive tittering whistling calls. Distant
Bar-tailed Godwits in winter plumage may be mistaken in
flight for similar-sized Whimbrel (though slighter and slimmer-
winged). Apart from bill and plumage differences, the godwits
have longer heads and necks in contrast to Whimbrel's and
Curlew's upwardly held heads and bulging breasts.

*migrating
flock*

RUFF *Philomachus pugnax*

122

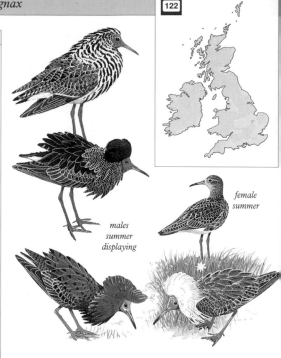

males summer displaying

female summer

KEY FACTS

Length: males 26-32cm; females 20-25cm. **Wingspan:** 46-58cm. **Weight:** males 130-230g; females 70-150g. **Habitat:** in Britain breeds mainly on lowland grassy meadows after winter floods; winter visitor/on passage, on marshes, wet meadows, muddy banks of lakes and reservoirs, small creeks in estuaries. **Movements:** passage migrant, mainly from N Sweden and Finland, late Mar-early Jun and, especially, mid Jul-Oct; winters in Mediterranean and (mainly) Africa; small but increasing numbers winter Britain and Ireland. **Population:** always rare breeder, but decline since 1970s; probably fewer than 5 females now breed each year at 10 irregular sites, most at Ouse Washes, Cambs and Norfolk. **Diet:** mainly insects and larvae in breeding season; otherwise wide range of invertebrates, frogs, small fish, seeds and other plant matter. **Voice:** generally silent; gruff, low 'wek' in flight. **Nest:** shallow scrape on ground, concealed among vegetation, lined with grass. **Eggs:** 4, pale olive with darker olive-brown blotches. **Incubation:** 20-21 days, by female. **Fledging:** 25-28 days. **Broods:** male several; female 1. **Maturity:** 1-2 years. **Confusion species:** Redshank (p162), especially juvenile (which has orange legs like many Ruffs), but has longer legs, longer, straight bill; also darker below and, in flight, prominent white trailing edges to wings and white lower back and rump. Female and juvenile Ruff resemble rarer Pectoral Sandpiper (p147), but latter smaller, less upright, with shorter legs, sharply defined breast band and double white 'V' on upper back. Juvenile Ruff also similar to rare Buff-breasted Sandpiper (opposite).

△ Males (ruffs) in breeding plumage (*c*Apr-Jun) have remarkable, boldly coloured, loose head tufts and huge ruff, unique among waders. Plumage extremely variable, with no two males exactly alike. Head tufts and ruff in different combinations of black, deep purple, chestnut, buff and white, often with barring of contrasting colour. Males gather together at traditional display sites (leks), each occupying his own small 'court', where they perform a strange dance, with head tufts raised and outspread wings fluttering, and indulge in chases and mock fights. Watching females (reeves) choose males to mate with. In summer, females lack head tufts and ruff; have variably dark-streaked head and hind neck, white throat with brownish spots, black or rufous back, with pale edges to feathers forming scaly pattern, greyish-brown wing coverts with paler tips; flanks mottled or barred dark brown and scaled with white; and white belly.

males moulting from breeding plumage

△ Head tufts grown and moulted quickly. Moulting males blackish above, marked with rufous, grey or white; breast and flanks lightly or heavily mottled blackish or chestnut, contrasting with white throat (and often foreneck) and belly.

| J | F | M | A | M | J | J | A | S | O | N | D |

▷ In winter plumage, adult males and females appear identical, except males noticeably larger. Upperparts more uniform greyish-brown than in summer, with scaly pattern restricted mainly to wing coverts; some individuals have pale head or white collar. Breast, sides of neck and flanks greyish; rest of underparts whitish. As in summer, legs and base of bill orange or pinkish; yellowish in some individuals. Odd shape compared with other superficially similar waders, having long, usually hump-backed, pot-bellied body and long legs but quite short, slightly downcurved bill, and neat, rounded head that seems too small for the longish, quite thick neck. Stands upright, but walks with body held almost horizontal; strides slowly and deliberately when searching for food among grass, probing in mud or wading in shallows, immersing head and bill below surface. Usually seen in small flocks or in ones and twos on passage. Frequently mixes with other waders, but quickly separates when they take wing.

female

winter

male

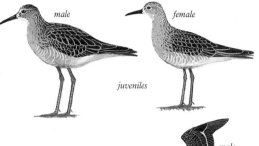

male

female

juveniles

◁ Juveniles have boldly but neatly scaled pattern on upperparts, blackish-brown feathers edged with warm buff; distinctive almost uniform deep buff throat, foreneck, breast and flanks. Base of bill pale brownish; legs greenish or yellow-brown, occasionally greyish.

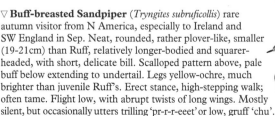

male

winter

females

▷ In flight, shows indistinct, narrow white wingbar on long, quite broad wings and distinctive oval white patches on sides of rump. Flight looks effortless and floating, with lazy, flicking, erratic wingbeats and occasional glides.

▽ **Buff-breasted Sandpiper** (*Tryngites subruficollis*) rare autumn visitor from N America, especially to Ireland and SW England in Sep. Neat, rounded, rather plover-like, smaller (19-21cm) than Ruff, relatively longer-bodied and squarer-headed, with short, delicate bill. Scalloped pattern above, pale buff below extending to undertail. Legs yellow-ochre, much brighter than juvenile Ruff's. Erect stance, high-stepping walk; often tame. Flight low, with abrupt twists of long wings. Mostly silent, but occasionally utters trilling 'pr-r-r-eeet' or low, gruff 'chu'.

Buff-breasted Sandpiper

adults

adult

juvenile

adult

REDSHANK *Tringa totanus*

188

KEY FACTS

Length: 27-29cm.
Wingspan: 45-52cm.
Weight: 85-155g. **Habitat:**
breeds in wet meadows inland
and on coastal saltmarshes; on
passage and in winter on
coasts, estuaries, saltmarshes,
freshwater marshes, muddy
shores of lakes and reservoirs.
Movements: British breeders
mostly resident, moving only
locally, mainly to coasts;
passage migrants and winter
visitors from Iceland and
N Europe Jul-May.
Population: 35 000-39 000
pairs breed; probably over
100 000 birds winter. **Diet:**
during breeding season chiefly
insects, earthworms; otherwise
crustaceans, molluscs, other
small invertebrates.
Voice: very noisy; sad musical
whistle 'teu' and ringing,
downslurred 'teu-hu' or 'teu-
heu-heu' of alarm in flight,
often rapidly repeated;
incessantly repeated high,
sharp 'tewk-tewk-tewk' of
alarm and scolding 'chip-chip-
chip'; song rapid, loud
yodelling 'tu-yoo, tu-yoo, tu-
yoo' starting slowly and
accelerating, in display flight.
Nest: shallow hollow, among
vegetation, often with
overhanging leaves and stems
intertwined to form canopy.
Eggs: 4, cream to buff,
spotted and blotched brown
and reddish-brown.
Incubation: 24 days, by both
sexes. **Fledging:** 23-25 days.
Broods: 1. **Maturity:** 1-2
years. **Confusion species:**
Spotted Redshank (opposite)
larger, more elegant, with
longer, finer, darker bill and
longer legs; summer plumage
very different, in winter paler
and greyer. Lacks white on
upperwings.

| J | F | M | A | M | J | J | A | S | O | N | D |

▷ Flight fast, erratic and
often tilting from side to side,
with shallow, jerky wingbeats.
Striking white wedge on
inner rear wings, and white
rump forming 'V' up back.

Abundant and widespread
wader on coasts; scarcer
inland. Body tapered, though
plumper than that of larger,
more elegant Spotted
Redshank and Greenshank.
Brown or greyish upperparts,
streaked white underparts,
fairly long red or orange legs,
longish straight orange-red
blackish-tipped bill, and
distinctive white wing and
tail markings in flight (see
below). Very wary, bobbing
neck when alarmed and
flying off with repeated, noisy
'teu-heu-heu' alarm calls.
Walks easily and steadily,
bobbing head and body with
swinging action and making
regular pecks at prey.

In display flight at breeding
grounds, male utters loud
yodelling song, often for
several minutes on end,
climbing to *c*40m above
ground before embarking on
switchback flight, alternately
gliding down on depressed
wings and rising again by
shivering wings rapidly below
level of body; this attracts an
interested female to join him.

summer

△ After moult Feb-Apr,
brown above, marked with
darker streaks and spots.
White underparts variably
but usually boldly barred and
mottled dark brown; legs
bright orange-red, brighter
than in winter. At breeding
sites, often perches on posts
and even on lower branches
of shrubs and trees.

adult winter   *juvenile*

△ After moult Jul-Jan, upperparts more uniform grey-brown,
with more white around eyes, finely streaked pale grey throat/
breast, less barred flanks, duller, more orange, legs. Juveniles
similar, but warmer brown above, with more buff fringes to
feathers and breast suffused greyish-buff. Legs orange-yellow.

winter

Tringa erythropus SPOTTED REDSHANK

189

male summer   *moulting from summer*

△ Breeding plumage unmistakable; males jet-black save for white spots on upperparts and undertail; females duller, with more white under tail; seen here late summer when birds pass through from Arctic breeding grounds and moult on our estuaries. Moulting birds look very odd – patchy black/grey/ white. Bill black, with dull red base; legs dark brownish-red.

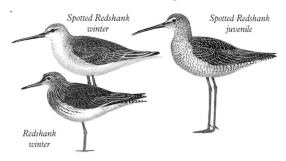

Spotted Redshank winter

Spotted Redshank juvenile

Redshank winter

△ After moult *c*Aug-Nov, mainly pale grey above, with broad white fringes to browner feathers of 'shoulders' and wing coverts; clear white stripe above dark eyestripe; underparts white, with pale grey wash on upper breast and flanks; much paler than Redshank; legs darker red, rarely orange. In juvenile plumage (seen only briefly, as quickly lost during autumn and much as winter adult by Nov), upperparts dusky brown, with neat whitish spotting and feather edges, underparts white with fine brown barring visible only at close range. Larger, more elegant, than Redshank; longer legs and longer, finer bill, with slight but sometimes obvious downward kink at very tip.

KEY FACTS

Length: 29-32cm.
Wingspan: 48-52cm.
Weight: 135-205g. **Habitat:** autumn passage migrants occur quite frequently at inland waters, but in winter almost entirely coastal. Breeds in forest marshes in N Eurasia. **Movements:** passes through British Isles Jul-Oct and Apr-Jun, on migration to and from SW Europe/Africa; also overwinters here in small numbers. **Population:** *c*1000 birds seen on autumn passage; *c*80-200 winter. **Diet:** as Redshank. **Voice:** loud, clear, sharp, disyllabic 'chu-it', rising in pitch, usually given in flight; constant soft quacking calls from feeding flocks. **Maturity:** probably 1 year. **Confusion species:** Redshank (see right and Key Facts opposite), Greenshank (p164).

J F M A M J J A S O N D

▽ Flight rapid, direct and purposeful; may tuck legs up into body feathers out of sight, when looks quite short-bodied and long-billed; also trails them behind tail. White rump extends in inverted 'V' up back; no wingbars.

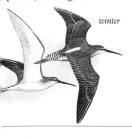

winter

winter, feeding

△ More lively than Redshank when pursuing prey; often wades up to belly, swims and up-ends like dabbling duck in shallows. Feeding birds favour estuarine creeks and channels. Often, suddenly gather together in dense flock at particularly productive spot and feed frenziedly, dashing about sideways or making rapid lunging runs.

GREENSHANK *Tringa nebularia*

summer

winter

190

△ Elegant grey and white wader with long, slightly upturned dark grey bill and long greenish legs. Looks very pale at distance. In summer (after moult Feb-May), upperparts grey with black patches arranged in longitudinal bands, head and breast with heavy blackish streaks, spots and arrowheads; rest of underparts white. In late summer, much of black on upperparts lost, and remnants give patchy, untidy look. In winter, even paler, with uniform pale grey upperparts, whitish face and finely streaked neck and breast. Walks with long strides, often wading deeply. Very active and energetic feeder, picking, probing and sweeping with bill and lunging after small fish, crabs and other prey, often running fast and suddenly and erratically changing direction with great agility.

juvenile

◁ Juveniles have upperparts tinged brown, with neat pattern formed by darker, more pointed feathers with pale buff edges. Head greyer than winter adult's, with neat speckling. Sides of neck and breast delicately streaked greyish. May show paler stripe part way up neck.

▽ In flight, looks heavier than Redshank and Spotted Redshank, with longer, narrower, more pointed wings. Shows large white V extending up back, white tail, barred darker; long legs project well beyond tail, adding to very elongated profile. Like Spotted Redshank but unlike Redshank, lacks white patches on upperwings. Spotted has smaller, more oval, white patch up back and darker tail. A noisy bird: usually gives loud, ringing calls when taking flight.

winter

Spotted Redshank

Greenshanks

Redshank

KEY FACTS

Length: 30-35cm.
Wingspan: 53-60cm.
Weight: 140-270g. **Habitat:** in Britain breeds mainly on boulder-strewn Highland blanket bogs with many small pools; some in young forestry plantations. **Movements:** some Scottish breeders winter here, others migrate as far as N Africa; passage migrants from N Europe end Jun-Aug (adults), Aug-Oct (juveniles); also some Apr-May.
Population: 1100-1600 pairs breed Scotland; 1000-1500 birds winter. **Diet:** mainly insects on breeding grounds; chiefly invertebrates and small fish on passage/winter. **Voice:** loud, ringing, evenly pitched 'tew-tew-tew' in flight; on breeding grounds, repeated 'chip-chip-chip ...' and rich whistling 'teu-i, teu-i, teu-i' song. **Nest:** shallow scrape on open ground, sparsely lined with vegetation and feathers.
Eggs: 4, off-white or buff, blotched and streaked brown.
Incubation: 24 days, by both sexes. **Fledging:** 25-31 days.
Broods: 1. **Maturity:** 2 years. **Confusion species:** Redshank (p162) smaller, shorter, less elegant, with shorter red legs, shorter, slenderer, straight bill, shorter red legs and white inner rear wings in flight. Spotted Redshank (p163) similar size, but has red legs and red on bill; white patch up rump and back narrower; legs project further beyond tail.

| J | F | M | A | M | J | J | A | S | O | N | D |

Tringa nebularia GREENSHANK

winter

Greenshank

Redshank

Spotted Redshank

▷ Larger, taller, more elegant, longer-billed, longer-legged and greyer than Redshank. Winter Spotted Redshank even paler above, with finer, straight bill, slightly downcurved at extreme tip, conspicuous white eyebrow ending just behind eye and all-white underparts. Redshank and Spotted Redshank have red legs.

Actitis hypoleucos COMMON SANDPIPER

158

Combination of short legs, long tail and crouched stance accentuates elongated look of this small wader. Tail projects well beyond wingtips in adults. Walks with distinctive, continuous rhythmic bobbing action of head and vertical swinging of hind body and tail. Usually seen singly or in pairs.

KEY FACTS

Length: 19-21cm. **Wingspan:** 32-35cm. **Weight:** 40-60g. **Habitat:** breeds by upland streams, rivers, lakes; on passage at edges of lakes, reservoirs, marsh creeks etc. **Movements:** summer visitor Apr-Aug; almost all our breeders winter Africa (a few winter here, mainly in SW Britain); passage migrants from N Europe late Mar-May, Jul-mid Oct. **Population:** c18 000 pairs breed. **Diet:** insects, molluscs, crustaceans, worms. **Voice:** shrill, loud, repeated, 'tsee-wee-wee' on take-off; song, given in display flight or on ground, by day or night, rapidly repeated series of clear, rhythmic 'kittiweewit, kittiweewit' notes. **Nest:** shallow scrape on ground, often in vegetation, sparsely lined with grass, debris. **Eggs:** 3-5, buff with dark spots. **Incubation:** 21-22 days, by both sexes. **Fledging:** 26-28 days. **Broods:** 1. **Maturity:** 1-2 years. **Confusion species:** Green and Wood Sandpipers (pp166-7).

| J | F | M | A | M | J | J | A | S | O | N | D |

summer

winter

△ In summer plumage (from Feb) upperparts olive-brown, faintly speckled black, underparts gleaming white and sides of chest strongly streaked brown, with distinctive white wedge between chest patch and bend of wing. In winter plumage (after moult Jul-Oct), more uniformly olive-brown above, with finer streaking on chest sides. Adults and juveniles have grey-brown bill with ochre base and grey-green (rarely yellow) legs.

▽ Juvenile like winter adult but more scaly above, buff fringes to feathers, wing coverts barred buff and sepia, sides of chest mottled.

summer

juvenile

△ Flight action very distinctive: low, with rapid, flickering, shallow wingbeats, alternating with brief glides on bowed, stiff wings. Readily distinguished from Green and Wood Sandpipers by bold white wingbar. Brown rump and tail with white sides distinctive. A noisy bird, giving loud, shrill piping calls almost continuously in flight.

GREEN SANDPIPER *Tringa ochropus*

Larger than Common and Wood Sandpipers, with shorter legs
than latter; stockier, plumper-bellied, larger-headed shape
than Wood, which together with often hunched posture makes
it look more like a large Common. Bobs head and rear up and
down frequently, but not continuously like Common. When
alarmed, bobs more vigorously before taking flight. Walks
steadily when feeding, pecking at prey on surface.

summer

winter

△ Always looks very dark above and white below (except for
dusky breast), appearing black/white at distance. Upperparts
very dark olive-brown; dark brown streaks form small,
prominent but diffuse breast band; streaked head; lacks
prominent eyebrow but has small white stripe in front of bold
white eyering; belly white. Legs greyish-green. In summer
(May-Aug) has whitish-buff spots on upperparts (much less
bold than on Wood Sandpiper). Winter adult more uniform
above, with fewer, vaguer buffish spots.

◁ Juvenile paler above, with
many small, dull buff spots;
best distinguished from
juvenile Wood Sandpiper
by structure, darker, bolder
breast band, lack of strong
chequered pattern of large
spots on upperparts, and
darker legs.

juvenile

winter

KEY FACTS

Length: 21-24cm.
Wingspan: 41-46cm.
Weight: 70-90g. **Habitat:**
breeds in N Europe in boggy
forests; on passage by
freshwaters, in muddy gullies
and ditches, along streams, on
watercress beds and at muddy
margins of lakes, reservoirs
and pools; in winter some on
estuary creeks. **Movements:**
passage migrants from NE
Europe to Mediterranean and
Africa, Jun-Nov, Mar-May;
some winter; has bred N
Britain. **Population:** usually
seen in ones and twos; flocks
of up to 30 recorded; autumn
total may reach 2000 birds;
200-600 birds winter. **Diet:**
insects, crustaceans, molluscs,
worms. **Voice:** loud, ringing,
mellow 'weet tluit weet weet'
of alarm on taking flight; also
more rippling 'tu-loo-ee'.
Maturity: 1 year. **Confusion
species:** Wood Sandpiper
(opposite) slimmer, paler
above, with shorter bill and
longer, paler legs; see also
Common Sandpiper (p165),
which has white wedge
between brown-streaked
breast and folded wing.

| J | F | M | A | M | J | J | A | S | O | N | D |

◁ In flight, wings uniformly very dark above and below,
contrasting dramatically with gleaming white belly and square
white rump; legs project only a little beyond barred tail. Looks
rather like outsized House Martin. Wings broader-based than
Wood Sandpiper's. Wing action clipped, rather like Snipe; has
similar escape flight: zigzagging low, then climbing fast and
high, with flickering, twisting action, before suddenly
plummeting to land. Excitable and noisy when disturbed,
usually giving loud, ringing, musical calls.

Tringa glareola WOOD SANDPIPER

125

Slimmer, more delicate than Green and Common Sandpipers, more like miniature Redshank. Has tapered profile but broad body, small head, long neck, finer, shorter bill and longer legs, especially above 'knee', than Green or Common Sandpipers. Bobs less than the other 2 species.

summer　　　*winter*

KEY FACTS

Length: 19-21cm.
Wingspan: 36-40cm.
Weight: 50-90g. **Habitat:** breeds in N Europe on tundra and in wet forests; tiny Scottish population breeds in bogs among trees; on passage at edges of lakes and pools, floodwaters, marshes, etc.
Movements: passage migrants from NE Europe to Africa Apr-May and (especially) Jul-mid Oct.
Population: small numbers on autumn passage, especially after E winds from Scandinavian breeding grounds; fewer in spring; fewer than 10 pairs breed Scottish Highlands. **Diet:** insects, other invertebrates. **Voice:** rapid, shrill, high, peevish 'chiff-iff' or 'chiff-iff-iff' of alarm on take-off; liquid 'tlui', rising in pitch; whistling 'tleea-tleea-tleea' in high song flight. **Nest:** scrape on ground among dense cover, lined with vegetation; occasionally in old nest of other bird. **Eggs:** 4, buff or greenish with bold dark spots and blotches.
Incubation: 22-23 days, by both sexes. **Fledging:** *c*30 days. **Broods:** 1. **Maturity:** 1 year. **Confusion species:** Green Sandpiper (opposite) and Common Sandpiper (p165). Juvenile Redshank (p162) also similar, but lacks clear pale eyebrow, has finer spots on darker breast, orange legs, and shows bold white wing patches and V-shaped white rump in flight.

J F M A M J J A S O N D

△ Much paler and browner above than Green Sandpiper, with more strongly spotted upperparts and clearer white eyebrows. In summer plumage (Apr-Jul), has dark brown upperparts (appearing grey-brown at distance), with large white and buff speckles; white throat; strongly dark-brown-streaked breast (though not usually as dark-looking as Green's); brown-barred flanks. In winter plumage (after moult Jul-Oct) upperparts less spotted, and breast brownish-grey with obscure streaks. Bill blackish, tinged green at base. Legs dull greenish (sometimes yellowish), paler than Green and Common Sandpiper's.

juvenile

◁ Juvenile resembles winter adult, but warmer brown above, with numerous prominent cream to rich buff markings; buff wash to intricately mottled breast; dark mottling on front flanks.

▽ In flight, distinguished from Green Sandpiper by more heavily barred tail, with less white on upper tail and rump, and, especially, paler brownish underwings (much paler than upperwings); looks much less dark/white than Green. Like Green, but unlike Common, lacks wingbar. Wings look relatively slim, compared with broader-based wings of Green. Feet project well beyond tail, further than on Green; feet of Common do not extend beyond tail. Flight rapid, agile, with fast, fluttering, shallow wingbeats. Usually calls loudly and excitedly on take-off, giving rapid series of 3-4 whistles. Escape flight erratic at first, but then less exaggerated than Green's.

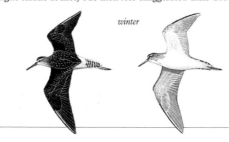

winter

167

PHALAROPES
Order Charadriiformes, Family Scolopacidae

Small birds distinguished from all other waders by habitual swimming; the 2 European species spend winter on the open sea, often far from land. Lobed toes, with small webs at base, and legs flattened from side to side help them swim well. Often spin around on water in tight circles, stirring up plankton and other diminutive prey, which they peck up with remarkable speed. Females slightly bigger, more brightly plumaged than males; take the lead in courtship, and leave males to incubate eggs and care for young alone. Summer plumage brighter than mainly grey winter plumage, in which there is a distinctive black stripe through eye.

● Note: bill shape, tone and pattern of plumage in winter. Most phalaropes seen here are juvenile/1st-winter birds.

GREY PHALAROPE *Phalaropus fulicarius*

Seen here about 10 times more often than Red-necked. Grey slightly larger, bulkier, with bigger head, thicker neck and distinctly thicker, shorter, less pointed bill, with small pale base. Swims with back held more level and tail higher than Red-necked. May resemble tiny gull on water.

female summer   *male summer*

△ Summer adult unmistakable: striking bright rust-red neck and underparts, black and white head, and black/buff patterned upperparts. Male duller, with browner, pale-streaked crown and mantle, duller cheeks and duller underparts, often with some white. Bill yellow with variable amount of black on tip (least in females). Legs pale bluish, toes with yellow lobes.

juvenile   *adult winter*

△ Juvenile has blackish-brown upperparts, streaked golden-buff; less strongly striped than juvenile Red-necked. Face/chest washed pinkish-buff. 1st-winter (from Sep) has grey-brown cap/mantle and patchy upperparts, with wing coverts and tertials still blackish and buff, contrasting with grey adult winter feathers on rest of upperparts. Adult winter has more uniform upperparts than Red-necked, with squarer, less curving blackish eyepatch. Winter Sanderling (p144) has no eyepatch, longer body and different behaviour. Bill blackish, often with yellowish base. Legs grey, toes with yellowish lobes.

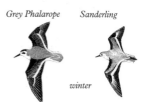

Grey Phalarope   *Sanderling*

winter

◁ In flight, very similar to Red-necked, but longer-winged. Also like winter Sanderling (see left and p144), but with longer wings and tail. White wingbar on dark wings; back grey.

KEY FACTS

Length: 20-22cm.
Wingspan: 37-40cm.
Weight: 50-75g. **Habitat:** on passage normally well out to sea, though autumn migrants may be driven inshore by westerly gales; rare inland.
Movements: on passage between breeding grounds in Iceland and Arctic and wintering areas in Atlantic Ocean off W Africa, late Sep-Nov; rare at other times.
Population: up to 500 birds recorded each year. **Diet:** chiefly invertebrates. **Voice:** shrill 'prip' or 'whit', higher-pitched than calls of Red-necked Phalarope. **Maturity:** 1 year. **Confusion species:** Red-necked (opposite) smaller, with thinner, slightly longer bill. Easy to distinguish in summer plumage, but very similar to Red-necked in winter and immature plumages (see opposite).

| J | F | M | A | M | J | J | A | S | O | N | D |

Phalaropus lobatus RED-NECKED PHALAROPE

207

Smaller, daintier, more delicately built than Grey Phalarope: thinner neck, very small head; fine needle-like bill, which is entirely black and never shows any yellow.

summer   male

female

△ In summer, females slate-grey above, with golden-buff lines forming Vs on back; white throat; and bright orange-red neck patches contrasting with a grey chest band. Rest of underparts white. Males much duller, with brownish upperparts, duller buff streaks on back, duller whitish throat and paler, less extensive orange on neck. Legs of both sexes slate-grey.

Red-necked adult winter

Grey adult winter

Red-necked adult winter

Red-necked juvenile

△ In winter plumage, rarely seen here, adult has pale blue-grey upperparts streaked white, white face with narrow pale grey crown and centre of hindneck. Juveniles much darker, with larger, blackish crown and blackish-brown upperparts, with striking golden-buff lines on back; pinkish-buff wash on throat, sides of breast and flanks. 1st-winter birds similar to adult winter, with blackish-brown mottled upper mantle contrasting with grey adult feathers of upperparts; cap usually larger and browner. In all these plumages, blackish eyepatch typically narrower than Grey's, and curves down at rear.

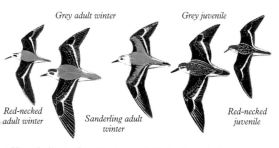

Grey adult winter

Grey juvenile

Red-necked adult winter

Sanderling adult winter

Red-necked juvenile

△ Very similar to Grey Phalarope in flight, but wingbars more prominent, plumage pattern more contrasting, flight action lighter and more buoyant. Over short distances, flight often erratic, bird suddenly ascending from water, fluttering rather weakly over surface and soon landing again suddenly.

KEY FACTS

Length: 18-19cm.
Wingspan: 31-34cm.
Weight: 25-50g. **Habitat:** in British Isles, breeds mainly by flooded peat cuttings and other shallow pools in Shetland, and usually hayfields or rough pasture near coastal pools in Hebrides and W Ireland; in N Europe, Siberia and N America breeds chiefly in marshy areas of sub-Arctic and Arctic tundra. Passage migrants mostly far out to sea; few visit coastal pools; very few driven inland by storms. **Movements:** almost all European breeders migrate SE in autumn via Caspian and Black Seas to winter in Persian Gulf, so rarely seen on W British coasts, unlike Grey Phalarope; most turn up along E coasts in spring (Apr-May) and early autumn (peak numbers Aug, much earlier than Grey Phalarope). British breeders arrive very late, few before Jun; most return S from late Jul onwards. **Population:** up to *c*30 pairs breed; fewer than 40 passage migrants recorded most years. **Diet:** small insects, molluscs, crustaceans. **Voice:** abrupt chirping 'twick', lower-pitched than call of Grey Phalarope; also more excitable, querulous 'kerrek kerrek'; feeding birds may twitter babble of twittering and chirping sounds. **Nest:** neat cup-shaped scrape, lined with leaves and stems, often in top of grass tussock, near water. **Eggs:** 4 (occasionally 3), buff, blotched brown. **Incubation:** 17-21 days, by male only. **Fledging:** 16-20 days. **Broods:** females 2; males 1. **Maturity:** 1 year. **Confusion species:** Grey Phalarope (opposite) bulkier, less delicate, with thicker, slightly shorter bill and plainer back. Winter Sanderling (p144) lacks dark eyestripe; also has much thicker bill and does not swim.

| J | F | M | A | M | J | J | A | S | O | N | D |

SKUAS
Order Charadriiformes, Family Stercorariidae

Medium to large seabirds with powerful hook-tipped bills. Toes webbed and strongly clawed. Long, narrow, angled wings; Great Skua's broader. Tail wedge-shaped, with central tail feathers usually elongated in adults, especially in the 3 smaller species, which also have variable plumage, occurring in dark and light forms (phases), plus intermediates. All show flash of white on both upper and underwings. Powerful and capable of fast flight, with piratical habits, chasing other seabirds until they disgorge their prey. Also, especially on breeding grounds, prey on small mammals and birds and their eggs. Breed on Arctic tundra and on moorland, mainly near sea; winter offshore, sometimes far out to sea. Nest on ground; parents boldly attack and even strike humans and animals approaching too closely. Sexes look alike; females slightly larger.

● Note: smaller species especially confusable, as great individual variation; look for structure and length/shape of adults' central tail feathers, if present.

POMARINE SKUA *Stercorarius pomarinus*

pale form autumn

female pale form summer

dark form summer

KEY FACTS

Length: 46-51cm (including tail streamers up to 10.5cm in breeding adult). **Wingspan:** 113-125cm. **Weight:** 550-900g. **Habitat:** on passage, usually well offshore or out to sea; few (especially juveniles) on moors, inland waters. Breeds Arctic tundra. **Movements:** passage migrant from Russian Arctic (chiefly late Apr-May and Aug-Nov); most seen off N Sea coasts, but also regular spring passage up English Channel and off NW Ireland and Outer Hebrides; winters in tropical oceans. **Population:** uncommon but regular passage migrant. **Diet:** chiefly fish at sea on passage and in winter, mainly pirated from other seabirds; kills birds and scavenges. Mainly lemmings on breeding grounds. **Voice:** usually silent at sea. **Maturity:** unknown. **Confusion species:** similar Arctic Skua (p172) slighter, more agile, wings more slender; Long-tailed (p173) even slighter, with longer, slimmer wings and more buoyant, tern-like flight. Great Skua (opposite) larger, bulkier; wings relatively shorter, broader, less pointed, with more prominent white flashes; shorter tail.

| J | F | M | A | M | J | J | A | S | O | N | D |

△ Larger, stouter than Arctic Skua; powerful, deep-bellied, with bigger head and bill. Summer adults have twisted, blunt-ended central tail feathers, like a blob or two spoons or trailing feet; make tail look thick-ended in side view. Flight heavier, more powerful than Arctic's, though can be very agile; wings broad-based, with long 'arms' tapering abruptly to pointed tips. Pale form much commoner. Adults (especially females) usually show a dusky breast band, and dark barred flanks, more prominent than on Arctic. Dark areas darker than on Arctic/Long-tailed. Cheeks and hindneck yellower than in Arctic. Scarce dark forms range from almost black, to dark brown with buff-grey fringes to feathers and buff-grey head. Winter birds have barred upper tail coverts; tail 'spoons' shorter or absent.

Pomarine juveniles

Arctic Skua juvenile

pale above

dark below

below

△ Juvenile usually darker than juvenile Arctic/Long-tailed, with greyer, more uniform, barred (not streaked) head and more heavily and evenly barred underparts; best distinction is double pale patch on underwing in flight. Juvenile Great Skua larger, heavier, with all-black bill, large white wing flashes.

Stercorarius skua GREAT SKUA

Larger and much bulkier than other skuas, with relatively shorter, broader, less pointed wings and shorter, rounder tail with only slightly elongated central feathers. Always all-dark, with bold white wing flashes, visible at long range. Thick black bill on smallish head. About same size as Herring Gull, but stockier and more compact, and has shorter tail.

◁ Dark brown upperparts with indistinct rufous streaks, bold yellowish streaks on sides/back of neck. Greyish-brown underparts, mottled rufous, with rufous and buff streaks on darker throat and on flanks; in winter (after moult Jul-Feb) loses yellowish streaks on neck.

▽ Flight quite slow and often laboured, rather like large gull or even Buzzard (pp110-11); accelerates to powerful, surprisingly fast, dashing action when chasing seabirds. Often flies low over sea, but may soar over land at breeding sites. Juvenile and 1st-year birds darker, more uniform than adults, with blacker head, no yellowish streaks on upperparts, more rufous underparts (may look orange-buff in sunlight), pale marks near tips of mantle/wing covert feathers; smaller wing flashes.

juvenile

adult

▽ Pirates fish and other prey from seabirds up to size of Gannet, buffeting them with wings and even seizing a wing or tail in bill. Sometimes hovers to pick up food from surface; settles on water more than other skuas. Eats more carrion and offal than other skuas, often following fishing boats.

Herring Gull

Great Skua

KEY FACTS

Length: 53-64cm.
Wingspan: 125-140cm.
Weight: 1.2-2kg. **Habitat:** breeds on moors near sea; at other times usually out to sea, though may visit coastal waters; rare inland.
Movements: summer visitor (end Mar-Sep). Many British breeders, along with those breeding Iceland and Faeroes, winter mid-Atlantic and coasts of S America and W Africa; some remain in N Atlantic, usually far out to sea; passage migrants Mar-Apr, Aug-Oct; rare here in winter.
Population: c8000 pairs breed Scotland. **Diet:** chiefly fish pirated from other seabirds, also birds, their eggs and young, mammals, fish, offal, carrion. **Voice:** silent at sea; on breeding grounds deep, barking 'uk-uk-uk', short, deep 'tuk tuk' of alarm and harsh, nasal 'skeerrr'.
Nest: shallow scrape on ground, in loose colonies.
Eggs: 2, olive, blotched or spotted dark brown.
Incubation: 29 days, chiefly by female. **Fledging:** 42-49 days. **Broods:** 1. **Maturity:** 7-8 years. **Confusion species:** larger, heavier than other skuas, with stouter black bill, larger white wing flashes and shorter tail without long central feathers; superficially similar to juvenile Herring and other large gulls (pp181-3), but much darker and sturdier, with deeper chest, white wing flashes and different habits.

J F M A M J J A S O N D

ARCTIC SKUA *Stercorarius parasiticus*

Commonest skua here; rakish, almost falcon-like, compared with gulls; smaller/slighter, with slenderer bill, than Pomarine, larger/heavier than Long-tailed. Adults have elongated central tail feathers: straight and pointed (not twisted and blunt, as in Pomarine, and not as long or fine as in Long-tailed).

adult pale summer

adult intermediate summer

adult dark summer

juvenile

△ Occurs in pale and dark forms, and intermediates. In summer plumage, pale form (least common here) has sometimes patchy sooty-brown cap, very pale yellowish cheeks and hindneck, dark brown upperparts and white underparts, except for grey-brown breast sides, flanks and undertail. Intermediate forms have a variable, usually rather indistinct, breast band. Dark form looks uniform sooty-brown, but at close range reveals blacker crown and yellowish streaks on cheeks and neck. Juveniles and 1st-winter birds very variable: head blackish or streaked brown/buff; upperparts all-dark or with variable pale barring; underparts all-dark, mottled or barred.

dark summer

intermediate summer

pale summer

△ Both pale and dark forms have white flashes near wingtips, especially prominent in immatures. In calm weather, flight steady and relaxed, wingbeats interspersed with glides; when chasing seabirds, it accelerates, with powerful, deep wingbeats, into a dashing chase, with sudden dives, swerves, stalls and somersaults. In strong winds, tilts and glides like shearwater.

juvenile

◁ Juveniles/1st winter birds usually less strongly barred on rump than immature Pomarine and Long-tailed, with pointed (not blunt) central tail feathers, shorter than adults'.

▷ Arctic Skuas are bold in defence of their eggs and young, dive-bombing intruders, and occasionally even drawing blood from unprotected human scalps.

KEY FACTS

Length: 41-46cm (including tail streamers up to 10.5cm in breeding adult). **Wingspan:** 97-115cm. **Weight:** 380-600g. **Habitat:** breeds on coastal moorland in N/W Scotland and on tundra in N Europe; on migration commoner along coasts than other skuas; winters at sea. **Movements:** widespread coastal migrant, chiefly Apr-May and Aug-Oct. **Population:** possibly fewer than 2000 pairs breed in Scotland since dramatic decline in sand-eel numbers. **Diet:** Scottish breeders feed mainly by robbing terns, auks and Kittiwakes of sand-eels and other fish; also eat small mammals, birds, insects and berries. On passage/winter, mainly fish, mostly pirated; also carrion and offal. **Voice:** silent at sea, but noisy at breeding grounds; various mewing and yelping calls, drawn-out, nasal 'eee-air', repeated rising 'ka-wow', short repeated 'kook' and dry 'tick-a-tick' when attacking intruder. **Nest:** shallow scrape on ground; in small colonies. **Eggs:** 2, brown to greenish with darker blotches. **Incubation:** 25-28 days, by both sexes. **Fledging:** 25-30 days. **Broods:** 1. **Maturity:** 2-7 years. **Confusion species:** Pomarine (p170) very similar, but heavier, thicker-billed and deeper-chested. Long-tailed Skua (opposite) daintier, with more buoyant, tern-like flight.

| J | F | M | A | M | J | J | A | S | O | N | D |

Although a few may be almost size of small Arctic Skua, generally by far the smallest-bodied and most slender skua. Almost tern-like in build, with smaller head, shorter bill, shorter neck, relatively longer, more pointed wings, narrower especially at base, and more wedge-shaped tail in all plumages.

summer

KEY FACTS

Length: 48-53cm (including tail streamers up to 22cm in breeding adult). **Wingspan:** 105-117cm. **Weight:** 250-450g. **Habitat:** on passage some in coastal waters, though migrates and winters further out to sea than other skuas; breeds on Arctic tundra.
Movements: passage migrant May-Nov, chiefly Aug-Sep, also May in far NW.
Population: by far our rarest skua; sometimes 300-400 birds per year, often fewer than 100. **Diet:** on passage/in winter, fish, usually caught direct rather than by piracy; also some offal and carrion; in breeding season chiefly small rodents, also other small mammals, birds, fish, insects and berries. **Voice:** silent at sea. **Maturity:** unknown.
Confusion species: pale/intermediate forms of Arctic Skua (opposite) larger, bulkier and less graceful, with much shorter, thicker central tail streamers in adults and shorter, less wedge-shaped tail in immatures.

J F M A M J J A S O N D

△ Adults in breeding plumage much more uniform than Arctic; dark form and intermediates almost unknown. Upperparts cold slate-grey, not dark brown, contrasting with black secondary and primary wing feathers; more contrasting, clearer-cut, darker cap than in pale/intermediate Arctic and Pomarine; cheeks and neck clearer yellow than in Arctic; underparts pure white apart from dusky lower belly and undertail. Central tail streamers very long, fine and flexible, whipping about in flight. Wing flashes much smaller, generally not visible at any distance. Underwings uniformly dark. Flight very graceful, with sudden changes in course and height. Often hovers. Regularly settles on water, when appears very buoyant, long wingtips combining with long tail to exaggerate angle at which tail is held.

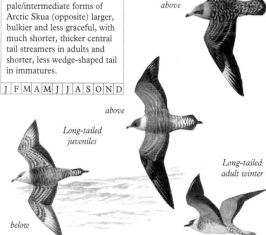

Arctic juvenile above

Long-tailed juveniles

above

below

Long-tailed adult winter

◁ Winter adult paler than Arctic, with strongly barred uppertail coverts and dark chest band. Juveniles more variable; very like juvenile Arctic. Plumage tone greyer, colder; paler, whitish barring on upperparts gives more contrasting, scalier pattern; often darker breast with white patch below; pale, greyish or even whitish patch on sides of head; heavier barring on underwing coverts and especially 'armpits'; usually blacker bill; white flash quite large on underwings (unlike adults') but much smaller on upperwings than in Arctic; tail projections blunt-tipped, often longer than in juvenile Arctic.

173

Long-winged seabirds, some also common inland. Plumage of adults mainly white, with grey or black backs and wings. Those with dark hoods in breeding plumage have mainly white heads in winter, with dusky patches; white-headed species usually have dusky streaks on heads in winter. Immatures take 1-4 years to lose mainly mottled brown plumage and acquire adult plumage (the smaller the species, the quicker it gains adult plumage). Bulkier, broader-winged and less graceful than terns, with less buoyant flight; their longer legs enable them to walk well. Nest on ground or cliff ledges, also on buildings; colonial. Roost on large areas of water. Sexes appear identical.

● Note: colour/pattern of wings; details of white spots ('mirrors') on black wingtips; bill size and colour; leg colour. Adult summer plumages generally distinctive, but winter adults and, especially, immatures can be very tricky to distinguish.

SABINE'S GULL *Larus sabini*

KEY FACTS

Length: 27-32cm.
Wingspan: 83-92cm.
Weight: 150-200g. **Habitat:** winters out to sea off coasts of Africa; occasionally forced inshore by autumn gales; breeds on Arctic tundra and islets. **Movements:** few storm-driven passage migrants seen here mainly Aug-Nov, rarely spring (Mar-Jun), very rarely winter; usually off W coasts, especially Cornwall. **Population:** several hundred may be seen in an exceptional year after severe Atlantic depression with northerly or westerly gales; otherwise 100 or so birds annually. **Diet:** invertebrates and small fish. **Voice:** harsh, grating, tern-like calls in breeding season, otherwise usually silent. **Maturity:** unknown. **Confusion species:** juvenile Kittiwake (opposite) has superficially similar wing pattern, but Sabine's lacks inner diagonals of inverted 'W' and has no dark collar.

summer / winter

△ Small and elegant, with small, rounded head and short, rather stubby bill. Looks rather pigeon-like at rest. Summer adult has entire head grey, edged with black collar; head white in winter apart from dark grey nape, and blackish crescents behind eyes. Bill black with yellow tip; legs dark grey.

juvenile / 1st-winter

△ Juvenile grey-brown and white; face and areas round eyes white; bill black; legs pinkish-grey. 1st-winter has head/back as adult winter, but wings still grey-brown.

Sabine's juvenile

Sabine's adult winter

Sabine's 1st-winter

Kittiwake juvenile

Sabine's adult winter

| J | F | M | A | M | J | J | A | S | O | N | D |

△ Flight light and buoyant, almost tern-like; bounding and banking in strong wind; feeds from surface of water. All plumages, including adult, show distinctive 3-triangle wing pattern, with grey inner wings (brownish in juvenile/1st-winter), white rear wings, and black outer wings – no dark diagonal markings as in immature Kittiwake. Sabine's Gull also lacks immature Kittiwake's dark collar. Grey back of 1st-winter Sabine's contrasts with brownish inner wings. Tail of adults all-white – slight fork usually difficult to distinguish except at close range. Tail of juvenile/1st-winter has black band near tip, further emphasizing fork.

Rissa tridactyla **KITTIWAKE**

summer

winter

KEY FACTS

Length: 38-40cm.
Wingspan: 95-110cm.
Weight: 300-500g. **Habitat:** breeds on sea-cliffs, locally on buildings, piers; otherwise most remain far out to sea, except on passage and during severe weather, when may rest on shore or even visit inland waters. **Movements:** British birds winter as far away as Newfoundland; passage migrants and storm-driven wanderers from Iceland/N Europe visit British waters, especially spring and autumn. **Population:** *c*550 000 pairs breed; sometimes as few as 1000 birds winter here close to shore. **Diet:** in breeding season, chiefly small fish; also fish offal; probably mainly invertebrates in winter. **Voice:** very distinctive far-carrying, rhythmic, nasal 'kitti-way-ake', in deafening chorus at large breeding colonies; also gruff 'kek-kek-kek' and quiet mewing calls. **Nest:** untidy mass of mud, grass, seaweed, with hollow in top, perched on tiny cliff ledge or projection of building or pier; colonial. **Eggs:** 2-3, bluish-grey to buff, blotched dark brown. **Incubation:** 25-32 days, by both sexes. **Fledging:** 33-54 days. **Broods:** 1. **Maturity:** 4-5 years. **Confusion species:** Common Gull (p180) has paler mantle/wing coverts, white 'mirrors' on black wingtips and longer, greenish or yellowish legs. Young Little Gull (p178 and below) rarer; has similar wing pattern but is smaller, with square tail, no neck band and lighter flight. See also much rarer Sabine's Gull (opposite).

△ Rather small and dapper, with long narrow wingtips crossing over tail at rest; perches upright, very short legs making it look 'tail-heavy'. Adult has dark grey mantle and inner part of wings, shading to white before all-black wingtips (without any white spots). Bill greenish-yellow, eyes blackish with orange-red rings; legs black. In winter plumage rear crown/hindneck grey, with blackish ear spot, often extending upwards over rear of crown, and small dusky crescent round eye.

juvenile

1st-winter

△ Juvenile paler grey than winter adult on hindneck; black half collar below; diagonal bar across closed wings. Bill and legs blackish. 1st-winter has reduced collar, and greyer hindneck. Bill blackish, often with some greenish-yellow. Legs blackish (some have wholly or partly orange or pinkish legs).

▽ Flight graceful, with rapid, springy beats of angled, tapered wings; in strong wind, rises and falls in long bounds; groups fly in single file low over sea. White head and neck protrude; short, very slightly forked, all-white tail. Distinctive pattern formed by grey wings shading to white, and clear-cut, triangular, black wingtips (lacking white 'mirrors'). Juveniles have striking dark inverted 'W' on wing, separating grey wing coverts at front of wing and white inner primaries and secondaries behind. Tail white with black tip which is wider at centre, emphasizing slight fork. By 1st summer, ear-marks and collar may be lost and 'W' wing pattern faded to pale brown. Feeds from surface in flight, plunges like a tern, or dives from water surface. Does not feed on shore or rubbish tips.

| J | F | M | A | M | J | J | A | S | O | N | D |

Kittiwake adult winter

Kittiwake juvenile

Kittiwake 1st-summer

Little Gull juvenile

MEDITERRANEAN GULL *Larus melanocephalus*

summer   winter

△ Larger, bulkier than Black-headed, with deeper chest, squarer head, heavier, drooping bill with blob-like tip, and longer red legs set well forward on body. High-strutting action, often with head hunched. Adults very pale, with gleaming white body and wingtips; latter lack black found in Black-headed and Common. Hood of summer adult (from March) black, not chocolate-brown as in Black-headed; extends further down nape (though appearance varies with posture). Prominent broken white eyering. Bill bright red; close view may reveal yellow tip with black band just behind it. In winter, head white with variable blackish patch through eye, often extended into narrow grey shawl over back of head. Bill and legs orange-red to blackish; bill often has yellowish tip.

Mediterranean juvenile

Common juvenile

Mediterranean 1st-winter

Mediterranean 1st-summer

△ Juvenile has almost pure white head, dark brown lower nape, brown mottling on sides of breast, and dark brown upperparts, scalloped with white, apart from plain pale grey panel along lower edge of closed wing. Thick black bill; legs reddish-black. Juvenile Common browner, less contrasting, with no grey wing panel, weaker bill and pale pinkish or greyish legs. 1st-winter Mediterranean has dark eyepatch on head like winter adult and also adult's pale grey mantle, but wings and tail faded version of juvenile's; base of bill pinkish, brownish or yellowish; legs blackish, greenish-grey or orange-red.

adult summer   adult winter   juvenile   1st-winter

△ In flight, heavy-bodied and bull-necked. Wingbeats stiffer than in Black-headed or Common, wings less angled; tail looks shorter and less spread. All-white upper and underwings, apart from minute black streak along leading edge of wingtips, make adult easy to identify. Juvenile and 1st-winter have more contrasting upperwings and 'cleaner' underwings than Common. 1st-winter has very pale grey back.

KEY FACTS

Length: 36-38cm.
Wingspan: 98-105cm.
Weight: 200-350g. **Habitat:** coastal lagoons, marshes and estuaries, rare inland.
Movements: regular though scarce passage migrant and winter visitor Jul-Apr; juveniles arrive later, generally Aug onwards; distinct spring passage of 1st-year birds, some remaining for summer.
Population: each year up to 15 or more pairs breed, and probably 100-150 birds winter, mostly S England.
Diet: fish, invertebrates, especially earthworms, snails and insects; also scavenges.
Voice: far-carrying, nasal 'eeu-err' calls in rising and falling rhythm, especially in spring and at breeding sites.
Nest: shallow depression on bare ground or among low vegetation, lined with grass or seaweed and a few feathers; colonial. **Eggs:** 3, pale buff or yellowish, spotted dark brown. **Incubation:** 23-25 days, by both sexes.
Fledging: 35-40 days.
Broods: 1. **Maturity:** 2-3 years. **Confusion species:** Black-headed Gull (opposite) slighter and smaller-/rounder-headed, with slimmer bill, outer wings with white leading edge and black trailing edge, and dark brown, not black, hood in breeding plumage; 1st-year Common Gull (p180) similar, but has darker back, broader tail band and less contrasting upperwing pattern.

| J | F | M | A | M | J | J | A | S | O | N | D |

Larus ridibundus **BLACK-HEADED GULL**

210

Smallest and palest common British gull; slim and neat, with small, rounded head and slender, pointed bill, tapered body, neat, rounded tail and longish legs. Walks gracefully and often briskly, holding head erect; has fast pattering run; perches easily; agile and quarrelsome. Follows plough on farmland. Swims buoyantly, with wings and tail usually held up at angle. Gregarious and often relatively tame.

summer   *winter*

KEY FACTS

Length: 34-37cm. **Wingspan:** 100-110cm. **Weight:** 225-350g. **Habitat:** breeds on inland and coastal marshes, moorland bogs, by flooded gravel pits, lakes, dunes; in winter very widespread, from coastal marshes, estuaries and shores to inland farmland, rubbish dumps, canals, towns and cities. **Movements:** most breeders disperse within British Isles; many passage migrants and winter visitors from Continent and Iceland Aug-Apr. **Population:** at least 200 000 pairs breed, *c*300 000 birds winter. **Diet:** chiefly invertebrates, especially worms; seeds, waste food. **Voice:** long, harsh, grating, angry 'kwarr' or 'kee-arr', brief 'kwuk' or 'kuk-kuk', melodious, nasal 'orr'; especially noisy at breeding colonies. **Nest:** scrape or cup of vegetation among tussocks or on bare ground; colonial. **Eggs:** 2-3, pale greenish or bluish to brownish, blotched dark brown. **Incubation:** 23-26 days, by both sexes. **Fledging:** 35 days. **Broods:** 1. **Maturity:** 2-3 years. **Confusion species:** Mediterranean Gull (opposite); Little Gull (p178) much smaller.

| J | F | M | A | M | J | J | A | S | O | N | D |

△ Adult in summer plumage (*c*Mar-Aug, some to Oct) has dark chocolate-brown hood covering front half of head (looks blackish at distance when fresh, but often fades to paler brown by midsummer), with white half-ring around rear of eye, and dark maroon-red bill and legs. Some show pale pink flush to underparts. Adult winter (*c*Aug-Mar) has white head with dark spot around eye and on ear coverts, with 1-2 dusky bands running up from these to crown. Bill tipped black. Wingtips appear mainly black when wings closed.

juvenile   *1st-winter*   *1st-summer*

△ Juvenile has much ginger-brown on head (where it forms partial hood), mantle and sides of breast; pale fringes to feathers give scaly pattern. Legs/bill dull pinkish or yellowish, bill with black tip. Tail has black band near tip. 1st-winter has head and body as adult, juvenile wings and tail. 1st-summer has brown hood, usually flecked with white, and faded version of juvenile wings/tail; bill and legs orange, bill with black tip.

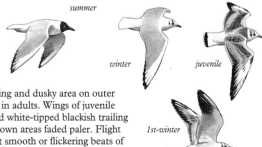

summer   *winter*   *juvenile*   *1st-winter*

▷ White leading edge to outer wing and dusky area on outer underwing; especially noticeable in adults. Wings of juvenile grey with brown diagonal bar and white-tipped blackish trailing edge; those of 1st-winter have brown areas faded paler. Flight light and buoyant, with quite fast smooth or flickering beats of pointed wings. Soars and glides; hawks for flying insects.

LITTLE GULL *Larus minutus*

summer

winter

△ The world's smallest gull, a dainty, neat little bird with a wingspan 20-30 per cent less than that of Black-headed Gull. Summer adults have jet-black hood completely covering the small rounded head. White underparts may be suffused pink. Short spiky bill, set low on head, brownish-red; legs, looking particularly short on the dumpy little body, scarlet. In winter plumage (*c*Aug-Apr), head white with dusky blackish remnants of hood on crown and small black ear spot, giving head squarer appearance; bill blackish, legs brownish-pink. Sides of upper chest washed grey.

juvenile   *1st-winter*   *1st-summer*

△ Juvenile has blackish crown, crescent round eye, spot on cheek, nape, breast sides and back (juvenile Kittiwake never has dark back). Bill black, legs brownish-pink. 1st-winters acquire grey nape and mantle; by 1st summer, head has usually dark brown (sometimes grey) hood, with white speckling around bill base; legs dull red.

juvenile

adult winter

adult summer   *1st-winter*

△ Flight buoyant and tern-like, sometimes direct but often with frequent dives and turns. Often picks insects from surface of water in flight, like Black Tern (p191). Very buoyant on water, floating like a cork. At all seasons, adults (less common here than immatures) have prominent blackish underwings, with broad white trailing edges, and uniformly pale grey upperwings with white trailing edges but without prominent black tips (some show small black marks). Juveniles have narrower wings than adults, with broad blackish W-shaped zigzag running from tips across inner wings to meet on rump; underwings white save for dusky tips; tail, which may look slightly forked, white with brownish-black band near tip, widest in middle. By 1st winter, back grey, wingtips streaked white, underwings darker and dark tail band reduced.

KEY FACTS

Length: 25-27cm.
Wingspan: 70-77cm.
Weight: 90-150g. **Habitat:** outside breeding season chiefly on coastal lagoons, coasts and estuaries, also on lakes and reservoirs inland; breeds on inland marshes.
Movements: may appear at any time, though passage migrants seen in spring (Mar-May) and, especially, autumn (Aug-Oct).
Population: 2 unsuccessful attempts at breeding in England, 1975-8; regular passage migrant and scarce winter visitor (*c*400-800 birds annually). **Diet:** insects, especially in summer, also other invertebrates; small fish. **Voice:** low 'kek-kek-kek', rapid, hoarse, tern-like 'ar-akar akar akar akar' with sound like squeaky toy. **Nest:** scrape lined with vegetation on ground; colonial. **Eggs:** 3, olive-brown to buff, blotched dark brown.
Incubation: 23-25 days, by both sexes. **Fledging:** 21-24 days. **Broods:** 1. **Maturity:** 2-3 years. **Confusion species:** immature Kittiwake (p175) and Sabine's Gull (p174) have similar zigzag wing pattern, but former has grey, not brownish, back (although Little has grey back by autumn), longer, more pointed wings, and black, not reddish, legs, while Sabine's has more clear-cut, grey/white/black wing pattern and distinctly forked tail.

J F M A M J J A S O N D

Larus delawarensis RING-BILLED GULL

Ring-billed adult winter   Common adult winter   Common 2nd-winter

KEY FACTS

Length: 43-47cm.
Wingspan: 120-155cm.
Weight: 500-750g. **Habitat:** on passage, chiefly on coasts, especially at harbours, sewage outlets and refuse dumps, but some inland e.g. on reservoirs or upland pastures with Common Gulls. **Movements:** a N American bird that wanders across Atlantic to our W and S coasts from autumn to spring. **Population:** recent increase in some parts of eastern N American breeding range, combined with improved knowledge of identification, has resulted in far more being seen at favoured sites since first discovered here in 1973; today *c*100 records each year, on average, mostly in SW England, S Wales and Ireland. **Diet:** worms, insects, molluscs, fish, refuse. **Voice:** usually silent outside breeding season; may utter soft, mellow 'kowk'. **Maturity:** 3 years. **Confusion species:** Common (p180); Herring (p181) larger, but immatures with 'ringed' bills often confusable; see also immature plumage differences (right).

| J | F | M | A | M | J | J | A | S | O | N | D |

△ Medium-sized gull; stands upright and has rapid, long-striding walk. Best identification feature at all ages/seasons is heavy-looking bill, whose parallel edges make it look as if it were open. Pale eyes give it fierce expression. Head generally less rounded than Common's. On water, sleeker and flatter-backed than Common. May be very tame. Adult winter has pale grey upperparts; white head spotted and streaked blackish. Bill yellower than Common's, with bold, clear-cut black band behind paler tip. Legs bright yellow (summer) or yellowish (winter). White crescent-shaped patch above tertials on closed wing (between grey and black) is much less obvious than on Common, which is neater, 'gentler'-looking, due to smaller, pointed bill and larger dark eyes, and has darker grey mantle.

Ring-billed 1st-winter   Common 1st-winter   Herring 2nd-winter

△ 1st-winter has heavy dark spotting down neck/breast as well as on head, and more spots on undertail than 1st-winter Common. Back/'shoulders' pale grey; pale greater wing coverts and narrow pale fringes to tertials. 1st-winter Common usually more lightly spotted on head/nape/ breast, with much darker back/'shoulders', darker greater coverts, and wider pale fringes to tertials. 2nd-winter Herring larger, stockier, with angular head, bigger bill, 'meaner' look; barred greater coverts and tertials; primaries do not project so far beyond tail.

Common adult winter

Ring-billed 1st-summer

Common 1st-summer

Ring-billed adult winter

Ring-billed 1st-winter

Common 1st-winter   Herring 2nd-winter

▷ In flight, Ring-billed has longer, broader wings than Common; wingtips more pointed. Adult winter paler grey above, with smaller white 'mirrors' on black wingtips. 1st-winter has much paler mantle, more contrasting dark/light wing pattern and less well-defined tail-band than 1st-winter Common, whose darker mantle forms distinct 'saddle', even more pronounced in 1st-summer birds. 2nd-winter Herring has quite uniform grey inner primaries, forming pale grey panel.

179

COMMON GULL *Larus canus*

summary summer · winter

△ Similar to Herring Gull, but much smaller, with rounded head and dark eye giving much gentler expression; much slenderer bill, yellowish or greenish without red spot; legs greenish-yellow, not pink. Wings project further beyond tail at rest. Walks more daintily. Adult summer has blue-grey upperparts, with large white patch between back and black wingtips; bill yellow-green, red rings around brown eyes; legs usually yellower than in winter. Adult winter (cAug-Mar) has dark streaks on head, and yellowish or greyish-green bill with darker base and faint darkish band near yellow tip.

juvenile · 1st-winter · 2nd-winter

△ Juvenile has heavily streaked and mottled head, breast and flanks, dull grey-brown upperparts, with pale greyish fringes forming scaly pattern, especially on mantle. Bill black with dull pinkish base; legs pinkish. 1st-winter acquires blue-grey mantle and loses much of streaking on head, breast and flanks; 2nd-winter more as adult, except head/flanks more streaked. As birds age, black of bill reduced to ill-defined, narrow band near tip; legs become yellowish or greenish.

▽ In flight, adults show much larger white 'mirrors' on black tips than Herring, and more black on tips of underwings; wings slimmer, flight lighter, more fluid than Herring, with less gliding and soaring. Easily distinguished at long range from slightly smaller Black-headed by absence of white leading edge to outer wing, less pointed wingtips and lack of hood or ear spot. Juvenile's wings show bands of brown, greyish-buff and blackish, darkest on outer wings and secondaries; tail white with clear blackish band near tip. 1st-winter has wing pattern faded to pale brown and whitish, and grey mantle.

KEY FACTS

Length: 38-44cm.
Wingspan: 106-125cm.
Weight: 300-500g. **Habitat:** breeds on moors and bogs, by lochs, and on shingle banks of rivers and lakes, often inland but some on coastal islands; winters chiefly on sheltered coasts, on lakes and reservoirs, farmland. **Movements:** many British breeders disperse S; passage migrants/winter visitors from Scandinavia/Baltic, Aug-Apr. **Population:** c71 000 pairs breed, over 700 000 birds winter. **Diet:** mainly worms, insects, molluscs, fish; also scavenges. **Voice:** shrill, squealing 'keee-ya'; short, soft 'gagaga'; nasal 'keow'. **Nest:** cup of vegetation or seaweed, usually on ground; colonial. **Eggs:** 2-3, greenish to dark olive, blotched dark brown. **Incubation:** 22-28 days, by both sexes. **Fledging:** 35-40 days. **Broods:** 1. **Maturity:** 2-4 years. **Confusion species:** Herring Gull (opposite). Immature like immature Ring-billed (p179). See also Kittiwake (p175), Key Facts, Confusion species.

| J | F | M | A | M | J | J | A | S | O | N | D |

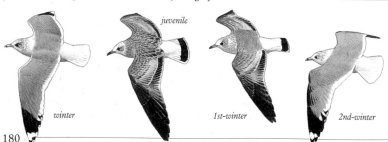

winter · juvenile · 1st-winter · 2nd-winter

Larus argentatus **HERRING GULL**

213

race argentatus *winter*

race argentatus
summer

*Yellow-legged
summer*

KEY FACTS

Length: 55-67cm.
Wingspan: 130-158cm.
Weight: 750-1250g.
Habitat: breeds mainly on cliffs, rocky islands, dunes or shingle beaches, moorland and on roofs of buildings; a few inland breeding colonies; otherwise widespread, with non-breeders especially found far inland, including towns.
Movements: most British breeders do not move far; passage migrants/winter visitors from N Europe chiefly Sep-Mar. **Population:** *c*200 000 pairs breed; perhaps as many as 500 000 birds winter. **Diet:** very wide, from fish and crabs to insects, from fish offal and garbage to birds, their eggs and young, and small mammals. **Voice:** loud wailing and squealing calls, short barks and deep 'kyow' or 'kyow-yow-yow'; nervous 'ga-ga-ga' of alarm. **Nest:** cup of grass or seaweed on cliff ledge, ground or building; colonial. **Eggs:** 2-3, pale green, blotched brown.
Incubation: 28-30 days, by both sexes. **Fledging:** 35-40 days. **Broods:** 1. **Maturity:** 3-5 years. **Confusion species:** Common Gull (opposite) smaller, with darker upperparts than race *argenteus*; immature Ring-billed (p179) similar but smaller. Immature Lesser Black-backed (p182) similar but darker, with darker bill. N race of Herring confusable with Glaucous and Iceland (pp184-5).

J F M A M J J A S O N D

△ Our commonest large gull. Heavily built, with large rounded or flattish head, powerful bill, thick neck. Usually slightly bigger, stouter and less elongated at rear than Lesser Black-backed. British race *argenteus* has pale grey upperparts; wingtips black with white 'mirrors'. Bill yellow with orange-red spot near whitish tip; legs dull pinkish; eyes pale yellow with orange or yellow rings. In winter plumage (*c*Sep-Jan/Mar) head streaked brownish. Scandinavian race *argentatus*, common winter visitor to N and E Britain, larger, with darker upperparts and less black in wingtips. Very close relative, **Yellow-legged Gull** *(L. cachinnans)*, formerly regarded as a race of Herring Gull, in small numbers in S Britain mainly Jul-Sep, also has darker grey upperparts, less white in black wingtips, plain white head in winter, greyish-yellow eyes with red eyerings, and yellow legs.

race argentatus

adult winter

1st-winter

2nd-winter

juvenile

juvenile

1st-winter

2nd-winter

△ Juvenile mottled grey-brown, with dark primaries, bar along secondaries and tail band, and blackish bill, paler at base. Inner primaries (behind bend of wing) paler than outer, forming pale 'window' above and below. Tail base pale grey-brown, contrasting less with blackish-brown band near tip than juvenile Lesser Black-backed's. 1st-winter has whiter head and more irregular pattern of dark bars on upperparts. 2nd-winter has strongly streaked white head; mainly white, variably dark-streaked underparts and rump; some pure grey on mantle and 'shoulders'; inner primaries/inner wing coverts greyish (with some brown on coverts); bill usually pinkish or yellowish, with dark area towards tip and sometimes with reddish spot.

LESSER BLACK-BACKED GULL *Larus fuscus*

214

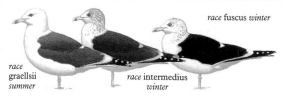

race fuscus winter

race graellsii summer

race intermedius winter

△ Almost as large as Herring Gull, but slimmer, more elegant, with longer, narrower wings reaching well beyond tail at rest, relatively longer legs and smaller, rounder head with less deep bill. Bill brighter yellow, eyering red, not yellow or orange. Legs bright yellow in summer, often creamy-yellow in winter (a few pinkish-grey). Adult of W European race *graellsii* has back and most of upperwings slate-grey (intermediate between Herring's and Great Black-backed's), contrasting with black wingtips; adult S Scandinavian race *intermedius* has back and most of upperwings almost as dark as Great Black-backed, contrasting slightly with black wingtips; adult N Scandinavian race *fuscus* has back/entire upperwings as black as Great Black-backed's, but looks longer-winged and more slender. In winter plumage (*c*Aug-Mar) head has dark streaks (few in *fuscus*).

juvenile   *1st-winter*   *2nd-summer*

△ Immatures very similar to immature Herring Gulls, but darker. Juveniles and 1st-winters have tertials fringed and tipped with white, not notched and barred like Herring's. Bill black (without Herring's pale base), eyes brown, legs pinkish-brown. 2nd-year birds have whiter heads and bodies and dark grey feathers on back and 'shoulders'; bill yellowish at base, eyes pale greyish, legs pale creamy-pink or pale yellowish.

adult winter   *juvenile*

2nd-winter

△ Flight slightly lighter, more graceful than Herring's. Adults have far less white in wingtips than Great Black-backed, usually only one small 'mirror' compared to latter's two much larger ones. When seen from below, complete dark trailing edge to otherwise white underwing – only outer primaries dark in adult Herring. Juvenile/1st-winter birds have darker, more uniform upperwings in flight, lacking pale inner primary 'window' of Herring and with 2nd dark band in front of dark secondary bar; also tail-band clearer, more contrasting. Grey on back forms distinct 'saddle', darker than on Herring, by 2nd year.

KEY FACTS

Length: 52-67cm.
Wingspan: 128-148cm.
Weight: 650-1000g.
Habitat: breeds on thickly vegetated areas above sea-cliffs (not often on ledges like Herring), shingle, dunes, also locally on buildings; unlike Herring, most breed inland, on moors and bogs; winters mainly inland, especially on arable farmland, rubbish tips and reservoirs, where it roosts.
Movements: chiefly summer visitor. Formerly almost all British breeders (race *graellsii*) migrated to winter as far away as Africa; now large numbers remain here. Passage migrants/winter visitors, of races *intermedius* and *fuscus* from Scandinavia, Jul-May.
Population: *c*89 000 pairs breed, *c*75 000 birds winter.
Diet: similar to Herring Gull.
Voice: similar calls to Herring Gull, but deeper, throatier.
Nest: as Herring Gull, but in thicker cover where available.
Eggs: 3, olive to dark brown, heavily blotched blackish.
Incubation: 24-27 days, by both sexes. **Fledging:** 30-40 days. **Broods:** 1. **Maturity:** 4 years. **Confusion species:** Herring Gull (p181); immatures very similar, but paler; adults have paler grey back and wings and usually pink legs. Great Black-backed Gull (opposite) much larger, with pale pinkish legs and larger, double white wingtip 'mirrors'. See also Yellow-legged Gull (p181).

| J | F | M | A | M | J | J | A | S | O | N | D |

Larus marinus GREAT BLACK-BACKED GULL

215

summer

3rd-winter

KEY FACTS

Length: 64-78cm.
Wingspan: 150-170cm.
Weight: 1.1-2.1kg. **Habitat:** breeds on sea-cliffs, rocky islands, very few inland by lochs and on moorland.
Movements: British breeders mainly resident; passage migrants and winter visitors from Norway Aug-Apr.
Population: *c*23 500 pairs breed, over 50 000 birds winter here. **Diet:** offal, carrion, refuse, fish, birds, their young and eggs, small mammals. **Voice:** deepest of all gulls, including characteristic short, hoarse, barking 'yowk', sometimes repeated, and guttural 'uk-uk-uk'. **Nest:** sometimes bulky mound of grasses/seaweed in hollow on clifftop or on ledge; small colonies. **Eggs:** 3, pale buff to olive, blotched dark brown. **Incubation:** 27-28 days, by both sexes.
Fledging: 49-56 days.
Broods: 1. **Maturity:** 4-5 years. **Confusion species:** Lesser Black-backed Gull (opposite). See right for differences from immature Herring/Lesser Black-backed.

| J | F | M | A | M | J | J | A | S | O | N | D |

△ Compared with other gulls, huge, with very heavy, strongly hooked bill on large, rounded head; broad, deep-chested body; legs relatively shorter than Lesser Black-backed's. Dominates other gulls. More often alone, though large groups form in winter at some sites, especially in N Scotland. Adult has uniformly almost black back and wings, contrasting with white of rest of plumage (unlike most other large gulls, has few or no streaks on head in winter). Large white tips to primaries always visible at rest. Wingtips relatively short, giving rather 'stumpy' look to rear end. Bill pale yellow with orange-red spot near tip; eyes pale yellow with red rings; legs pinkish or creamy-pink.

juvenile   *1st-winter*

2nd-winter

△ Juveniles and 1st-years best distinguished from young Herring and Lesser Black-backed by much larger black bill, standing out sharply against mainly whitish head and underparts. Upperparts more clearly barred or chequered grey-brown and whitish, generally paler than Herring and, especially, Lesser Black-backed. Bill often has pale base and tip by 1st summer, with black restricted to tip by 2nd year.

adult summer   *juvenile*   *1st-winter*

2nd-winter

▷ Flight heavier than other gulls', more ponderous, with slower wingbeats; despite great wingspan, broader wings look shorter proportional to body than Lesser Black-backed's. Large white 'mirrors' on outer 2 primaries of adults stand out on black wingtips as large white patch. Immature birds have coarser dark markings on back and wings than immature Herring/Lesser Black-backed, and vaguer tail-band, usually consisting of several diffuse narrow lines. 2nd- and 3rd-year birds have black on back and large black blotches on wings.

GLAUCOUS GULL *Larus hyperboreus*

adult winter   *1st-winter*   *2nd-winter*

△ Only gull, apart from smaller Iceland, that lacks black on wings and tail at all ages. Varies in size, but most are slightly bigger than Herring Gull; structure more like Great Black-backed, with large head, long, powerful, deeply hooked bill over half length of head, heavy body with deep chest and long, sturdy legs. Sloping or angular forehead, combined with massive bill and small glittering eyes, gives fierce expression. Adult has pale grey mantle and all-white wingtips; head and upper breast usually strongly streaked brown in winter; eyes pale yellow with yellowish or orange rings; bill yellow with red or pale orange spot near tip; legs pink. 1st-winter birds look pale coffee-coloured or sandy-brown at distance; closer view reveals delicate grey-buff mottling and dirty whitish wingtips; eyes dark brown; basal two-thirds of bill pale pink, with clear-cut black tip; legs pale pinkish. 2nd-winters less closely barred, with patchy buff, grey-brown and white feathers on back and 'shoulders'; bill usually has less black at tip and may be yellowish; eyes often pale.

KEY FACTS

Length: 62-70cm.
Wingspan: 142-162cm.
Weight: 1-2kg. **Habitat:** winters among flocks of other gulls, mainly on coasts, feeding at harbours and fish docks; also inland, at rubbish tips and reservoirs on edges of towns; breeds on Arctic sea-cliffs and islands.
Movements: winter visitor from Arctic, Oct-Apr; a few seen other months.
Population: c200-700 birds each year; most in Shetland and Orkney. **Diet:** chiefly carrion, offal, refuse, fish, crabs, molluscs, worms.
Voice: generally silent in winter, but may give wailing and yapping calls, like Herring Gull's but hoarser. **Maturity:** probably 4 years. **Confusion species:** Iceland Gull (opposite) rarer and smaller, with smaller head, 'gentler' expression, much shorter bill, longer wingtips.

J	F	M	A	M	J	J	A	S	O	N	D

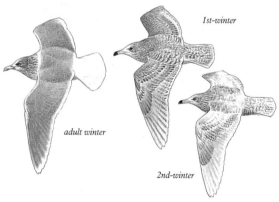

1st-winter

adult winter

2nd-winter

△ Flight heavy, almost as ponderous as Great Black-backed's; wings have broad 'arm' and relatively short 'hand'. Whiter primaries show up at tips of wings on immature birds, which, like immature Iceland Gulls, lack the distinct dark bars on secondaries of upperwings and dark tail-band of other immature gulls.

▷ N race *argentatus* of Herring Gull, common winter visitor from Scandinavia to N and E Britain, may be as large as some Glaucous and may show little or no black in wingtips, especially of underwings, and especially when seen in flight at long range. However, they have much darker back and upperwings.

winter

Herring Gull, race argentatus

Larus glaucoides ICELAND GULL

adult winter

1st-winter

2nd-winter

KEY FACTS

Length: 52-60cm.
Wingspan: 130-145cm.
Weight: 750-1000g.
Habitat: in winter similar to Glaucous Gull's. Breeds rocky coasts NW Canada and Greenland (not Iceland, though common in winter there). **Movements:** scarce winter visitor from Greenland Nov-Apr; very few other months. **Population:** 100-300 birds in a good year, when hard weather drives them S from Iceland. **Diet:** chiefly fish, also worms, crabs, molluscs, offal, carrion, refuse. **Voice:** usually silent in winter; calls similar to those of Herring Gull (p181) but much shriller. **Maturity:** 4 years. **Confusion species:** Glaucous Gull (opposite).

| J | F | M | A | M | J | J | A | S | O | N | D |

▷ May be confused with Glaucous (and, to a lesser extent, Herring), especially in flight. Flight slightly more buoyant and energetic than that of Glaucous or Herring. Looks quite heavy-bodied but wings proportionately longer, slimmer, with broad bases. Seems to be no consistent difference in plumage between Glaucous and Iceland at any age; however, on average, 1st-year Iceland slightly greyer-brown and less coffee-coloured than 1st-year Glaucous, with more neatly barred wings and upper and undertail coverts.

△ Much rarer than Glaucous, the same size as or smaller than most Herring Gulls, with deep chest and belly but tapering rear end; longer wingtips, extending beyond tail more than the length of the bill (though moulting Iceland Gulls in autumn may have shorter wingtips). Iceland also has rounder head, with much shorter, slighter bill which, with larger, darker eyes, gives it a far less fierce, often dove-like expression. Adult's plumage pattern very like that of Glaucous, with head and breast streaked in winter. Legs pinkish, slightly greyer than in Glaucous. Legs of immatures greyer than in Glaucous. 1st-years have mainly black bills, appearing all-dark at long range, with only small, inconspicuous dull pinkish or greyish area at base, merging with black extending back in wedge, unlike Glaucous with its 'dipped-in-ink' bill. By 2nd winter, black area reduced and bill resembles that of 2nd-year Glaucous.

Iceland adult winter

Iceland 1st-winter

Iceland 2nd-winter

Herring 1st-winter

TERNS
Order Charadriiformes, Family Sternidae

Smaller relatives of gulls, with slenderer bodies, narrower wings and forked tails. Bills slim, sharply pointed. Flight buoyant; do not glide or soar. Feet short and webbed. Swim and walk/run far less often than gulls. 'Sea terns' hover above waves and plunge in to catch small fish; have grey/white plumage with black caps (foreheads white outside breeding season and in immatures) and deeply forked tails, often with long outer feathers ('streamers'); nest on ground. 'Marsh terns' darker, with short, shallowly forked tails; nest among floating vegetation in freshwater habitats. Sexes similar.

● Note: colour of bill and legs; pattern of dark/light on wings.

LITTLE TERN *Sterna albifrons*

220

adult summer *adult autumn* *juvenile*

△ Tiny compared with other terns, and unlike them has white forehead in all plumages; bill uniquely yellow with tiny black tip in summer; legs usually yellow. Relatively compact body and very short legs give it squat appearance; large head and thick neck; bill relatively long, spike-tipped. Summer adult pale, with grey upperparts, white forehead contrasting sharply with neat black cap and black eyestripe, and white underparts. Legs bright orange-yellow; in summer may appear reddish-yellow. After moult from Aug, loses black stripe from bill to eye, rear crown becomes grey, merging into black of cap at nape; grey of upperparts extends onto centre of tail; bill may be partly black by autumn; legs dull yellowish or reddish-brown. Juvenile has dark horseshoe-shaped markings on sandy-buff upperparts, forming scaly pattern; background colour soon fades to produce more black and white effect; bill brown, legs dull yellowish-buff.

KEY FACTS

Length: 22-24cm.
Wingspan: 48-55cm.
Weight: 50-65g. **Habitat:** breeds on sand and shingle beaches; winters along African coasts. **Movements:** summer visitor mid Apr-late Sep; winters W Africa. **Population:** *c*2800 pairs breed. **Diet:** sand-eels, herrings, other small fish; invertebrates, especially crustaceans, insects. **Voice:** high, quick, quite liquid 'kit-kit'; rapid, chattering 'kirri-kirri-kirri ...'; high, rasping 'kree-ik'. **Nest:** scrape on sand or shingle; small, loose colonies. **Eggs:** 2-3, buff, spotted/blotched brown. **Incubation:** 19-22 days, by both sexes. **Fledging:** 15-17 days. **Broods:** 1. **Maturity:** 1-2 years.

adult summer *adult autumn* *juvenile*

△ Flight fast and direct, on long, slender wings; careers along with whirring wingbeats, producing less graceful, more flickering effect than other terns. Prominent black strip along leading edge of outer wing. Rather short tail only shallowly forked, without fine streamers. Excitable and noisy, frequently giving loud, raucous calls. Less gregarious than other terns.

▷ Unlike other terns, hovers for long periods with steeply angled body before diving, often suddenly dropping and then halting to hover again, before plummeting fast to hit surface with dramatic splash. Fond of diving into breaking waves at edge of steeply shelving shingle beach.

J F M A M J J A S O N D

summer

Sterna sandvicensis **SANDWICH TERN**

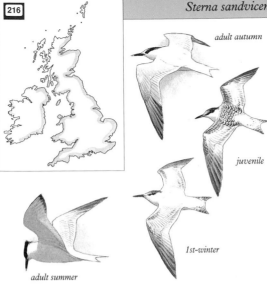

216

adult autumn

juvenile

1st-winter

adult summer

KEY FACTS

Length: 36-41cm.
Wingspan: 95-105cm.
Weight: 210-260g. **Habitat:**
breeds mainly among sand
dunes and on shingle beaches
and rocky islets; a few on
artificial islets in coastal
lagoons, and inland by large
loughs in Ireland; winters
along African coasts and
estuaries. **Movements:**
summer visitor late Mar-Sep,
wintering W Africa; passage
migrants Mar-May, Jul-mid
Oct. **Population:** *c*18 000
pairs breed. **Diet:** chiefly
small fish, especially sand-
eels and herrings. **Voice:**
distinctive loud, shrill, grating
'ki-er-ink'; also short 'kik' or
'kirr-kit'. **Nest:** scrape in
open or among vegetation;
in large, dense colonies, often
with Black-headed Gulls.
Eggs: 1-2, whitish to buff,
blotched, streaked and
spotted dark brown and grey.
Incubation: 21-29 days, by
both sexes. **Fledging:** 28-30
days. **Broods:** 1. **Maturity:**
3-4 years. **Confusion
species:** smaller, much rarer
Roseate Tern (p190) also has
long black bill and may also
have rosy tinge to underparts,
but has red, not black, legs,
very long tail streamers;
juveniles have very similar
plumage pattern, but Roseate
much smaller.

J	F	M	A	M	J	J	A	S	O	N	D

△ Flight stronger, faster, less buoyant than that of smaller terns,
with stiffer, quite shallow wingbeats; often at some height.
Usually holds bill level in flight when not hunting. Wings long,
narrow; usually show distinct bend at 'wrists'. Tips of upperwings form streaky darkish wedge. Juvenile shows prominent
chequered 'saddle' on back in flight and has much less strongly
forked tail (with dark 'corners') and shorter, less pointed
wings. 1st-winter resembles adult winter, patterned 'saddle'
becoming plain grey, and black 'shawl' over rear of head.

adult autumn

1st-winter

adult summer

△ Distinctly larger than other regular British terns, and paler
than all except Roseate; looks very white below compared with
Arctic and Common. Has long wings and short (though
deeply forked) tail with only short streamers, and looks large-
headed, with rough crest at nape. Crest may look smooth,
especially in flight, but is prominent, shaggy or spiky, when
erected. Long, thickish-based, black bill with yellow spiked
tip; black legs. Particularly noisy, with frequent harsh rasping
calls. With moult mid Jun-Sep adult gains winter plumage,
forehead gradually becoming completely white and forecrown
streaked with white; black 'shawl' from eye back over nape.
Juvenile has completely black cap at first, but this soon
becomes speckled with buff and then white; very small crest;
shorter bill than adult's, lacking yellow tip; wings and tail
mainly greyish, rest of upperparts distinctively chequered
blackish-brown, sandy-buff and white.

▽ Often flies quite high; hovers
only briefly before plunging
steeply, often vertically, onto
prey, striking water abruptly
with loud splash, sending up
distinct spray.

summer

COMMON TERN *Sterna hirundo*

adult summer

adult autumn

juvenile

△ Very similar to Arctic Tern. Common has longer, more angular head than Arctic, with flatter forehead; longer neck; longer bill, stouter along whole length; shorter tail (wings extend to tip of tail streamers at rest); longer legs. Contrast between paler grey inner primaries and darker grey outer primaries of wingtips. Adult in spring has bright orange-red bill with black or brownish tip, slightly paler grey underparts than Arctic, sometimes with pinkish tinge, and vivid red legs. After moult Jul-Aug onwards, adult acquires white forehead; bill may be mainly blackish, with red only at base. Juvenile also has white forehead (tinged gingery at first), but bill blackish with basal half pinkish or orange-yellow, unlike almost all-black bills of juvenile Arctic; mantle gingery; legs dull pinkish-red or yellow-orange (not red or dark brown).

adult summer

adults autumn

juvenile

△ Flight quick, direct, with body quite stable; more protruding head and neck and shorter (though still deeply forked) tail than Arctic, so there is more in front of wing and less behind. A slightly heavier-looking bird than Arctic, with broader-based wings; inner part of wing ('arm') quite long compared with outer part ('hand'). Small dusky wedge formed by darker primaries towards wingtip distinctive. From below, only inner primaries translucent, forming pale patch behind bend of wing; dark trailing edge to outer primaries smudgier, broader, more uniform in shape than on Arctic. Fast, powerful downstroke and slower, more noticeable upstroke. Juvenile has gingery tinge to upperparts, bold blackish leading edge to upperwing and grey band across hindwing; palest part of upperwing is at centre; pale grey rump.

▷ When feeding, fly *c*3-8m above water, stopping and hovering, usually once only, before moving on and repeating process. On spotting fish, generally swoop upwards and turn back slightly before diving more abruptly than Arctic into water with a splash.

summer

KEY FACTS

Length: 31-35cm.
Wingspan: 82-95cm.
Weight: 90-150g. **Habitat:** breeds mainly on shingle coasts, also on rocky islets, among dunes and on saltmarshes; also inland, on banks, islands and artificial platforms in flooded gravel pits and lakes, and on gravel bars in rivers in Scotland; winters mainly along African coasts.
Movements: summer visitor mid Apr-Oct, wintering mainly W and S Africa; passage migrants Apr-May, Jul-Oct.
Population: *c*16 000 pairs breed. **Diet:** mainly small fish, also crustaceans, insects and other invertebrates. **Voice:** long, grating 'kreee-yair' alarm call, with downward inflection; abrupt 'kik'; many calls at breeding colonies, including long, ringing 'krreeeer', rapid 'kirrikirrikirri' and 'kye kye kye', chattering 'kikikikik'; voice generally fuller and throatier than Arctic's. **Nest:** shallow scrape on ground; in colonies. **Eggs:** 2-4, cream to buff, blotched dark brown. **Incubation:** 22-26 days, by both sexes. **Fledging:** 21-26 days. **Broods:** 1. **Maturity:** 1-2 years. **Confusion species:** Arctic Tern (opposite) very similar, but has rounder head, shorter bill, neck and legs, longer tail, different flight and fishing style, and distinct calls. Roseate Tern (p190) much paler, with longer body, bill and tail.

J F M A M J J A S O N D

Sterna paradisaea ARCTIC TERN

adult summer *adult autumn* *juvenile*

KEY FACTS

Length: 32-35cm.
Wingspan: 80-95cm.
Weight: 80-110g. **Habitat:**
breeds on rocky and boulder-strewn beaches, also on moorland in N isles of Scotland; winters mainly at sea and on pack ice in S Hemisphere. **Movements:** summer visitor, end Apr-mid Oct, wintering from S Africa to Antarctic; passage migrants end Apr-Jun, Jul-Oct.
Population: *c*45 000 pairs breed. **Diet:** mainly small fish, especially sand-eels, crustaceans, insects. **Voice:** most calls similar to (though usually higher and harder than) those of Common, including grating 'kee-yah' (shorter, less slurred), 'kik', and 'kreer'; but piping 'pee-pee', with rising inflection, distinctive. **Nest:** scrape on ground; colonies mainly small, some very large, especially in Orkney and Shetland. **Eggs:** 2, cream to buff, spotted and blotched dark brown and black. **Incubation:** 21-22 days, by both sexes.
Fledging: 21-26 days.
Broods: 1. **Maturity:** 2 years.
Confusion species: Common Tern (opposite) very similar. See also Roseate Tern (p190).

J F M A M J J A S O N D

△ Rounder, shorter head than Common, with steeper forehead; shorter, deeper-based but sharp-tipped bill; longer tail, extending slightly beyond wings at rest (though not as far as Roseate's); shorter legs. Underparts greyer, contrasting more with white cheeks (forming white streak), though this depends on light. Bill blood-red or deep scarlet, without black tip; legs deep red. Moults primary wing feathers later than Common, not until after it has migrated; at all times of year wingtips pale, with no contrast between inner and outer primaries as in Common. Late autumn birds may show some white flecks on forehead and all-dark bill. Juvenile has clear white (never gingery) forehead, purer grey-and-white patterned upperparts (without gingery tinge), black bill with only a little pinkish-red at base, and red or dark brown legs.

adults summer *adult autumn* *juvenile*

△ Compared with Common, has shorter head and bill and shorter, thicker neck. These combine with longer, more angled wings and longer, whippy tail streamers to give different flight shape; less in front and more behind, with an 'all wings and tail' look, and short head merging straight into body. Shorter 'arms' and longer, more pointed wingtips. More bouncy, butterfly-like flight, body rising and falling with wind; faster, more abrupt, more emphatic upstroke, with a slower, more noticeable downstroke. Upperwings more uniform; paler wingtips, lacking dark wedge. From below, all flight feathers (not just central patch) appear translucent in good light. Dark trailing edge to outer primaries narrower, clearer cut and tapered. Juvenile's upperwings whitest at rear, without grey band of juvenile Common, rump pure white (not grey).

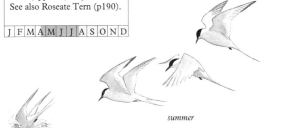

summer

◁ When fishing, flies at about same height as Common, but its feeding style is more hesitant. Typically hovers, drops down a few metres, hovers again, maybe slips to one side or pauses, hovers once more, then, when it has sighted prey, makes final quick plunge into water.

ROSEATE TERN *Sterna dougallii*

adult summer   *adult autumn*   *juvenile*

△ Very scarce and highly maritime. Although sharing Common's and Arctic's neat black caps and red legs, more like a small Sandwich Tern in some ways (except for very long tail), with a long, spiky, mainly black bill on a long, rounded head; neck longer than Common's or Arctic's and upperparts paler grey; strikingly white (not grey) underparts and a rosy tint to breast in spring; stands out as much paler when seen in mixed flock with Commons or Arctics. Smaller, more delicate-looking than Common. Has much longer tail streamers than Common or Arctic, extending far beyond wingtips at rest. Also has longer legs than both. Adult in spring has almost entirely black bill, with dark red only at very base; red increases through summer, but rarely occupies more than basal half of bill. Legs very bright orange-red. May acquire white forehead and all-black bill before migrating in autumn. Juvenile has heavier, brown markings on upperparts, dark forehead with little or no white, and black legs; looks like miniature juvenile Sandwich.

KEY FACTS

Length: 33-38cm.
Wingspan: 75-80cm.
Weight: 95-130g. **Habitat:** breeds on rocky islets and sandy beaches. **Movements:** summer visitor, late April-Sep; winters W African coasts.
Population: massive decline in recent decades; now fewer than 90 pairs in Britain, *c*400 pairs in Ireland. Main colony at Rockabill, Co Dublin.
Diet: mainly small fish, especially sand-eels, herrings, sprats. **Voice:** distinctive rich, musical 'zraaak' call; also loud, harsh 'kraak' of alarm.
Nest: scrape on sand or shingle, often concealed in hollow among vegetation; in colonies, always with other species of terns. **Eggs:** 1-2, cream to buff, speckled reddish-brown/grey.
Incubation: 21-26 days, by both sexes. **Fledging:** 22-30 days. **Broods:** 1. **Maturity:** 2-3 years. **Confusion species:** much paler than Common and Arctic Terns (pp188-9); more like Sandwich (p187).

| J | F | M | A | M | J | J | A | S | O | N | D |

juvenile   *Sandwich adult summer*   *adult summer*   *adult autumn*

△ Flight faster than Common's or Arctic's, more stable, more direct. Wings shorter, straighter, blunter-tipped, appearing more centrally placed; together with long bill, slightly more projecting head/neck and very long, spike-like tail streamers give different effect. Stiffer wingbeats, with upstrokes and downstrokes of equal speed and emphasis. Dark outer primaries by summer, forming blackish wedge contrasting with very pale rest of upperparts. Like Sandwich, lacks well-defined dark border to tips of underwings. Juvenile has mainly whitish wings; has dark bar along inner part of leading edge of upperwing but lacks prominent dark tips to underwing.

▷ When fishing, usually flies higher than Common or Arctic Tern, hovering briefly in strong wind, but, in calm weather, staying in one spot for a few seconds only, hovering rather awkwardly, with very fast, almost whirring wingbeats. On spotting a fish, simply turns and flies steeply down straight into water at greater speed than Common or Arctic, submerging slightly deeper and for longer.

summer

Chlidonias niger BLACK TERN

adult male summer

adult autumn

juvenile

KEY FACTS

Length: 22-24cm. **Wingspan:** 63-68cm. **Weight:** 50-75g. **Habitat:** on passage at lakes, reservoirs, flooded gravel pits; estuaries, saltmarshes, coasts; breeds on marshes, lakes etc; winters mainly on African coasts. **Movements:** passage migrant mid Apr-May, Jul-Oct; winters W Africa. Usually several hundred birds each year; occasional mass movements of hundreds or thousands. **Population:** bred SE Britain until mid 19th century, after which the odd pair has bred sporadically. **Diet:** on passage and in winter, mainly small fish, some insects and crustaceans; when breeding, mainly insects, other invertebrates; also small fish, amphibians. **Voice:** generally silent on passage; may utter short, squeaky 'kik' or 'kik-keek'. **Maturity:** probably at least 2 years. **Confusion species:** White-winged Black Tern (see below).

| J | F | M | A | M | J | J | A | S | O | N | D |

△ Small, delicately built, with slender bill, almost as long as neat rounded head, and short legs combining to give low, elongated stance. In all plumages has grey (never white) rump and uppertail. Summer male has black head and upper breast, blackish-grey body, grey wings/rump and uppertail; white undertail, whitish patch at bend of closed wing. Summer female greyer below, without pale wing patch. By Jul-Aug, usually has some pale feathers on head and mottled black and white underparts; plain grey upperparts. By autumn has black cap with white forehead, collar and underparts; distinctive small blackish patch on side of breast in front of wings. Bill black, legs reddish-brown. Juvenile like winter adult, but has brownish tinge to forehead and collar; darker, mottled brown and grey, above, with pale fringes to feathers. Base of bill and legs dark yellowish.

juveniles

adult summer

adult autumn

△ Size of Little Tern, but bulkier, with longer, broader wings tapering to a point, and short, hardly forked tail. Flight buoyant, erratic, with frequent side-sweeps and swoops; wingbeats loose and shallow. Adults have plain grey upperwings; in autumn and winter, dark bar along leading edge of inner wing; pale grey underwings in all plumages. Juvenile has brownish 'saddle' and whiter underwings. Unlike sea terns, rarely dive into water when feeding. Instead, fly low over water (or sometimes marsh or other land), rhythmically rising and falling, dipping down to surface to snap up small fish or insects in their bills; also hawk flying insects in mid-air like giant swallows.

> **White-winged Black Tern** *(Chlidonias leucopterus)* rare but annual spring/autumn passage migrant, usually in SE England, with Black Terns. Similar length to Black (20-23cm); in full breeding plumage, easily distinguished by striking white upperwing coverts and tail contrasting with jet-black of most of body, and black (not pale grey) underwings. Autumn plumage similar to Black's, but nearly always retains traces of white on upperwing coverts and black on underwing coverts; lacks Black's dark smudge on breast; tail less forked. Juvenile has strongly contrasting dark brown 'saddle' and paler wings. All plumages have white (not grey) rump and uppertail; bill slightly shorter than Black's, black, tinged crimson in spring adult, with yellow base in juvenile; legs red.

adult autumn

juvenile

White-winged Black Terns

AUKS
Order Charadriiformes, Family Alcidae

Small to medium seabirds, with black and white plumage, short narrow wings and legs set far back on bodies. Superficially resemble penguins, but can fly, travelling fast and direct on rapidly whirring wings. Superb divers, chasing fish and other prey deep underwater, propelled by wings; feet used for steering. Usually stand upright on land; Puffin (and sometimes other species), like most birds, stands and walks on feet alone, but others often shuffle along, using legs (held horizontally) as well as feet. Nest on cliff ledges, among rocks or in burrows; otherwise, only on sea unless storm-blown inland. Sexes look identical.

● Look for: length/shape/colour of bill; amount of white on face.

LITTLE AUK *Alle alle*

237

KEY FACTS

Length: 17-19cm.
Wingspan: 40-48cm. **Weight:** 140-170g. **Habitat:** marine outside breeding season, mainly in large groups, or 'flights', well out to sea; small numbers turn up offshore and occasionally even inland after severe gales, on freshwaters or even in fields, gardens etc; breed in huge colonies among boulder screes on Arctic islands. **Movements:** winter visitor, mid Sep-mid Mar; mainly Nov-Feb; most remain far out at sea well to N and W of British Isles, but small numbers reach North Sea.
Population: irregular except in N; largest numbers in Shetland area. Strong onshore winds bring chance of birds close to E coasts Britain. May be several thousand in exceptional years with particularly stormy weather.
Diet: plankton, small crustaceans and small fish.
Voice: usually silent away from breeding colonies.
Maturity: possibly 2 years.
Confusion species: despite small size, may be confused with other auks, especially juveniles, particularly juvenile Puffin (pp196-7). Most other auks have partly white, not all-dark, underwings; Puffin also has dark underwings, but has different face pattern, complete collar and lacks short white lines across 'shoulders'.

| J | F | M | A | M | J | J | A | S | O | N | D |

Tiny auk, only size of Starling, but much plumper. Big head, very short, thick neck, very short, stubby bill and hunched body give curious frog-like appearance. Neck extended and short tail cocked when alarmed. Buoyant on water and more agile on land than other auks.

Little Auks adults winter · *Puffin juvenile* · *Guillemot juvenile* · *Razorbill juvenile*

△ In winter, narrow white lobe extends from throat and curves forwards onto ear coverts, leaving dark patch below eye; 3-4 short horizontal white lines on back; broader angled or vertical white line (formed by white tips to secondary wing feathers) not always noticeable, and shared by Guillemot and Razorbill. Summer adults (rare here) have entire head and chest black.

Little Auks · *Puffin* · *winter* · *Guillemot* · *Razorbill*

△ More agile in flight than other auks, taking off from water easily and flying fast, with frequent changes of direction like small waders and backward-flicking wing action. Plumage detail on relatively long wings hard to see as wingbeats very fast. Small white lines on sides of back. Underwings dark (with whitish 'armpits' and silvery tips of flight feathers giving paler impression in strong light); Puffins have even darker underwings and are longer-bodied, with broader outer wings and more forward-flapping wing action, very much larger, triangular bills (though smaller in juveniles) and dusky face/rear flanks. Other auks have mainly pale underwings.

Cepphus grylle BLACK GUILLEMOT

233

summer

KEY FACTS

Length: 30-32cm.
Wingspan: 52-58cm.
Weight: 340-450g. **Habitat:**
breeds on rocky and boulder-
strewn coasts and feeds in
inshore waters; otherwise out
at sea, but not as far from
shore as other auks.
Movements: relatively
sedentary; some wander S in
winter, rarely more than
100km from breeding site.
Population: *c*20 000 pairs
breed. **Diet:** mainly fish, also
crustaceans, worms, molluscs,
other marine invertebrates.
Voice: various shrill whistling
calls, often rapidly repeated
into a trill. **Nest:** none; lays
eggs on bare rock deep under
boulders, in caves or in rock
crevice; occasionally beneath
driftwood or in ruined
buildings, holes in harbour
walls or other artificial
structures. Usually in small,
loose colonies. **Eggs:** 1-2,
white (often tinged cream,
buff or blue-green), blotched
and spotted black, rufous or
grey. **Incubation:** 21-24 days,
by both sexes. **Fledging:** 35
days. **Broods:** 1. **Maturity:**
2 years. **Confusion species:**
though distinctive in breeding
plumage, could be confused
with Velvet Scoter (p95), but
latter much bigger, with only
small white bar on closed
wing and white on rear (not
front) of wing in flight. In
winter plumage, at long
range, may be confused with
grebes in winter plumage
(pp47-51).

△ Smaller, rounder-headed and plumper-bodied than Guillemot
(p194), with brilliant red legs in adults, visible through water.
Unmistakable in summer: deep brownish-black with large
white wing patches. Vermilion mouth contrasts dramatically
with black bill when latter opened during courtship or threat
displays. As with Guillemot, bill slim and pointed, but shorter
and finer. Much less gregarious than other auks; usually seen
singly, in pairs or small groups. Walks more easily than
Guillemot or Razorbill and stands at angle as well as upright.

*adult
winter*   *juvenile*   *1st-summer*

△ Adult in non-breeding plumage (from late July) at first
mainly black above and mottled white below, then finely
barred blackish and white above (looks very pale, grey and
white, at distance), with white wing patches, black flight
feathers and tail, and all-white below apart from dusky streaks
on flanks. Juvenile darker above than winter adult, with rows
of dusky spots visible on white wing panels at close range. 1st-
summer resembles adult summer, but black areas browner,
white wing panels still mottled and underparts often flecked
white. Very buoyant on water, dives suddenly. Stays closer
inshore than other auks outside breeding season.

juvenile

adult summer   *adult winter*

△ In all plumages, white wing patches large and prominent in
flight, which is fast and very low over water, with flickering
effect produced by white panels on whirring wings.

J F M A M J J A S O N D

GUILLEMOT *Uria aalge*

KEY FACTS

Length: 38-45cm.
Wingspan: 64-73cm.
Weight: 850-1130g.
Habitat: breeds on sea-cliffs on mainland and islands, feeding in coastal waters; otherwise often well out to sea, though may be blown ashore or rarely inland.
Movements: at breeding colonies from Jan (mainly Mar) to early Aug; then disperse, most adults locally, but young as far as Norway or N Spain; few winter visitors from N Europe. **Population:** *c*600 000 pairs breed. **Diet:** mainly fish, especially sprats, sand-eels; crustaceans, molluscs, marine worms.
Voice: very noisy at colonies; trumpeting and moaning calls and harsh growls produce deafening chorus; most common call is long, angry-sounding growling 'arrr'; juveniles utter far-carrying, plaintive 'plee-o'. **Nest:** lays eggs directly on bare cliff ledge or occasionally among boulders. Dense colonies; many large, some smaller.
Eggs: 1, very variable in colour, from white to blue, green, reddish or ochre, and from completely unmarked to heavily blotched; individual variation helps adults to recognize their own eggs in crowded colonies.
Incubation: 28-34 days, by both sexes. **Fledging:** young leave for sea at 14-21 days before properly fledged; able to fly well at *c*7-10 weeks.
Broods: 1. **Maturity:** usually 5 years, a few at 4 years.
Confusion species: Razorbill (opposite). Winter Long-tailed Duck (pp92-3) may look similar, especially in flight.

| J | F | M | A | M | J | J | A | S | O | N | D |

Our commonest auk; slim-bodied, with triangular head tapering into long, slender, pointed bill, quite long, slender neck and short, squared-off tail. Looks long and low-bodied on water, neck hunched or upright; often rises partly out of water to flap wings, 'standing on tail'. Dives with flick of wings and tail. Gregarious all year.

summer

'bridled' form

△ At breeding colonies, narrow cliff ledges densely packed with noisy, jostling birds. Stand upright, resting or shuffling with legs held horizontally on ledge, but sometimes waddling along on feet alone; also rest horizontally on rocks. In breeding plumage (from late winter/early spring), adults in S Britain and Ireland (race *albionis*) have chocolate-brown upperparts; colour gradually becomes darker further N, with N race *aalge* almost black above, with deep chocolate head, in Shetlands. Narrow white bar across folded wing. Flanks streaked brown, more heavily in N race. 'Bridled' individuals, more common in N, have thin white 'spectacles'; typical birds have much less obvious furrow, same colour as rest of head, behind eye. At all seasons, bill brownish-black, unmarked.

adult winter   *adult winter 'bridled'*   *juvenile*

△ In winter plumage (only in autumn in S birds) has white chin throat, sides of neck and cheeks, latter divided by dark indented line behind eyes; some show complete dark collar at base of neck; bridled form still reveals white around eyes at close range; S race greyer-brown above. Juvenile like winter adult, but smaller, shorter-billed, browner above, with unstreaked flanks.

▷ Flight fast and direct. Shares Razorbill's white trailing edge to inner wing, but has slim, dagger-like bill, longer neck, narrower white sides to rump, streaked flanks and dark marked 'armpit'.

winter

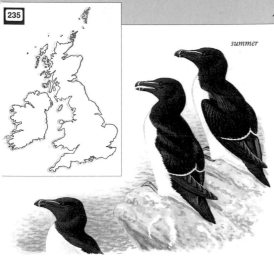

summer

KEY FACTS

Length: 37-39cm.
Wingspan: 63-67cm.
Weight: 590-730g.
Habitat: breeds on sea-cliffs and boulder- strewn shores on coasts and islands, feeding in adjacent waters; otherwise often well out to sea, though may be blown ashore or even inland by storms.
Movements: at breeding colonies from Jan (usually Mar or Apr) to mid Aug; then disperse, adults to waters off British Isles or as far as N France, young as far away as Norway, Atlantic off Iberia or NW Africa and Mediterranean. Ledges visited Oct/Nov at some E Scottish colonies. Winter visitors from N Europe and France.
Population: up to 90 000 pairs breed. **Diet:** mainly fish, especially sand-eels, also crustaceans, marine worms and molluscs. **Voice:** a variety of growls and grunts, some shrill, others deep, at breeding colonies; most common calls a prolonged growl and a quiet, tremulous snoring sound; juveniles give quieter whistles than those of Guillemot.
Nest: lays eggs directly on bare rock crevices in cliffs or beneath boulder scree lower down; sometimes on sheltered cliff ledges. A few large colonies, but mostly in small colonies or single pairs among Guillemots. **Eggs:** 1, brown or buff to white, variably marked dark brown.
Incubation: 33-36 days, by both sexes. **Fledging:** leaves ledges at *c*18 days before fully grown and properly fledged; able to fly well at *c*7-10 weeks.
Broods: 1. **Maturity:** 4-5 years. **Confusion species:** Guillemot (opposite) has rounder head, slimmer, more pointed bill and thinner neck; in winter black line from eye across cheeks; juveniles much more difficult to distinguish, though Razorbills tend to have darker throats than Guillemots.

Similar size and plumage pattern to Guillemot; best distinguished by much deeper, square-ended, blade-like bill, black with vertical broken white line across middle and horizontal white line joining bill and eye; also has heavier, squarer head, with flatter forehead and thicker neck. Adult summer has velvety-black upperparts, looking distinctly blacker than S race of Guillemot, except for chocolate-brown sheen to lower head and sides of neck, visible only in strong sunlight. White bar across folded wing, as with Guillemot. Generally less numerous than Guillemot.

adult winter   juvenile

Winter adult (Aug-Oct to *c*Mar) has brownish-black upperparts, and prominent white chin, throat and sides of neck. Dark area on head larger than Guillemot's, less sharply demarcated from white. Also lacks brown streaks on flanks found in Guillemot, and has shorter black collar. Usually looks less swollen-chested on water, with longer, pointed tail held cocked. Juvenile's bill much smaller than adult's (but larger than juvenile Guillemot's), without white markings; throat darker than juvenile Guillemot's.

winter

In flight, shows more white on sides of rump than Guillemot and rear end looks longer and broader, as body, longer tail and feet all spread to increase lift provided by very fast-whirring, relatively smaller, narrower wings. Body slightly tilted upwards. Like Guillemot, has white edge to rear wing. Unstreaked flanks; underwing coverts whiter than Guillemot's.

J F M A M J J A S O N D

PUFFIN *Fratercula arctica*

summer

△ Unmistakable in summer, with huge triangular colourful bill continuing profile of forehead, big rounded head with greyish-white face bordered by black of crown and upperparts, white underparts and short bright orange-red legs. Bill made up of red, blue and yellow plates, forming bands of colour, with a frilly swollen yellow edge to the gape. Red eyering, with blue-grey appendages above and below. In all plumages, lacks white bar across closed wing. Stands and walks upright, but rests and displays horizontally. Paired birds clash bills noisily. Extremely gregarious, waddling comically across grassy slopes outside breeding burrows, often chasing one another excitedly, and even tumbling downhill with bills interlocked. Often cock heads on one side, as when peering out of burrow at intruder. They use their powerful, sharply clawed, webbed feet for excavating burrows as well as for swimming and as rudders when braking as they come in to land.

▷ At the colony, breeding birds are constantly coming and going, bringing beakfuls of gleaming silver sand-eels and other small fish to their hungry young; able to carry up to 12 or more fish, held crosswise in the powerful, specially hinged mandibles; as each fish is caught, it is gripped between tongue and upper mandible, freeing lower mandible for further catches. Roof of mouth bears small hooks that further secure fish. In flight, more manoeuvrable than Guillemot and Razorbill. If chased by gulls or skuas seeking to steal their catch or kill them, they may dive into the sea to escape.

Fratercula arctica **PUFFIN**

adult winter

juvenile

KEY FACTS

Length: 26-29cm.
Wingspan: 47-63cm.
Weight: 310-500g. **Habitat:**
breeds on clifftops, mainly on
islands, and feeds in adjacent
waters; otherwise usually well
out to sea. **Movements:** at
breeding colonies Mar-mid
Aug; then disperse widely,
wintering as far away as
Newfoundland, Greenland,
Italy and Canary Islands.
Population: *c*470 000 pairs
breed. **Diet:** mainly fish,
especially sprats and sand-
eels, also crustaceans, marine
worms and small squid.
Voice: deep, nasal, groaning
'karr-orr-arr' in burrow,
similar growling grunts in
open; generally silent outside
breeding season. **Nest:** usually
in a 1-2m long burrow on
grassy slopes at or near tops of
cliffs, excavated either by
Puffin itself or Manx
Shearwater; may take over
rabbit burrow. Sometimes
lined with dry grass or
feathers; some nest in cliff
crevices. Colonies mostly
large. **Eggs:** 1, white, usually
unmarked, but sometimes
with extensive lilac-brown
markings. **Incubation:** 39-43
days, by both sexes.
Fledging: 38-56 days.
Broods: 1. **Maturity:** 4
years. **Confusion species:**
summer adults unmistakable,
but smaller bill outside
breeding season means it may
be confused with other auks
when seen far out to sea. Grey
face helps distinguish them
from other winter auks; they
are smaller and much
dumpier-bodied than
Guillemots (p194) and
Razorbills (p195), with dark
underwings, no white hind
margins to inner wings, and
orange or yellow legs; large
head makes it look front-
heavy, with much stubbier tail
behind. Juveniles have smaller
bills than adults; Little Auks
(p192) have different head
pattern and tiny bills.

J F M A M J J A S O N D

△ In winter plumage (after moult Aug-Sep) cheeks darker
grey, blackish between eyes and bill. Bill becomes smaller and
less colourful (grey-brown, yellow and orange) as coloured
plates at base and around edges of bill are shed; yellow gape
shrinks until small and unswollen. Red eyering remains, but
appendages around them lost. Legs become yellow. Juvenile
smaller and duller than adult winter, with darker grey cheeks
and almost black in front of eyes; bill much smaller, less deep,
more pointed, uniformly dark grey; pinkish legs.

▷ By 1st winter, bill has
started to acquire shape and
colours of adult's, with outer
part dull red, but is still
distinctly smaller and duller.
Soon gains red-brown
eyering and grey-blue
appendages above and below
it. Legs yellowish.

1st-winter

▽ Large head, short neck and massive bill give big-fronted
appearance in flight; combined with stocky body and narrow
but broad-ended wings gives unique profile. Flight action also
distinctive; although wings whirred like other auks, broad
outer half flapped more loosely, and body moves up and down
more definitely with wingbeats. Like Little Auk, flight more
agile, takes off more easily and lands more abruptly than larger
relatives. Often flies higher than other auks. Underwings
darker than in other auks; though Little Auk's may look very
dark, too, they usually appear paler; also Little Auk is much
smaller, with much smaller bill.

winter

PIGEONS AND DOVES
Order Columbiformes, Family Columbidae

Small to medium, often plump-bodied, with small heads and cere (fleshy bulge at base of upper mandible of bill, containing nostrils). Plumage of British species mainly grey or brown. Walk easily on ground, bobbing head; flight strong and direct, sometimes with glides on V-shaped wings; often take off with loud clatter of wings, and clap wings together audibly over back in display. Feed on leaves, seeds and fruits. Build flimsy nests in trees or in holes in trees, buildings, cliffs etc. Usually lay 2 white eggs. Feed small young (called 'squabs') on 'crop milk', a milk-like substance formed from sloughed-off cells of the crop (pouch leading off gullet used for food storage and found in many other birds). Sexes very similar. Words 'pigeon' and 'dove' loosely used and do not represent different groups of birds, though 'pigeon' often used in names of larger species with larger square or round-ended tail, and 'dove' for smaller, slimmer species with longer, graduated tails.

● Note: amount of white on rump or tail and, at close range, markings on neck. May be confused with smaller birds of prey in flight at distance.

ROCK DOVE/FERAL PIGEON *Columba livia*

22

▽ 'Pure' wild Rock Doves are now found only on the more remote rocky windswept coasts and islands of N and W Scotland, and N, W and S Ireland; because of extensive interbreeding with their feral relatives, it is possible there are now only a few genuine Rock Doves left, in the most isolated of the breeding colonies. Truly wild Rock Doves have blue-grey head and underparts, paler, ash-grey back and inner wings, two broad black wingbars, blue-grey tail with broad blackish band at the tip, and prominent white rump. Nape, neck and upper breast have green and purple gloss. Adults have red or orange eyes (dark brown in Stock Dove), grey-black bill with white cere (Stock Dove's bill mainly yellow or whitish-yellow with red at base) and purplish-red legs. In flight, darker head and underparts contrast strikingly with silvery-white underwings (those of Wood Pigeon and Stock Dove are grey). Juveniles are duller and darker than adults, with brown tinge to plumage, no glossy feathers and greyer underwings.

The wild Rock Dove is the ancestor of the domestic pigeons kept for hundreds of years to supply food, as well as of racing pigeons and other, more colourful, 'fancy' domestic pigeons. All belong to the same species. Over a long period, many of the domesticated birds escaped, or were lost or abandoned by their owners. These birds survived in the wild, breeding on quarries, ruins, bridges, inland cliffs and sea-cliffs, and in greatest numbers in towns and cities. These birds are known as Feral Pigeons.

Rock Doves

Columba livia ROCK DOVE/FERAL PIGEON

Feral Pigeons, plumage variations

△ Feral Pigeons come in a great variety of colours and patterns, reflecting mixed ancestry. Some closely resemble their wild cousins, but others range from all-black through a variety of piebald types and blue-grey, brown, sandy and reddish forms to all-white; many chequered or irregularly patterned; often have white (or whitish) rump, but not all show the double wingbar of wild birds. Although frequently seen on roofs and ledges of buildings, bridges etc, as well as on cliffs, like their wild ancestors they usually avoid trees, though sometimes perch on them and may use them as daytime roost.

Feral Pigeons

◁ Like wild Rock Doves, Feral Pigeons are fast and agile in the air, making frequent dramatic swoops and glides, as well as suddenly spiralling down to a perch or the ground with wings raised above back in a V, then final flutter on landing. Take-off explosive, with loud clattering of wings when alarmed. Distinctive shape in flight, with more pointed, protruding head, less stocky body and swept-back wings compared with more compact shape of Stock Dove. In display flight, male makes series of exaggerated, slow wingbeats, then claps wings together loudly over back several times, before planing down in long glide on V-shaped wings.

▷ Well-known and easily observed display on ground: male struts round, bowing and pursuing female, his crown, neck and back feathers puffed out, as he utters his familiar throaty, crooning cooing song, which is audible even above city traffic.

Feral Pigeons

male *female*

KEY FACTS

Length: 31-35cm.
Wingspan: 63-70cm.
Weight: 250-350g. **Habitat:** wild Rock Doves very local breeders at coastal and island sea-cliffs with caves and crevices in N and W Scotland and NW and S Ireland, and feed in adjacent fields etc; feral Rock Doves (Feral Pigeons) abundant in towns and cities, also breeding on quarries and cliffs inland and by the sea, feeding mainly on farmland. Homing pigeons (same species) also widespread. **Movements:** mainly sedentary.
Population: difficult to distinguish between truly wild and feral birds; total probably over 100 000 pairs. **Diet:** grain, seeds, buds, crops, seaweed, molluscs; feral birds eat wide range of scraps and other food. **Voice:** moaning 'oh-ooh-oor' or 'oohr'; song is longer, more crooning 'oo-roo-coo' given in display.
Nest: wild Rock Dove often uses just a few scraps of material, but sometimes builds a loosely constructed, untidy cup of heather stems, seaweed, grass etc, usually in ledge or crevice in sea cave, occasionally on sheltered cliff ledges, under boulders or in ruined buildings or other artificial sites. Feral Pigeon builds similar nest of locally available materials on ledges or in roof spaces of buildings, ledges on bridges and other crevice-like sites. **Eggs:** 2, white. **Incubation:** 16-19 days, by both sexes.
Fledging: 35-37 days.
Broods: 3, sometimes more; able to breed all year round.
Maturity: 1 year. **Confusion species:** Stock Dove (p201) similar, but lacks white rump, has pale pink breast, thick black border to trailing edge of wings and wingtips, less marked double black wingbars, and dark blue-grey underwings.

| J | F | M | A | M | J | J | A | S | O | N | D |

WOOD PIGEON *Columba palumbus*

Usually very gregarious, seen in huge flocks on arable land and when flying to and from roosts in trees. Feeds in shrubs and trees (where remarkably agile) as well as on ground.

adult　*juvenile*　*adult*

△ Largest, commonest and most widespread of our pigeons, from farmland and woodland to city centres. Large plump body, small rounded head, broad 'shoulders', deep chest and long tail. Plumage basically blue-grey, but back greyer, breast pinkish-mauve; bold white patch between glossy green and purple patches on side of neck. Thick white line along bend of closed wing. Eyes pale yellow; bill yellow with red base and mainly white cere; feet deep purplish-red. Juvenile has browner plumage, lacks white patch on neck and has duller, greyer eyes, duller bill, duller greyish legs. Looks short-legged on ground, with deliberate, low-slung, almost waddling gait.

△ In flight, wings and tail look long, chest deep; dainty head protrudes and generally angled slightly upwards. Often flies higher than other pigeons and may resemble bird of prey such as Sparrowhawk, but smaller-headed and bigger-bodied. Best identified by bold white bar across middle of upper wing; outer wings black, with white outer fringes to primary feathers showing as thin lines at close range and making primaries appear paler than primary coverts. Upper tail grey with broad black tip. Underwings blue-grey. Undertail has pale central band and dark tip. When disturbed, takes off explosively, rocketing into air with loud clatter of wings. Flies steadily and direct with continuous fast wingbeats or alternately flaps and glides, following a slightly undulating course.

male, displaying

◁ In frequently seen display, male climbs steeply, claps wings together loudly over back one or more times, then glides down with wings held out straight and tail fanned.

KEY FACTS

Length: 40-42cm.
Wingspan: 75-80cm.
Weight: 480-550g. **Habitat:** highest concentrations in farmland near woods, but breed almost everywhere except on higher hills and mountains; increasingly in city centres. **Movements:** mainly sedentary, with local movements; some movement from SW Britain to Ireland; some winter visitors from Continent. **Population:** about 3.5 million pairs breed; perhaps almost 10 million birds at end of breeding season. **Diet:** cereals, clover, peas, brassicas and other crops; seeds, leaves, buds, berries and nuts of a wide variety of wild plants.
Voice: series of lazy-sounding, muffled, husky cooing notes, 'coo *cooo* coo, coo-coo cook', the last note much briefer. Wings make loud clatter on take-off; clapped together loudly in display flight. **Nest:** thin, untidy platform of sticks, usually in tree or shrub, often built on previous nest. **Eggs:** 2, white. **Incubation:** 17 days, by both sexes. **Fledging:** 20-35 days. **Broods:** usually 1, sometimes 2. **Maturity:** 1 year. **Confusion species:** Stock Dove (opposite) smaller, without white patch on neck (though juvenile Wood Pigeon lacks this) and white wingbars, rounder head, shorter tail and shorter, more triangular wings; faster wingbeats. Different call.

| J | F | M | A | M | J | J | A | S | O | N | D |

juvenile　　　　*adult*

KEY FACTS

Length: 32-34cm.
Wingspan: 63-69cm.
Weight: 290-330g. **Habitat:** farmland, parkland and woodland edges with old trees; also around cliffs and ruins in wide range of habitats, from moorlands to sea coasts, and dunes. **Movements:** mainly sedentary; some winter visitors from Continent. **Population:** c240 000 pairs breed. **Diet:** mainly weed seeds, also leaves, buds, flowers, berries of various wild plants, and some crops. **Voice:** deep, gruff 'ooo-woo', repeated up to 10 times or more in accelerating series. **Nest:** in hole or cavity in old tree, thatched roof, building or rabbit hole, cavity in steep bank, old nest of other bird or squirrel drey, or on sheltered cliff ledge; small platform of sticks, rootlets, straw and leaves, though often uses no material when laying eggs on soft debris in tree hole. **Eggs:** 2, white. **Incubation:** 16-18 days, by both sexes. **Fledging:** 20-30 days. **Broods:** 2-3, sometimes more. **Maturity:** 1 year. **Confusion species:** Wood Pigeon (opposite) larger, longer-winged and longer-tailed, relatively smaller-headed, with prominent white patch on neck (lacking in juveniles) and white wingbar, slower flight action; wings make loud clatter on take-off. Different call. See also Rock Dove (p198 and right).

J F M A M J J A S O N D

△ Smaller and darker than Wood Pigeon, without any white markings on neck or wings. Shape more compact and evenly proportioned, with rounder head and smaller bill, stocky, rounder body and shorter tail. Head and most of body dark grey, with blue hue to head and underparts in good light. Back, rump and most of upperwing paler grey; breast with mauve-pink tinge (duller than and lacking sheen of Wood Pigeon's breast); glossy emerald-green patch on hindneck; 2 short black bars (and often trace of a third) near wingtips, far less noticeable than on Rock Dove; tail grey with broad black band at tip. Bill yellow or whitish with bright red base, eyes dark (not pale yellow as in adult Wood Pigeon), legs bright coral-red, duller in some females. Juvenile browner, without gloss on neck and duller breast; bill dull greyish or brownish.

▷ Stock Doves are the only British pigeons that regularly nest in holes. Most use holes in old trees, and supply of suitable sites severely reduced in some areas due to Dutch elm disease and hedgerow clearance.

Although they feed in fields and locally in town parks, Stock Doves do not usually associate with Feral Pigeons, though they sometimes join feeding flocks of Wood Pigeons in winter. Most often seen in pairs or small flocks, and never in such huge numbers as their larger relatives.

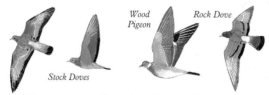

Wood Pigeon　　　*Rock Dove*

Stock Doves

△ In flight, structure of body (see above) and shorter, more triangular wings and shorter tail help distinguish Stock Dove from Wood Pigeon; best distinguishing features are lack of white wingbars and thick black border right round end and rear of wing surrounding pale grey panel; 2 black bars on each wing near body small and insignificant; dark grey underwing (silvery-white in Rock Dove and some Feral Pigeons) and no white rump as in Rock Dove/Feral Pigeon. Display flight horizontal, unlike Wood Pigeon's. Wings beat slowly and deeply at first, then are clapped over back before bird glides along with wings held at slight upward angle.

COLLARED DOVE *Streptopelia decaocto*

adult

juvenile

KEY FACTS

Length: 31-33cm.
Wingspan: 47-55cm.
Weight: 150-220g. **Habitat:** gardens, allotments and other sites in villages, towns and city suburbs, parks, farmland near farm buildings, with good cover, especially coniferous trees. **Movements:** mainly sedentary, with some westerly movement within Britain and from Britain to Ireland, and small numbers continuing to arrive from Continent (though immigration much declined since dramatic range expansion tailed off in 1970s). **Population:** phenomenal spread from original range in Asia and SE Europe since 1930s, aided by birds taking advantage of spilled grain around farmyards. Unknown here before 1950s; now *c*200 000 pairs breed.
Diet: chiefly cereal grain, much of it spilled from barns, silos and poultry-breeding units on farms; also invertebrates, weed seeds and seed from bird tables.
Voice: monotonous, deep 'coo-coo-kuk', usually accented on 2nd syllable and repeated rapidly for long periods; also nasal, harsh 'kwurr' and 'ghee ghee' calls of alarm and during gliding display flight. **Nest:** flimsy platform of twigs in trees (especially conifers), sometimes shrubs, often near trunk; occasionally on buildings. **Eggs:** 2, white. **Incubation:** 14-16 days, by both sexes. **Fledging:** 17-18 days, often before fully grown. **Broods:** 2-3, sometimes up to 6 or more (even as many as 9). **Maturity:** 1 year.
Confusion species: Turtle Dove (opposite), summer visitor only, smaller, darker and less uniformly patterned above and with less white in shorter tail (particularly underside); different flight, with jerky, flickering wingbeats; very different call.

△ Smallish, slim-bodied; small round head, with steep forehead, and long tail, longer than Turtle Dove's. Uniform pale greyish-brown upperparts, with pinkish face (more buff in female), narrow black half-collar, edged with white, especially above, on hindneck. Rest of neck and most of underparts pinkish, fading into whitish-buff belly and undertail. Blackish wingtips contrast with rest of plumage. Eyes ruby-red, bill narrow and black, legs deep red. Juvenile paler and duller; upperparts scaled with pale buff edges to feathers; no neck collar; underparts buff-grey to pinkish-grey. Feeds on ground on spilled grain and visits bird tables; often perches on overhead wires. Monotonous, unmusical cooing very distinctive.

male, display flight

△ Flight direct and normally fast, less tilting than Turtle Dove's, with rapid, rhythmic beats of rather bowed, rounded wings. Tail long, quite broad but usually held closed; has distinctive pattern (different from Turtle Dove's) from below, with broad white tip and black base; from above, looks same colour as upperparts, showing white corners when opened. In dramatic display flight from roof, tree, TV aerial or other perch, male rises steeply, then glides down in spiral, tail fanned, giving harsh nasal calls, and lands on perch, cocking tail.

Barbary Dove

△ **Barbary Dove** (*Streptopelia 'risoria'*) domesticated relative, similar to Collared Dove but smaller (*c*29cm), paler; wings without contrasting dark primary flight feathers. Has 3-note cooing call usually accented on 1st, not 2nd, syllable.

Streptopelia turtur TURTLE DOVE

35

KEY FACTS

Length: 26-28cm.
Wingspan: 47-53cm.
Weight: 130-180g. **Habitat:** lowland farmland on light fertile soils, with thick hedges, woodland edge, scrubland, young plantations.
Movements: summer visitor, end Apr-Sep, wintering in Africa; some passage migrants from Continent, mid Apr-May, mid Aug-mid Oct.
Population: *c*65 000 pairs breed. **Diet:** almost entirely weed seeds. **Voice:** repeated, deep, lazy-sounding, purring 'roorrrr roorrrrr'. **Nest:** flimsy platform of twigs and stalks, lined with rootlets and grass, typically in hawthorn or other bush, often in hedge, sometimes in low branches of tree. **Eggs:** 2, white.
Incubation: 13-14 days, by both sexes. **Fledging:** 19-21 days. **Broods:** 2, sometimes 3.
Maturity: 1 year. **Confusion species:** Collared Dove (opposite) larger, relatively longer-tailed, uniform, unpatterned upperparts and narrow black half collar at back of neck; more white on tail, especially beneath (half white towards end); also often calls in flight, unlike Turtle Dove. Kestrel (p115), especially male, has similar plumage pattern, but very different shape and flight action; also habitually hovers, which Turtle Dove never does. Mistle Thrush (p253) has different plumage, more undulating flight, straighter wings/square tail.

△ Unlike our other pigeons, summer visitor only. Small and slender, with neat round head and longish graduated tail; like Collared Dove, perches across overhead wires, with body at slanting angle but often remains hidden deep in dense hedge or thicket, from which it utters its distinctive long, lazy, purring song on warm summer days. Darker than Collared Dove, with neat, bold scaly pattern of black and rich chestnut on 'shoulders' and wing coverts; bold black and white neck patch; head and outer wing coverts blue-grey; outer wings brownish-black; back and rump brown, tinged with grey; breast pink, belly white and tail blackish, tipped with white. Eyes vary from yellow-brown to orange-red, surrounded by reddish-purple ring; neat bill blackish; legs purple-red or crimson. Often in small flocks when migrating along coast in spring and when feeding on arable land in late summer.

△ Rises quickly and steeply from ground or cover with slight clattering of wings. Flight agile, wings flicked sharply backwards in abrupt, jerky, clipped action, wingbeats alternating with brief glides in which bird tilts from side to side; spreads tail, showing broad white edges, as it lands with a flurry of wings.

▷ In display flight, male climbs steeply with tail spread, then glides down in a circle on outspread wings.

male, display flight

juvenile

◁ Juvenile duller and browner, with grey-brown head, no neck patches, less contrasting duller chestnut and less grey on inner wings and back, and buff, not pink, breast.

J F M A M J J A S O N D

PARROTS
Order Psittaciformes, Family Psittacidae

This very large family (containing some 350 species), restricted mainly to the tropics and other areas with hot climates, has only one representative living here in the wild. Some other very similar species escape, but have not become established in the wild.

RING-NECKED PARAKEET *Psittacula krameri*

Originating from escaped aviary birds introduced into the country from Africa and from India, Pakistan and other south Asian countries, where the species occurs naturally, the feral population of Ring-necked Parakeets is now well established and continues to expand its range. There are also small feral populations in Belgium, the Netherlands and Germany. The feral birds are thought to have three sources: birds escaping from pet shops and exotic-bird breeding centres; aviary birds allowed to fly free that failed to return; and birds deliberately released by sailors and other travellers who brought them back from their voyages and did not want the expense or trouble of keeping the parakeets in quarantine as the law demands. Although it might seem surprising that a member of a bird family so associated with the tropics could survive in the wild through our cold winters, some parrots do have a natural range that includes quite harsh weather, and British Ring-necked Parakeets take advantage of food provided by people in winter at bird tables etc. Also called Rose-ringed Parakeet.

female

male

▷ Large head, fairly slim body, with very long tail. Plumage bright emerald-green, with blackish outer wings and bluer-green tail. Bill crimson. Male also has narrow rose-pink and black neck ring, the black broadening onto throat, and bluish nape. Female lacks these 2 features but otherwise identical. Juvenile resembles female but has coral-pink bill with pale tip.

▽ Flight fast with shallow, quick, flickering wingbeats; makes sudden changes of direction and rapid dives; large, blunt head, narrow, quite pointed wings, and very long tail distinctive. Frequently gives loud screeching calls in flight (also when perched). Like other parrots, it clambers about with great agility on branches and trunks, using its powerful bill as a 'third foot'; waddles clumsily on ground. Usually gregarious.

females

KEY FACTS

Length: 38-42cm. **Wingspan:** 42-48cm. **Weight:** 100-150g. **Habitat:** open woodland, parks, gardens, orchards, fields with trees, mostly in suburban areas. **Movements:** some local feeding movements. **Population:** first recorded living here in the wild in 1969; original feral population concentrated mainly in Kent and Thames Valley. Since then, slow but steady expansion in range and local increases in numbers, especially in outer London area. By 1983, population estimated at 500-1000 birds. Currently, several thousand individuals are thought to breed in Britain. **Diet:** fruits, berries, seeds, nuts, scraps. **Voice:** loud, shrill, rasping screech 'keeo- keeo-keeo' or 'kee-ak kee-ak kee-ak'. **Nest:** eggs laid on layer of wood dust or other debris inside tree hole, often old nest hole of owl, woodpecker or Jackdaw; sometimes in cavity in roof or wall. **Eggs:** 2-4, white. **Incubation:** 22-24 days, by female. **Fledging:** 40-50 days. **Broods:** 1. **Maturity:** 2-3 years.

| J | F | M | A | M | J | J | A | S | O | N | D |

CUCKOOS
Order Cuculiformes, Family Cuculidae

A single species breeds and occurs here regularly; like almost half the world's 127 species of cuckoo, it is a brood parasite, laying its eggs in other birds' nests and leaving the host to incubate them and rear its young.

Cuculus canorus CUCKOO

adult

juvenile

36

KEY FACTS

Length: 32-34cm.
Wingspan: 55-65cm.
Weight: 105-130g. **Habitat:** woodland, farmland, heathland, moorland, sand dunes, reedbeds. **Movements:** summer visitor mid Apr-Jul, early Aug; juveniles do not leave until late Aug or Sep.
Population: 16 000-32 000 pairs breed. **Diet:** mostly caterpillars, especially hairy ones (poisonous to and rarely eaten by other birds; Cuckoo has protective stomach lining which can be shed and renewed); also other insects.
Voice: male utters familiar, far-carrying 'cuc-coo', sometimes 'cuc-cuc-coo'; also short, hoarse 'wha-wha-wha' of excitement; female has long, rich, liquid bubbling chuckle. Young can be located by distinctive begging calls – at first, thin, squeaky 'seep' only when host brings food, but later much louder, persistent, piercing, sibilant 'si-si-si-si ...' **Nest:** none – lays its eggs in nests of other birds. **Eggs:** each female lays 1-25 (average 9) eggs, 1 (rarely 2) per host nest.
Incubation: 11-12 days, by hosts only. **Fledging:** 17-21 days; usually leaves nest at 17 days. **Maturity:** 2 years, sometimes 1. **Confusion species:** superficially similar to male Sparrowhawk (see right and p109). Juvenile and rare rufous female could be mistaken for female Kestrel (p115), which has similar shape, but streaked (not barred) underparts and dark moustache stripe, and which frequently hovers.

△ Much less frequently seen than heard. Adults usually have plain grey head, breast and upperparts, and always have strongly barred underparts (fewer bars on creamy-white vent and undertail coverts). Long, dark, white-spotted tail. Males have blackish-brown barring; females usually very similar, but with browner barring on buffer breast and brown tinge to upperparts. Bill blackish with yellow base; eyes and short legs yellow. Juveniles have variable plumage, with two types common: one with dark grey-brown upperparts with little barring above, the other rufous-brown and strongly barred all over. Both types differ from adults in having whitish fringes to feathers of upperparts, prominent white patch on nape, barred throat and breast. When perched, especially on overhead wire, they look awkward and unbalanced, frequently shifting body, tail and wings. Wings often drooped and tail fanned and moved from side to side. Waddle or hop on ground.

Cuckoo adult

Sparrowhawk male

Kestrel male

△ With long tails and small heads, Cuckoos in flight frequently mistaken for small falcons and hawks – especially Sparrowhawks, whose basic plumage pattern they share. Unlike Sparrowhawk, they have pointed, not broad-tipped, wings and graduated tail with white spots, not dark bars. Flight direct, usually low and straight (but often looking rather unstable and rolling), with fast shallow beats of pointed wings (never rising above level of back); often glides with wings extended or drooped; makes final glide to perch and droops wings and raises tail on landing.

OWLS

Order Strigiformes, Families Tytonidae, Strigidae

Mainly nocturnal predators, unrelated to diurnal birds of prey (raptors), though some species regularly hunt by day. Small to large, with big heads; flattened faces have distinct 'facial discs'. Eyes forward-facing, usually large (and often yellow or orange); sharply hooked bill half-hidden in face plumage. Strong, sharp-clawed feet usually feathered. Silent flight, due to sound-deadening effect of extra-soft, fringed flight feathers. Swallow prey whole and regularly regurgitate pellets of indigestible material (bones, fur, feathers, beetle wing-cases etc) via bill. Two families: the barn owls (Tytonidae) have heart-shaped faces; the typical owls (Strigidae) have rounder faces and mainly have camouflaged plumage, typically barred, mottled and streaked in browns and greys. Some species of typical owls have 'ear' tufts, tufts of feathers near top of head that can be erected when bird is alarmed or excited; these have nothing to do with ears or hearing. Nest in tree holes, old buildings etc, in old nests of crows and other birds, or on ground. Sexes usually look identical.

● Note: presence/absence of 'ear' tufts, pattern of markings on facial disc, colour of eyes, plumage patterns in flight.

BARN OWL *Tyto alba*

37

race guttata

race alba

△ Big rounded head, with slim body and short tail. Distinctive heart-shaped face, with relatively small dark eyes. Legs long and neatly white-feathered, with 'knock-kneed' appearance from front. Adults of pale-breasted W European race *alba*, breeding in Britain, pale golden-buff above, mottled with grey (especially females), and white below, with buff tinge and fine dark spots (especially females). Adults of dark-breasted C and E European race *guttata*, a few of which reach here in autumn and winter, generally darker and greyer above and rich buff with more spots below. Unlike other owls, lacks streaks or bars on underparts. Although active primarily at night, also frequently hunts in late afternoon and evening, especially when feeding young in summer, and even throughout day in winter.

▽ In flight, looks very pale. Wings slightly rounded; big head/short tail make it look front-heavy. Flight graceful, buoyant, often wavering, but sometimes steadier. When hunting, patrols slowly low (1-5m) above ground, alternating quick wingbeats with elegant glides, frequently changing direction and sometimes hovering. Often drops briefly to ground; plunges head-first onto prey in grass. When going in for the kill, lowers long legs and swings feet up, spreading talons wide to grip prey.

hunting sequence

Tyto alba **BARN OWL**

KEY FACTS

Length: 33-39cm.
Wingspan: 85-93cm.
Weight: males 290-340g;
females 330-460g. **Habitat:**
hunts mainly over open
farmland with hedges/rough
grassland, also over other
open habitats, including sand
dunes, saltmarshes; needs
barns, old/ruined buildings,
haystacks, hollow trees or
holes in cliffs/quarries, or
nestboxes, for nesting and
roosting. **Movements:** mainly
sedentary; immatures wander
a bit further; a few immigrants
from Continent in autumn/
winter, rarely including
dark-breasted race *guttata*
(especially Oct-Dec,
SE Britain). **Population:**
possibly as few as 5000 pairs
now, since major decline over
past 100 years (1932 survey
estimated 12 000 pairs); hard
to count because of annual
fluctuations related to cycles
of abundance/scarcity of vole
prey. **Diet:** mainly rodents
(especially voles, except in
Ireland, where voles absent),
also other small mammals,
birds, insects. **Voice:** various
shrill, blood-curdling shrieks;
also variety of snoring, hissing
and yapping sounds at nest
site; young beg food with
drawn-out hissing. **Nest:**
scrape in debris, in hole or
hollow in tree, in crevice in
quarry or cliff, in church
towers, ruins, in barn or other
outbuilding, or in haystack;
also takes to suitable
nestboxes. **Eggs:** 4-7, white.
Incubation: 30-32 days, by
female. **Fledging:** 55-65 days.
Broods: 1-2. **Maturity:** 1
year. **Confusion species:**
Snowy Owl (see right).

J F M A M J J A S O N D

▷ Often active in daytime.
Flight powerful, often fast
and low, with long glides and
sudden dashes after prey;
long, broad wings, tapered to
tips; wingbeats slow on
downstroke, fast on upstroke.

△ Prey often carried in bill as owl takes off, but usually deftly
passed to one foot to be carried to the nest, then passed to bill
as owl flies up to feed chicks. Owlets are different sizes
because, as with other owls, female Barn Owls lay their eggs at
intervals of 2-3 days and begin incubation with the first egg
laid; in a typical family of 5, the owlet that hatched first will be
8 days older than the one that hatched last.

▷ Pellets dark, large, smooth,
cylindrical, rounded at both
ends. Contain bones, fur
and feathers of small rodents
or birds, highly compressed.

*30-70mm
x 15-40mm*

▽ **Snowy Owl** (*Nyctea scandiaca*) rare wanderer to moors,
saltmarshes and other open country in Britain from Arctic
breeding grounds: usually annual in N Scotland, especially
Cairngorms and N isles (has bred Fetlar, Shetland, 1967-75),
very rare elsewhere. Very large (53-66cm), powerful-looking,
mainly white owl with yellow eyes (which look dark at
distance) in cat-like face, big, rounded or flattened head,
heavy barrel-shaped body and massive, heavily feathered feet.
Female larger, with dark brown barring over crown, nape and
much of body and wings; male all-white apart from a few
scattered spots and bars. Juvenile dark grey, at first speckled
with protruding greyish-white down; later, acquires white face
and white flight and tail feathers barred brown; very well
camouflaged when on ground. 1st-winters resemble adult
female, but male less and female much more heavily barred.
Perches slanted or more upright on rocks, posts or other low
lookout; often sits on ground, resting on breast just like a cat.

male

female

female

male

LITTLE OWL *Athene noctua*

38

KEY FACTS

Length: 21-23cm.
Wingspan: 50-56cm.
Weight: males 140-180g;
females 150-200g. **Habitat:**
mainly lowland farmland,
parkland, orchards and other
semi-open habitats with
scattered old deciduous trees.
Movements: British breeders
mainly sedentary. **Population:**
introduced from Continent
1842 and extensively during
1870s; well established as
breeding bird in England and
Wales after population
explosion 1910-30; today
6000-12 000 pairs breed,
18 000-36 000 individuals in
midwinter. **Diet:** chiefly
rodents and other small
mammals, insects and
earthworms; also small birds.
Voice: song a repeated loud,
liquid, plaintive, 'keeeoo' call,
slightly rising, often given by
pair as duet; also shriller,
shorter version of this sound,
sharp, ringing or yelping
'werro' call and excited
'kip-kip-kip' of alarm; young
beg for food with steady
hissing. **Nest:** mainly in
hollow deciduous trees; also in
holes in quarries, cliffs, banks,
ruins, farm buildings, or in
rabbit burrows or even
haystacks ; will also use
nestboxes. No nest material.
Eggs: 2-5, white. **Incubation:**
27-28 days, by female.
Fledging: 30-36 days.
Broods: 1. **Maturity:** 1 year.

| J | F | M | A | M | J | J | A | S | O | N | D |

△ By far our smallest owl;
only the size of plump thrush.
Often seen during day, on
regular and often conspicuous
perch, where it may hardly
move for hours. Hunts mainly
during twilight and night.
Moves easily on ground, can
run; catches insects and
earthworms. Squat, with
broad, flat head; combination
of yellow eyes and white
eyebrows gives fiercely
frowning expression; short
tail. Upperparts dark brown,
spotted and barred with white;
underparts whitish, with
broad dark brown streaks.

juveniles

△ Typical nest site a hole low
down in old or pollarded tree,
often in hedgerow. Juvenile
paler brown above than adult,
with spots and bars more buff
than white; and pale buff, not
whitish, underparts, with
narrower streaks; downy.

agitated

relaxed   *alert*

△ Favourite perches include
posts, fences, tree branches,
rocks and overhead wires and
associated poles. When
relaxed, looks dumpy-bodied
and broad-headed; when
curious or agitated, stretches
body upright on long legs,
jerking it from side to side,
bobbing head up and down,
even turning it upside-down.

▽ Pellets small, elongated
and pointed at one end,
usually containing many
beetle wing-cases and other
hard insect remains.

15-40mm x 10-15mm

△ Short, but portly and heavily built – looks quite large in
flight, which is usually low and fast. In contrast to other owls,
has heavy, deeply bounding flight, like woodpecker's; quick
wingbeats in between glides. Occasionally hovers clumsily.
Blunt head and broad rounded wings distinctive in flight.

Strix aluco **TAWNY OWL**

Blackbird male

Wren

KEY FACTS

Length: 37-39cm.
Wingspan: 94-104cm.
Weight: males 330-440g;
females 420-590g. **Habitat:**
old woodland, especially
deciduous, also urban parks,
large gardens with trees.
Movements: highly
sedentary. **Population:**
25 000-50 000 pairs breed;
70 000-175 000 individuals in
midwinter. **Diet:** chiefly
rodents and other small
mammals, also birds (main
diet of urban Tawnies), frogs,
fish, insects, earthworms.
Voice: commonest call a
loud, sharp, 'ke-wick'; male's
song far-carrying, long
multiple hoot, 'hoo-hooh…
hooo, hoo-hoo-hoo, hooooo-
o-o-o-o-o', the 2nd part
quavering and following the
1st after a pause of 1-4
seconds. Female usually
replies to male's song with
'ke-wick' call; this duet is the
popularly rendered 'tu-whit,
to-whoo'. Male sometimes
gives an extraordinary long
bubbling trill. Young beg food
with loud, wheezy 'sheee-eep'
calls. **Nest:** in hole in tree,
sometimes in chimney or
other part of building, hole in
rocks, in old nest of Magpie,
in rabbit hole or even on
ground. No nest material.
Eggs: 2-5, white.
Incubation: 28-30 days, by
female. **Fledging:** 32-37 days.
Broods: 1. **Maturity:** 1-2
years. **Confusion species:**
Long-eared Owl (p210)
slighter, with orange eyes and
ear tufts (though latter not
always visible); Short-eared
(p211) paler, more buff, with
yellow eyes, often seen
hunting during day.

| J | F | M | A | M | J | J | A | S | O | N | D |

juvenile

△ Most widespread and common British owl; not found in
Ireland. Generally strictly nocturnal – its familiar quavering
hoots heard far more often than bird is seen – but may be
disturbed in daylight from roost site in tree hole, among ivy or
on branch against trunk. Despite superb camouflage, Tawnies
(like other owls) often harassed ('mobbed') by mixed flocks of
tits and other small birds, which fly around the predator,
calling excitedly. At dusk, Tawny Owl may be seen silhouetted
on prominent perch within its territory, from which it sings
and which it uses as vantage point when hunting; has several
such perches on regular hunting 'beat'. Largest common owl;
very big head, bulky body. Plumage variable, from
reddish-brown (most common in Britain) through tawny-buff
to greyish; upperparts streaked/marbled, underparts streaked.
Lack of ear tufts and black eyes in rounded facial discs
distinctive, as are conspicuous creamy-white stripes forming
V on front crown, whitish crescents between eyes and bill
and whitish moustaches. Also has whitish patches on
'shoulders'. Usually looks squat and hunched, but when
alarmed or excited can appear much more slim and upright.

▷ Looks bulky and very front-
heavy on the wing, with very
large head and short tail,
giving it great manoeuvrability
in dense woodland. Slow
flier, regular beats of broad,
rounded wings alternating
with short glides. Can look
very pale in car headlights.

20-50mm x 10-25mm

◁ Pellets medium-sized,
grey, irregularly shaped and
usually tapering at one end,
with bones of vole and
mouse prey often protruding.
Usually widely scattered.

▷ Young make distinctive, hoarse, hissing food-begging calls
continuously through night. Can scramble around trees and
flutter about well before they can fly. (If you come across an
owlet, leave it for its parents to find.) Recently fledged young
often still very downy, their shaggy, loose plumage finely barred;
overall colour as variable as in adult.

LONG-EARED OWL *Asio otus*

83

alert

relaxed

very relaxed

KEY FACTS

Length: 35-37cm. **Wingspan:** 84-95cm. **Weight:** males 210-270g; females 240-330g. **Habitat:** breeds mainly in coniferous trees, chiefly in isolated copses, younger plantations and overgrown hedges; in Ireland, where it is commonest owl and there are no Tawny or Little Owls to compete with it, often breeds in broadleaved woodland. In winter also on saltmarshes, heathland, moorland, etc. **Movements:** our breeders largely sedentary, but young disperse randomly. Winter visitors from N Europe, Oct-mid May. **Population:** 2200-7200 pairs breed, half in Britain, half in Ireland; *c*7500-25 000 birds in midwinter. **Diet:** mainly small rodents in breeding season; roosting birds important in winter. **Voice:** song of male drawn-out, low, moaning or cooing 'oo...oo...oo'; other calls in breeding season include squeals, screams and barks. Juveniles beg for food with distinctive, far-carrying, mournful squeaking 'eee-oo', sounding like unoiled hinge. **Nest:** usually uses old nest of Magpie or other crow, Sparrowhawk or other bird, or squirrel's drey, though in more open habitats often nests in scrape on ground under bushes, brambles or bracken. **Eggs:** 3-5, white. **Incubation:** 25-30 days, by female. **Fledging:** 30 days or more. **Broods:** 1, occasionally 2. **Maturity:** 1 year. **Confusion species:** Short-eared Owl (opposite).

| J | F | M | A | M | J | J | A | S | O | N | D |

△ Secretive and generally strictly nocturnal, though migrants may turn up on coasts at any time of day. May also be seen leaving or returning to communal roosts in trees, thickets, etc. Long ear tufts (though these may be held flat and not visible), narrowed eyes and slanting white eyebrows. Body usually more slender, head smaller than Tawny's; eyes glowing orange. Wingtips reach beyond tail. When alarmed, adopts very upright, thin posture. Upperparts mottled grey, brown and warm buff with fine streaking; underparts slightly paler, with dark streaks and bars. Facial disc golden-buff.

△ Flight quicker than Tawny's, with longer wings and tail. Bursts of a few deep, stiff wingbeats alternate with long glides, in which wings usually held straight out (even arched) and not raised above level of body, unlike Short-eared Owl. Looks darker, more uniform than latter, with less contrasting wing pattern from above: dark patches on 'wrists' not so obvious; orange-buff, not buff/whitish, patch along centre of primary feathers; no pale trailing edge to upperwings; evenly barred outer primaries rather than black wingtips; and more uniform, densely barred greyish-buff tail. Underparts more uniformly streaked, without Short-eared's contrast between darker neck/breast and pale belly. Ear tufts not visible in flight.

juvenile, threat posture

▷ Pellets long and slender with rough surface; contain mainly small mammals and birds, with fur much more digested than Tawny's.

30-60mm x 15-20mm

◁ Young have heavily barred downy grey plumage and prominent, very dark facial discs. They adopt a dramatic posture when threatened. From late May to July, they beg for food with distinctive 'rusty-gate' calls.

Asio flammeus SHORT-EARED OWL

KEY FACTS

Length: 34-42cm.
Wingspan: 90-105cm.
Weight: males 260-310g;
females 290-350g. **Habitat:**
breeds chiefly in open heather
moorland and young forestry
plantations in uplands, some
on rough grassland, coastal
marshes and hollows ('slacks')
between sand dunes; winters
more widely, including chalk
downlands, rough farmland,
inland marshes and other
wetlands and saltmarshes.
Movements: wanders far and
wide in winter in search of
food; many immigrants from
Continent arrive in autumn.
Population: at least 1000
pairs breed, with up to 3500
or more pairs in years when
vole prey especially plentiful;
at least 5000 and possibly up
to 25 000 individuals in
midwinter. **Diet:** chiefly field
voles; also other rodents and
other small mammals and
birds. **Voice:** calls heard
chiefly on breeding grounds,
including high-pitched nasal
bark 'kee-aw', hoarse
'gwee-ek' of female; and
male's song, a repeated, soft,
deep, pumping 'boo-boo-boo-
boo-boo' usually given during
circular display flight, when
also claps wings loudly . **Nest:**
scrape on ground, no nest
material. **Eggs:** 4-8, white.
Incubation: 24-29 days, by
female. **Fledging:** 24-27 days.
Broods: 1-2. **Maturity:** 1
year. **Confusion species:**
Long-eared Owl (opposite)
generally strictly nocturnal.

J F M A M J J A S O N D

△ Movements hard to predict but, when bird located, easily observed: regularly hunts in broad daylight over moors, rough grasslands, marshes and other open country. Often perches on ground, with horizontal or sloping posture unlike other owls; also perches more upright on low posts and other lookout points. Plumage paler, often more golden, than Long-eared, with bolder, blotchier, more contrasting dark markings above. Blazing yellow eyes surrounded by black patches give it fierce expression. Very short ear tufts rarely visible. At first, owlets creamy-buff; older juveniles darker than adults, with cream barring on upperparts, buffer underparts with less streaking, and dark facial disc.

△ When hunting, quarters ground usually at height of only 1-2m, but sometimes up to 10m or more. Flight very buoyant, with a few slow wavering beats of stiff wings, as if rowing, alternating with long wavering glides, wings held up in shallow V; often turns, banks and side-slips abruptly, and sometimes hovers slowly. Even at distance, fierce expression with glaring yellow eyes very distinctive. Wings longer and slimmer than Long-eared's. A paler and more contrasting bird than latter, with very prominent dark carpal patch at 'wrist' (bend of forewing), in front of conspicuous pale golden-buff patch on bases of primary feathers, tips of which more solidly black; also pale trailing edge to upperwings. As in Long-eared, black carpal patches stand out strikingly against pale underwings, but latter do not contrast with dark body as in Long-eared; belly of Short-eared appears same pale colour as underwings; only breast noticeably streaked. Tail strongly barred, less uniform-looking than Long-eared's.

35-70mm x 15-25mm

◁ Pellets quite large, elongated, rounded at one end, tapered at other; often segmented. Grey with slight sheen. Contain entire skulls, especially of voles, also other small mammals and birds.

NIGHTJARS
Order Caprimulgiformes, Family Caprimulgidae

Medium-sized, with broad flattened heads, big eyes, tiny bills with huge gape which they hold open to snap up flying insects in flight, detected/funnelled in by surrounding bristles (which may also protect birds' eyes from damage); active at dusk and dawn and during night. Tiny feet. Long narrow wings. Plumage has intricate 'dead leaves' pattern, giving superb camouflage when they remain immobile during day, resting on ground or lengthways along branch. Nest on ground. Sexes similar. Only 1 species breeds here.

NIGHTJAR *Caprimulgus europaeus*

KEY FACTS

Length: 26-28cm.
Wingspan: 54-60cm.
Weight: 75-100g. **Habitat:** breeds mainly in newly felled and young conifer plantations, also on heathlands, moorland, sand dunes. **Movements:** summer visitor May-Sep; winters Africa. **Population:** c6000 pairs breed (very few, maybe only c30 pairs, in Ireland). **Diet:** flying insects, especially moths, beetles. **Voice:** from dusk through night, male utters very distinctive, loud, mechanical-sounding churring song, alternating between 2 main pitches, sounding like distant small motorbike, given for hours on end with only brief pauses; has ventriloquial quality. Also often claps wings loudly in display flights. Flight call a soft, nasal 'koo-ick' or 'goo-eek'. **Nest:** scrape on ground, no nest material. **Eggs:** 2, superbly camouflaged with grey, yellow-brown and darker marbling and spotting. **Incubation:** 17-18 days, mainly by female. **Fledging:** 16-17 days. **Broods:** 1 or 2. **Maturity:** 1 year. **Confusion species:** owls (pp206-11) have much broader, more rounded wings.

| J | F | M | A | M | J | J | A | S | O | N | D |

male, churring

△ Secretive, mysterious summer visitor, heard far more often than seen. Distinctive loud, dry churring song of male, which starts as light fades and may continue for several hours on end, helps locate it; usually given as bird perches lengthways along branch. More active on still, warm, dry nights when plenty of moths and other flying insect prey about. Can look quite large in dim light. Long, squat head, with tiny, hardly visible bill and big, dark eyes; tiny feet not visible.

△ During the day when asleep or on nest on ground, superbly camouflaged plumage of mottled and barred browns, buffs, greys, black and cream renders bird invisible against dead leaves, heather, bracken etc.

female

male display

males

△ Flight silhouette rather falcon- or cuckoo-like, with long, pointed wings and long tail that may look almost as large as wings. Flight silent, floating, ghostly, with frequent long glides on stiff wings, and remarkable dips, side-slips and hovers as it hawks for flying insects from dusk through night, trapping them in its huge mouth. Often fans tail in flight. Male has prominent white spots on wings and corners of tail. In courtship display flights, he claps wings loudly over back, and often gives frequent nasal, rather frog-like 'koo-ick' calls; also glides with wings raised in a V and tail spread wide, drawing attention to white spots on wings and tail.

SWIFTS
Order Apodiformes, Family Apodidae

Very small to medium-sized, most aerial of birds, feeding exclusively on insects and spiders in flight, and even sleeping on the wing. Cigar-shaped body, bill very small but with extremely wide gape to trap flying insects. Legs very short, feathered, feet tiny but strong and able to grasp onto vertical surfaces (bird unable to take off from ground without great difficulty). Sexes alike. Nest mainly in roofs of buildings, originally in tree holes (rarely now) or crevices in cliffs. Only 1 species breeds here.

△ Superb fliers, often very high in air. Never perch on wires, roofs etc like Swallow and martins. Bigger than latter, with longer, narrower, scythe-shaped wings; short, blunt head; slim, cigar-shaped body tapering to pointed or forked tail gives distinctive 'anchor' silhouette. Plumage blackish-brown (looks black except at close range in strong light), apart from whitish throat (often difficult to see at distance, and most obvious when head-on); underwings flash pale in sun.

△ Flight action very distinctive and different from Swallow and martins: short burst of very rapid, flickering, wingbeats (in which wings may appear to beat alternately) followed by long, slow glide on stiff wings, held flat or distinctly depressed; often tilts from side to side. Silhouette of gliding, wheeling or stalling bird, with straighter wings and fully open forked tail, looks stubbier than flying bird with its anchor shape and longer, slim, pointed, closed tail.

△ Excited parties of Swifts career madly at high speed around rooftops and houses, often low, especially towards dusk, giving distinctive thin, high, screaming calls.

KEY FACTS

Length: 16-17cm.
Wingspan: 42-48cm.
Weight: 36-50g. **Habitat:** spends most of life in air; common over villages/towns, where churches, houses and other buildings provide nest sites, and over water, where insect food numerous, but very widespread and seen in every habitat. **Movements:** summer visitor and passage migrant (late Apr-Aug, with stragglers until Oct); winters in C and SE Africa. Some immatures remain in Africa right through to summer; others migrate N, but wander widely across Europe.
Population: possibly *c*100 000 pairs breed here.
Diet: flying insects and airborne spiders. **Voice:** prolonged shrill screaming call in flight; also rapid chirruping at nest. **Nest:** shallow cup of leaves, feathers, straw, scraps of paper and other materials gathered on wing; in small scattered colonies; nest chiefly in hole in eaves (or in stonework or under thatch) of houses, church towers or in other buildings; a few still nest in crevices in cliffs (formerly also nested in tree holes).
Eggs: 2-3, white. **Incubation:** 18-25 days (the longer periods in cooler weather), by both sexes. **Fledging:** 37-56 days (depending on weather).
Broods: 1. **Maturity:** 4 years.
Confusion species: unrelated Swallow (pp226-7) and martins (pp224-5) superficially similar; see p227.

| J | F | M | A | M | J | J | A | S | O | N | D |

KINGFISHERS AND RELATIVES
Order Coraciiformes, Families Alcedinidae, Meropidae, Upupidae

Varied group of brilliantly coloured birds, most of which feed on large insects. Occur mainly in warmer parts of the world; 1 species, Kingfisher (Family Alcedinidae), breeds regularly here, and 2 others, Bee-eater (Family Meropidae) and Hoopoe (Family Upupidae) are rare but annual wanderers from the Continent. Members of the order have big heads, long and pointed (sometimes downcurved) or stout and slightly hooked bills, short necks, sturdy bodies and short legs. Middle toe fused with inner at base and with outer for most of its length. Tails may be short or long with projecting streamers. Sexes alike. All nest in holes.

KINGFISHER *Alcedo atthis*

male *female*

△ Small, dumpy-bodied, with big head and long, heavy, dagger-like bill, tiny stubby tail and tiny feet. Perches on branches, posts etc above or near water, with head/bill angled forwards or down and tail depressed. When suspicious and when on lookout for fish, bobs head and flicks tail. Despite bright plumage, can be very hard to spot in shade against foliage or water. Often pinpointed by shrill whistling calls. In good light, upperparts brilliant blue-green with particularly vivid pale blue streak on back. Long crown and nape, long, broad moustache and wing coverts spotted paler blue; chestnut through eye; white throat and neck patches. Wing and tail tips blackish. Underparts orange chestnut. Female has red base to lower mandible of bill; male's bill all-black.

△ Pair dig out nest tunnels with bills. When feeding young, they fly straight in without perching or hesitating. Nest chamber soon becomes foul-smelling with regurgitated fish bones and scales; often a giveaway white streak of droppings below tunnel entrance. Each chick needs 12-18 fish daily.

juvenile

◁ Juvenile has duller, greener upperparts than adults, especially on crown and moustache; paler below with pale speckling on breast; bill shorter, all-black; legs duller.

KEY FACTS

Length: 16-17cm (of which bill 4cm). **Wingspan:** 24-26cm. **Weight:** 35-40g. **Habitat:** unpolluted, shallow, still or slow-flowing rivers, streams, canals etc, also lakes, ponds and small ditches; in winter also along estuaries and sheltered coasts, especially when freshwater haunts frozen. **Movements:** largely sedentary, though young birds wander further in autumn after breeding season. **Population:** 4600-7600 pairs breed here; 8500-13 000 individuals in winter. Short-term declines after severe winters; pollution, unsympathetic river management and drying-up of rivers also reduce numbers. **Diet:** chiefly small freshwater fish, also some aquatic insects and small marine fish; occasionally crustaceans, molluscs and amphibians. **Voice:** long, loud, shrill whistle 'cheeeee' or 'chi-keeeee', often repeated; also shrill, aggressive, piping 'shrit-it-it'; very noisy in spring and autumn when defending nesting and wintering territory. **Nest:** long narrow tunnel (typically 45-90cm long, with entrance hole typically 5-5.5cm diameter), excavated by both sexes in sand or earth bank, usually above water. **Eggs:** 5-7, white. **Incubation:** 19-21 days, by both sexes. **Fledging:** 23-27 days. **Broods:** 2. **Maturity:** 1 year.

| J | F | M | A | M | J | J | A | S | O | N | D |

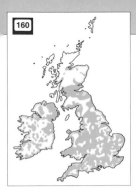

△ Waits patiently on perch or hovers until prey spotted, then flies (not drops) straight into water, plunging beneath it with bill open and eyes shut, and often making audible splash. After seizing fish in bill, it powers itself out of the water with strong wingbeats, then returns to the same perch, beating its prey before swallowing it head first.

◁ Flight typically very fast and direct, bird shooting along low over water, with whirring beats of stubby wings, interspersed with short glides. Usually seen as a 'blue streak'. Flies high in spring display, calling loudly.

▷ **Hoopoe** (*Upupa epops*) very scarce but regular visitor from Continent, especially in spring (most late Apr-May); a few stay to breed; smaller numbers in autumn (Aug-Oct). Size of Mistle Thrush (26-28cm), with pinkish-brown body, black and white wings and tail, long, black, downcurved bill and long pinkish-brown crest with white and black tips to feathers. Crest usually closed, giving 'hammerhead' head profile, but raised into Indian war-bonnet shape in flight, on landing and when excited or alarmed. Surprisingly difficult to see when waddling about on short grey legs, probing rapidly into ground for insect larvae with long bill. Perches on tree branches, walls etc and can climb up tree trunks and other rough surfaces. Named after its deep, soft but far-carrying quick 'oop-oop-oop' song; also has mewing, cawing and chattering calls. In flight, resembles huge butterfly, with very broad, boldly pied wings. Undulating, erratically flitting flight action, wings alternately open and closed.

Hoopoe

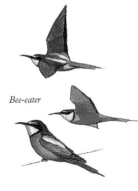

Bee-eater

◁ **Bee-eater** (*Merops apiaster*) rare but annual wanderer to Britain; exotic-looking, thrush-sized (27-29cm); vividly coloured, with long downcurved bill and projecting central tail feathers. Chestnut and yellow upperparts, blue-green primary wing feathers and tail, brilliant yellow throat and blue-green underparts. Juvenile has green upperparts except for brownish-red crown; lacks central tail feathers. Gregarious. Often perches crosswise on telephone wires, head and bill projecting forwards, body angled or horizontal. Distinctive flight call: far-carrying, constantly repeated, throaty, liquid 'quilp', with penetrating, bell-like quality. Hawks for bees and other insects in flight; rises quickly with burst of rapid beats of long, stiff, pointed wings, then stalls before slow curving glide on outstretched wings. Flies faster/more direct on migration.

215

WOODPECKERS AND WRYNECKS
Order Piciformes, Family Picidae

Small to medium; feed mainly on wood-boring insects and larvae, obtained by hacking into wood with strong, chisel-like bills. Catch prey on extremely long tongues, armed with barbed or sticky tips. Large, strong feet, with 2 toes pointing forwards and 2 backwards, provide stable support when climbing jerkily up trees. Pointed tail; stiffened feathers serve as prop (except in Wrynecks). Flight undulating, with broad, rounded wings closed between each burst of wingbeats. In most species, including our two spotted woodpeckers, both sexes drum loudly with bills on trunks/branches to advertise/defend territory. Almost all excavate nest holes in trees, usually new one each year; no nest material apart from wood chips. Sexes similar.

● Note: in all except Wryneck, colour/pattern of head markings; varies between species, and within species with sex and age; pattern of white markings on backs of two spotted species; calls distinctive, as are length and speed of drumming in spring.

LESSER SPOTTED WOODPECKER *Dendrocopos minor*

62

male

female

KEY FACTS

Length: 14-15cm. **Wingspan:** 25-27cm. **Weight:** 18-22g. **Habitat:** deciduous woodland, copses, trees in hedgerows and along river banks, large wooded gardens. **Movements:** sedentary. **Population:** decline since 1980 as many elms, important nesting trees, have died from Dutch elm disease; now only c3000-6000 pairs breed; c12 000-24 000 birds in midwinter. **Diet:** mainly insects, especially adults and larvae of wood-boring beetles. **Voice:** slow, nasal 'pee pee pee pee', weaker, less ringing than similar call of Wryneck (p219); also abrupt 'tchick' call, much feebler than Great Spotted's; drumming weaker, more rattling than Great Spotted's, each burst longer, c1-1$\frac{1}{2}$ seconds. **Nest:** small hole excavated in tree, entrance diameter only c3cm, 1-25m above ground, usually in thick dead branch, often on underside. **Eggs:** 4-6, white. **Incubation:** 12-14 days, by both sexes. **Fledging:** 18-20 days. **Broods:** 1. **Maturity:** possibly 1 year. **Confusion species:** Great Spotted (opposite) much larger, with big white shoulder patches, red undertail, unstreaked flanks.

△ Smallest of our 3 woodpeckers, only size of sparrow. Secretive; usually stays high up on smallest branches of tree canopy, searching for insect food with rapid 'sewing-machine' action of small pointed bill. Has fluttering, flitting action when feeding, more like perching bird than woodpecker, though has typical stiff woodpecker posture. Climbs trunks and branches less jerkily than other woodpeckers, with creeping action. Upperparts closely barred black and white in 'ladder' pattern; underparts whitish-buff, with few dark streaks on flanks. White cheeks with black moustache stripe extended into inverted T. Male has dull red crown; female has whitish-buff to pale brown forecrown, sometimes flecked red, and black rear crown.

▷ Flight undulating, rather slow and weak, with hesitant flitting action. All-barred wings and back distinctive.

males

male   female

juveniles

◁ Juvenile has front of crown whitish, mottled black; rear crown red in young male, flecked red in female. Flanks more heavily streaked/spotted.

| J | F | M | A | M | J | J | A | S | O | N | D |

216

Dendrocopos major GREAT SPOTTED WOODPECKER

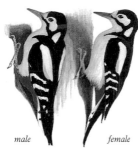

male   *female*

KEY FACTS

Length: 22-23cm.
Wingspan: 34-39cm.
Weight: 70-90g. **Habitat:**
deciduous, coniferous and
mixed woodland, copses,
hedgerow trees and gardens
with trees, latter especially in
winter, when visits bird tables.
Movements: British breeders
chiefly sedentary; some
immigrants from Scandinavia
Sep-Apr, especially
N and E Britain Sep-Oct;
rare wanderer to Ireland.
Population: may have bred
as far N as Sutherland, NW
Scotland, until late 18th
century, but by early 19th
century had disappeared
completely from Scotland and
largely retreated from N
England. Then recolonized
N during late 19th/early 20th
centuries. Today, *c*25 000-
30 000 pairs breed; *c*125 000-
150 000 individuals in
midwinter. **Diet:** mainly
insects, especially beetles and
their wood-boring larvae; also
eggs and chicks of hole-
nesting birds, and seeds of
trees, especially conifers.
Voice: usual call a loud,
abrupt 'tchick', which may be
repeated when bird alarmed
or excited into a rapid chatter;
occasionally accelerated
further into a dry rattle;
drumming (especially
Mar-May) much faster than
that of other woodpeckers,
each burst rarely lasting longer
than 1 second, followed by
interval of several seconds.
Nest: hole excavated in tree,
usually 3-5m above ground,
entrance diameter 5-6cm.
Eggs: 4-7, white.
Incubation: 15-16 days, by
both sexes. **Fledging:** 20-24
days. **Broods:** 1. **Maturity:**
possibly 1 year. **Confusion
species:** Lesser Spotted
Woodpecker (opposite) much
smaller, lacks large white
shoulder patches and red
undertail, has back as well as
wings barred white, and
streaked flanks.

△ Our most widespread and numerous woodpecker. Heard
more often than seen; sharp calls and frequent rapid
drumming in spring help pinpoint birds. Distinctly smaller
than Green Woodpecker, with shorter bill; much bigger than
Lesser Spotted. Smaller than Blackbird. Boldly pied plumage;
distinguished by 2 prominent large white shoulder patches
standing out against black back, and red undertail coverts.
Black crown joined by black band to black moustaches,
isolating two areas of buffy-white. Underparts unstreaked
white with variable buff tinge. Not often seen on ground. Male
has small red patch on nape; red undertail coverts extend to
lower belly; female lacks red nape.

juvenile

◁ Juvenile has entire crown
red and smaller area of pink
(not red) on undertail
coverts. Black moustache
narrower, streaked white;
often a few black streaks on
shoulder patches and flanks.

▷ Less wary than Green
Woodpecker, often visiting
garden bird tables in winter,
especially in wooded areas,
where it relishes suet, fat and
peanuts. Wedges pine cones in
cracks in branches to hammer
out seeds with audible blows
of its powerful bill.

male

males

◁ Flight deeply undulating,
shooting up to land abruptly
on tree trunk. Distinctive
features: bold white shoulder
patches, white spots on black
primary and secondary wing
feathers and flash of red on
undertail coverts. Underwing
coverts whitish.

Usually, a new nest hole excavated each year, by both sexes,
typically in dead oak or birch trunk; this process takes birds
1-2 weeks, depending on hardness of wood. Later, the young
draw attention to their presence by almost continuous,
insistent, squeaking 'sirrr-sirrr-sirrr . . .' calls.

| J | F | M | A | M | J | J | A | S | O | N | D |

GREEN WOODPECKER *Picus viridis*

female

male

60

△ Largest of the 3 British woodpeckers (about size of town pigeon but slimmer), brightly coloured, exotic-looking. Dull yellowish-green above and pale greyish-green below, with striking crimson-red crown, black patch on face surrounding prominent pale eye, black moustache stripe, with red centre in male, greenish-brown barring on rear flanks and vent. Strikingly bright greenish-yellow rump. Tail blackish with greenish barring, feathers often worn and frayed at tips.

▷ Juveniles greyer above and mottled: black and grey streaks and bars on head and neck, whitish spots and bars on upperparts, and bold blackish bars and streaks on underparts. Moustache shorter, speckled, partly red on young males.

juvenile

droppings

female

◁ Often seen feeding on ground far from trees, digging for ants in grass or ant hills. Hops clumsily upright and frequently looks round warily. Distinctive droppings, each containing remains of hundreds of ants, look like cigarette ash.

▷ Flight markedly undulating, with wings closed after only a few beats; sweeps up to land on tree trunk or branch. Flight profile distinctive, with pointed head/bill and pointed tail; most striking plumage feature is bright greenish-yellow rump (brightest in males), which looks brilliant in good light; primary feathers dark brown with cream mottling. Underwings strongly barred.

females

KEY FACTS

Length: 30-33cm.
Wingspan: 40-42cm.
Weight: 180-220g. **Habitat:** parkland, farmland, orchards, large gardens and other open deciduous or mixed woodland, with open grassy areas for feeding and mature trees for nesting. **Movements:** sedentary. **Population:** spreading in N England and Scotland since 1920s, after fluctuations in range since 19th century; now *c*15 000 pairs breed; rough estimate of 40 000 individuals in mid-winter. **Diet:** mainly ants and their pupae. **Voice:** unlike most other woodpeckers, rarely drums (and then weak and tremulous), but often gives territorial call ('yaffle'), a loud, ringing, slightly descending laugh, 'kleu-kleu-kleu...' (female's version thinner than male's); flight call shrill 'keu-keu- kook'. **Nest:** hole excavated in tree, usually 2-6m above ground, entrance *c*6.5cm diameter. **Eggs:** 5-7, white. **Incubation:** 17-19 days, by both sexes. **Fledging:** 23-27 days. **Broods:** 1. **Maturity:** 1 year. **Confusion species:** female Golden Oriole (*Oriolus oriolus*), rare passage migrant/breeder, also has green upperparts and yellow rump, but much smaller, relatively narrower-winged and longer-tailed, and lacks red crown; also has contrasting dark wings, red bill and very different call.

| J | F | M | A | M | J | J | A | S | O | N | D |

KEY FACTS

Length: 16-17cm.
Wingspan: 25-27cm.
Weight: 30-45g. **Habitat:** breeds in a few places in semi-natural open pine and birch forests in Scotland. **Movements:** summer visitor (Apr-Oct), also passage migrant from N Europe in spring (Apr-May) and, especially, autumn (Aug-Oct); winters in N tropical Africa (a few winter Mediterranean and Middle East). **Population:** formerly quite widespread breeder England and Wales; decline from early 19th century until by 1960 restricted as breeder to Kent, with fewer than 200 pairs; only *c*12 pairs by 1965, and none by 1979; during early 1970s Scandinavian birds colonized several sites in Scottish Highlands, but since 1980 only a few pairs have bred there. **Diet:** chiefly ants, larvae and eggs; also other insects; spiders, woodlice, molluscs and occasionally birds' eggs, frog tadpoles and berries. **Voice:** monotonous, weak, plaintive, nasal or piping 'kyeu-kyeu- kyeu…', similar to calls of Lesser Spotted Woodpecker (p216) or distant small falcon, especially Hobby (pp116-17), and quite similar to one of Nuthatch (p286). **Nest:** natural or artificial hole in tree, wall or bank, or nestbox; does not excavate own nest hole; quite often steals hole from tits or other birds, pulling out nest; uses no lining. **Eggs:** 7-10, white. **Incubation:** 12-14 days, by both sexes. **Fledging:** 18-22 days. **Broods:** 1, sometimes 2. **Maturity:** 1 year. **Confusion species:** with only brief views, could be mistaken for large warbler, especially immature Barred Warbler (p266), but bigger, with different markings and different arrangement of toes (see above left; Warbler has three toes pointing forward, one back).

△ At a distance, resembles long-bodied warbler or other perching bird, in between warbler and thrush in size, with dull grey-brown upperparts and paler underparts. Closer views reveal intricate mottled, barred and streaked pattern of black, brown, rufous, buff and lilac-grey on upperparts, striped head; buff underparts with darker bars, spots and arrowheads. Bill quite short, pointed. Perches across branches and clings to trunk, but does not climb trees like woodpeckers. Feet, however, resemble those of woodpeckers, with two toes pointing forwards and two backwards (unlike feet of perching birds). Elusive, secretive, creeping about unobtrusively and often hard to see because of camouflaged plumage. More likely to be heard than seen: distinctive monotonous calls. Unlike woodpeckers, migratory, wintering in Africa.

threat display

◁ Acquired name from curious habit of twisting and turning head right round when alarmed or if handled, to deter predators. Also twists head, erects crown feathers, stretches body and raises tail feathers when displaying.

▷ Hops clumsily on ground with tail raised; often remains motionless for long periods. Feeds mainly on ants, snapping them up in sharp bill or darting out long, mobile, sticky-tipped tongue to winkle them out of crevices in bark etc.

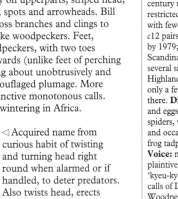

◁ Flight slightly undulating and rather hesitant, flicking wingbeats alternating with long glides on closed wings. Long barred tail with rounded tip distinctive; looks rather like large, long-tailed lark or small thrush in flight.

| J | F | M | A | M | J | J | A | S | O | N | D |

PERCHING BIRDS
Order Passeriformes

This major group includes some 60 per cent of all the world's bird species. Contains over 80 families of land birds, of which representatives of 24 breed and occur regularly in British Isles. All have feet with 4 unwebbed toes, 3 of them directed forwards and 1 rearwards – an adaptation for perching (though some, such as larks, pipits and many buntings, spend much or all of their time on the ground). Live in almost every habitat, from woods and marshes to deserts and from remote mountains to city centres. Size varies greatly, from tiny 9cm-long Goldcrest to 64cm-long raven. In main subgroup popularly known as songbirds (Oscines), only group found here, muscles of syrinx (the avian 'voicebox') highly developed and arranged so that (with a few exceptions) these birds can utter sophisticated songs. Bill shape varies from conical bills of seed-eaters such as finches and thin, pointed bills of insect-eaters such as flycatchers to stouter, general-purpose bills of omnivores, such as many crows. Nest sites varied: e.g. on ground, in reeds, in holes, in forks of tree/shrub branches; nests vary from simple stick or twig platforms to neat lined cups and more complex structures. Many species migratory, making long annual journeys between N Hemisphere and tropics.

House Martin · Skylark · Yellowhammer · Ring Ouzel · Goldcrest · Great Tit · Grey Wagtail · Tree Sparrow · Raven · Brambling

LARKS
Family Alaudidae

Small birds of open habitats, mainly treeless, where they can walk and run freely. Most brown, streaked, with quite short, moderately pointed bills for feeding on small seeds and insects. More stoutly built, thicker-billed and shorter-tailed than similarly plumaged pipits (pp228-31). Many are fine songsters and most sing in the air. Ground nesters. Sexes alike or very similar in almost all species (including all British ones).

● Note: can be tricky to identify; look for shape of bill, presence or absence of crest, presence or absence of white hindwing, plumage pattern of underparts, particularly on breast and shoulders; songs and calls very important identification clues.

SKYLARK *Alauda arvensis*

plumage variations

◁ By far our commonest lark, found in wide variety of open habitats, from farmland and downland to saltmarshes and dunes; indeed, still one of our commonest birds despite major declines. Bigger than sparrow, smaller than Starling, usually looks sturdy and plump-bellied but long-bodied. Upperparts brown, heavily streaked blackish; underparts buff/white with breast boldly streaked blackish. Plumage variable in hue, from greyish to reddish-brown. Longish tail with conspicuous white outer feathers. Rather obscure pale stripe above eye continues round ear coverts, isolating them from neck; short, blunt crest not always visible, but prominent when raised; long, thick-based, pointed bill. Legs yellowish-brown. Walks steadily or shuffles along rather aimlessly with body held low and legs bent. Also runs and hops over obstacles. Often crouches when approached, then suddenly explodes into air.

▽ In remarkable song flight, male ascends into air from ground, climbing vertically to great height, hangs stationary for several minutes on outstretched fluttering wings, then spirals or parachutes down with final headlong plunge to ground. Pours out continuous stream of loud warbling and trilling song throughout ascent and hovering and sometimes also during descent.

△ Distinctive white trailing edge to wings, except in juveniles. In flight, erratic rhythm of alternating bursts of floppy wingbeats and brief glides, or periods with wings almost closed, produces long, shallow, irregular undulations. More fluttering and aimless-looking than other larks, with quite laboured take-off and fluttering hover before landing, though on migration flight more thrush-like. Wings wide, broader at base than tail, leading edge usually angled backwards, hind edge straighter and tip rather square, with splayed feathers; look longer and narrower when fully extended.

juvenile

△ Juvenile distinctive: until late summer, pale edges to feathers of upperparts produce strongly spotted, speckled and scaly appearance; throat almost unstreaked (adult's has fine speckling); chest more spotted than streaked. For some time after fledging, tail shorter than adult's.

KEY FACTS

Length: 18-19cm. **Wingspan:** 30-36cm. **Weight:** 33-45g.
Habitat: very wide range of open habitats, including fields, downs, moors, heaths, dunes, saltmarshes, even rough ground in built-up areas; leaves high ground in winter.
Movements: British/Irish breeders mainly resident, though some move as far as Continent; many passage migrants/winter visitors from NE Europe, Sep-Apr.
Population: drastic decline due to intensive farming practices; *c*2.5 million pairs breed. **Diet:** seeds, grain, leaves and other plant matter, insects and other invertebrates.
Voice: liquid, rippling 'chirr-rr-up' call, especially in flight; also whistled 'tsee' or 'skee-oo' from winter flocks. Song a continuous stream of rapid, high-pitched musical trills and warbles, usually uttered in song flight; occasionally sings from low perch or ground. **Nest:** cup of grass, lined with fine grass or hair, on ground, often built into side of grass tussock.
Eggs: 3-5, white, heavily speckled with greys and browns. **Incubation:** 11-12 days, by female. **Fledging:** 18-20 days. **Broods:** 2, sometimes 3. **Maturity:** 1 year. **Confusion species:** Woodlark (p222) smaller, shorter-tailed, smaller-crested, wings more rounded without white trailing edges, plumper body, tail with white only at corners, pale eyebrows meeting at back of head, and black and white mark at bend of wing; very different calls and song, in different song flight.

| J | F | M | A | M | J | J | A | S | O | N | D |

In autumn and winter, immigrants from N Europe may occur in large flocks, especially on lowland stubble, searching for cereal and weed seeds. These visitors rarely mix with local Skylarks.

WOODLARK *Lullula arborea*

adult

juvenile

93

△ Smaller and stockier than Skylark, with finer, pointed bill and very short tail. More contrasting head pattern, with bold eyebrows, narrow and pale buff in front of eye but whitish behind it and meeting at nape, creating capped appearance; crown feathers can be erected to form small but prominent crest. Variable but usually prominent dark eyestripe extending down rear edge of rusty-buff ear coverts. Distinctive white/black/white patch on edge of closed wing. Upperparts buff, strongly streaked blackish, underparts whitish, with strongly streaked breast. Legs pinkish. Juvenile has strongly scalloped pattern on upperparts, with pale-edged, rounded feathers, and less contrasting face pattern. Unlike Skylark, perches readily on branches of trees and shrubs, even walking along them. Voice distinctive, with sweet, liquid, fluty calls and song, quite different from Skylark's (see also Key Facts).

△ Very distinctive shape in flight, with broad, rounded wings and very short tail. Flight action strongly undulating, recalling Lesser Spotted Woodpecker (p216), jerky and wavering, with wingbeats in very loose bursts and floppy swoops with wings completely closed; buoyant but hesitant action resembles small bat. Lacks Skylark's white trailing edge to wings and has only whitish corners to tail, often obscure. White/black/white at bend of wing very distinctive.

△ Male sings beautiful, rich, mellow song with repeated melodious, descending, yodelling phrases, given in much lower song flight than Skylark's: spiral ascent on fluttering wings, then circles widely before descending.

Eremophila alpestris **SHORELARK**

male winter

male late spring

juvenile

female winter

KEY FACTS

Length: 14-17cm.
Wingspan: 30-35cm.
Weight: 33-45g. **Habitat:**
has bred in Scotland on stony
mountain tops (and does so
regularly in S Europe, N
Africa and Asia; in N Eurasia
breeds on tundra and in N
America in wide variety of
open habitats). **Movements:**
passage migrant/winter visitor
from Scandinavia/Finland
Oct-Apr, especially Oct-Nov,
especially to E coasts,
particularly N Norfolk coast.
Population: a few pairs bred
in Scotland 1973-7. In typical
winter, probably *c*300 birds at
most, but in past good years
up to 1500 birds wintered.
Highest numbers in late
autumn as passage migrants
visit our coasts before moving
on to winter on Continent.
Diet: seeds, insects, some
crustaceans and molluscs on
shorelines/saltmarshes. **Voice:**
weak, piping, pipit-like
'tseeep', clear wagtail-like
'tseep-tseep'; warbling song
like much quieter, more
tinkling version of Skylark's,
often prolonged, usually given
from ground, rarely in high
song flight like Skylark's.
Nest: cup of grass, lined with
fine grass or hair, on ground
in shelter of grass tussock.
Eggs: 4, variable pale colours,
but usually greenish-white,
speckled and lined brown and
black. **Incubation:** 10-14
days, by female. **Fledging:**
12 days. **Broods:** 1 or 2.
Maturity: 1 year.

| J | F | M | A | M | J | J | A | S | O | N | D |

△ Smaller than Skylark, with very distinctive black and yellow
face pattern and bold black crescent-shaped breast band;
duller in winter adults and immatures. Upperparts quite
uniform pinkish-brown, with lengthy mottling rather than
streaking; underparts below breast band whitish, faintly
spotted on chest and tinged dusky-pink on chest sides. Bill
quite stubby, pointed. Male brighter than female, especially in
breeding plumage (only seen here in late spring migrants),
when has tiny black 'horns' extending from sides of black
band across crown. Juvenile darker, blackish and golden-buff
above, with bold whitish spots; breast and flanks also spotted;
only trace of adult's yellow and black face pattern.

*Snow Buntings
in flight*

Shorelarks

Snow Buntings

△ Scarce passage migrant and winter visitor, mainly to
saltmarsh, shingle or along E coasts. Usually in small flocks,
often with Snow Buntings (p313), Lapland Buntings (p314),
Skylarks (pp220-1) or finches. When feeding, constantly walk,
shuffle or hop fast but unobtrusively with mouse-like actions;
can be difficult to see until they suddenly take flight.

winter

female

male

△ Flight more undulating than Skylark's; wingtips and longer
tail narrower. Uppertail blackish with pale pinkish-brown
centre and thin white edges. From below, white body and black
centre to undertail distinctive. Action light, fast wingbeats
alternating with dips on almost completely closed wings; flocks
usually flicker quite low over ground. Quieter voice than other
larks, with shrill but weak, pipit-like or wagtail-like calls.

SWALLOWS AND MARTINS
Family Hirundinidae

Small, highly aerial birds, with light, graceful, aerobatic flight, slim, streamlined bodies, long pointed wings and forked tails. Spend much of time catching flying insects in air; very short, flattened bills have very wide gapes to trap prey. Perch on wires, reeds, roof tiles etc but do not walk well, and usually visit ground only to gather nest material. Most nest colonially on buildings or cliffs, building nests of mud strengthened with grass or straw. Sexes similar or alike. Make long migrations.

● Note: tail shape important (deeply forked in Swallow with long streamers in adults, distinctly, but not deeply, forked in House Martin, and barely forked in Sand Martin); also colour of upperparts, presence/absence of contrasting rump or breast band.

SAND MARTIN *Riparia riparia*

juvenile

adults

KEY FACTS

Length: 12cm. **Wingspan:** 26-29cm. **Weight:** 13-14g. **Habitat:** feeds mainly over rivers, lakes, reservoirs, flooded sand and gravel pits, other fresh waters; breeds in sandy river banks, sand and gravel quarries and earth banks; migrants roost in reedbeds. **Movements:** summer visitor mid Mar-Oct, with stragglers to end Nov, also passage migrant Mar-early May and Aug-Oct; winters Africa in Sahel region on S fringe Sahara. **Population:** dramatic decline since population crashes 1968-9 and 1983-4, due to drought in Sahel winter quarters; c400 000 pairs breed here. **Diet:** insects and spiders caught on the wing. **Voice:** dry, rasping 'chrrrrp' and sharper, shorter 'brrt' of alarm; song a weak, harsh, chattering twitter. **Nest:** colonial; in tunnel, excavated by birds in sand/soil bank or cliff; nest cup, made of feathers, leaves, grass etc, in chamber at end of tunnel. **Eggs:** 4-5, white. **Incubation:** 14 days, by both sexes. **Fledging:** 19 days. **Broods:** 2. **Maturity:** 1 year. **Confusion species:** House Martin (opposite) slightly bigger, with conspicuous white rump, blackish, not brown, upperparts, and no breast band.

| J | F | M | A | M | J | J | A | S | O | N | D |

△ Smaller and slenderer than House Martin and Swallow. Distinctive plumage, with sandy-brown upperparts and white underparts bisected by brown breast band. Juvenile has pale fringes to wing covert and rump feathers, giving brighter appearance, and buff tinge to throat. One of our earliest summer visitors. Perches on wires, and on vegetation on soft banks and cliffs where it nests in burrows which it excavates; sometimes settles on ground to drink or bathe. Always gregarious, in noisy, twittering flocks.

◁ Looks more delicate in air than Swallow or House Martin; flight action similar to latter's but slightly weaker and more fluttering, with jerky, flicking beats of long, more angled wings; tail quite short and, unlike House Martin and Swallow, barely forked; no white rump. Feeds mainly over fresh waters.

▷ Migrants roost from dusk in large flocks in dense reedbeds, often in company with Swallows.

Swallow

Sand Martins

Delichon urbica **HOUSE MARTIN**

3

KEY FACTS

Length: 12.5cm. **Wingspan:** 26-29cm. **Weight:** 15-21g. **Habitat:** feeds over wide variety of open and semi-open habitats, often around houses and over lakes and other fresh waters; breeds mainly under eaves of houses etc or other artificial structures, such as bridges; a few still choose natural nest sites under overhangs in cliffs. **Movements:** summer visitor Apr-mid Oct (stragglers to Dec), also passage migrant (early Apr-mid May and late Aug-Nov); winters Africa. **Population:** 320 000- 640 000 pairs breed here. **Diet:** almost entirely insects caught in flight. **Voice:** clear, hard, chattering 'prrrit', 'tchirrip' or 'tchitchirrip'; shrill 'tseep' of alarm; song a weak, soft, sweet, melodious chirruping twitter, based on calls, less varied, less often heard, than Swallow's. **Nest:** colonial; dome of mud pellets mixed with a little dried grass and lined with feathers and fine plant material collected in air, closed except for small entrance hole at top, and built onto eaves of house, occasionally elsewhere. **Eggs:** 4-5, white. **Incubation:** 14-16 days, by both sexes. **Fledging:** 22-32 days. **Broods:** 2 or 3. **Maturity:** 1 year. **Confusion species:** Sand Martin (opposite) slightly smaller, lacks white rump; has brown (not blackish) upperparts, and brown breast band.

J F M A M J J A S O N D

△ Smaller than Swallow, more compact and plump-bodied than Swallow or House Martin; looks black and white at a distance, though closer view in good light reveals upperparts actually blue-black except for brownish-black wings and tail. Most distinctive identification feature striking white rump. White underparts tinged buff in autumn. Unlike Sand Martin or Swallow, short legs and feet neatly clothed in white feathers. Wings broad at base, tail moderately but distinctly forked. Often flies high, frequently circling, with flickering beats of stiff, almost triangular wings interspersed with flat glides. Often feeds over fresh waters. Gregarious. Roosts in trees, or possibly in nests or even on the wing, but rarely with Swallows or Sand Martins in reedbeds. More likely to be seen in urban areas than Swallow or Sand Martin.

△ To build a nest, a pair must collect some 2500 separate tiny pellets of mud, gathering it in their bills from puddles etc. During periods of drought, nest-building may be delayed.

◁ Distinctive, cup-shaped nests adorn the eaves of houses, usually in colonies. Old nests may be patched up and reused, and artificial nests may tempt birds to colonize a house. Fledglings of earlier broods often help feed later arrivals.

▽ House Martins are fond of sunning themselves on roofs; also frequently perch on wires, where they feed fledged young (also fed on the wing). Juveniles browner above, with brownish-grey wash to underparts.

SWALLOW *Hirundo rustica*

KEY FACTS

Length: 17-19cm, including elongated tail streamers (2-7cm). **Wingspan:** 32-35cm. **Weight:** 16-25g. **Habitat:** feeds over wide variety of open and semi-open habitats; breeds in open habitats with buildings for nesting (except for most remote islands and high mountains), especially in mixed, traditional farmland, around villages and suburbs, on moorland, marshes etc; often feeds over fresh waters. **Movements:** summer visitor, late Mar-Oct (stragglers to Dec) and passage migrant (late Mar-mid May and Aug-Oct); winters Africa (British breeders mainly in S Africa). **Population:** c820 000 pairs breed here. **Diet:** flying insects, especially bluebottles, horseflies, robberflies, hoverflies and other large flies. **Voice:** sharp 'tswit tswit', 'vit-vit-vit-vit' or 'tsee-tsewit', running into a rapid twitter when excited; song much more prolonged, mixture of melodious rapid twittering and warbling notes. **Nest:** untidy open cup of mud pellets and dry grass or straw, lined with feathers, on rafter or ledge in cowshed, stable, barn, garden shed, porch, garage, other outbuilding; sometimes under bridges, in culverts, chimney stacks, wells, mineshafts; occasionally in kettles, hats etc; or during drought when no mud available, in old nests of other birds; very few still nest in caves and trees. Often breed in loose groups, with nests a few metres apart. **Eggs:** 4-6, white, speckled dark reddish. **Incubation:** 14-16 days, by female. **Fledging:** 17-24 days. **Broods:** 2, sometimes 3. **Maturity:** 1 year. **Confusion species:** related House Martin (p225) and Sand Martin (p224) and completely unrelated Swift (p213); see right for comparison.

△ Easily distinguished by combination of metallic blue-black upperparts, rich deep red patches on forehead and throat and whitish to pinkish-buff or darker orange-pink underparts, with very long spiky streamers on deeply forked tail, unlike any other small British bird. Frequently fly just above ground or water, especially when feeding. Fast, very agile though relaxed flight, with graceful, easy swooping action; regular, fluid, rowing beats of long, swept-back wings alternate with glides, purposeful and direct or with frequent changes in direction. Long tails give them great manoeuvrability when flying low or avoiding farm buildings, grazing animals and other obstacles.

adult males

adult female

juvenile

△ As with martins, Swallows regularly perch crossways on overhead wires, TV aerials, thin branches etc. They also squat on roofs and visit ground to collect mud pellets and dried grass or straw for nest building. Usually, males have longer tails than females, but there is some overlap; also, underparts of females generally paler than those of males, with less shiny, more mottled, breast band. Juveniles have only very short tail streamers, shorter than those of extreme female, and are duller, with pale orange or pinkish-buff forehead patch and throat.

| J | F | M | A | M | J | J | A | S | O | N | D |

△ Less urban than House Martin, particularly favouring farms with old barns, stables etc for nesting, and traditionally reared herds of livestock, ensuring healthy population of flies, their main food. Modern concrete and steel buildings, intensive animal rearing, improved farm hygiene and pesticides all contribute to declining numbers. Typically nest on rafter or ledge in cowshed or other outbuilding, or porch, flying in and out through gap in door or half-open window. Female does most of nest building while male mainly brings materials. Nest may be used for several years in succession, birds navigating back from Africa each spring to exactly same spot. Though often gregarious when feeding and especially when roosting on migration, Swallows nest separately, though up to 5 nests often quite closely though loosely grouped together.

Familiar sight in autumn, from September onwards: large numbers of Swallows gathering together in restless, twittering groups on overhead wires, prior to journeys to the coast where they will embark on first leg of long migration to Africa. British breeders winter mainly in E and S parts of South Africa, together with Swallows from Russia and central Europe.

△ At night, migrants roost in reedbeds, often along with Sand Martins; some of the autumn roosts hold thousands of birds. Here they face danger in the form of predatory Hobbies and Sparrowhawks. They may respond to this threat by uttering loud alarm calls and even flying up and diving at the bird of prey. Small groups of migrating birds may be seen following coastlines and heading out to sea; the following spring they can be welcomed again as they make their way inshore.

Swifts

House Martins

Sand Martins

Swallows

◁ Could be confused with martins and Swift, especially at distance. House Martin has bold white rump; Sand Martin brown above with brown breast band; both smaller than Swallow, with white, not buff, underparts, no red on throat and forehead, much shorter forked tails without streamers and less swooping, more flitting flight, often higher (especially House Martin). Swift looks uniformly dark, with long scythe-shaped wings and different flight action, with series of rapid wingbeats alternating with long glides.

PIPITS AND WAGTAILS
Family Motacillidae

Small, mainly ground-dwelling birds, with slender bills and longish, slender legs; spend much time walking or running on ground, though some perch in trees, shrubs etc. Pipits brown or brownish, streaked, paler beneath; they wag their tails, which have white or pale outer feathers, up and down. Sexes look identical. Nest on ground. Wagtails larger, slimmer, with much longer tails which they wag more conspicuously; much brighter and more boldly patterned; sexes similar; most nest in walls, banks etc.

TREE PIPIT *Anthus trivialis*

94

KEY FACTS

Length: 15cm. **Wingspan:** 25-27cm. **Weight:** 20-25g. **Habitat:** needs trees for song posts and open ground for feeding. In S and E, in young conifer plantations, woodland clearings, coppice, heath/scrub with scattered trees. In N and W, in open sessile oak, birch and old native pine woodland. **Movements:** summer visitor, Apr-early Oct, winters tropical Africa. Passage migrants from N Europe, mainly Aug-Oct. **Population:** *c*120 000 pairs breed. **Diet:** mainly insects and larvae; some small seeds in autumn/winter. **Voice:** hoarse, buzzing 'bizzt', thinner 'zeep'. Song louder, fuller than Meadow Pipit's, ending with distinctive loud 'seea, seea, seea'. **Nest:** cup of grass, with hair in lining, on ground, hidden in bank or grass tussock. **Eggs:** 4-6, bluish, pinkish or greenish, with dark markings. **Incubation:** 13-14 days, by female. **Fledging:** 12-13 days. **Broods:** 1, sometimes 2. **Maturity:** 1 year. **Confusion species:** Meadow Pipit (opposite).

| J | F | M | A | M | J | J | A | S | O | N | D |

Summer visitor and passage migrant only. Best distinguished from very similar Meadow Pipit by calls and song. Unlike Meadow, restricted as breeder to habitats with scattered trees and shrubs. Slightly larger, more elegant, sleeker than Meadow, with slimmer rear body exaggerating longer tail; slightly longer, stouter bill. More erect walk/run, not shuffling like Meadow; wags tail gently. Feeds on ground but, when disturbed, tends to fly up and perch on outer branches of tree/shrub. Not gregarious like Meadow.

adult

juvenile

△ Flight less jerky, more purposeful than Meadow's, with less erratic wingbeats and more bounding action; has slightly longer, more pointed wings and longer tail; white outer tail feathers, as in Meadow.

△ Upperparts olive to buff-brown, streaked darker, less strongly than in Meadow; bolder, neater streaks on breast, fewer, finer streaks on flanks. Face pattern usually bolder: conspicuous, pale yellowish eyebrow, creamy eyering, thin dark stripe between bill and eye, bolder dark stripe behind eye. Usually has yellower or more orange-buff breast and pale pinkish legs, but juvenile Meadow can show these features, too. Often has prominent black/white pattern formed by median coverts near bend of wing. Juvenile browner above, with bolder blackish streaks, less yellowish breast, less streaked flanks.

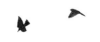

△ Distinctive song usually given in parachuting descent after initial silent ascent, usually starting or finishing from tree or shrub.

grey adult *buff adult*

KEY FACTS

Length: 14.5cm. **Wingspan:** 22-25cm. **Weight:** 16-25g. **Habitat:** breeds on moors and upland farmland, rough meadows, downs, heaths, bogs, fens, saltmarshes, dunes. Winters mainly in lowlands, from fields and urban parks to marshes and coasts. **Movements:** many N breeders migrate S to winter in S and SW England and Ireland and as far S as Spain. Passage migrants from Iceland/ N Europe arrive autumn (from mid-Aug) and some winter here. **Population:** *c*2.8 million pairs breed. **Diet:** mainly insects and larvae; some small seeds in autumn/winter. **Voice:** when flying off, repeated, sharp, rather weak 'peest' or 'tseep' calls, usually repeated; also in flight, thin chirping 'tyit' and coarse 'chut-ut-ut-ut'; alarm call a persistent 'stit-it'. Song simpler, more mechanical than Tree's, usually quiet at first, then accelerating into a trill, given in parachuting song flight. **Nest:** cup of grass, on ground, hidden in grass tussock. **Eggs:** 4-5, white, heavily spotted grey and brown. **Incubation:** 13-14 days, by female. **Fledging:** 13-14 days. **Broods:** usually 2. **Maturity:** 1 year. **Confusion species:** Tree Pipit (opposite) very similar; best distinguished by less strongly streaked flanks and different calls and song.

△ On moorlands and other uplands, generally most abundant bird in summer, constantly fluttering erratically into air with repeated, thin, squeaky 'peest peest' calls. Also common in open lowland habitats in winter. Smaller, weaker-looking than Tree Pipit, with plump breast and belly, slightly finer bill and shorter tail. Has distinctive, shuffling, mouse-like gait; twitches tail, but less often than Tree Pipit. Mostly seen on ground and on rocks, but migrants in particular will perch in trees. Plumage variable: upperparts greyish to olive-buff, underparts pale grey or buff to yellowish. Mantle and rump more strongly streaked than Tree's and dark/light bar near bend of wing less prominent; streaks on breast smaller, denser, more untidy; flanks, especially, more strongly streaked. Legs darker, browner, than Tree's; longer rear claw visible only at close range. Face pattern less prominent than Tree's. Outside breeding season, more gregarious than Tree.

▷ Juvenile darker above with bolder streaks than adult, and often much yellower below ; legs often pinkish; more easily confused with Tree Pipit than adult.

juvenile

◁ Weak-looking in flight, as if struggling to maintain height, with erratic wingbeats and distinctive, jerky, rising and falling action. Often ascends high in air. Less pointed wings and shorter tail than Tree's; shares latter's white outer tail feathers.

▽ Song flight both starts from and returns to ground; bird sings during both initial fluttering ascent and parachuting descent; sometimes also sings from bush, post or boulder.

J F M A M J J A S O N D

ROCK PIPIT *Anthus petrosus*

race petrosus

adults summer

238

△ Larger, bulkier, more upright than Meadow Pipit, with darker, duller, more obscurely streaked plumage, fuller tail with grey, not white, outer feathers, heavier, mainly blackish bill and longer, much darker legs. Rarely occurs far from rocky shores, typically clambering confidently over rocks, searching seaweed for food, flying up to cliffs; flicks tail. Often hard to see against background. Usually in pairs or small flocks.

▷ British race *petrosus* has dark olive-brown upperparts, indistinct, often broken pale eyebrow and eyering, dull buffy wingbars and dingy buff underparts with large, dense brown streaks on breast and flanks. Juvenile browner, more mottled, above, with clearer brown streak bordering throat. In winter, darker overall, duskier upperparts contrasting less with buffer underparts.

juvenile

adult winter

race petrosus

race littoralis

adult spring

◁ Scandinavian race *littoralis* distinguishable only in spring, when many have prominent pale eyebrow, greyer upperparts and paler, plainer underparts, with creamy or pinkish tinge; some strongly streaked but others with almost unstreaked breast, which, with blue-grey tinge to head, makes them look like Water Pipit; unlike latter, have creamy or buff outer tail feathers, with only tips whitish.

▷ Flight much more confident than Meadow's: more frequent, fuller, stronger wingbeats; often ends with long, curving sweep to land among rocks or seaweed.

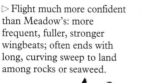

race petrosus

◁ Song flight quite similar to Meadow Pipit's, but with slower 'parachuting' descent, usually starting and ending on rock or cliff edge.

KEY FACTS

Length: 16.5cm. **Wingspan:** 22.5-28cm. **Weight:** 20-30g. **Habitat:** breeds on rocky coasts; on passage and in winter also on other types of coast, saltmarshes; a few on rivers and at inland reservoirs. **Movements:** British breeders (race *petrosus*) largely resident, though some disperse to coasts where do not breed; Scandinavian race *littoralis* passage migrant and winter visitor, mainly to E and S coasts England. **Population:** *c*46 500 pairs breed; *c*100 000 birds winter here. **Diet:** mainly insects and larvae, sandhoppers, other small crustaceans, small molluscs etc; also some small seeds. **Voice:** strong, loud, shrill 'feest' or 'pseep', usually given singly (unlike Meadow Pipit's most frequent, thinner call). Song, given in descending song flight, like Meadow's but louder, less tuneful, more regular, with stronger trill. **Nest:** cup of grass, lined with hair, in sheltered rock crevice. **Eggs:** 4-5, whitish, spotted grey and brown. **Incubation:** 14 days, by female. **Fledging:** 16 days. **Broods:** 1, often 2. **Maturity:** 1 year. **Confusion species:** Water Pipit (see opposite and above left). Tree and Meadow Pipits (pp228-9) smaller, paler, browner, shorter-billed, with paler legs and white, not grey, outer tail feathers; different calls and song.

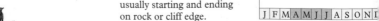

J F M A M J J A S O N I

Anthus spinoletta **WATER PIPIT**

Water Pipit

Rock Pipit race petrosus

winter

△ Passage migrant/winter visitor mainly to freshwater habitats. In winter, very similar to much more common, resident and almost entirely coastal Rock, but has paler, greyer (not olive) upperparts, more prominent, whitish wingbar, whiter underparts with deeper bib and streaking confined chiefly to breast, and bold pale eyebrow. Legs usually dark brown.

Water Pipit spring

◁ Striking appearance in spring, with bluish-grey head, generally prominent pale eyestripe and paler, faded version of winter upperparts; underparts virtually unstreaked except for breast sides and flanks; breast has peachy tinge. Legs blackish.

KEY FACTS

Length: 17cm. **Wingspan:** 22.5-28cm. **Weight:** 20-36g. **Habitat:** on passage and in winter, by watercress beds, lakes, reservoirs, freshwater marshes; breeds in Alps and other mountains of C and S Europe. **Movements:** passage migrant and winter visitor Oct-Apr. **Population:** usually *c*100 per year. **Diet:** mainly insects, larvae, other invertebrates. **Voice:** short, sharp 'fist', thinner than call of Rock Pipit; short 'drrt'. **Maturity:** 1 year. **Confusion species:** Scandinavian race of Rock Pipit similar, especially in spring (see opposite).

| J | F | M | A | M | J | J | A | S | O | N | D |

▷ Has whiter wingbars than Rock, almost white, not brown, underwing coverts, and white outer tail feathers. Generally shy, flying off high and far when some distance away. Usually solitary in winter; may occur in small groups in spring.

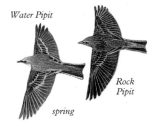

Water Pipit

Rock Pipit

spring

◁ **Richard's Pipit** (*Anthus novaeseelandiae*) regular but rare passage migrant from Siberia (mainly mid Sep-Nov), chiefly to E, S and W coasts Britain. Much larger (18cm) than common pipits, with almost thrush-like appearance; long stout bill, long, sturdy yellowish-pink legs and feet with long hind claws, bold dark streaks on upperparts, prominent, broad pale eyebrow, pale, unmarked area between bill and eye, and wide black stripes down sides of throat. Underparts gingery-buff, with sparsely streaked breast band. White outer feathers on dark tail. Loud, rasping call. Juvenile has bolder blackish/buff pattern on back, and paler but more strongly streaked breast.

Richard's Pipit

▷ **Tawny Pipit** (*Anthus campestris*) regular but rare passage migrant (mainly May and late Aug-Sep), mostly S and SE coasts Britain. Large (16.5cm), but slimmer, more wagtail-like than Richard's, with smaller, slimmer bill and slightly shorter, thinner, yellower legs, with very long, curved hind claws. Adults easily distinguished, with pale, sandy, faintly streaked upperparts, prominent row of dark spots on median coverts near bend of wing; underparts creamy, almost unstreaked. Juvenile has scalloped back, spotted breast/flanks; dark line from bill to eye, and darker ear coverts than Richard's.

Tawny Pipit

PIED/WHITE WAGTAIL *Motacilla alba*

Pied Wagtails summer

male　*female*

△ Pied (race *yarrellii*) commonest wagtail here, abundant breeder and resident, in wide variety of open habitats, from farmland to urban car parks. Very distinctive: boldly pied plumage and long tail, almost constantly wagged up and down; head moves back and forth, especially when walking. Loud flight calls often draw attention to its presence. Chases after flying insects with agile, high-stepping, trotting walk or run, including frequent stops and starts, or short fluttering flights; also hops and leaps. Male in breeding season has rear crown, upperparts, throat and breast black; most of underparts, forecrown and sides of face white; flanks dusky; black wings with white edges to feathers; black tail with white outer feathers; thin black bill and black legs. Female in breeding season has back dark grey (sometimes tinged olive), not black, and black of hind crown and breast less extensive.

Pied Wagtails winter

male

female

△ Male in winter plumage has mottled black forehead and partly grey crown, black of throat replaced with white, resulting in narrower, crescent-shaped black bib on breast; back greyer than in breeding plumage, but still with very little contrast between back and head; rump remains solid black. Winter female as male, but entire crown grey, white of face takes on dusky (sometimes olive-tinged) mottling, and back has more grey feathers, though still with little overall contrast between colour of back and head.

KEY FACTS

Length: 18cm. **Wingspan:** 25-30cm. **Weight:** 19-27g. **Habitat:** wide range of open habitats, from city parks to farmland, often near water. **Movements:** N breeders move S to winter in C and S England, France, Spain and Morocco. White Wagtail, race *alba*, passage migrant from Iceland/Scandinavia Mar-May, Aug-Oct. **Population:** *c*430 000 pairs of Pied breed here; perhaps over 1 million birds winter; White Wagtail breeds rarely mainland Britain, quite often Shetland, regularly Channel Islands. **Diet:** chiefly insects and larvae (especially flies) and other invertebrates, some small seeds. **Voice:** emphatic, shrill 'tchizzick' (more like 'pe-vit' in race *alba*) in flight, liquid 'shirree', abrupt 'tchik' or 'tslee-vit'; song infrequent, often quiet, simple twittering warble, incorporating variants of calls. **Nest:** bulky cup of grass and moss lined with hair and feathers, in hole or crevice in wall, bank or bridge, among ivy, in sheds and other outbuildings. **Eggs:** 5-6, pale grey with dark speckles. **Incubation:** 13-14 days, by female. **Fledging:** 14-16 days. **Broods:** 2-3. **Maturity:** 1 year. **Confusion species:** immature birds, particularly those with strong yellowish tinge to white of face or underparts, could be mistaken for immature Grey or Yellow Wagtail (pp234-5), or even spring Water Pipit (p231). Grey distinguished by intense yellow undertail. Yellow has smaller black bib, buffer upperparts, yellower underparts.

| J | F | M | A | M | J | J | A | S | O | N | D |

△ Outside breeding season, Pied Wagtails roost together, often in large numbers. Small flocks may be seen flying overhead at dusk, en route to communal roost, often in reedbed or dense thicket of bushes or small trees. In some areas, the wagtails have taken to roosting on ledge or roof of city building or on cross beams inside large commercial glasshouses; do not seem bothered by noise or bright lights. Generally assemble first in nearby tree, roof, fence, roadside or other suitable gathering place, calling to one another noisily.

Pied Wagtail juvenile

Pied Wagtail female 1st-winter

male spring

White Wagtails

female spring

White Wagtail female 1st-winter

△ Juvenile Pied Wagtails have brownish-grey or olive-grey crown, upperparts, breast sides and flanks and an untidy narrow blackish stripe running down from chin to a broader, smudged blackish breast band; white areas of plumage, especially cheeks and throat, have buff or sometimes yellowish tinge, which may remain into winter. Rump of juvenile generally looks darker grey than on White Wagtail (see below), but back may be almost as pale, and immature birds of the two races can be very difficult to distinguish until September, when most young Pieds have at least some black on crown, unlike immature Whites, which have all-grey crowns (except for some males). Grey areas on Whites look brighter, cleaner than on Pieds. In spring, some 1st-year female Pieds may have upperparts almost as pale as, but duller than, Whites but, in Pied, grey replaced by black on rump.

White Wagtail (race *alba*), breeding across rest of Europe, regular passage migrant and rare breeder (sometimes hybridizes with Pied). Breeding male has pure, pale grey back/rump, sharply demarcated from black of rear crown/nape and tail. Otherwise resembles Pied, but browner on wings and much paler on flanks (sooty-black in male Pied). Female like male, but back/rump duskier grey, flanks duskier, blackish mottling on forehead, white mottling on chin; often some grey feathers in black crown, so that demarcation between crown and back not as sharp.

▷ Most White Wagtails seen here on passage in autumn have already moulted into winter plumage. Males have partly grey crowns with mottled black foreheads, and white chin and throat leaving black crescent-shaped breast band, as in winter Pied. Lack the white line between bib and flanks which male Pied has. Winter White females may have all-grey crowns with little or no black.

male winter

White Wagtails

female winter

Pied Wagtail male summer

White Wagtails males summer

◁ Flight direct, with dramatic bounding action, rising and falling with alternating brief bursts of fast wingbeats and long downward swoops. Looks deeper-chested than other wagtails.

GREY WAGTAIL *Motacilla cinerea*

161

male   *female*

summer

△ Seldom ventures far from water. Has most slender, tapering shape of wagtails, with longest tail, often fanned and almost constantly and energetically quivered up and down, especially when landing after one of frequent sallies into air after insects. Perches on overhanging trees. Unlike Yellow, not gregarious; usually singly or in pairs. Mainly blue-grey above and yellow below, with narrow white eyebrow, mainly black wings, yellowish-green rump and black tail with white outer feathers. Legs pinkish or pale brown. Male summer has black chin and throat separated from white-flecked grey cheeks by white stripe, and bright yellow underparts. Female summer has white throat, sometimes with some black and yellow mottling, cheeks tinged greenish and paler, duller breast.

male   *female*

winter

△ In winter, male loses black throat, and yellow breast becomes duller, more buff; female's underparts vary from pale yellow to pale buff or peachy; both retain bright yellow on undertail coverts and have buff tinge to eyebrow and throat.

juvenile   *1st-winter*

△ Juvenile similar to winter female, but olive-brown tinge to upperparts, duller, more buff face markings and chest, greyish mottling on breast sides, grey flanks, buff-tinged rump and 2 narrow buff bars on wings, visible at close range. 1st-winter as adult female, except for duller chest.

△ In flight, looks very slim and streamlined; rises rapidly, then shoots off in series of long, shallow bounds, with tail whipping up and down. Single broad white wingbar (Yellow and Pied have 2 narrower wingbars).

KEY FACTS

Length: 18-19cm.
Wingspan: 25-27cm.
Weight: 15-23g. **Habitat:** fast-flowing upland streams, rivers, also by weirs, millstreams, waterfalls, canal locks etc; in winter briefly on puddles on roofs, in car parks etc, also by reservoirs, lakes, slower-flowing waters, coastal marshes. **Movements:** some N breeders leave uplands to winter in lowlands and in S; passage migrants, including birds from Continent, Mar-Apr, Aug-Oct.
Population: c56 000 pairs breed here. **Diet:** mainly insects and larvae, also small crustaceans, molluscs and other invertebrates. **Voice:** sharp 'tzit' or 'tziz-eet', more metallic, emphatic, higher-pitched and clearer than similar calls of Pied Wagtail; song infrequent, louder, more trilling warble. **Nest:** cup of grass, small roots and twigs, often moss, lined with hair, or ledges and in holes and crevices in walls, banks and bridges near water. **Eggs:** 4-6, buff with greyish-brown spots. **Incubation:** 13-14 days, by female. **Fledging:** 12 days. **Broods:** usually 2. **Maturity:** 1 year. **Confusion species:** Yellow Wagtail (opposite) shorter-tailed, with greenish, not blue-grey, upperparts, less intense yellow underparts (though juvenile Grey Wagtails may have yellow only under tail), black legs and different voice.

J F M A M J J A S O N

127

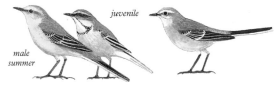

juvenile

male summer

△ Summer visitor/passage migrant only, mainly to grassland with fresh water. Smallest wagtail, graceful, with tapering rear end to body and medium-length tail, wagged constantly but less dramatically than other wagtails. Slender black legs. Greenish upperparts and yellow underparts; wings blackish with 2 narrow white wingbars; tail black with white outer feathers. Male of British race *flavissima* has bright yellow eyebrow and underparts, yellowish-green crown, cheeks and back. Female duller, browner-green above, and buff-yellow below. Juvenile even duller, buff above, pale buff-yellow below, with pale buff cheeks surrounded by blackish bib.

KEY FACTS

Length: 17cm. **Wingspan:** 23-27cm. **Weight:** 16-22g. **Habitat:** breeds mainly in water meadows, damp pastures grazed by cattle, also marshes, margins of lakes, gravel pits etc, boggy moors, damp heaths; passage migrants more widespread, including coastal marshes. **Movements:** race breeding here (*flavissima*) is summer visitor (Mar-mid Oct), wintering in Africa; also passage migrant (late Mar-Jun, Aug-mid Oct), along with Continental races, chiefly 'Blue-headed', *flava*, from S Scandinavia and NW Europe (see bottom right). **Population:** *c*50 000 pairs breed England and Wales; only a few pairs in Scotland and Ireland. **Diet:** mainly insects and larvae, also some other small invertebrates. **Voice:** most common call is loud, musical but quite shrill 'tsweep' or 'tswi-weep', also clear, ringing 'see-see-see' and brief 'pseet'. Song a simple, brief repetition of chirping notes, e.g. 'tsip-tsip-tsipsi'. **Nest:** cup of grass, lined with hair, on ground, hidden among vegetation. **Eggs:** 5-6, buff, with darker spots. **Incubation:** 13 days, by female. **Fledging:** 13 days. **Broods:** usually 2. **Maturity:** 1 year. **Confusion species:** Grey Wagtail (opposite). Juveniles look rather like juvenile Pied/White Wagtail (pp232-3) and adult summer Water Pipit (p231).

▷ Often associates with cattle, feeding on insects disturbed by them. Gregarious; often in bustling flocks, darting about and fluttering up after flies. In winter plumage, after moult Aug-Sep, crown, cheeks and upperparts browner, eyebrow and throat tinged buff, chest buff and flanks greener; females duller than males.

males summer

◁ Looks less elongated, shorter-tailed in flight than other wagtails, more like longer-tailed pipits. Flight bounding but not as 'shooting' as Grey or Pied; fans tail on landing.

▽ Various races from Europe and beyond occur on passage (see also Key Facts). Breeding males readily identifiable; non-breeding males, females and immatures indistinguishable, except for male and female 'Blue-headed' and 'Black-headed'. Most regular is 'Blue-headed': male has blue-grey crown and darker bluish cheeks, white eyebrows and throat; female has browner crown and cheeks, buff or yellow tinged eyebrows and throat. Few 'Grey-headed' on passage most years; dark grey crown, blackish cheeks, no eyebrows.

'Yellow'
flavissima
male

'Yellow'
flavissima *female*

'Blue-headed'
flava *male*

'Black-headed'
feldegg *male*

'Grey-headed'
thunbergi
male

WAXWINGS
Family Bombycillidae

This family contains 8 species, 3 of which – the plump, crested, short-tailed, Starling-sized waxwings – breed in forests of N Eurasia and N America. Only 1 waxwing species occurs here, as an erratic winter visitor, especially when its staple winter diet of berries fails in its northern homelands. Sexes very similar.

WAXWING *Bombycilla garrulus*

male   *female*   *male*

△ Exotic-looking, generally scarce winter visitors, usually seen in small flocks feeding acrobatically on berries. Also perch on aerials/wires. Tame, allowing close views. Mainly pale pinkish-brown, with striking swept-back crest, black bib and eyepatch separated by narrow white moustache streak on 'foxy' face, colourful yellow and red markings on wings, grey rump, cinnamon undertail coverts and short, yellow-tipped tail. Upperparts darker than underparts. Males tend to have larger, more clear-cut black bib and brighter, more complete, yellow and white V-shaped tips to primary wing feathers, more numerous and larger red waxy tips to secondary wing feathers, and brighter, broader yellow tail-band than females.

▷ Immatures duller, especially on wings. Juveniles have distinctly shorter crests, no black bib, buff-streaked underparts; waxy red tips to secondaries smaller or absent; only outer edges of primaries tipped with paler yellow, and narrower, paler yellow tail-band (especially in young females).

juvenile

male
1st-winter

▽ Flight strong, undulating; triangular wings and very short tail. Silhouette very like Starling, but action faster, more graceful. Clear view from above in good light shows distinctive grey rump; unlike Starling's, underwing coverts greyish.

Waxwings   *Starlings*

KEY FACTS

Length: 18cm. **Wingspan:** 32-35.5cm. **Weight:** 45-70g. **Habitat:** in winter in Britain, anywhere with berry-bearing shrubs or trees, from rural hedgerows to city parks; often in suburban gardens. Breeds in remote coniferous forests of N Scandinavia and Russia. **Movements:** irregular winter visitor from N Scandinavian/ Russian breeding grounds, chiefly to E fringes of Britain, especially NE, and smaller concentrations in W Midlands suburbs. In invasion years, much more widespread, reaching W Britain and even Ireland. **Population:** probably up to 100 birds winter most years; in invasion years, may be several thousand. **Diet:** in winter, mainly berries of a variety of trees and shrubs, especially rowan; also some insects caught in flight (exclusive diet in breeding season). **Voice:** usually silent, but may utter high, trilling, 'tzreeee' calls. **Maturity:** probably 1 year. **Confusion species:** distant flying birds could be mistaken for Starlings (see left and p297).

| J | F | M | A | M | J | J | A | S | O | N | D |

DIPPERS
Family Cinclidae

Small, plump, short-tailed, short-winged, stout-legged/strong-clawed birds found in Eurasia and the Americas, mainly along fast-flowing streams. Unique among perching birds in diving, and walking underwater to feed. Swim well, despite having unwebbed feet, by 'flying' underwater. Build domed nests. Sexes identical. Only 1 species found here.

162

race gularis

race cinclus

race hibernicus

KEY FACTS

Length: 18cm. **Wingspan:** 25.5-30cm. **Weight:** 55-75g. **Habitat:** mainly fast-flowing upland streams; in winter, some on lowland rivers etc; in severe weather, a few on coasts. **Movements:** British race *gularis* and Irish and W Scottish race *hibernicus* sedentary, apart from hard weather movements; a few Continental birds, mainly N European race *cinclus*, on E coasts/S England in winter. **Population:** *c*8750-26 000 pairs breed; recent decline due to acidification of streams, as result of conifer plantation and acid rain, and to water pollution. **Diet:** aquatic invertebrates, especially mayfly, stonefly, caddisfly larvae; also some small fish, crustaceans, molluscs, especially in winter. **Voice:** repeated short, piercing, rasping 'zit', loud, metallic 'chink' calls; song very loud, disjointed mixture of liquid warbling and high, explosive, grating notes; sings almost all year. **Nest:** bulky domed structure of moss and grass, lined with leaves, in crevice under overhanging bank or in bridge, among tree roots or behind waterfall. **Eggs:** 4-6, white. **Incubation:** 16 days, by female. **Fledging:** 19-25 days. **Broods:** usually 2. **Maturity:** 1 year.

△ Always associated with water, typically fast-flowing upland streams and rivers, usually on boulders and stones or actually in water. Rotund, with hunched head, sloping back, short wings, short tail (sometimes cocked), sturdy legs and feet; resembles giant wren in shape. Looks pied at distance, with dazzling white chin, throat, foreneck and breast; closer view reveals head and rear underparts dark brown, while upperparts have dark slate-grey tinge. Frequently bobs and curtseys entire body, as if on springs, flicks tail downwards, and blinks, showing striking white eyelids. British race *gularis* has chestnut band on belly, between white of breast and dark rear underparts. Continental race *cinclus*, scarce winter visitor, has belly as well as rear underparts blackish-brown, with only trace of chestnut tinge at most; Irish and W Scottish race *hibernicus* darker above, with a narrower, duller belly band.

Walks, leaps or even flies into water to search for food; swims or submerges, flicking wings to propel it upstream forwards and downwards; walks along stream bed, holding on and avoiding being swept away in currents using its strong feet and claws. Pops up again like a cork with prey to eat it on boulder, though deals with small items underwater.

◁ Juvenile has slate-grey upperparts, with scaly whitish markings on wings; underparts dirty white, with grey crescents.

J F M A M J J A S O N D

▷ Flies fast and low over water, with rapid whirring beats of short wings, often uttering loud 'chink' calls. Flight direct along straight stretches of stream, but swerves round bends or over boulders. Highly territorial, defending stretch of stream as pairs when breeding, but often as individuals in winter.

WRENS
Family Troglodytidae

Small, slender-billed insect-eaters, mostly plump with very short, often cocked, tails, short wings and sturdy, strong-clawed legs; feed near ground and move deftly through dense undergrowth. Only 1 species found here. Build domed nests. Sexes alike or similar.

WREN *Troglodytes troglodytes*

5

KEY FACTS

Length: 9-10cm. **Wingspan:** 13-17cm. **Weight:** 8-13g. **Habitat:** among undergrowth in wide range of habitats, from woods and gardens to moorland and sea-cliffs. **Movements:** mostly only local movements in winter, but in severe weather birds may move further, chiefly S, a few as far as Continent. Small numbers of passage migrants/winter visitors from Continent, late Sep-mid Apr, chiefly SE. **Population:** in typical years almost 10 million pairs breed here. **Diet:** mainly insects, also spiders. **Voice:** hard, dry 'chit' or 'chiti', often run together into a rattle; rolling 'churrr'; song remarkably loud, explosive, prolonged warbling, usually ending with a trill. **Nest:** ball of leaves and bracken or other vegetation and moss, in thick vegetation; typical sites include brambles, overgrown banks, among ivy on walls or trees; several built by male, chosen one lined with feathers. **Eggs:** 5-6, white, with reddish-brown spots. **Incubation:** 14-15 days, by female. **Fledging:** 16-17 days. **Broods:** female usually 2, male (with more than 1 mate) up to 4. **Maturity:** 1 year.

| J | F | M | A | M | J | J | A | S | O | N | D |

One of our most widespread birds – found almost everywhere there is low cover, from city parks to remote sea-cliffs – and often our most abundant species, except after severe winters, when population may be reduced by 70 per cent. Numbers recover very quickly after one or two mild winters. Not gregarious, except when roosting.

juvenile

adult

△ Tiny, stumpy-bodied, with very short, cocked tail, slender, slightly downcurved bill. Extremely active, restlessly hunting with mouse-like movements among dense ground cover for small insects and other prey; often presence betrayed only by loud calls and song. Usually quite tame, allowing close approach. Upperparts rusty-brown and buff, with darker barring on back and wings, mottled throat and pale eyebrow. Underparts paler, buffy, with barred flanks; tail barred; undertail spotted white. Juvenile has more densely mottled crown/throat, less distinct eyebrow, unspotted undertail.

▷ On some of Scotland's N islands there are 4 separate races, differing slightly from mainland race. Those on St Kilda and Fair Isle greyer above; those on Outer Hebrides and Shetlands darker, more barred, above and paler and more strongly barred below. Also, length of bill, wings, tail and legs increases towards N.

Fair Isle race

Outer Hebrides race

△ Flight low, fast and direct, on whirring wings; quickly dives into cover again.

Small, rather secretive, ground-feeding birds with slender, pointed bills and shuffling gait. Sexes very similar. Nest in bushes or among rocks. Only 1 species (apart from very rare vagrant, Alpine Accentor *P. collaris*) found here.

6

Generally unobtrusive small brown bird with grey head and breast, thin dark bill and prominent reddish eyes and reddish-pink legs. Remains in or near cover, but not at all shy. When foraging on ground, has very distinctive jerky, mouse-like, creeping shuffle, with legs almost hidden, body often horizontal; also makes short hops; often flicks wings and tail rapidly and restlessly. Also seen bustling about in hedges, sometimes on top, especially when singing in spring.

male *female* *juvenile*

KEY FACTS

Length: 14.5cm. **Wingspan:** 19-21cm. **Weight:** 19-24g. **Habitat:** hedges, open woods and woodland edges, gardens, parks, scrub; some on moorland, rocky islands. **Movements:** our breeders highly sedentary; passage migrants from Continent to E Britain late Sep-mid May. **Population:** *c*2.8 million territories; up to *c*12 million birds in midwinter. **Diet:** mainly insects in breeding season, seeds in winter. **Voice:** loud, penetrating, high, piping 'tseep'; song a clear, high, broken series of warbling phrases. **Nest:** cup of twigs, moss, leaves, grass, rootlets, lined with hair, feathers, moss, wool. **Eggs:** 4-5, deep blue. **Incubation:** 12 days, by female. **Fledging:** 12 days. **Broods:** 2, sometimes 3. **Maturity:** 1 year. **Confusion species:** despite old name Hedge Sparrow, completely unrelated to sparrows and with much thinner bill and blue-grey underparts (streaked in juvenile). Young Robin (pp240-1) less grey. Dunnock also has shuffling gait.

△ May appear nondescript, but a closer look reveals subtle plumage pattern. Upperparts rich brown, streaked blackish; head, neck, throat and breast slate-grey, with brown on crown and ear coverts; sides of breast/flanks streaked blackish and rufous, rest of underparts greyish-white. Male brighter than female, especially in spring: grey clearer, without female's brown tinge, upperparts more rufous, more strongly streaked. Juvenile browner, especially on head; duller, with whitish throat, entire underparts streaked.

males, 'wing-waving'

△ Usually solitary, but in loose groups at good feeding sites. Groups of males perform remarkable 'wing-waving' display, signalling aggression by flicking up wings, sometimes both at once but often alternately. Sex lives complex: both male and female may have up to 3 mates, and sometimes several males pair with several females. When mating, male stimulates female with bill to eject sperm from any previous liaison.

◁ Flight usually low, fast, whirring and rather undulating, generally soon dives into cover; wings rounded and tail looks quite long and full.

J F M A M J J A S O N D

CHATS AND THRUSHES
Family Turdidae

Large family of birds with rather plump bodies, quite slender bills and, generally, square-tipped tails. Feed mainly on insects and other invertebrates, chiefly on ground, in breeding season, also on berries and other fruit in trees/shrubs in autumn/winter. Hop or run fast on ground. Sexes usually similar, but easily distinguished in some species (particularly chats). Chats are small, with striking plumage patterns and bright colours; nest on ground, in holes in trees, walls, ground etc. Thrushes are larger, often with spotted underparts; build cup nests in bushes, trees etc.

● Note: chats – plumage colour and patterns of face, breast and tail; thrushes – head pattern, colour of flanks and underwings.

Chats (pp240-9)

Stonechat

Wheatear

Nightingale

Thrushes (pp250-5)

Mistle Thrush

Blackbird

ROBIN *Erithacus rubecula*

Familiar, jaunty, neckless, very upright little bird with long legs. Very plump when feathers fluffed out in winter, but can look quite slim in summer. Feeds mainly on ground; often drops from perch to ground and darts back. Hops rapidly, pausing upright with drooped wings and head cocked on one side, then dipping forward to resume hopping or seize beetle or other prey; often flicks wings and tail; when excited or alarmed, bobs and bows with cocked tail. Solitary for much of year; outside breeding season, both sexes defend individual territories. Sings mainly from perch in cover in shrub, hedge or tree, but sometimes from higher, more exposed branch, especially in winter; often uses regular song-perch. Males sing all months except July, when moulting; unusually for birds, females sing too, in autumn and winter.

▽ Quite often, Robins sing at night, near street lamps or other artificial lights; often mistaken for singing Nightingales.

▷ Adults warm olive-brown above, with reddish-orange face and breast, separated from upperparts by blue-grey band; flanks buff; rest of underparts whitish. Sexes look identical. Extremely pugnacious. Outside breeding season, both sexes usually drive off intruders, though some neighbours of opposite sex that are parents, offspring or former mates tolerate one another. Males more aggressive than females in breeding season. Threat postures centre on displaying red breast to rival; plumage often puffed out, body swayed and tail cocked; often accompanied by bursts of song with strange, strangled quality, and loud 'ticc, ticc' or 'seee' calls.

males, threat postures

British race

Continental
race

KEY FACTS

Length: 14cm. **Wingspan:**
20-22cm. **Weight:** 16-22g.
Habitat: chiefly gardens,
woods, hedges, other areas
with trees, but can breed in
other habitats with shrub layer.
Movements: our breeders
mainly sedentary, though
some upland breeders winter
in lowlands; very few migrate
to Continent; immigrants from
Continent late Sep-Apr,
especially E Britain.
Population: *c.*4.4 million
pairs breed. **Diet:** mainly
insects and larvae (especially
beetles), worms, other
invertebrates, berries, seeds.
Voice: main calls loud, sharp
'tic' of alarm/ territorial
defence, often persistently
repeated, with clockwork
quality, and very high-pitched,
thin 'tseee' or 'tseeep' of alarm
when predators nearby; song
beautiful flow of brief, liquid,
warbling notes and longer,
shriller notes, with sudden
changes in tempo. Autumn
song thinner, more wistful.
Nest: domed structure of
leaves lined with fine roots,
hair, well hidden in hollow in
ivy-covered bank, at base of
tree, in hedge etc. **Eggs:** 4-6,
whitish, with fine pale reddish
spots. **Incubation:** 13-14
days, by female. **Fledging:**
12-15 days. **Broods:** 2,
sometimes 3. **Maturity:**
1 year. **Confusion species:**
juvenile like juveniles of
Nightingale (p242), Bluethroat
(p243), Redstart (p244); see
also above right.

J F M A M J J A S O N D

△ In British Isles, Robins, though aggressive towards small birds
– especially other Robins – are tame and confiding towards
humans, except briefly during summer moult. Continental
Robins, by contrast, are much wilder and more skulking. This
difference in behaviour may help to distinguish winter visitors
from Europe, which are also slightly paler and greyer above
and have somewhat paler, duller breast than our birds.

△ Robins' nests usually well concealed in bank, hole or ledge;
sometimes they use shelf in garden shed or other outbuilding,
and occasionally nest in such objects as old kettles or tin cans.

Bluethroat   Redstart   Robin

juveniles

△ Juveniles very different from adults, without red breasts. Have
brown upperparts, heavily spotted pale buff on head, mantle
and shoulders, and buff underparts with dark crescents, giving
scaled appearance. Unlike juvenile Nightingales, Bluethroats
and Redstarts, they lack any reddish in the tail.

△ Flight usually low and flitting, though strong and fast, often
with half-cocked tail giving jerky action, especially over longer
distances; turns or dives rapidly into cover.

NIGHTINGALE *Luscinia megarhynchos*

63

△ Generally very secretive and difficult to see; mainly brown plumage conceals it well in the tangled bramble thickets and other dense cover it favours. Remarkably loud, rich and varied song, given by day as well as by night, usually from dense cover. Males arrive here from Africa before females and sing during daytime only at first to warn off rivals and establish territories. Later, they deliver longer, more complex songs at night to attract newly arrived females to mate with them. On a still night song may carry for up to 1.6km.

△ Rather like a large, all-brown Robin but with relatively smaller head and longer, fuller tail, making it appear less portly, more thrush-like. Vital distinction is rich chestnut tail. Upperparts warm russet-brown, underparts buff, whiter on throat and belly. Large, dark eyes also distinctive; pale eyering emphasizes 'gentle' expression. Sexes look identical. Actions similar to Robin's, with frequent flicking of wings and tail and cocking of head; tail usually raised, showing orange-buff undertail; often raises crown feathers; hops among leaf litter on long brownish legs, searching for food.

▷ Juvenile spotted, like juvenile Robin, but larger, with rufous tail and paler underparts; tail not as bright as juvenile Redstart's and lacks latter's dark centre.

juvenile

◁ Reddish tail particularly noticeable as bird dives into thick cover. Flight action similar to Robin's, but faster, more floating, less flitting, with longer wings and, especially, longer, fuller tail.

KEY FACTS

Length: 16.5cm. **Wingspan:** 23-26cm. **Weight:** 18-27g. **Habitat:** breeds in areas with dense undergrowth, chiefly overgrown broadleaved coppice woodland, old hedgerows, scrubland and young conifer plantations. **Movements:** summer visitor, Apr-Sep, wintering Africa. **Population:** *c*5000 pairs breed. **Diet:** insects and larvae, worms, berries. **Voice:** liquid 'hweet', harsh 'tack tack', croaking 'krrr', grating 'tschaaa'. Beautiful, rich, loud song: a long, abruptly varied sequence of clear notes, including distinctive slow, sad, fluting 'peeoo' in crescendo, fast, deep, staccato 'chok chok', hard trills, croaks, musical chuckles. **Nest:** cup of leaves, lined with hair, fine grasses, hidden in cover on or near ground. **Eggs:** 4-5, olive-brown. **Incubation:** 13-14 days, by female. **Fledging:** 12-13 days. **Broods:** 1. **Maturity:** 1 year. **Confusion species:** juvenile similar to juveniles of Robin (pp240-1), Bluethroat (opposite), Redstart (p244). All are smaller; Robin lacks red in tail, has darker underparts and is generally tamer; Bluethroat has red at base of tail only and streaked, not scaled and mottled, underparts; Redstart has redder tail with dark central feathers. Cetti's Warbler (p256) has shorter, less reddish tail and very different song/calls; usually by water.

| J | F | M | A | M | J | J | A | S | O | N | D |

race svecica
male summer

race cyanecula

male summer

female summer

KEY FACTS

Length: 14cm. **Wingspan:** 20-22.5cm. **Weight:** 15-23g. **Habitat:** passage migrants mainly along coasts, in scrub and other low vegetation. Breeds in damp heaths and tundra of N Eurasia and Alaska, and mainly in moist woodlands on Continent. **Movements:** scarce but regular passage migrant, chiefly to E coasts Britain, mainly in spring (Mar-May); some in autumn (late Aug-mid Oct), including red-spotted N European race *svecica* and white-spotted C and S European race *cyanecula* (latter much scarcer, most on NE British coasts and islands in early spring, especially Shetland, with some on E and S British coasts autumn). Winters SW Europe and Africa. **Population:** typically only *c*100 birds, but in some springs a much greater influx with prolonged easterly winds (as in 1970, 1981 and, especially, 1985, when at least 590 birds recorded). Has attempted to breed in Scotland on a few occasions. **Diet:** insects, small seeds, berries. **Voice:** sharp 'tak', soft 'wheet', guttural 'turrc', often run together. **Maturity:** 1 year. **Confusion species:** juvenile resembles juveniles of Robin (pp240-1), Nightingale (opposite), and Redstart (p244) but these are all scaled and mottled, rather than streaked, below, and lack Bluethroat's tail pattern.

| J | F | M | A | M | J | J | A | S | O | N | D |

△ Resembles a slim, long-legged Robin, but with dark brown upperparts, whitish eyebrows, variable throat/breast, rest of underparts buff-white, darker flanks and distinctive rufous patches at sides of blackish tail at base. Shy and skulking, creeping mouse-like among dense cover, though hops upright over more open ground; often tilts forward and cocks or fans tail, or moves it from side to side, flashing reddish patches at sides. In breeding plumage (from Mar-Apr), male of red-spotted race *svecica* has brilliant blue throat with chestnut-red spot in centre and bands of black and chestnut below, separated by thin white band. Male of white-spotted race *cyanecula* has smaller white spot in centre of blue throat. Females of both races usually lack all but trace of male's blue throat and red or white spot; instead have blackish moustache joined to blackish necklace, broken along lower edge, and with some rufous-buff (or sometimes blue) feathers in necklace.

female winter

male winter

◁ In winter plumage (from mid Jul-late Sep), males variable, but throat/breast pattern less distinct, duller, with blackish mottling on upper throat. Races cannot be safely distinguished in non-breeding plumage. Females rarely have any blue on throat/breast.

▷ Juvenile dark brown above, boldly streaked/spotted pale buff; dull buff below, with dark brown streaks/spots; same distinctive tail pattern as adult. 1st-winter birds resemble non-breeding females, but still have juvenile's buff tips to outermost greater wing-coverts; males usually have some blue and red on breast and throat; females duller, with little red and no blue.

juvenile

female

male   *1st-winter*

female winter

◁ Flight fast, direct, low, ending with sweep or glide into cover; broad dark tail shows distinctive rust-red patches at base.

REDSTART *Phoenicurus phoenicurus*

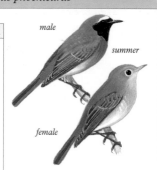

male

summer

female

04

KEY FACTS

Length: 14cm. **Wingspan:** 20.5-24cm. **Weight:** 12-20g. **Habitat:** breeds in open mature woodland, especially sessile oakwoods in W and N Britain, parkland, large gardens, old hedgerows, other areas with trees, including moorland streamsides, heaths etc. **Movements:** summer visitor (Apr-Sep), wintering Africa; also passage migrants from Continent late Mar-mid Jun, Jul-Oct, especially E and S coasts. **Population:** probably *c*100 000-200 000 pairs breed. **Diet:** mainly insects and larvae, some spiders, worms, and berries in autumn. **Voice:** plaintive, ascending 'hueee' (male) or 'hweet' (female), in male often combined with 'tic' or 'tk' calls, as, e.g. 'hueee-tic-tic'; also sharp, scolding 'tchuk' and rasping calls. Song a brief, clear, rather melancholy warbling, nearly always introduced by 'hueee' note, followed by rolling 'tuee-tuee- tuee-tuee', and petering out into weak metallic trill. **Nest:** cup of moss, grass, etc, lined with feathers, hair etc, in hole in tree, walls, rocks or building, occasionally among tree roots or in bank; readily takes to nestboxes. **Eggs:** 5-7, pale blue. **Incubation:** 13-14 days, by female. **Fledging:** 14-16 days. **Broods:** 1. **Maturity:** 1 year. **Confusion species:** females/immatures may be mistaken for female and juvenile Black Redstarts (see right and opposite), but latter resident and only scarce, local breeder mainly at urban sites in S England (though passage migrants and wintering birds more widespread on coasts), and plain slate-grey, with little contrast between upper and underparts; juveniles far less spotted. See also juveniles of Robin (p241), Nightingale (p242) and Bluethroat (p243).

△ Elegant, with flattish, gently rounded head and full chest tapering to prominent, strikingly orange-red rump and tail, latter with dark brown central feathers and almost constantly and rapidly quivered (not flicked). Rather shy; mostly in trees, often high up, where may perch half-upright; much more upright, with Robin-like actions, on ground. Feeds from trunks, branches and among foliage of trees; on ground, often after short flight from perch; and (especially males) by chasing aerial insects in brief flight from perch; returns to perch to eat food. Male striking, with black face and throat, brilliant white forehead and eyebrow, blue-grey upperparts, brown wings, orange-chestnut breast and flanks; in autumn (after moult Jul-Sep), black throat/chestnut breast partly mottled with white, forehead and eyebrow less distinct, duller upperparts with brownish feather tips. Female duller, with greyish-brown upperparts, darker on wings, almost white throat, pale orange-buff or peach breast and flanks and whitish belly; pale eyering and gentle expression. Paler, browner than female Black Redstart, which also lacks whitish chin.

▷ Juvenile mottled like juvenile Robin, but distinguished by rust-red rump and tail, quivered as in adult; juvenile Nightingale also spotted, but larger, with more rounded, duller reddish tail without dark brown centre, which it does not quiver. Juvenile Black Redstart has similar tail, but body plain slate-grey, not spotted.

juvenile

Black Redstart juvenile

male

female

◁ Flight agile, usually brief, with flitting action; often ends with a sudden turn or sweep into cover; over longer distances gently undulating. Loosely held, often fanned tail looks long and flashes reddish. Sometimes hovers by foliage when feeding.

Phoenicurus ochruros **BLACK REDSTART**

summer

male

female

KEY FACTS

Length: 14.5cm. **Wingspan:** 23-26cm. **Weight:** 14-20g. **Habitat:** breeds in Britain mainly in derelict buildings and part-built houses in urban areas, waste ground, industrial sites, power stations, railway yards etc; passage migrants/ wintering birds mainly coastal, in open country along cliffs, sheltered beaches, ploughed fields, gardens etc.
Movements: summer visitor and passage migrant, Mar-Oct; few winter. **Population:** from 1923 onwards, handful of colonists from Continent bred on Sussex and Cornwall cliffs, then during 1940s expanded into bombed areas in London and other urban areas in SE England; as bombsites cleared, moved into present habitats; increased range and numbers after 1969 but now declining again: only 30-100 pairs breed, mainly SE England, E Anglia and W Midlands; probably no more than 500 birds winter here. **Diet:** mainly insects, larvae, also small molluscs, earth-worms, other invertebrates, fruit and seeds in autumn/ winter. **Voice:** usual call short 'tsip', often preceding scolding 'tucc-tucc'; also rapid, stuttering, rattled 'tititicc' of alarm; song very hurried warble like Redstart's but simpler, quieter, thinner, less musical, usually followed by strange spluttering, crackling, like scrunching gravel or rattled ballbearings, and ending in loud burst of musical ringing or warbling notes. **Nest:** cup of grass, moss etc, lined with wool, hair, feathers, usually on ledge in building or hole in wall. **Eggs:** 4-6, white. **Incubation:** 13-17 days, by female. **Fledging:** 12-19 days. **Broods:** 2. **Maturity:** 1 year. **Confusion species:** female and juvenile may be mistaken for female and juvenile Redstart (see opposite).

△ Usually looks plumper, heavier than Redstart, but with same flattish head, tapering rear, and orange-red rump and tail with dark central feathers in all plumages. Tail quivered, but less often than Redstart's. Unlike Redstart, not in woodland – coastal passage migrant and scarce breeder, mainly in urban areas, industrial sites in S England – and mostly on ground, though often perches on rocks, walls, buildings etc. Unlike Redstart, runs as well as hops. Male in breeding plumage striking: head, back, breast and upper belly sooty-black, with whitish wing flash on browner wings, dusky-grey flanks and lower belly, and orange-buff undertail. Has distinctive song (see Key Facts). Female grey, almost as dark below as above, without whitish wing flashes: some paler and browner than others, but always dirtier, duller, greyer than female Redstarts, and never have pale buff or peach on underparts.

male winter

juvenile

△ In winter plumage (after moult Aug-Sep), males paler, duller, dark grey rather than black, due to grey feather tips, though face/throat remain blackish; underparts dirty whitish-grey. Juvenile similar to female, but browner, with dark bars and flecks on upperparts, chest and flanks; juvenile Redstart has pale spots above and is paler and browner.

▷ 1st-summer males variable: some very like females, others with blackish throat and breast, sometimes with small whitish wing flashes. Young males can sing and hold territories; may breed.

male
1st-summer

female

male

◁ Flight similar to that of Redstart, but with more compact shape, less flickering wing action and much less 'loose'-looking tail.

| J | F | M | A | M | J | J | A | S | O | N | D |

STONECHAT *Saxicola torquata*

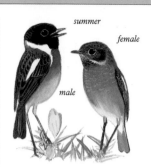

summer

female

male

KEY FACTS

Length: 12.5cm. **Wingspan:** 18-21cm. **Weight:** 14-17g. **Habitat:** breeds on rough ground, moors, heaths, commons, especially with gorse and near coast; some among young conifers. **Movements:** British breeders (race *hibernans*) mainly resident, but many N and upland birds move to coasts and S in autumn, a few as far away as Mediterranean; E races *maura* and *stejnegeri* rare vagrants (Sep-May, especially Oct-Nov) to N and E coasts Britain. **Population:** 16 000-40 000 pairs breed here. Similar numbers in winter. **Diet:** mainly insects and larvae, also worms, other invertebrates; some seeds and berries in autumn and winter. **Voice:** persistent, scolding, hard 'tsak' or 'tsak tsak', like 2 stones being clinked together; clear 'weet'/'weet-tsak-tsak'. Song a series of irregular, rapidly repeated phrases, containing short, twittering double notes, one sharp and clear, the other deeper, throatier; usually from exposed perch, also in song flight. **Nest:** cup of grass and moss, lined with hair, feathers, sometimes wool, in gorse or other thick cover; often hidden deeply, with tunnel leading to it. **Eggs:** 5-6, very pale blue-green, speckled reddish-brown. **Incubation:** 14-15 days, by female. **Fledging:** 14-16 days. **Broods:** 2, sometimes 3. **Maturity:** 1 year. **Confusion species:** Whinchat (opposite) slimmer, longer-winged, squarer-headed, less upright; males distinct, but females and immatures quite similar: Whinchats have distinct pale eyebrow and white sides to base of tail. See also E races of Stonechat (opposite page).

| J | F | M | A | M | J | J | A | S | O | N | D |

male

summer

female

△ Very upright, quite plump little bird with large rounded head, short wings and short tail. Usually seen perched on top of shrub (especially gorse) or fence post, giving harsh scolding calls, bobbing body and flicking wings and tail; restless and irascible, quite tame and inquisitive. Darts to ground from perch to seize prey, returning to same perch or new one. Male in summer plumage has distinctive black head/throat, like a guardsman's busby, contrasting white neck patches forming half-collar, blackish-brown upperparts and tail, with brown streaks on back, white line on inner wing and white mottling on rump, and deep orange-chestnut breast. Female far less distinctive, like faded version of male, with much smaller, duller, whitish markings on neck and wings and no white on rump; darker head (lacking pale eyebrow) and redder underparts than female Whinchat.

winter

female

male

△ In winter plumage (after moult Aug-Sep), male duller, with more prominent, rufous, streaks on upperparts, smaller, less bright white, neck and wing markings, buff mottling on black throat and duller, deeper reddish breast. Female in winter plumage even duller, with dark throat and whitish neck patches obscure or absent.

▷ Juvenile quite like juvenile Robin (pp240-1), with pale buff streaks on upperparts and blackish speckles on breast, but shorter-tailed, bigger-headed, generally darker, with orange or rufous-buff tinged breast. Throat greyish-buff, speckled darker.

juvenile

◁ Flight low, fast, direct and agile, with whirring action; male resembles giant bumblebee. Sometimes hovers briefly. Song given in dancing song flight, as well as from perch.

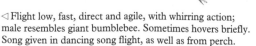

96

male *summer* *female*

KEY FACTS

Length: 12.5cm. **Wingspan:** 21-24cm. **Weight:** 16-24g.
Habitat: open country with bushes, including heaths, rough agricultural land, bracken-covered hillsides, moorland, railway embankments, young conifer plantations. **Movements:** summer visitor Apr-Sep, wintering Africa; passage migrants from Scandinavia Apr-May, mid Jul-early Oct, especially E and S Britain.
Population: 15 000-30 000 pairs breed here; major decline C and S England.
Diet: mainly insects and larvae, some seeds and blackberries. **Voice:** short, scolding 'tictic' and 'tu-tic-tic' calls; also clicks and rattles; song brief, rather metallic warbling, like Stonechat's or Redstart's (p244) but sweeter, more broken. **Nest:** cup of grass, sometimes lined with hair, on ground, by tussock or bush. **Eggs:** 5-6, greenish-blue, often speckled reddish.
Incubation: 13 days, by female. **Fledging:** 13 days.
Broods: usually 1, sometimes 2. **Maturity:** 1 year.
Confusion species: females/immatures confusable with female/immature Stonechat (opposite). See also 'Siberian Stonechat' (right).

J F M A M J J A S O N D

△ Similar to Stonechat but summer visitor/passage migrant only. Slimmer, longer, with longer wings and less rounded head; less upright, perching at an angle, often on top of low bush, thistle etc. Often active at dusk. In all plumages, has pale eyebrow, dark cheek patch and pale moustache, and white sides to base of tail; adults also have 2 white patches on each wing. Summer male has most contrasting plumage, with blackish-brown crown and cheeks separated by broad white eyebrow, white moustache below cheek patch and warm orange-buff throat and breast; back dark rufous-brown, strongly streaked blackish. Female summer duller, paler, with buff tinge to eyebrow and moustache, brown cheek patch, smaller, duller white wing and tail patches.

male winter

◁ In winter plumage (after moult Jul-Sep), sexes similar, with duller eyebrows, wing and tail patches, browner cheek patches and often fine streaks and spots on breast.

▷ Juvenile's upperparts more reddish-brown, with contrasting pale streaks and more rufous wings; duller buff underparts, with dark mottling on throat/breast; less distinct face pattern. Paler than juvenile Stonechat, especially underparts. Lacks white on wings but has white tail patches. This plumage is moulted before migration.

juvenile

male

female

◁ 'Siberian Stonechat' (E races), rare vagrant to N and E coasts in Oct; female resembles Whinchat, but has pale gingery or whitish rump, no white basal tail patches, plainer back, fainter eyebrow; also dumpier, bigger-headed than Whinchat.

'Siberian Stonechat' winter

▷ Flight action similar to Stonechat's, but stronger, more direct, less 'buzzing'; often from one perch to another. Male in particular shows white wing and tail flashes, very noticeable when landing.

female *male* *summer*

WHEATEAR *Oenanthe oenanthe*

▷ Bold, upright, ground-loving; widespread summer visitor to open country, especially uplands. Best identification feature is very distinctive pattern at rear, with inverted black 'T' at tip of short white tail and rump. Distinctly larger, longer-bodied and longer-winged than Stonechat or Whinchat; elegant, restless and active, mainly on ground, rarely perching higher than rock or fence post. Frequently bobs body up and down, while flicking wings and flirting or wagging tail. Characteristic feeding action: makes fast run or series of long hops, then pauses to dip down to ground for insect prey, then stretches upwards and continues process. Also flutters up into air to catch insects in flight and may hover when searching for food or looking for predators. Often first migrant to appear here, sometimes as early as mid Feb.

female

S birds summer

male

N birds summer

female

male

◁ Male in summer plumage (Jan-Mar) striking, dapper, with blue-grey crown and back, blackish face mask and wings, white eyebrow, sandy-buff breast and white belly. In S, males smaller and paler, with almost pure white underparts; N males bulkier and with rich buff underparts. Females duller, with dark brown face mask, cream eyebrow, grey-brown upperparts and wings and rich buff underparts. Both sexes have long black legs.

▷ Male often delivers his brief, rather lark-like song, containing wheezy creaking and rattling sounds as well as warbling, from boulder, fence or other perch, but also in a dancing and hovering song flight. Song often includes mimicry of other nearby breeding birds, such as Meadow Pipit (p229). Calls also distinctive, especially loud 'chak-chak' and 'weet-chak-chak'.

male summer, song flight

female summer

◁ Unlike Stonechats and Whinchats, which nest in thick cover, Wheatears nest deep in rabbit burrow, hole among rocks or in drystone wall, under corrugated iron etc. Drystone walls particularly favoured, providing song posts and lookout perches as well as breeding sites.

▷ Juveniles have similar basic plumage pattern and colours to females, but at first have numerous pale/dark spots and/or dark brown scale-like markings on crown, back, lesser wing coverts, sides of neck and breast. By time juveniles ready to migrate in autumn, they look very like females.

juvenile

Oenanthe oenanthe WHEATEAR

112

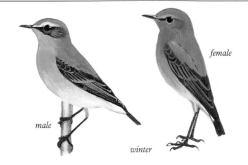

male

female

winter

KEY FACTS

Length: 14.5-15.5cm.
Wingspan: 26-32cm.
Weight: 17-30g. **Habitat:**
open country, including
mountains, moors and upland
pastures with rocks, scree or
walls for nesting, downs,
breckland, dunes, shingle.
Movements: summer visitor,
Mar-Sep, wintering Africa;
passage migrants from Iceland,
Greenland, Mar-early Jun,
late Jul-Oct. **Population:** at
least 67 000 pairs breed. **Diet:**
chiefly insects and larvae,
some other invertebrates;
berries and sometimes seeds
in autumn. **Voice:** main calls
harsh 'chak-chak' or 'weet-
chak-chak'; brief song of
melodious warbling notes,
harsh, scratchy sounds and
whistles, often mixed with
mimicry of other bird calls/
song, frequently given in
dancing song flight. **Nest:** cup
of grass and other vegetation,
lined with hair, feathers etc,
in hole in wall or among
rocks, or in rabbit burrow or
hole in ground (chiefly in
lowlands). **Eggs:** 5-6, pale
blue. **Incubation:** 10-16
days, by female. **Fledging:**
10-21 days. **Broods:** 1-2.
Maturity: 1 year.

J F M A M J J A S O N D

> Flight fast and more fluid
than smaller chats', with
longer body and wings; dashes
low over ground, then swoops
up onto boulder or other
prominent perch, flashing
distinctive rump/tail pattern.

△ Male in winter plumage (after moult Aug-Sep) not as neat
and contrasting as in breeding season, with much browner
upperparts, buff or whitish edges and tops to wing feathers,
creating scaly pattern on shoulders, narrow pale wingbar just
below and a more obvious pale panel below this, along tertials
and inner secondaries; rear of face mask mottled greyish,
producing indistinct edge. Underparts darker, more buff,
more uniform, with little trace of white belly. Although much
more similar than in summer, can still be distinguished from
female by more distinct, whitish eyebrow, black between bill
and eye and blacker wings. Female changes less in winter than
male, but more uniform, with browner crown and upperparts,
often with rufous tinge, and darker, all-buff, underparts,
nearer in tone to upperparts; face pattern less contrasting;
reddish-buff fringes to wing feathers.

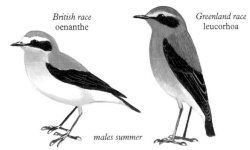

British race
oenanthe

Greenland race
leucorhoa

males summer

△ Birds belonging to race *leucorhoa*, regular on passage from
Greenland and Iceland in late spring and autumn, larger, with
more richly coloured, darker, more uniform underparts than
British breeders (race *oenanthe*). Tend to stand more erect
than 'our' birds. Longer wings help them make long sea
crossings on remarkable journeys to winter quarters in Africa;
e.g. Icelandic breeders make nonstop sea crossings to Spain,
where they rest and refuel before setting off again.

males summer

BLACKBIRD *Turdus merula*

male

female

10

△ Medium-sized, often looks stocky and plump-bellied; hops or runs, pausing to look with head on one side; usually not so erect as Song or Mistle Thrushes. Often tilts tail slowly upwards and droops wings. Sometimes perches high up, especially male when singing, but also skulks in or near cover. Although often tame, easily alarmed. Not really gregarious except on migration. Male unmistakable, with glossy, jet-black plumage and bold orange-yellow bill and eyering. Female dark brown above, paler and often more reddish-brown below, with variable dark mottling and paler, often almost whitish, throat, with dark streaks. Bill varies from dark brown to almost completely yellow or orange-yellow. In all plumages, legs dark brown.

juvenile male

1st-winter male

△ Juvenile like female, but more rufous, with pale reddish-buff streaks on head, mantle, 'shoulders' and forewings, and bold mottling on whitish to reddish-buff underparts. Juvenile males usually darker, with brighter rufous streaks. Bill pinkish-grey with darker tip. By early Dec (earlier, by Oct, in migrants), has acquired 1st-winter plumage, males brownish-black above with paler, browner wings and underparts. Bill stays dark at first, becoming yellower in late winter/early spring. 1st-winter females very similar to adult females, but usually paler, with juvenile wing pattern and darker bill.

males

△ Flight usually low, rather wavering, though fast and agile, with hurried bursts of uneven wingbeats and sudden bursts of acceleration. Take-off often hurried and panicky, with noisy wingbeats and alarm calls. Wings held more forward than other thrushes; wings/tail have more rounded tips. Wings of males appear paler than body in flight, especially against strong light or dark background. On landing, has distinctive habit of drooping wings and raising fanned tail. Migrants have stronger, more direct, higher flight.

KEY FACTS

Length: 24-25cm. **Wingspan:** 34-38cm. **Weight:** 80-110g. **Habitat:** gardens, woods, hedges, scrub, from city centres to remote islands. **Movements:** many British breeders resident, but most N breeders migrate to winter as far as Ireland and France; also huge number of winter visitors from Continent. **Population:** *c*4.6 million pairs breed here; *c*12-18 million birds winter. **Diet:** mainly insects, worms, small snails and other invertebrates in summer, berries and other fruits in winter. **Voice:** distinctive, low, scolding 'chook' anxiety calls, and run together into hysterical, harsh, screaming rattle of full alarm; groups utter chorus of 'chink chink' calls at dawn and dusk. Song a mellow, rich, fluty warbling, usually ending in loud, harsher chuckling or creaky notes. **Nest:** cup of mud and moss lined with grass, in tree, bush or hedge, usually quite low down, sometimes in garden sheds or other buildings. **Eggs:** 3-5, pale greenish-blue, variably spotted pale reddish-brown. **Incubation:** 13-15 days, by female. **Fledging:** 12-15 days. **Broods:** commonly 2-3; 4 and even 5 recorded. **Maturity:** 1 year. **Confusion species:** Ring Ouzel (opposite); female and immature sometimes confused with Song Thrush (p252), but latter much paler, more spotted below.

| J | F | M | A | M | J | J | A | S | O | N | D |

Turdus torquatus **RING OUZEL**

113

KEY FACTS

Length: 23-24cm.
Wingspan: 38-42cm.
Weight: 95-130g. **Habitat:**
breeds in mountains,
moorland, in wild open
country with rocky gullies/
crags; on migration, in open
country, especially near coast.
Movements: summer visitor
(Apr-Sep), winters in S
Europe/N Africa; passage
migrants from Scandinavia
(Mar-May, end Aug-Nov),
especially E Britain.
Population: *c*5600-11 300
pairs breed here. **Diet:** chiefly
insects, also berries and fruit.
Voice: distinctive loud, hard,
rattling 'tak-tak-tak', often run
on into long chattering, also
chuckling, piping and trilling
calls. Song a simple series of
phrases of 2-4 fluty notes,
separated by pauses. **Nest:**
cup of grass, earth and heather
twigs, lined with grass, among
rocks, crevices, on overgrown
banks, or in old buildings.
Eggs: 5-6, blue-green,
blotched reddish-brown.
Incubation: 12-14 days, by
both sexes. **Fledging:** 14-16
days. **Broods:** usually 2.
Maturity: 1 year. **Confusion
species:** Blackbird (see
opposite page and below).

| J | F | M | A | M | J | J | A | S | O | N | D |

*Blackbird
partial albino
male*

*Ring Ouzel
male summer*

Has been called the 'mountain blackbird'; differs from
Blackbird in being summer visitor and passage migrant only,
with restricted breeding habitat and wild, restless character.
Usually very shy and wary, often flying off a long way when
disturbed. Normally more upright than Blackbird, with
slimmer, more streamlined body, usually straighter back,
slightly longer legs, longer, more pointed wings and longer,
squarer tail. Often raises head and cocks tail; droops or flicks
wings. Migrants tend to skulk in dense cover.

female   *male*

autumn

summer

male

female

△ Male sooty or brownish-black, with striking white crescent
across breast and distinctive, long, pale panel on wing due to
silvery and greyish fringes to feathers. After autumn moult
(Jul-Sep) gains pale scaling on underparts, with white edges to
feathers; breast crescent flecked brown. Female browner, with
duller pale scaling all year; breast crescent narrower, duller,
with brown feather tips; like male, has distinctive pale wing
panel. Bill yellowish, brighter in summer and brightest in males.

▷ Juveniles lack white breast
crescent and scaling; look
quite like juvenile Blackbirds,
but have greyer, much less
rufous-brown upperparts and
more heavily spotted and
barred underparts; often look
chocolate and cream.

juvenile

male summer

◁ Flight rapid, powerful
and direct, the bird hurtling
recklessly up and down
cliffs and over boulders to
hide among cover. Like
Blackbird, often cocks tail on
landing. Wings have long
points, tail sharp-cornered.

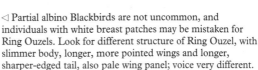

◁ Partial albino Blackbirds are not uncommon, and
individuals with white breast patches may be mistaken for
Ring Ouzels. Look for different structure of Ring Ouzel, with
slimmer body, longer, more pointed wings and longer,
sharper-edged tail, also pale wing panel; voice very different.

SONG THRUSH *Turdus philomelos*

11

△ Most familiar of the spotted thrushes, though declining, especially on farmland. Smaller than Blackbird, with compact shape, upright stance. Hops or runs, frequently pausing upright, often with head cocked on one side. Flicks wings and tail. Not really gregarious except during migration. Adult has warm brown upperparts, uniform apart from 2 faint wingbars; lacks bold face pattern apart from dark streak contrasting with almost white throat. Breast and flanks suffused golden-buff, heavily marked with blackish, mainly arrowhead-shaped, spots; belly whitish with fewer spots. Sexes look identical.

▷ Evidence of presence often indicated by anvil – such as concrete step or large stone – on which the bird smashes snail shells to get at the soft body within, leaving shell fragments scattered around it. Snails are an important food, especially during droughts and in hard winter weather, when other animal food is scarce.

juvenile

◁ Juveniles heavily streaked and speckled above, with dark tips to feathers of crown and face, pale buff streaks and dark tips to back feathers and yellowish tips to wing feathers; underparts have smaller, less diffuse spots.

▽ Shows distinctive golden-buff underwing coverts in flight (darker, rufous-buff in race *hebridensis*, though not as red as in Redwing). Flight outline compact; over long distances fast, with more constant wingbeats/less frequent wing closures, and few glides compared with larger thrushes; short-range flight into cover low and agile, often with sudden turns.

Song very distinctive, with loud, clear, ringing repeated phrases; usually given from conspicuous perch such as treetop in early spring, but later often from hidden perch within tree or shrub.

KEY FACTS

Length: 23cm. **Wingspan:** 33-36cm. **Weight:** 70-90g. **Habitat:** most habitats except completely open ones; especially in woods, hedges, gardens. **Movements:** mainly resident, though some, chiefly N and upland breeders, winter S Britain and Ireland (smaller numbers, mainly immatures, as far as Spain). **Population:** *c*1.35 million pairs breed here; *c*2.54 million birds winter. Major decline over last 20 years, due to agricultural changes, cold winters and probably effects of pesticides (especially slug pellets). **Diet:** worms, snails, fruit, berries. **Voice:** 'tchuk' or 'tchik', rapidly repeated as alarm call; flight call a soft 'tsip', shorter than Redwing's (more Redwing-like 'tseep' from Continental immigrants). Song very loud, consisting of short, varied phrases (from musical whistles to guttural croaks) repeated 2-4 times, with brief pause between each sequence of phrases. **Nest:** neat cup of leaves and twigs, lined with mud, in tree or bush. **Eggs:** 3-5, blue, lightly spotted black. **Incubation:** 12-14 days, by female. **Fledging:** 12-16 days. **Broods:** 2-3, sometimes 4. **Maturity:** 1 year. **Confusion species:** Mistle Thrush (opposite). Redwing (p255) slightly smaller, with bold creamy eyebrow and reddish flanks and underwing coverts.

J F M A M J J A S O N D

Turdus viscivorus **MISTLE THRUSH**

12

Song Thrush

Mistle Thrush

KEY FACTS

Length: 27cm. **Wingspan:** 42-48cm. **Weight:** 110-140g. **Habitat:** open woods, parks, gardens, fields, upland scrub. **Movements:** mostly resident, though Scottish birds highly migratory, wintering SW to Ireland and S to France. English/Welsh breeders partly migratory in 1st winter. Irish breeders sedentary. **Population:** *c*320 000 pairs breed here; *c*500 000 birds winter. **Diet:** berries, fruit, worms, slugs, insects. **Voice:** distinctive rasping chatter, like wooden rattle, also staccato 'tuk-tuk-tuk'; dry rattling 'trrrrr-rrr-rrr-rrr' and variants, louder and more intense with alarm. Song loud, far-carrying, with similar tone to Blackbird's but wilder, more disjointed, less varied, each brief phrase consisting of 3-6 fluting notes, with distinct pauses between phrases. **Nest:** cup of roots and grass in fork of tree. **Eggs:** 3-5, pale blue-green, spotted reddish-brown. **Incubation:** 12-15 days, by female. **Fledging:** 12-15 days. **Broods:** usually 2, sometimes 3. **Maturity:** 1 year. **Confusion species:** Song Thrush (opposite) smaller, darker, less grey, with warm brown upperparts, warm yellowish or golden-buff wash on breast, smaller, neater spots on underparts and slight but noticeable eyebrow. Fieldfare (p254) has bold dark/light plumage pattern, different calls.

△ Our biggest thrush, much larger than Song Thrush: longer, less neatly proportioned, with longer wings and longer, fuller tail, and deeper chest. Looks tall when it stands very upright, with tail down; powerful bill and sturdy legs; neck often looks quite long, compared to almost neckless Song Thrush. Moves in long, bouncy, leaping hops. Flicks wings/tail when excited. Bolder, less skulking than Song Thrush, often well away from cover. Calls and song very different. Plumage much greyer, less uniform above than Song Thrush's, with paler rump and pale edges to wing coverts and tertials; underparts more boldly, more irregularly marked with larger spots (those on breast often merging in a dark band). Tail has whitish tips to outermost feathers. Sexes look identical.

juvenile

◁ In autumn, forms small loose flocks/family groups. Juveniles look very pale: strong spotted pattern above, created by white tips/dark streaks on feathers.

▷ Though wary, Mistle Thrushes fearless and belligerent in defence of their nests, even attacking humans; males, in particular, also drive off other thrushes from berry-bearing trees, especially in winter, with loud, angry rattling calls.

Mistle Thrush

Redwings

One of the earliest birds to start nesting, with eggs laid as early as Feb; far-carrying song can be heard from Dec onwards. Male often chooses topmost branch of tall tree as songpost and will sing in all weathers, including strong wind (hence old country name of 'Stormcock').

△ In flight, has small protruding head, stout, 'pot-bellied' body tapering to long tail. Flight direct, powerful, buoyant, often bounding, bursts of loose wingbeats alternating with long swoops on closed wings; often reaches treetop height soon after take-off (very different from low dash for cover of Song Thrush). Often swoops to ground from trees. Distinguished from Song Thrush by white underwing coverts and whitish tips to outer tail feathers; wings less rounded.

J F M A M J J A S O N D

FIELDFARE *Turdus pilaris*

42

Large, long-tailed thrush with strikingly contrasting plumage pattern; most colourful of our thrushes. Almost as long as but less bulky than Mistle Thrush (p253). Wary, though bold towards other birds when feeding and when defending nest. Highly gregarious. Noisy, with distinctive harsh chackering calls. Often seen feeding with Redwings (opposite) in winter, when large numbers of both of these thrushes visit from N Europe, stripping berries from shrubs/trees and taking slugs, worms and other invertebrates from open fields. Run or hop on ground, frequently pausing upright with drooped wings.

adults

juvenile

△ Blue-grey head and nape contrast with dark reddish-brown back, mainly blackish-brown wings, grey rump and almost black tail. Chin creamy-white, throat, breast and flanks orange-buff, with blackish spots on throat and chest grading into larger arrowheads on lower breast and flanks (latter almost solid black on some birds in spring); rest of underparts white. Indistinct creamy eyebrow; black markings on crown and face, more prominent in males, which are slightly brighter, and less contrastingly spotted than females. Juveniles much duller, browner, than adults, with stronger face pattern.

△ When disturbed feeding in field, flocks fly off, calling noisily, typically making for clump of tall trees and perching on topmost bare branches. Flight action loose, leisurely; bursts of floppy wingbeats alternate with brief glides on open wings and short, faster glides with wings closed (wing-closures briefer than Mistle Thrush's, so flight not so undulating; also angle of tail changed more often). Grey head and rump contrast dramatically with chestnut back/wings and blackish tail.

Redwing

Blackbird male

Fieldfares

KEY FACTS

Length: 25.5cm. **Wingspan:** 39-42cm. **Weight:** 80-130g. **Habitat:** in winter and on passage in open country, feeding in fields, along hedges and in trees on berries, also on windfalls in gardens and orchards; breeds along edges of woods or in clearings. **Movements:** passage migrant and winter visitor from Scandinavia, Finland, Russia (Sep-May, mainly Nov-Mar); a few summer. **Population:** maybe as many as 1 million birds winter; tiny numbers have bred most years (probably 25 pairs in a year at most), almost all in Scotland, since first nested Orkneys, 1967. **Diet:** worms, insects, slugs, berries, fallen apples, grain. **Voice:** distinctive, harsh, slurred 'tchacker-tchak-tchak' or 'tchak-tchak-tchak-tchak' calls, nasal, Lapwing-like 'weeip', and thin, drawn-out 'tseee' in flight. Song weak, tuneless series of squeaks, chuckles and whistles. **Nest:** cup of twigs and grass, usually in fork of tree. **Eggs:** 5-6, pale blue, variably speckled reddish. **Incubation:** 10-13 days, by female. **Fledging:** 12-15 days. **Broods:** 1-2. **Maturity:** 1 year.

| J | F | M | A | M | J | J | A | S | O | N | D |

◁ By late winter, when berries have gone, Fieldfares visit gardens together with Redwings and other thrushes to feast on windfalls etc, especially in hard weather.

adult

adult

juvenile

KEY FACTS

Length: 21cm. **Wingspan:** 33-35cm. **Weight:** 55-75g.
Habitat: on passage and in winter in fields, open woods and woodland edges; breeds in scrub, open woodland.
Movements: passage migrant/winter visitor from N Europe. Icelandic birds of dark, heavily streaked race *coburni* winter mainly Ireland and Scotland; Scandinavian/ Finnish breeders mainly England and Wales.
Population: *c*1 million or more birds winter; tiny breeding population established Scottish Highlands since 1925; currently perhaps 40-80 pairs breed. **Diet:** worms, insects, berries and fallen apples in winter. **Voice:** flight call distinctive, thin, long 'tseeeeeip' or 'seeeeze', more penetrating than Song Thrush's; alarm calls sharp 'kewk' and harsh 'chittuk' or 'chi-tic-tik'. Song very variable; monotonously repeated phrases of 3-4 fluty notes, rising and falling, followed by weak, throaty chuckle. **Nest:** cup of twigs and grass in shrub or tree. **Eggs:** 4-6, pale blue to greenish-blue, speckled reddish-brown. **Incubation:** 10-14 days, by female.
Fledging: 8-12 days.
Broods: 2. **Maturity:** 1 year.
Confusion species: Song Thrush (p252) bigger and Mistle Thrush (p253) much bigger; both paler, with spotted underparts and no eyebrow or reddish flanks.

J F M A M J J A S O N D

△ Smallest and slightest of our thrushes, generally shy and nervous; winter visitor in large flocks, often with Fieldfares. Like latter, feeds both in fields and on berries (and, when other food unavailable, on windfall apples). Face can have 'cross' look due to distinctive bold cream eyebrow, contrasting strongly with dark crown and broad dark band through eye onto cheeks; below this, whitish stripe, with line of blackish spots beneath. Upperparts darker than Song Thrush's, uniform dark brown. Underparts silvery-white, apart from small yellowish-buff area on sides of chest; dark spots on breast, flanks and sides of belly run together to form pattern of streaks; distinctive rusty-red flanks. Bill blackish-brown with yellowish base to lower mandible. Sexes look identical. Juvenile has boldly spotted buff upperparts, whiter eyebrow than adult's and paler reddish flanks and underwing.

△ Little larger than Skylark, with rather similar fluttery flight. Like Fieldfare, flies off quickly when disturbed, up into tall hedges or treetops. Flight silhouette and action resemble Starling's: sharply pointed wings and tail corners and faster flight than other thrushes, with longish periods of closed wings between bursts of fast flaps, producing quite undulating path. Reddish flanks extend onto underwing coverts, distinguishing Redwing seen from below or side from other thrushes.

△ As loose flocks of migrant Redwings pass overhead at night in autumn and spring, above urban as well as rural areas, they utter distinctive, soft but far-carrying 'tseeeeeip' contact calls, more drawn out than those of Song Thrush.

WARBLERS
Family Sylviidae

Small, active birds with short, slim bills. Primarily insect eaters, but many also relish berries in autumn. Several main types here: bush warblers, *Cettia*, p256; grass or grasshopper warblers, *Locustella*, p257; reed warblers, *Acrocephalus*, pp258-61; tree warblers, *Hippolais*, p262; scrub warblers, *Sylvia*, pp263-7; leaf warblers, *Phylloscopus*, pp268-71; and 'crests' or kinglets, *Regulus*, pp272-3; latter sometimes classified in a separate family (Regulidae) of their own. Sexes look identical, except in many *Sylvia* warblers. Difficult to identify: many are classic 'little brown birds' with few obvious distinctive markings; plumages wear rapidly, adding to confusion. Also, many are shy, and remain hidden in cover. Most nest on or near ground among low vegetation, *Acrocephalus* among reeds and other tall vegetation. Most are summer visitors/passage migrants only, making long migrations to winter mainly in Africa; two British species resident.

● Note: shape/proportions and behaviour help distinguish between different groups; calls of different species within a group often similar, but song important aid to identification.

CETTI'S WARBLER *Cettia cetti*

KEY FACTS

Length: 14cm. **Wingspan:** 15-19cm. **Weight:** 12-18g. **Habitat:** dense, tangled, low scrub near water, reedbeds (especially in winter). **Movements:** sedentary, though a few wander to atypical habitats, such as heathland and orchards. **Population:** colonizer from the Mediterranean; first recorded 1961, first bred 1972 or 1973, spread rapidly; today *c*330 pairs may breed. **Diet:** insects, spiders, snails, some seeds. **Voice:** distinctive, very loud, brief bursts of song consisting of staccato notes 'chee-cheweecho-weecho-weecho-weecho-chew(ee)'; calls much quieter, including stuttering 'chich-ich-ich-ich-ich'. **Nest:** deep cup of leaves and grasses, low in dense vegetation. **Eggs:** 3-5, brick-red. **Incubation:** probably 16-17 days. **Fledging:** 15-16 days. **Broods:** 1-2. **Maturity:** 1 year. **Confusion species:** Savi's, Reed and Marsh (pp257, 260, 261) have paler upperparts and different calls/song; Savi's and Marsh rarer. Nightingale (p242) and female Redstart (p244) have longer, redder tails and different calls/song/habitat.

J F M A M J J A S O N D

△ Scarce resident in S and E Britain. Larger, stouter than other wetland warblers, with plump body, domed head, sturdy legs, broad, rounded tail. Creeps about low down in dense, tangled waterside vegetation, though sometimes emerges briefly into view, flicking tail. Typical view is of bird tilting forward, then diving into cover, flicking tail downwards or cocking it, revealing barred undertail coverts. Looks rather like small Nightingale, but tail shorter, less reddish than back, and eyebrow pale. Reddish-brown above, brightest on back, greyish and white below. Juvenile very similar, though less reddish above and less white below. Male usually utters loud, explosive song from dense cover. Cetti's (pronounced 'Chetti's') Warbler has biggest size difference between sexes of any European perching bird: males up to 30 per cent heavier.

▷ Flight fast and low, with rounded tail fanned and flirted, and rounded wings whirring; darts from one patch of dense cover to another.

Locustella naevia GRASSHOPPER WARBLER

typical individual

faintly streaked individual

KEY FACTS

Length: 12.5cm. **Wingspan:** 15-19cm. **Weight:** 11-15g. **Habitat:** dense, low vegetation in marshes, fens, scrub, damp farmland, young forestry plantations, sand dunes. **Movements:** summer visitor (Apr-Oct); winters Africa. **Population:** decline over past 25 years; now c16 000 pairs breed. **Diet:** insects, spiders. **Voice:** remarkable song, a rapid, dry, sustained, mechanical reeling sound, like fishing reel or cricket, with ventriloquial quality due to bird turning its head; heard day and night. Usual call a sharp 'tchik', run into chatter of alarm. **Nest:** cup of grass, leaves, moss, in low, tangled vegetation. **Eggs:** 5-6, white, speckled purplish. **Incubation:** 13-15 days, by female. **Fledging:** 10-12 days. **Broods:** usually 2, sometimes 3. **Maturity:** 1 year. **Confusion species:** rare Savi's Warbler (below); Sedge Warbler (p258) has bolder creamy eyebrows and more boldly streaked upperparts.

J F M A M J J A S O N D

Savi's Warbler

Reed Warbler

△ Small, slim summer visitor, with rounded tail which it often bobs and sometimes cocks. Very secretive, spending most of time in dense cover on or near ground: has distinctive, prolonged, monotonous reeling song, best heard at dawn or dusk; very high-pitched and hard to hear against other noises; at close range, sounds more rattling. Plumage very variable. Typically, upperparts olive-brown, with darker streaks on crown, mantle, 'shoulders', rump; faint eyebrow. Tail usually reddish-brown, faintly barred. Underparts buff, with browner, faintly streaked chest and flanks; brown streaks/mottling on undertail coverts. Legs pale pink or orange. Some birds have more buff or yellowish upperparts, with heavier or fainter streaking, and yellower underparts, with bolder or less obvious ground colour/streaking on chest/flanks. A few much browner above/below with no obvious streaking visible except at closer range: then very like Savi's Warbler (below).

▽ Flight brief, flitting jerkily; often 'bucks' rear end, emphasizing long, wide rump and rounded tail, which is often flicked and fanned, especially as bird twists and turns or dives into cover.

△ Creeps or runs mouse-like through tangled vegetation with remarkable speed and agility; long central toe enables it to grasp more than one stem at a time. Often impossible to see for more than a moment, though not particularly shy and may sing from an exposed perch.

◁ **Savi's Warbler** *(Locustella luscinioides)* has, since 1960s, become a rare/local breeder in dense reedbeds in parts of S and E England, after 100-year gap as British breeding bird. Larger (14cm), more heavily built/pot-bellied and fuller-tailed than Grasshopper, with unstreaked plumage. Superficially resembles large Reed Warbler (p260), but has very uniform, darker, duller reddish-brown upperparts; underparts whitish with olive-brown wash on breast sides and flanks, and reddish-buff undertail. Legs dark pinkish-brown. Song similar to Grasshopper's but faster, lower-pitched, more buzzing, often preceded by low 'tick' notes. Calls include hard, scolding chatter, abrupt 'pswit' and 'chink chink' like Great Tit's.

SEDGE WARBLER *Acrocephalus schoenobaenus*

129

KEY FACTS

Length: 13cm. **Wingspan:** 17-21cm. **Weight:** 10-13g. **Habitat:** tangled undergrowth, mainly by water, including drier edges of reedbeds with shrubs, in lowlands; some breed in dry scrub, including hawthorn and bramble thickets. **Movements:** summer visitor (mid Apr-mid Oct), wintering Africa. **Population:** *c*360 000 pairs breed. **Diet:** insects, berries in autumn. **Voice:** sharp, explosive 'tucc', often run together into stuttering rattle of alarm, also harsh 'tchurrr'. Song very loud, very varied in tempo; prolonged series of sweet, clear warbles and trills suddenly alternating with harsh, strident chattering calls and mimicry of other birds' calls and song. Often utters snatches of song in brief vertical display flight or while moving about in dense cover; also sings full song from perch; often sings at night. **Nest:** deep cup of grass, spiders' webs, lined with reed flowers, hair and plant down, among dense vegetation, just above ground. **Eggs:** 5-6, pale green, with yellowish-brown blotches and thin dark lines. **Incubation:** 13-14 days, mainly by female. **Fledging:** 10-14 days. **Broods:** 1-2. **Maturity:** 1 year. **Confusion species:** Grasshopper Warbler (p257) has similar plumage but lacks strong crown pattern and has very different song; Reed Warbler (p260) has similar song but without melodic phrases, and lacks crown pattern and streaked back; rare Marsh Warbler (p261), very similar to Reed, but has much more melodic song; rare Aquatic Warbler (opposite) has more strongly streaked back and different head pattern, with clear-cut pale crown stripe, longer pale eyebrow and slightly thicker bill. Aquatic often shows a spikier tail.

spring

autumn

△ Most widespread and easily observed member of reed warbler group *(Acrocephalus)*. Small, quite plump summer visitor; has flat-topped head and 'frowning' expression, striking, broad, creamy eyebrow contrasting with dark crown and dark eyestripe; unstreaked rich ginger rump contrasts with dark brown tail, often revealed as bird droops buff and dark brown wing feathers. Pale yellowish or buff fringes to greater covert and tertial feathers of folded wing sometimes form pale panel. Underparts whitish, with reddish-buff wash on breast and rear flanks. Tail graduated, but not spiky like Aquatic Warbler's; frequently flicked. By autumn, plumage worn, looking more uniform grey-brown, with very dark crown. Bill blackish, with bright yellowish-pink base to lower mandible. Legs greyish-brown.

▷ An inquisitive little bird; though often remains hidden among thick cover, will sidle up a nettle, reed or other stem to investigate intruder. Can become very agitated, scolding an observer with harsh rattling or churring (can be attracted by imitation of its calls), or may respond to intrusion by bursting into song. Often feeds from exposed stems or branches or even on ground. Feeds and sings most actively around dawn and dusk; some individuals sing at night.

spring

juvenile

◁ Juvenile brighter than adult, more yellowish or buffish. Some individuals have pale centre to dark crown, duller, yellower eyebrow and paler, yellower legs, so they closely resemble rare Aquatic Warbler (see opposite for distinctions).

J F M A M J J A S O N D

Acrocephalus schoenobaenus **SEDGE WARBLER**

male, song flight

male, singing

◁ Male has remarkably loud and varied chattering song of alternating series of harsh and sweet notes. Sometimes gives this from perch, either prominent (e.g. top of reed stem or outer branch of bush) or from within cover. As pours out song, may turn from side to side, throat feathers puffed out and whole body trembling with the effort. At other times, performs brief, dancing song flight, ascending vertically, then turning and spiralling down slowly back to perch with outspread wings and tail. The most sustained songs come from perched birds, but those given in song flights are more complex.

Usual flight jerky, low, ⟩ong but quite fluttering; ⟩ks compact, with short tail ⟩ned and often lowered; ⟩n dives deep into cover.

⟩atic Warbler
1st-winter

Sedge Warbler juvenile

◁ **Aquatic Warbler** *(Acrocephalus paludicola)* rare but annual autumn passage migrant, most often 1st-winters seen at reedbeds along S and SW coasts of England. Same length (13cm) as Sedge, but slightly slimmer and rounder-headed, with slightly thicker bill. Much more heavily streaked: back has yellower or golden-buff background contrasting with heavy black streaks to produce distinctive 'tiger-stripe' effect extending to rump and uppertail coverts (only faintly marked on Sedge); usually 2 broad creamy stripes along mantle. Broad, bold creamy stripe along centre of crown, dark lateral crown stripe and long, pale golden-buff eyebrow. Lacks dark area between bill base and eye that makes Sedge look 'fiercer'. Breast streaked at sides (often also in centre). Legs pale pinkish (usually greyish in Sedge). Tail often looks spiky; Sedge's more rounded. Juvenile Sedge, with cream-buff central crown stripe and pale, bright buff legs, can look very similar, but lacks distinctive boldly streaked crown, back and rump pattern.

Adult Aquatics may turn ⟩ in worn autumn plumage: ⟩rk above, much duller than ⟩t-winter, breast more ⟩eaked, may show dark line ⟩tween bill base and eye, ⟩ore like Sedge; much ⟩eaker than Sedge and legs ⟩uch paler, pinkish-buff.

Aquatic Warbler 1st-winter

Aquatic Warbler adult autumn

REED WARBLER *Acrocephalus scirpaceus*

130

spring

△ Locally common summer visitor, mainly to reedbeds, throughout south/central England and Wales; often seen well away from reeds/water on migration. Extremely similar to Marsh, best distinguished by song (see Key Facts); Reed's less varied and musical, with less mimicry of other species; some birds, possibly hybrids with Marsh, have much more similar musical song. Reed has slightly longer, spikier bill than Marsh, longer, lower forehead but often with high-peaked crown behind eye level, slightly shorter wingtips (not reaching tip of tail coverts) and slimmer body. Upperparts warm brown, slightly darker/more rufous than Marsh, especially on rump. Underparts less uniform, with white throat and belly, buff breast sides and undertail, and reddish-buff flanks. Legs usually greyish-brown, slightly darker in spring than Marsh's. Reed tends to perch more horizontally than Marsh; highly acrobatic climber of reed stems, often adopting vertical, head-down posture. Male often sings from deep within reeds but may use exposed perch, when adopts upright, plumper-bodied posture.

▷ Nest a deep cup of grasses woven around living reed stems, incorporated into its structure; differs from Marsh's shallower cup bound to surrounding stems by 'jug handles'.

autumn

◁ By end of summer, with worn plumage, upperparts less olive-brown, though rump retains warm rufous-orange colour; underparts paler.

▷ Juvenile brighter, with more rufous upperparts than adult, especially on rump, and duskier underparts. Rarely possible to distinguish from juvenile Marsh, though legs usually darker.

juvenile

◁ Flight bounding, jerky, brief and low; tail often spread and lowered, especially when diving into cover.

KEY FACTS

Length: 13cm. **Wingspan:** 17-21cm. **Weight:** 10-15g. **Habitat:** breeds mainly in lowland reedbeds, some among other tall vegetation such as willowherbs and arable crops like rape; often feeds in waterside willows. **Movements:** summer visitor (mid Apr-early Oct); winters Africa. **Population:** expansion in range to N and W over last 20 years; now *c*40 000-80 000 pairs breed England/Wales, *c*40-50 singing males recorded Ireland. **Diet:** insects, berries in autumn. **Voice:** calls include low 'churr' and longer, harsh 'ztcharr' of alarm. Song similar to Sedge's, but fussier and gruffer, consisting mainly of harsher, chattering notes and infrequent, less sustained mimicry; typical repeated phrases include 'chirruc chirruc', 'jag-jag-jag'. **Nest:** deep cup of grass, reed flower and other vegetation, lined with finer materials such as hair, woven around living reed stems or other tall vegetation, usually above water; often breeds in loose colonies. **Eggs:** 3-5, greenish-white, blotched olive-green and grey. **Incubation:** 11-12 days, by both sexes. **Fledging:** 10-14 days. **Broods:** 2. **Maturity:** 1 year. **Confusion species:** Marsh Warbler (opposite) looks extremely similar, but voice differs. See also Savi's Warbler (p257).

J F M A M J J A S O N

Acrocephalus palustris MARSH WARBLER

131

Reed Warbler

Marsh Warbler

spring

KEY FACTS

Length: 13cm. **Wingspan:** 18-21cm. **Weight:** 11-15g. **Habitat:** tall, dense vegetation, in overgrown ditches, stream banks, disused farmland etc, often near water. **Movements:** summer visitor (late May–early Oct); winters Africa. **Population:** always scarce and local; marked decline over last 20 years, and now found chiefly in small, isolated populations in SE England; currently fewer than 12 pairs breed most years. **Diet:** insects, berries in autumn. **Voice:** most calls differ from Reed's, including soft, quiet 'stit' and 'tuc', stuttering 'st-t-t-t-t' and 'tic-tirric' and loud, repeated 'tchuc'; also 'churr', softer than Reed's harsh 'ztcharr'. Song remarkable, distinctive musical outpouring of varied notes, including sweet high-pitched warbles and trills, harsh grating and chattering notes, and featuring superb mimicry of songs/calls of many European birds and even African species heard in winter quarters. **Nest:** cup of grass, lined with fine grass and hair, suspended in dense vegetation near ground by 'jug handles' woven round stems. **Eggs:** 4-5, very pale blue-grey, spotted darker. **Incubation:** 12 days, by both sexes. **Fledging:** 10-14 days. **Broods:** 1. **Maturity:** 1 year. **Confusion species:** Reed Warbler (opposite); Savi's Warbler (p257).

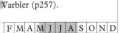

F M A M J J A S O N D

△ Though common in Europe, one of Britain's rarest and most localized breeding birds: population declining, unlike Reed Warbler, which is abundant in suitable habitats and may be increasing. Summer visitor to a few isolated breeding colonies. Unlike Reed, not found in reedbeds; breeds in areas of tall, dense vegetation such as nettles, willowherbs and willows. Usually plumper-bodied, more pear-shaped, with slightly shorter bill, flatter crown, 'gentler' expression, longer wingtips, reaching tip of tail coverts. Tends to perch more upright and be less agile and energetic. Lacks Reed's rufous tinge to paler, more olive-brown upperparts, especially rump, more uniformly pale below, making it look neater; eyering and front of eyebrow whiter. Paler ends to wingtip feathers; Reed's wings look more uniform.

▷ Best distinguished from almost identical Reed by song: Marsh's far more melodious and varied, with many sweet warbling notes. Finest mimic of all British birds; can imitate over 70 bird species in half-hour song bout. On arrival, male sings day and night. Throat may look bigger and whiter especially when male sings from prominent perch, often opening bill wider than Reed to reveal bright orange mouth.

spring

autumn

◁ By end of summer, when plumage worn, looks duller and greyer, even more like Reed, though rump still usually less rufous.

▷ Juvenile more warmly coloured above than adult with rusty tinge, usually indistinguishable from juvenile Reed except by structure, though feet often look paler, usually pinkish-brown or buff-yellow.

juvenile

1st-winter typical individual

1st-winter brighter individual

△ **Icterine Warbler** (*Hippolais icterina*) very scarce but regular passage migrant from E Europe, mainly in autumn (Aug–Oct), few spring, to S/E coasts Britain and S Ireland; mostly 1st-winters. Very like Melodious Warbler (below): both have distinctive, long, broad-based, mainly orangey bill, 'open-faced' expression, greenish and yellowish plumage with yellow eyebrow and eyering, abrupt undertail and square-ended tail. Icterine slightly larger (13.5cm) but slimmer-bodied; long forehead accentuates long bill, giving front-heavy look, but crown often peaked; wings longer, reaching tip of tail coverts. Pale greyish-green above, sometimes brighter; yellowish-white to pale buff below, with pale yellow on chin and throat. Unlike Melodious, usually shows conspicuous pale wing panel. Legs usually blue-grey. Bolder than Melodious, often perching in full view; leaps and hops clumsily through cover, swaying stems; pulls off berries with upward tugs of bill. Usual call short, hard 'tek'; song forceful, repetitive, with harsh notes as well as whistles and musical phrases.

▽ Autumn adults dull olive above, with greener rump, pale yellow below; pale win panel largely lost. Spring adults, rare here, much brighter greenish-olive abov yellower below, with bright wing panel. Juvenile/autum adult Willow Warblers (p268) also green and yello but brighter, smaller, more restless than autumn Icterine/Melodious, with shorter, weaker bill and dar eyestripe extending to bill.

Icterine Warbler adult

autumn

Willow Warbl bright individu

Icterine Warbler

Melodious Warbler

◁ Icterine looks slimmer in flight than Melodiou Warbler, with longer, more pointed wings. A more accomplished flyer, with faster, stronger, more dashing flight, often swerving abruptly int cover. Melodious has distinctly weaker, more fluttering flight action, sometimes so much so that it resembles that of a fledgling.

▷ **Melodious Warbler** (*Hippolais polyglotta*) very scarce but regular passage migrant from SW Europe, almost all in autumn (Aug–Oct), mostly 1st-winters; mainly in S and W, especially along coasts W from Dorset and around Irish Sea. Slightly smaller (13cm) but plumper-bellied than Icterine, with shorter wings, not reaching tip of tail coverts; bill same colour but shorter. Head more rounded, less peaked. Usually lack distinct wing panel. Most have brownish, not bluish-grey, legs. Much more skulking than Icterine, often remaining within same cover for long periods. 1st-winter typically darker, browner-green above than Icterine, and paler, more uniform yellowish-white or cream below. A few almost brown above and creamy-buff below. Not very vocal, but may utter sparrow-like chattering; song soft, smooth, fast series of babbling or twittering notes after hesitant start.

1st-winter typical individual

1st-winter browner individu

autumn

spring

◁ Autumn adults have worn, bleached plumage dull pale brownish-grey above with slightly greener rump, and pale buffy-yellow to yellowis white below. Spring adults (rare here) rich, war greenish-brown above and rich yellow below, with olive or buff wash to breast sides and flank

Sylvia undata **DARTFORD WARBLER**

male

male, song flight, spring and autumn

autumn to spring

female

KEY FACTS

Length: 12.5cm. **Wingspan:** 13-18.5cm. **Weight:** 9-12g. **Habitat:** dry southern heaths with dense gorse bushes and heather. **Movements:** resident; some make short-distance movements; probably also few immigrants from Europe. **Population:** fluctuating, dependent on severity of winters and dryness of summers; up to c1800 pairs breed annually. **Diet:** insects, also spiders (especially in winter) and other invertebrates. **Voice:** long, buzzy 'tchaairr', hard, emphatic 'tuk' and combination of two, e.g. 'tchaairr-ik-tuk'. Song short, scratchy warbling mixed with sweeter notes, frequently repeated. **Nest:** cup of grass, young gorse and heather shoots, moss, wool, lined with fine grass, feathers and hair, often adorned with spiders' cocoons, well hidden among gorse or heather. Males also build several flimsy 'cock's nests'. **Eggs:** 3-5, yellowish or greenish-white, speckled grey and brown. **Incubation:** 12-13 days, mainly by female. **Fledging:** 13-15 days. **Broods:** usually 2, sometimes 3. **Maturity:** 1 year.

J F M A M J J A S O N D

△ Resident, sparsely scattered in heathlands on England's S fringe, chiefly New Forest and Dorset; mainly Mediterranean species, on edge of range here, vulnerable to human disturbance, habitat loss, uncontrolled fires and severe winters. Tiny body with short wings and very long, slim tail, half total length, which it often cocks, moves sideways, and flicks. Body can look slim or round. Crown feathers often raised in high peak; combine with puffed-out throat feathers to give big-headed appearance. Elusive, skulking among dense gorse and heather, though males often sing from tops of gorse bushes or in short, dancing songflight. When glimpsed in distance pausing to perch atop a gorse spray before darting into it again, looks very dark; closer to, male reveals slate-grey head, dark brownish-grey upperparts with grey fringes to brownish-black wing feathers; underparts dull wine-red, apart from white on belly and white spots on throat (may form indistinct moustache stripe), visible at close range. Spiky dark brown bill with yellow base, red eye/eyering, yellowish legs. Female has browner crown, face and upperparts, paler, duller, pinkish underparts; eye/eyering yellow-brown.

juvenile

◁ Juvenile like female but duller, rustier-brown above and brownish-buff below, darker on sides of breast and flanks. Dull eyering.

▷ By Jun-Jul, when plumage worn, brown feather tips mostly gone, and upperparts darker slate-grey, underparts more uniform; loses white spots on throat. Plumage becomes brighter again after moult Aug-Oct.

male summer

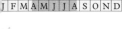

◁ Flight weak, undulating, on short, whirring wings, with long tail bobbing, usually brief and very low, almost touching ground; dives abruptly into cover. Looks very dark in flight.

WHITETHROAT *Sylvia communis*

male

female

spring

△ Medium-sized, large-headed, slim-bodied, with quite long tail, which it frequently flicks or cocks as it darts rapidly in and out of hedge or other cover. Often-raised crown feathers and pale eyes give it 'cross' or 'glaring' expression. In spring, male has pale grey head with pale yellowish or brownish eye, prominent white throat, grey-brown upperparts with distinctive, large, bright rufous panel on dull brown wings; dark brown tail has prominent white outer feathers. Underparts pale creamy-buff, with pinkish wash on breast; belly white. Indistinct whitish eyering; greyish-buff bill, pinkish at base; bright, pale pinkish-brown legs. Female duller, less contrasting, with browner head and less pink breast, dusky brown eye; some females especially dull, with duller whitish outer tail feathers, while others brighter in spring, almost like males. Though often skulking, also restless and inquisitive, emerging to perch briefly on hedge-top or other prominent perch and scold observer with harsh 'churr's.

▷ Males often deliver their scratchy warbling songs during short, jerky, dancing song flight upwards from hedge-top, or from prominent perch.

male, song flight

male summer

◁ By June/July, male has drabber grey head, duller, greyer upperparts, deeper wine-pink breast, and little or no white on outer tail feathers. Autumn adults browner, less pink on breast, more like typical female.

▽ Flight erratic, alternately jerky and darting, and flitting and undulating; burst of uneven wingbeats followed by brief glides and dodges to one side, flitting low over hedge-top and diving back into cover; often fans or flicks longish tail.

juvenile

△ Juvenile like typical female, but upperparts warmer brown, with particularly bright orange-brown wing panel; underparts duller, lacking pink, with darker brown wash to flanks; white outer tail feathers duller.

44

KEY FACTS

Length: 14cm. **Wingspan:** 18.5-23cm. **Weight:** 12-18g. **Habitat:** sunny open areas with bushes, brambles, nettles and other cover for nesting, including hedges, scrubland, coastal clifftops and young deciduous woods and woodland edges. **Movements:** summer visitor (mid Apr-early Oct), and passage migrant (Apr-May, Aug-Oct), wintering in arid Sahel region S of Sahara. **Population:** huge decline 1968-74, due to drought in Sahel winter quarters, then fluctuating numbers, though has never regained former status; currently *c*780 000 pairs breed. **Diet:** insects; berries and fruit in autumn. **Voice:** harsh 'tcharr', lower-pitched, more drawn-out, scolding 'churrr', sharp 'tak-tak' of alarm and, most distinctive, sweeter 'wheet wheet whit-whit-whit-whit'. Typical song lively, hurried, scratchy warbling, mixture of harsher sounds and sweeter notes, often given in short dancing song flight. **Nest:** low cup of dry grass, rootlets, lined with fine grass and hair, hidden low among brambles. **Eggs:** 4-5, pale blue or green, speckled olive-grey. **Incubation:** 9-13 days, by both sexes. **Fledging:** 10-12 days. **Broods:** 2. **Maturity:** 1 year. **Confusion species:** Lesser Whitethroat (opposite) lacks rufous wings; see also Garden Warbler (p266).

J F M A M J J A S O N D

Sylvia curruca **LESSER WHITETHROAT**

male *female*

spring and autumn

KEY FACTS

Length: 13.5cm. **Wingspan:** 16.5-19cm. **Weight:** 10-16g. **Habitat:** tall, overgrown hedges, small thickets, patches of scrub. **Movements:** summer visitor (late Apr-Sep) and passage migrant (mid Apr-Jun, mid Aug-Nov), including a few birds of larger Siberian race *blythi*; winters NE Africa/SW Asia. **Population:** *c*80 000 pairs breed Britain, only one breeding record from Ireland. **Diet:** insects; berries and fruit in autumn. **Voice:** usual calls hard 'tak tak', like Blackcap's ('p267), but thinner, lower-pitched, more abrupt; scolding 'tchurrr', like Whitethroat's; also distinctive, sharp, thin, very high notes, like sounds of bats or shrews. Song monotonous, loud rattle on a single note, often preceded by soft, low-pitched musical warbling, with occasional squeaks and stutters. **Nest:** cup of fine twigs and grass, lined with fine roots, hair etc; low in shrub; smaller, flimsier than Whitethroat's. **Eggs:** 4-6, cream, blotched grey or brown. **Incubation:** 10-14 days, by both sexes. **Fledging:** 10-14 days. **Broods:** 1, sometimes 2. **Maturity:** 1 year. **Confusion species:** Whitethroat (opposite).

F	M	A	M	J	J	A	S	O	N	D

△ Slimmer, neater, more compact than Whitethroat, with less peaked crown and shorter, slimmer tail; lacks rufous in wings, has greyer upperparts, dark eyepatch, duller, whiter underparts, much darker legs, vaguer pale eyering (often only beneath eye, sometimes missing altogether) and very different song. Grey-brown above, greyer on crown, nape, rump and upper tail-coverts; prominent dusky-grey or blackish patch from bill base onto cheeks; dark greyish-brown wings; white outer tail feathers (narrower, less obvious than in Whitethroat); underparts greyish-white, with pink tinge to breast and flanks in spring; eye brownish-grey; bill blackish, without pale base, and legs dark blue-grey. Shyer, much more skulking than Whitethroat, less excitable; more often in trees, especially males in spring, which sing from higher branches.

male summer

◁ In worn plumage, between May and Jul, crown and upperparts cleaner, darker; breast sides and flanks greyer, less tinged with buff; rest of underparts drabber, sometimes greyer, lacking any warm pink tinge.

▷ Birds of Siberian race *blythi* occasionally turn up here, chiefly on E coasts from Shetland to Kent, Oct-early Nov. Tend to be larger than usual (W European) race, with warmer, browner upperparts; darker head, contrasting less with dark eyepatch and more with throat, and short partial eyebrow in front of eye.

Siberian race blythi

juvenile

◁ Juvenile very similar to adult, but crown browner, duller, same colour as back, paler, less contrasting eyepatch, darker brown wings and dingier underparts washed with buff.

◁ Flight more direct, less jerky and dancing than Whitethroat's, with more regular, faster wingbeats; smaller head, more compact body and shorter, slimmer tail. Shows less white in outer tail feathers.

GARDEN WARBLER *Sylvia borin*

65

Medium-sized warbler with plump body, rounded head and stubby bill; face has 'gentle' expression, with large dark eyes. Lacks any obvious plumage features. Misleading name: not normally a bird of gardens.

△ Plain plumage and sturdy, rounded shape are main identification features, but close view reveals obscure pale greyish or buff eyebrow and eyering, which emphasizes dark eye; greyer sides of neck on otherwise drab grey-brown upperparts; pale tips to tertial and primary wing feathers; brownish wash to sides of belly on otherwise whitish-buff underparts. Bill brown with paler base; legs greyish-brown. Generally shyer than Blackcap, skulking in cover for long periods, though singing males often use conspicuous perches in trees. Song and calls very like Blackcap's, but can be distinguished with experience. Does not flick wings or tail except when excited.

▷ Juvenile very similar to adult, but with rusty or yellowish tinge to upperparts, and darker buff underparts; warm brown or even chestnut hue to fringes of larger inner wing feathers.

juvenile

◁ Flight fast, flitting, rather like Robin's (pp240-1); bulky body and full tail. Has glowing-buff underwings.

▽ **Barred Warbler** *(Sylvia nisoria)* very scarce autumn passage migrant from E Europe (Aug-mid Oct), mostly to E coasts; rare in spring. Large warbler (length 15.5cm), stout-bodied, with strong bill and sturdy legs, big head and steep forehead, rounded back and long, full, square-ended tail. Often slower, less agile than smaller warblers; sometimes looks rather like small shrike (pp288-9). Generally shy and skulking, but sometimes hops heavily to top of bush. Most British records are of 1st-winters: plain birds, rather like oversized Garden Warblers, but with more sandy-coloured or greyer upperparts, 2 faint pale wingbars, paler fringes to tertial wing feathers and rump, narrow white corners to tail and variable barring on shoulders, flanks and undertail (often only on latter). Adults, rare here, greyer, with whitish underparts boldly marked with dark crescents, and staring yellow eyes.

1st-winter   *adult male autumn*

J F M A M J J A S O N

66

female

male

KEY FACTS

Length: 13cm. **Wingspan:** 20-23cm. **Weight:** 14-20g. **Habitat:** broadleaved/mixed woods, overgrown hedges, copses, parks, gardens, with dense undergrowth; wintering birds visit bird tables. **Movements:** summer visitor (Apr-Sep); passage migrant (late Mar-Jun, mid Aug-Oct); British breeders winter in S Europe and N Africa, but some central European birds winter here, especially in W and SW. **Population:** *c*580 000 pairs breed Britain, *c*40 000 Ireland; probably over 3000 birds winter. **Diet:** insects; berries and fruit in autumn, also fat, cheese etc from bird tables in winter. **Voice:** main alarm call a hard 'takk', often repeated, harder and more emphatic than Garden Warbler's; also a scolding 'tcherrr'. Song beautiful rich, clear warbling, usually shorter, deeper, more mellow and varied than Garden's (though can mimic latter). **Nest:** cup of plant stems, lined with fine grasses etc, low in brambles etc. **Eggs:** 4-5, pale buff, spotted dark brown. **Incubation:** 10-12 days, by both sexes. **Fledging:** 10-14 days. **Broods:** usually 2. **Maturity:** 1 year. **Confusion species:** male quite similar to Marsh and Willow Tits (pp282-3), but these smaller, usually plumper, bigger-headed, with bigger caps, and different actions and voice. Similar song to Garden Warbler (opposite).

△ Medium-sized, looks flatter-headed, slimmer than Garden Warbler (opposite), with thinner, sharper bill, and prominent cap contrasting with rest of plumage. Less secretive than Garden, generally more restless, with more upright posture, especially singing male. Song very similar to Garden's but can be distinguished with experience. Greyer than Garden, especially on cheeks, nape, throat and breast; bill black, legs slate-grey. Male has glossy black cap, grey-brown upperparts (with olive tinge in fresh spring plumage), olive-brown wings, silvery-grey underparts with darker flanks and dull white belly, and blackish tail. Female as male, but with bright red-brown cap, more olive-brown tinge to upperparts and browner cheeks, nape and underparts.

juvenile female

1st-winter male

△ Juvenile resembles female, but has duller, yellow-brown to blackish-brown cap, less grey upperparts, often showing rusty tinge, and duskier underparts, especially breast and flanks. Although young females usually have yellow-brown caps and young males blackish-brown ones, this is not always a reliable distinction. By their 1st winter, males have dull black caps with some brown feathers, while 1st-winter females sometimes distinguishable from adult females by more orange crown.

▷ Small numbers of Blackcaps remain here over winter instead of migrating to Mediterranean or Africa; fond of visiting garden bird feeders, where often surprisingly aggressive towards other birds.

Blackcap male

Marsh Tit

male

◁ Flight quick, flitting; looks very similar to that of Garden Warbler, though lighter, with slightly longer, slimmer tail.

J F M A M J J A S O N D

WILLOW WARBLER *Phylloscopus trochilus*

67

Small, slender, restless leaf warbler with sad, sweet song; our most abundant summer visitor, by far the commonest and most widespread of all our warblers. Very similar to Chiffchaff, best distinguished by totally different songs, but usually looks neater, cleaner and paler, with longer, clearer, yellower eyebrow, greener upperparts, paler underparts, and usually pale brown legs. Bill usually looks slightly longer, head flatter and wings a bit longer.

W race trochilus
spring

◁ Adults of W race *trochilus*, common breeders/passage migrants, bright in spring, olive-green above, often with brownish tinge, and pale whitish-yellow below.

▷ Plumage less variable than Chiffchaff's but, as it wears, does become duller, greyer-green above and duller yellow below, by about Jun. Later (Jul-Sep) moults body feathers and becomes much greener above and lemon-yellow beneath, with equally yellow eyebrow; easier to distinguish by plumage from Chiffchaff at this time than in spring. Like Chiffchaffs, Willow Warblers constantly flick wings and tail (but without former's distinctive downward tail dip/wag), and flit through trees, hovering to pick insects from leaves.

summer   *W race* trochilus

autumn

juvenile

◁ Juveniles variable, but usually bright green above, often strikingly yellow below and on eyebrow; bill and legs have orange tinge lacking in Chiffchaff. Bright green/yellow pattern leads to confusion with Icterine, Melodious or Wood Warbler (pp262, 270).

▷ Some Willow Warblers, particularly passage migrants from N/E Europe, and many Scottish breeders, look pale, washed-out, with much browner upperparts and whiter underparts, and barely any yellow visible. Best distinguished from dull autumn Chiffchaffs and 'Siberian Chiffchaffs' by structure/leg colour.

autumn

Willow Warbler
N/E race acredula

Chiffchaff
W race collybita

KEY FACTS

Length: 10.5-11.5cm.
Wingspan: 16.5-22cm.
Weight: 6-10g. **Habitat:** woods (especially along edges and in clearings), copses, bushes, scrub, young conifer plantations, overgrown hedges and gardens. **Movements:** summer visitor (Apr-Sep) and passage migrant (late Mar-Apr and Jul-Oct); British breeders winter W Africa. **Population:** c3.1 million pairs breed. **Diet:** small insects and their larvae. **Voice:** call a plaintive, distinctly disyllabic 'hoo-eet'; distinctive, musical, wistful song a rippling cascade of descending silvery notes, starting softly, growing louder, then dying away in a terminal flourish, '...swee-sweeotoo'. **Nest:** dome of grass, lined with feathers, hidden among vegetation on or near ground. **Eggs:** 6-7, white, speckled red-brown. **Incubation:** 13 days, by female. **Fledging:** 13-14 days. **Broods:** 1, sometimes 2. **Maturity:** 1 year. **Confusion species:** Chiffchaff (opposite) very similar, though usually duller, greyer/browner above, whiter/buffer/less yellow below, clearer eyering and much darker legs. Very different songs best distinction; calls subtly different.

| J | F | M | A | M | J | J | A | S | O | N | D |

Flight low, quite weak-looking, but fast and agile; often chases other small birds. Action slightly stronger than that of Chiffchaff.

68

spring

summer

△ Very similar to slightly larger Willow Warbler, but generally appears plumper, with rounder head, smaller-looking bill, slightly longer tail, and slightly shorter, more rounded wings. Most have dark greyish legs, which often look slimmer than Willow's usually paler legs; bill generally looks all-black. Surest distinction totally different song, repeating its name. Plumage more variable than Willow's. In spring, our breeders and many passage migrants, belonging to W race *collybita*, dull brownish-olive above, dingier than Willow, with slightly brighter, yellower rump, and buff-white below, with yellowish wash; eyebrow shorter, less distinct than Willow's, cheeks darker, more uniform, and pale eyering often more noticeable. Usually shows blackish mark just below 'shoulder'. From about Jun, worn plumage loses most or all of yellowish tinge, being browner, then duskier, above and more buff, then whiter, below. Like Willow, flicks wings/tail almost constantly; tail movement when feeding distinctive; tail lowered below body level and wagged sideways. Often sings from higher in trees. Summer visitor, but a few overwinter, mainly in SW.

autumn

◁ After summer/autumn moult (Jun-Oct), typical W European birds brighter, more greenish above and yellowish below, although not nearly as bright as typical autumn Willow Warblers.

▽ Scandinavian race *abietinus*, regular on passage, browner or greyer above, paler below. Siberian race *tristis*, rare here late autumn/ winter, even greyer above and whitish below, with bolder eyebrow and subtle wingbar (less distinct than Greenish Warbler, p271).

juvenile

△ Juveniles browner above, with yellower, less olive tone, often suffused grey, and yellower throat/breast; usually look darker, much less green above, much less yellow below, and dingier overall than juvenile Willow Warblers. Often look 'scruffy' compared to adults.

*Siberian race
tristis autumn*

▽ Flight more fluttering than that of Willow, with shorter, more rounded wings (does not migrate as far as longer-winged Willow).

Willow Warbler

Chiffchaff

WOOD WARBLER *Phylloscopus sibilatrix*

69

▷ Our largest leaf warbler, distinctly bigger, sleeker, longer, brighter, more elegant than Willow Warbler and Chiffchaff, with longer, more pointed wings which it often droops (not flicks) below proportionately shorter tail. From below, shape particularly distinctive: elliptical body and drooped wings tapering to short, almost triangular tail. Male gives very distinctive song (of 2 types) while moving about high in tree or in slow, butterfly-like display flight.

spring

▽ Much bolder plumage pattern than Willow Warbler or Chiffchaff, with bright green upperparts (tinged golden-yellow in fresh spring plumage) and sulphur-yellow eyebrow and breast contrasting with white of rest of underparts. Dusky-green stripe through eye; bright yellowish fringes to wing feathers. Large head; prominent bright brown bill with orange-yellow lower mandible; yellowish to brownish legs. Has very different song and calls from Willow Warbler or Chiffchaff; much scarcer than either, chiefly restricted to open oak or beech woods, especially in W. Spends much time among leaves, where well camouflaged, usually high in trees; moves by short leaps and flutters beneath leaf canopy.

Willow Warbler bright individual

Wood Warbler spring

juvenile

▷ Juvenile very similar to adult, but upperparts drabber with grey-brown tinge, and underparts paler yellow.

◁ Flight light, agile, stronger than that of smaller relatives; longish wings and rather short, broad tail produce more compact shape. Very agile when hovering to pick insects off leaves or darting out to catch fly in mid-air.

KEY FACTS

Length: 12.5cm. **Wingspan:** 19.5-24cm. **Weight:** 7-12g. **Habitat:** mature broadleaved woods, chiefly upland oak and beech with little ground cover. **Movements:** summer visitor (mid Apr-Aug) and scarce passage migrant from Continent (Apr-Jun, Aug-Sep), wintering Africa. **Population:** c17 000 pairs breed Britain, c30 singing males Ireland. **Diet:** insects and larvae. **Voice:** main call sad, piping 'piu', also soft 'wit wit wit' and sharp 'see see see'. Song of two types: first and most common a series of remarkably powerful 'stip' notes, slowly repeated at first, then accelerating to a loud, silvery grasshopper-like trill; second type, uttered less frequently, a dramatic repetition of clearer and more liquid version of the 'piu' call. **Nest:** dome of grass and leaves, lined with fine grass, built into ground, often against slope. **Eggs:** 6-7, white, speckled purplish-brown. **Incubation:** 12-13 days, by female. **Fledging:** 11-12 days. **Broods:** 1. **Maturity:** 1 year. **Confusion species:** Willow Warbler (p268) and Chiffchaff (p269) smaller, more restless, less elegant, with shorter wings and longer tails. Melodious and Icterine Warblers (p262) lack Wood's white underparts and have longer bills, steeper foreheads and darker (not pinkish) legs. All these have very different calls and songs.

| J | F | M | A | M | J | J | A | S | O | N | D |

Greenish Warbler *(Phylloscopus trochiloides)* rare but annual and increasing wanderer from E Europe/Asia, traditionally autumn (especially late Aug-Sep), but also recently in increasing numbers late spring/early summer (late May/early Jun), mainly to E coasts Britain in autumn, though spring/summer records scattered throughout coastal counties. Most records are of 1st-winter birds, though adults have been recorded, including singing males in spring.

*Greenish Warbler
1st-winter*

autumn

*Greenish
Warblers*

spring

*Chiffchaff
Siberian
race* tristis
autumn

◁ Rather like greyish Chiffchaff (p269); indeed, Chiffchaffs of greyer, E races with faint wingbars have been mistaken for this species, though they usually do not appear here until late autumn (Oct onwards), have different structure, are black-billed, and their wingbars are never as noticeable as those of Greenish. Smaller (10cm) than Arctic Warbler (below); like Arctic, has larger, longer, flatter head than Chiffchaff; 1st-winters have greyish-green upperparts and whitish underparts with duller, greyer flanks and yellowish tinge sometimes visible at close view on breast and flanks. Thinner eyebrows than Arctic, usually meeting over bill and sometimes kinked up at rear (though less noticeably than on Arctic). Short but distinct wingbar. Bill has yellow or orange-pink lower mandible. Legs usually look darker, browner, than Arctic's. Autumn adults greyer above, whiter below, with wingbar faint or missing. Spring adults brighter, greener. Call very different: wagtail-like 'chee-vit'. Song rapid, high-pitched, beginning with call, then jerky chattering, accelerating towards final Wren-like trill.

Arctic Warbler *(Phylloscopus borealis)* rare but annual autumn wanderer (Aug-Oct, with peak in Sep) from N Eurasia/Alaska, mainly to Shetland, with small numbers down E coast Britain and SW coast England. Most are 1st-winter birds, but adults do turn up, usually in worn plumage.

*Arctic Warbler
1st-winter*

*Arctic Warbler
autumn*

*Willow Warbler
race* acredula
autumn

◁ Larger (11cm) and stouter than Greenish Warbler (above), Willow Warbler (p268) and Chiffchaff (p269), with heavier, broader-based bill. Very similar to Greenish, with large, long, flattish head, but tends to have greener upperparts; longer creamy eyebrows, often not meeting above bill, and extending almost as far back as nape, where often kinked upwards or downwards. Like Greenish, has dark eyestripe, contrasting with eyebrow; cheeks tend to be darker, blotchier, and breast duller, greyer. Often shows 2 wingbars, the upper smaller, fainter (rare on Greenish). Legs yellowish, paler than in Greenish. Autumn adults in worn plumage paler, browner above, especially on wings and tail, and often have only hindmost wingbar, whiter below. Call very different from that of Greenish: hard, metallic 'tzik'. Has stronger, more dashing flight than Greenish, with bulkier body and longer wings.

*Arctic Warbler
autumn*

*Greenish Warbler
autumn*

*Chiffchaff
autumn*

*Willow Warbler
autumn*

GOLDCREST *Regulus regulus*

male   *female*

84

△ Britain's (and Europe's) smallest bird, weighing no more than 5p coin. Looks like cross between warbler and tit, with big rounded head, tiny, rotund, neckless body, short wings and tail and minute, spiky bill. Compared with Firecrest, rather dingy, though passage migrants and wintering birds from N Europe somewhat brighter (and slightly larger). Coloured 'crest' frequently raised and spread in excitement; otherwise, may not be very obvious. Has very distinctive 'open-faced' appearance due to pale greyish area around large, prominent, beady black eye, producing 'surprised' expression. Heard more often than seen, usually remaining high among dense conifers; very high-pitched calls and song.

male   *female*

△ Adults have yellow crown, raised when bird excited, with black border; in male, crown has bright orange centre, becoming orange to red at rear. Otherwise sexes look the same, with dull dark greenish upperparts, narrow black moustache stripe, broad black band and 2 white bars on wing; underparts dull whitish, suffused buff and yellow.

▷ Juvenile lacks coloured crest, though crown has dark mottling at sides; browner above than adults, with duller wing pattern, and less buffish below.

juvenile

▽ Very agile, especially when feeding, hovering like leaf warbler to pick aphids from beneath leaves or when catching flying insects; also, like leaf warblers, frequently flicks wings. Restless, constantly fluttering about or moving in tiny hops, so seems to be creeping fast; often flits from tree to tree, with whirring beats of short rounded wings, when dumpy little body contrasts with slim, slightly forked tail. Mainly high up in trees, but also searches for food low down. In winter, often joins flocks of tits roaming woods in search of food. Usually very tame, seeming unaware of humans.

female   *male*

KEY FACTS

Length: 8.5-9cm. **Wingspan:** 13.5-15.5cm. **Weight:** 5-7g.
Habitat: breeds in woods, mainly coniferous but also mixed or deciduous, especially in Ireland, also in gardens with large conifers; in winter also occurs in hedges, scrub and smaller gardens.
Movements: our breeders mainly resident, though some dispersal, chiefly SE, often across Irish Sea; many immigrants from N and E Europe in winter.
Population: *c*860 000 pairs breed; may be as many as 4 or even 5 million birds in winter.
Diet: spiders, insects. **Voice:** shrill, thin and very high-pitched 'see-see-see' call, weak and difficult to pinpoint; song of similar quality, a rhythmical, rising and falling 'seedla-seedla-seedla-seedla-sissi-peesoo', ending in flourish. **Nest:** tiny deep cup of moss and cobwebs, lined with feathers, usually suspended from twigs at end of conifer branch; sometimes among ivy. **Eggs:** 7-8, white, finely spotted reddish-brown.
Incubation: 16 days, by female. **Fledging:** 18-20 days.
Broods: 2. **Maturity:** 1 year.
Confusion species: Firecrest (opposite) much brighter, with more striking, complex head pattern, bronzy 'shoulders' and different song. See also Pallas's and Yellow-browed Warblers (opposite), both rare passage migrants only.

J	F	M	A	M	J	J	A	S	O	N	D

male   *female*

△ Similar to Goldcrest in shape, habits and size, but has much brighter, cleaner plumage -- brighter olive-green upperparts and whiter, 'silkier' underparts – and, in adults, striking pattern of stripes on head. As well as larger, brighter crown stripe with broader black edges, has broad white eyebrow and dark eyestripe; short black moustache stripe. Crown fiery orange-red in male, yellow at rear; bright yellow in female; also have orange and yellow patches respectively just above bill. Another distinction from Goldcrest (and small leaf warblers) is bronzy shoulder patch, though this is duller in females/immatures.

▷ Juvenile lacks bright crown patch, but has whitish eyebrow and blackish eyestripe, distinguishing it from juvenile Goldcrest.

juvenile

▽ **Pallas's Warbler** *(Phylloscopus proregulus)* looks no larger (9.5cm) than Goldcrest/Firecrest and quite similar, especially to latter, with boldly striped head, plump body and restless actions; rare but annual vagrant from Siberia, mainly Oct-Nov, mostly to E and S coasts, from Shetland to Scilly. Upperparts bright green, with 2 bold yellow wingbars emphasized by blackish bands. Distinguished from Yellow-browed (below) by dumpier shape, bold yellow central crown stripe and yellow eyebrow, separated by blackish-green sides to crown and eyestripe. Pale yellowish rump clinches identification, best seen when bird flicks wings or hovers, which it does frequently. Call slightly rising 'wseeet'.

Yellow-browed Warblers   *race humei 1st-winter*   *Pallas's Warbler 1st-winter*

1st-winter

△ **Yellow-browed Warbler** *(Phylloscopus inornatus)* tiny (10cm), very scarce but annual, in greater numbers than Pallas's; similar range, also S Ireland; regular Scilly; some overwinter; often with Goldcrests. Longer/slimmer than Pallas's, with longer wing-point; crown stripe and contrasting rump absent or faint; never distinctly yellow. Long pale yellow eyebrow, dusky eyestripe; quite bright greenish or brownish-olive above, with 2 conspicuous whitish wingbars emphasized by blackish bands; dull whitish below. Calls with loud, rising 'tsweeest', rather like Coal Tit. Race *humei* rare, drabber, usually with only one wingbar.

KEY FACTS

Length: 9cm. **Wingspan:** 13-16cm. **Weight:** 5-7g. **Habitat:** breed in various types of woodland, including conifer plantations, though much less tied to conifers than Goldcrest, and occurs widely in both summer and winter in mixed or broadleaved woodland. Winters chiefly in scrub along S and W coasts Britain; a few inland along river valleys. **Movements:** movements of British birds uncertain; most wintering birds probably from Continent. **Population:** c80-250 singing males establish territories each year, though at least half of these may fail to breed; c200-400 birds winter (great variation between years). **Diet:** invertebrates, especially springtails, spiders and aphids. **Voice:** 'see see see' call indistinguishable from Goldcrest's, but rhythmically repeated 'zit' and loud, piping, tit-like 'peeppeep' distinct. Song like Goldcrest's but shorter, louder, lower, 'zi-zi-zi-zi-zi-zi-zit' without flourish at end. **Nest:** like Goldcrest's, but sometimes in broadleaved trees. **Eggs:** 7-11, pinkish-buff, with very fine red-brown spots. **Incubation:** 14-16 days, by female. **Fledging:** probably 22-24 days. **Broods:** 2. **Maturity:** probably 1 year. **Confusion species:** Goldcrest (opposite), Yellow-browed and Pallas's Warblers (right).

| J | F | M | A | M | J | J | A | S | O | N | D |

85

FLYCATCHERS
Family Muscicapidae

Small, short-legged birds that specialize in catching insects by watching motionless from a perch, then flying out to seize them in their bills in mid-air or dropping onto the ground to catch them there. Small, rather flattened bills have very broad gape for trapping insects; bristles around gape may detect prey and protect birds' eyes from damage as they deal with large, struggling, tough-skinned insects. The three regular British species are easy to distinguish from one another.

RED-BREASTED FLYCATCHER *Ficedula parva*

male 1st-summer *1st-winter*

△ Plump little bird, much smaller than other flycatchers – only size of Blue Tit, easily distinguished from relatives by striking tail pattern; brownish-black tail has bold white patches on either side at base. Round head, short, sharp, brown bill with broad base, often shining yellow in light. Big dark eyes emphasized by whitish eyering. Narrow wingtips often drooped either side of slim, often cocked, tail; wings and tail often flicked. Very alert and restless, with actions rather like Willow Warbler or other leaf warbler, feeding from foliage; lively and usually not at all shy. Frequently darts out from perch to snap up fly in mid-air or seize beetle from ground. Most birds passing through here are immatures. 1st-winter birds have grey-brown upperparts, with rusty-buff tips and edges of greater coverts and tertials, and creamy- or yellow-buff underparts, with diffuse grey bib. By 1st summer, males may show just a tinge of red on throat, but may not acquire full red throat until 2 or even 3 years old.

male *female*

△ Adult male (rare here) like tiny Robin, with grey or greyish head (almost blue-grey on face and sides of neck) and buff-red to orange-red throat. Adult female similar to 1st-winter bird, but lacks rusty-buff tips on wings.

▷ Flight very agile when feeding, able to perform tight circles; broad wings beat fast and tail often looks quite long. Otherwise usually flies fast to cover.

1st-winter

KEY FACTS

Length: 11.5cm. **Wingspan:** 18.5-21cm. **Weight:** 8-13g. **Habitat:** migrants mainly in coastal scrub/trees; breeds Europe in deciduous/mixed forests. **Movements:** scarce but regular autumn passage migrant from E Europe, mid Aug-mid Nov, especially early Oct, with a few in spring; winters Indian subcontinent and SE Asia. **Population:** *c*50-200 birds reported each year. **Diet:** mainly insects, also spiders, earthworms, other invertebrates. **Voice:** calls include abrupt, hard 'dzik', loud 'pfitt', softer, rising, melancholy 'tlee' and short chattering rattle, like Wren's (p238) but not so loud. **Maturity:** probably 1 year. **Confusion species:** plumage pattern of male similar to Robin's (pp240-1), but latter much bigger, and lacks all-grey head and bold black/ white tail pattern. Female could be mistaken for small chat or warbler, but she also has distinctive tail pattern.

| J | F | M | A | M | J | J | A | S | O | N | D |

Ficedula hypoleuca **PIED FLYCATCHER**

female   summer

male

KEY FACTS

Length: 13cm. **Wingspan:** 21.5-24cm. **Weight:** 10-15g. **Habitat:** mature open deciduous woodland, especially sessile oak woods on hillsides or valleys; also well-wooded parkland and gardens; usually near water.
Movements: summer visitor, almost entirely to W and N Britain. Spring/autumn passage migrants from Continent, late Apr-early Jun, Aug-mid Oct. Winters tropical Africa. **Population:** 35 000-40 000 pairs breed Britain, 1-2 pairs Ireland. **Diet:** mainly insects, especially flies, beetles, wasps/bees/ants; many caterpillars, especially for feeding young; small amounts of fruit and seeds in late summer and on migration. **Voice:** commonest calls loud, sharp, penetrating 'whit', like Chaffinch (p301), softer 'pwheet'; also repeated, abrupt 'tic', often combined with other calls as 'whit-tic' or 'pwheet-tic'. Song a brief, sweet warbling repetition of 'psee-chee' notes, clearly separated, ending in brief liquid jangling trill. **Nest:** cup of leaves, moss, lined with hair and other finer materials, in natural hole or old wood-pecker hole in tree; readily takes to nestboxes. **Eggs:** 5-9, pale blue. **Incubation:** 12-13 days, by female. **Fledging:** 14-17 days. **Broods:** 1. **Maturity:** 1 year. **Confusion species:** male unmistakable; only other regular small British birds with pied plumage are Pied Wagtail (pp232-3), not in woods and with much longer, constantly wagging tail, and Dipper (p237), much larger, plumper, in or by streams and rivers. Juveniles similar to those of Spotted Flycatcher (p276), but have white edges to flight feathers. Female and young Red-breasted (opposite) smaller, with larger white patches at base of blackish tail.

Slightly smaller and more compact than Spotted Flycatcher, with stubbier bill and shorter tail. Spends more time hidden in cover than Spotted, rarely uses same lookout perch more than once; as well as catching insects in flight, also takes them from leaves, trunk or branches while hovering or clinging to bark, and from ground. Frequently moves tail up and down and flicks entire wing from shoulder. In summer, males boldly pied, with jet-black upperparts relieved only by small white patch on forehead and large white wing patches; black tail with white outer feathers. Underparts white. Females drab brown above, whitish below, without white on forehead and with less white on wings; become more buff below in autumn; usually show faint moustache stripe on throat. From autumn (after moult Jul-Aug), males resemble females closely but have blackish rumps and tails and more white on wings; most lose white forehead patch. Bill and legs black.

male 1st-summer

juvenile

Juvenile similar to juvenile Spotted, with scaled and spotted plumage, but distinguished by white markings on wings and tail. 1st-summer males distinguished from adult males by having brown mixed with black on upperparts (some all brown), less white on forehead and duller wings.

Dramatic population increases have been achieved in some areas where large numbers of nestboxes provided. (By the time the Pied Flycatchers arrive here from Africa, the best natural tree nest holes often already taken by tits.)

male

female

◁ Looks short-tailed in flight and more compact than Spotted; white wing markings and white outer tail feathers conspicuous, particularly in breeding male. Spend much time darting in and out of tree canopy.

| J | F | M | A | M | J | J | A | S | O | N | D |

SPOTTED FLYCATCHER *Muscicapa striata*

13

△ Commonest/most widespread of our flycatchers. Spends much of time perched very upright on bare branch, overhead wire, fence or another favourite vantage point, often just beneath foliage where light and shade meet, watching for flying insects. Usually solitary except after breeding and on migration. Adults have grey-brown upperparts, with short streaks on crown, and whitish underparts, with buff wash to breast sides and flanks; close view reveals breast marked with quite long, soft dull brown streaks. Blackish-brown wing feathers have narrow, pale edges, not bold white markings as in Pied Flycatcher.

△ When it sees fly or other insect approaching, Spotted Flycatcher darts out smartly with flurry of wingbeats, followed by a glide, to seize it with audible snap of broad-based bill before gliding back to same or nearby perch, where it deals with prey. It beats large or venomous insects against perch to subdue them before eating them.

juvenile

◁ Juveniles earn the species' name, being truly spotted, heavily marked with round buffish-white spots above; more buff below than adult; throat, breast and flanks spotted or scaled dark brown. At first, plumage often looks loose and fluffy and tail distinctly shorter than adult's. Wing covert feathers have reddish-buff edges.

▷ Flight over any distance rapid, with bursts of wingbeats and slightly undulating path; could be confused with large warbler such as Garden Warbler. No distinctive plumage pattern, lacking white wingbars of Pied Flycatcher and black and white tail pattern of Red-breasted.

KEY FACTS

Length: 14.5cm. **Wingspan:** 23-25.5cm. **Weight:** 14-19g. **Habitat:** open woodland, especially along edges and in clearings, also parks and gardens with trees. **Movements:** summer visitor; also spring and autumn passage migrants from Continent (late Apr-early Jun, Aug-mid Oct); winters tropical Africa. **Population:** *c*155 000 pairs breed. **Diet:** mainly flying insects; also berries in autumn. **Voice:** usual calls thin, scratchy, high 'tzee' and louder 'tzee-zuk-zuk' of alarm. Song feeble, simple series of 6 or so squeaky notes, with pause between each. **Nest:** cup of moss and other vegetation, lined with feathers etc, among ivy, creepers, on ledges, walls, in tree holes; sometimes in old nests of other birds; uses open-fronted nestboxes. **Eggs:** 3-5, white, blotched red. **Incubation:** 12-14 days, by female. **Fledging:** 12-16 days. **Broods:** 1-2. **Maturity:** 1 year. **Confusion species:** juvenile Pied Flycatcher (p275). Garden Warbler (p266) also brown and whitish, but different structure, with longer legs; different posture.

| J | F | M | A | M | J | J | A | S | O | N | D |

BABBLERS
Family Timaliidae

Large and varied family of mainly thrush-like, long-tailed, highly sociable birds found mostly in woodland in tropical Asia and, to lesser extent, Africa; only one occurs here, the Bearded Tit, which, despite name, is not related to the true tits. It is a member of a subgroup of 20 species of babblers with stubby bills that live in reedbeds and bamboo thickets; all the others found in Himalayan region, China and SE Asia.

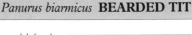

Panurus biarmicus **BEARDED TIT**

adult male *adult female*

juvenile male

KEY FACTS

Length: 12.5cm (including 7cm tail). **Wingspan:** 16-18cm. **Weight:** 12-18g. **Habitat:** breeds/winters only in extensive reedbeds, but also feeds in tall vegetation nearby. **Movements:** resident, but many birds, especially immatures, disperse from breeding sites in autumn. Some migration to and from Continent, especially Netherlands; occasional large-scale irruptions after food supply exhausted. **Population:** down to only a few pairs after hard winter of 1947 and flooding of E Anglian reedbeds in 1950s. Expansion since mid 1960s after immigration from colonies in newly created Dutch polders. Today *c*400 pairs breed; 2000-2500 birds winter (maybe as many as 10 000 during large-scale irruptions). **Diet:** insects, especially midges and wainscot moth larvae/pupae (live in reed stems) in summer; mainly reed seeds in winter. **Voice:** commonest call a unique, explosive, twanging, metallic 'ping'; also has ticking and churring calls. Song a quiet series of 3 squeaky notes similar to calls. **Nest:** deep cup of dead leaves of reeds and other marsh plants, lined with reed flowerheads and feathers, low down among reeds. **Eggs:** 5-7, white, speckled black. **Incubation:** 10-14 days, by both sexes. **Fledging:** 12-13 days. **Broods:** 2-3, occasionally 4. **Maturity:** 1 year.

| J | F | M | A | M | J | J | A | S | O | N | D |

△ Has unique combination of tit-like body, conical, stubby bill and long tail; never seen away from reedbeds except when feeding or on migration. Very acrobatic, grasping adjacent reed stems with feet and moving nimbly up and down them. On ground, jumps and creeps over mud, with long tail often raised and fanned. Upperparts bright sandy or tawny-reddish, streaked with black and cream or white on wings; underparts paler. Male has striking pale blue-grey hood, bold drooping black moustache and black undertail coverts. Female paler, without contrasting head pattern or black undertail. Bill bright orange or straw-yellow in male, duller, browner or greyer in female; eyes pale orange, brightest in male during breeding season; legs black. Juveniles resemble females but are smaller, slimmer-tailed, and have much more black on upperparts, extending to back as well as on wings, and black on sides of tail, too. Juvenile males have black between eye and bill.

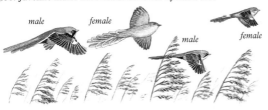

male *female* *male* *female*

△ Usually remain low among reeds in windy weather, but otherwise flocks can often be seen flying fast and low over reeds, looking like tiny pheasants with wings whirring and long tails trailing; tails look loose in flight and are often fanned and then suddenly twisted; progress uneven and flight may be straight or undulating – birds often disappear behind reeds to emerge a moment later. First clue to flock's presence is often their distinctive twanging calls.

LONG-TAILED TITS
Family Aegithalidae

Very small relatives of true tits, with tiny, stubby bills and extremely long tails. Agile feeders, eating small insects; live mainly in woodland and scrub, rarely visiting ground, and build distinctive domed nests in trees and bushes. Four species in the Himalayas and China, one in Africa and one in N America; the most widespread, found across Eurasia, is the only British species, the Long-tailed Tit. Sexes look alike.

LONG-TAILED TIT *Aegithalos caudatus*

adult

juvenile

adults

juvenile

KEY FACTS

Length: 14cm (including 9cm tail). **Wingspan:** 16-19cm. **Weight:** 7-9g. **Habitat:** breeds chiefly in thick hedges, bushy heaths, scrub; in winter, especially, in deciduous woods; scarce in gardens and urban areas. **Movements:** mainly resident, with some local movement; N/E European race *caudatus* rare vagrant. **Population:** can suffer severely from effects of hard winters, with up to 80 per cent mortality; *c*250 000 breeding territories; *c*90 000 birds in winter. **Diet:** almost entirely small insects, especially bugs and butterfly and moth eggs/caterpillars; occasionally seeds in winter. **Voice:** distinctive low, soft, abrupt 'tpp' and rippling 'tsirrrrup', given constantly by flocks, also high, rather nasal 'tzee' or 'tzee-tzee-tzee'; infrequent song a mixture of last 2 calls. **Nest:** unique, oval purse-shaped structure of moss, spiders' webs and lichens, lined with feathers, in dense, low, usually thorny bushes/ brambles, or much higher, in fork of tree or against trunk. **Eggs:** 8-12, white, some with tiny reddish speckles. **Incubation:** 13-14 days, by female. **Fledging:** 14-18 days. **Broods:** 1. **Maturity:** 1 year.

| J | F | M | A | M | J | J | A | S | O | N | D |

△ Tiny, almost spherical body combined with very long, slim tail gives unique 'ball-and-stick' appearance. Loose, fluffy plumage patterned in black, white and pale pink. Bill minute, stubby, black; legs black. Extremely active, restless family parties or larger flocks constantly jumping and flitting through trees and bushes, calling excitedly with rippling and trilling sounds. Only rarely seen on ground; not often attracted to bird tables and feeders but, once a group has learnt to exploit 'hand-outs', the birds will return for more; although not so often around houses and gardens as true tits, can be tame and approachable at close range

▷ British and Irish race *rosaceus* has broad dark band above eye from forehead to join up with black of upperparts on nape. Much paler N and E European race *caudatus*, with all-white head, more white on wings and less pink, is rare wanderer to E England and possibly to Shetland and other N isles of Scotland.

race rosaceus

race caudatus

adults, roosting

△ Both parents may roost together in the extraordinarily elastic nest with their brood of up to a dozen young. Being so small, Long-tailed Tits can suffer badly from effects of severe winter weather, especially at night, when not bustling about. They counteract this by roosting communally in flocks side by side on a branch, huddled closely together in series of fluffy balls to keep warm. These winter roost sites typically situated in dense thorn bushes, which help protect the tiny birds from predators as well as from effects of cold.

juveniles

△ Nest, which may take a pair 3 weeks or more to build, is a remarkable, oval, purse-like construction of moss, bound together with spiders' webs, camouflaged with lichen (or occasionally unusual items such as polystyrene fragments), and lined with up to 3000 or more feathers.

△ Juvenile has distinctly shorter tail than adult; plumage darker, with less pink (and brown tones at first). Crown and centre of forehead white; broad eye-band and face brown. Legs dull pinkish or brownish.

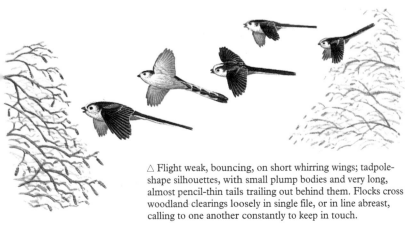

△ Flight weak, bouncing, on short whirring wings; tadpole-shape silhouettes, with small plump bodies and very long, almost pencil-thin tails trailing out behind them. Flocks cross woodland clearings loosely in single file, or in line abreast, calling to one another constantly to keep in touch.

TRUE TITS
Family Paridae

Small, plump, short-billed insect eaters that live among trees. Use small but strong bills for hammering open seeds held firmly under strong feet, but also eat many insects in breeding season. Extremely agile and acrobatic, often hanging upside-down when feeding. Regular visitors at bird feeders, generally very easy to approach. Most species are hole nesters, and readily use nestboxes; they often raise large broods. Outside breeding season, roam about in mixed feeding flocks (which may also contain Goldcrests, Nuthatches, Treecreepers and other species). Plumage colourful or drabber combination of brown and buff, with contrasting cap and bib. Sexes look the same or similar.

CRESTED TIT *Parus cristatus*

86

KEY FACTS

Length: 11.5cm. **Wingspan:** 17-20cm. **Weight:** 10-13g. **Habitat:** in Britain, found only in mature open Scots Pine forest in Highland Scotland, especially Speyside (some in mature plantations, e.g. on Moray coast). **Movements:** highly sedentary. **Population:** *c*900 pairs breed Scotland; *c*3600 birds in winter. Total of *c*10 birds reported from England, probably all vagrants from Continent. **Diet:** mainly insects, spiders; pine seeds, stored in spring, also eaten outside breeding season. **Voice:** distinctive, soft, quite deep, purring trill: also thin 'zee-zee-zee' like calls of other tits; song a combination of sharp, higher-pitched 'keerr-it' and repetition of trill. **Nest:** cup of moss, lined with hair, wool and sometimes feathers, in tree hole, usually in decaying pine stumps, some in living pine, few in holes in other trees, against fence posts, in squirrel's drey or in hole in ground; mostly less than 3m above ground. **Eggs:** 5-7, white, with reddish spots/blotches. **Incubation:** 13-16 days, by female. **Fledging:** 18-22 days. **Broods:** 1. **Maturity:** 1 year. **Confusion species:** in British Isles, almost unknown outside a few Scottish pine forests; other brown/buff tits have black caps and lack distinctive trilling call.

| J | F | M | A | M | J | J | A | S | O | N | D |

△ Though widespread on Continent in suitable habitat, found here only in Caledonian pine forests of Scotland (apart from handful of vagrants to England over the years). Often very hard to see high in tall trees; distinctive purring calls help locate them. If seen lower down, appearance unique – only British bird of its size with a crest, though as this changes angle frequently, it is not always immediately obvious. Large head and plump little body, with slim tail. Very active, climbing up trunks and bustling about among pine needles or among bark on ground in search of insect food. Generally shyer and less gregarious than other tits. Upperparts greyish-brown, underparts whitish, with buff flanks; head dingy white, with crest speckled black/white; small black bib joins narrow black collar, and thin curving black line through and behind eye.

▷ Juvenile distinguishable at close range by shorter, duller, less pointed crest, browner bib with white flecks, and lack of black collar.

juvenile

◁ Flight action similar to Blue Tit's, but has stronger wingbeats and more undulating progress; crest makes head look larger, and tail looks narrower.

280

juvenile   *race* britannicus

adult

△ Smallest of the true tits, slightly smaller than Blue Tit (p284), with large, neckless head (though this can look sleeker and slimmer) and short narrow tail. Readily distinguished from other black-capped tits by bold white or yellowish patch extending from rear crown to nape, and by 2 prominent white wingbars (each appearing as row of white spots at close range). Upperparts of British race *britannicus* olive-grey, underparts dull white, washed buff on flanks; crown and large bib black (glossier after moult Aug-Sep), cheeks and prominent nape patch white. Juvenile has browner upperparts and yellowish underparts; crown and smaller bib brownish-black; cheeks, nape patch and wingbars yellowish. Spends less time in tree canopy than Blue Tit; often busily investigates rough bark in search of insect food, clinging to or climbing trunk, as well as exploring holes in walls or vegetation on ground. A great hoarder, making endless visits to bird feeder for nuts or suet and zooming off to hide them for later consumption.

race hibernicus

race ater

△ Adults of Irish race *hibernicus* look more like juveniles, with yellowish tinge to cheeks and nape patch and yellowish-buff flanks. Adults of Continental race *ater*, irregular here in winter in small numbers, have pure white cheeks and nape patch and slate-grey upperparts (though rump brownish-buff).

▷ Occurring in greatest numbers among conifers, Coal Tits are adaptable nesters; if no suitable natural or woodpecker hole available, as in many new plantations, they use hollow among tree roots or mouse-burrow or other hole in ground. Also take readily to nestboxes.

◁ Flight very fast and flitting, with prominent double white wingbars. Looks smaller-headed than other tits (partly due to white/yellowish nape patch), and also has much shorter, narrower tail.

KEY FACTS

Length: 11.5cm. **Wingspan:** 17-21cm. **Weight:** 8-10g. **Habitat:** woods, especially conifers but also mixed and broadleaved woods, common in sessile oak in W and birch in N; also in gardens with conifers, scrub in Scottish Highlands. **Movements:** highly sedentary; small-scale immigration from Continent of race *ater* in winter. **Population:** *c*880 000 pairs breed; up to 3.5 million birds in winter. **Diet:** chiefly insects, especially aphids, moth eggs/ larvae/pupae, and spiders; also conifer seeds and some nuts. **Voice:** most common call is sad, piping 'tseu' or 'tseu-ee'; also more vigorous 'psueet', quiet, thin 'tzee', often repeated, and sweet, clear 'see-weet-wee-tit-tit'. Most common song a repeated, sweet, piping 'weecho-weecho-weecho', with accent on 2nd syllable, not 1st as in Great Tit (p285). **Nest:** cup of moss, lined with hair and wool, in hole in tree, tree stump, rocks, wall or ground (especially in old mouseholes or among tree roots); uses nestboxes. **Eggs:** 7-11, white with reddish spots. **Incubation:** 14-16 days, by female. **Fledging:** 18-20 days. **Broods:** 1, occasionally 2. **Maturity:** 1 year. **Confusion species:** other brown/fawn black-capped tits (pp282-3) lack white nape patch, are larger, and have smaller black bibs and different calls.

| J | F | M | A | M | J | J | A | S | O | N | D |

MARSH TIT *Parus palustris*

72

Extremely similar to Willow Tit, and often indistinguishable unless characteristic calls or song are heard. Despite name, Marsh not found in marshes or very damp woodland, preferring deciduous woodland, especially beech and oak; rarely occurs in coniferous woods or scrub like Willow. Like latter, ranges from upper tree canopy to lower undergrowth, but differs in frequently foraging on ground. Another difference is that it does not excavate own nest; rarely uses nestboxes. Non-breeders join roving mixed flocks of tits and other woodland birds in winter; breeding pairs do so temporarily, but leave them when they reach boundaries of their territory, which they defend throughout winter.

adult

juvenile

△ Subtle structural and plumage differences from Willow. Generally looks slimmer, sleeker than Willow, with smaller, shorter head and slimmer neck; tail usually more forked or square-ended, rather than rounded. Usually lacks pale wing panel of Willow, and has paler flanks. Cap glossy black and bib small and neat; smaller area of white on cheeks, grading into dusky-brown ear coverts. Juveniles have dull brownish-black caps and bibs and are greyer above and paler below; usually impossible to distinguish from juvenile Willows.

▷ Marsh Tits are great food hoarders, and regularly visit bird feeders, carrying away large quantities of peanuts and other food which they hide in crevices in tree bark or bury in ground. When times are hard in the depths of winter, they find this stored food by memory.

◁ Deals with tough, struggling insects and hard seeds by hammering at them with bill (slightly stouter than Willow's) while holding food item in one foot on perch.

▷ Flight flitting, less whirring than Blue Tit's; often looks stronger than Willow's; latter often hovers while searching tree trunks for insect food.

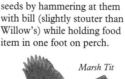

Marsh Tit

Willow Tit

KEY FACTS

Length: 11.5cm. **Wingspan:** 18-19.5cm. **Weight:** 10-12g. **Habitat:** deciduous woods, copses, parks and gardens with trees; very scarce in urban areas. **Movements:** highly sedentary. **Population:** *c*60 000 breeding pairs in Britain; *c*200 000 birds in winter. **Diet:** mainly insects and spiders in breeding season; beechmast and other tree seeds important in winter, also berries and nuts. **Voice:** distinctive commonest call a loud, high-pitched, sneezing 'pit-chew', often followed by deep, harsh, nasal 'tchair-tchair-tchair . . .', similar to Willow Tit's but fuller toned; also 'chicka-dee-dee-dee . . .' Usual song a repeated ringing, liquid, bubbling or bell-like 'schip-schip-schip . . .' **Nest:** cup of moss, lined with hair or fur in hole, usually low down in tree, tree stump, wall or ground. **Eggs:** 6-8, white, spotted reddish. Incubation: 13-15 days, by female. **Fledging:** 17-20 days. **Broods:** 1. **Maturity:** 1 year. **Confusion species:** Willow Tit (opposite) almost identical, but subtle differences in structure and plumage and major difference in voice.

| J | F | M | A | M | J | J | A | S | O | N | D |

Parus montanus WILLOW TIT

73

Not recognized as separate species from Marsh Tit in Britain until turn of century, Willow Tit looks extremely similar. Despite name, does not favour willows, but does live in greater variety of woodland than close relative, including coniferous woods. During breeding season, more likely to be seen in damp woodland, where it can find rotting tree stumps, as it excavates own nesthole instead of using existing one like Marsh and most other tits. Does not seem to hammer with bill at tough seeds and other food like Marsh Tit, and not often on ground. Rarely seen together with Marsh Tit.

adult

juvenile

KEY FACTS

Length: 11.5cm. **Wingspan:** 17-18cm. **Weight:** 9-11g. **Habitat:** woods, clumps or lines of trees, coniferous and mixed, and especially damp birch/alder woodland and among elders; also hedges, gardens, heaths, scrub in winter. **Movements:** highly sedentary. **Population:** c25 000 breeding pairs in Britain; c175 000 birds in winter. **Diet:** mainly insects in breeding season, seeds and berries in autumn and winter. **Voice:** distinctive, quiet, buzzing 'eez-eez-eez'; also very nasal, grating 'tchay tchay tchay', like Marsh Tit's but sounding 'angrier', more 'questioning'; occasionally thin, very high, sibilant 'tzee-tzee-tzee-tzee'. Song not often heard, often incomplete; short, sweet, rich warbling, rather like song of Nightingale (p242), Canary or Goldfinch (p307), or repeated, slow piping notes 'piu piu piu' like Wood Warbler's (p270). **Nest:** loose structure mainly of plant fibres, including strips of bark and dry grass, lined with finer fibres such as plant down and animal hairs; often on base of wood chips in hole excavated by female with bill in rotten tree stump or trunk. **Eggs:** 6-9, white, with reddish-brown spots. **Incubation:** 13-15 days, by female. **Fledging:** 17-20 days. **Broods:** 1. **Maturity:** 1 year. **Confusion species:** Marsh Tit (opposite).

J F M A M J J A S O N D

△ Only reliable way to distinguish the 2 species is by their distinctive voices (see Key Facts). Plumage differences very slight, particularly in summer when adults have worn feathers, and only discernible at close range; as well as subtle differences in head plumage (see below), Willow tends to have pale panel on wing (though this may be missing in late summer birds in worn plumage, and Marsh in fresh plumage in winter and spring may show faint wing panel); Willow's flanks slightly darker buff. Slight structural differences can sometimes help: Willow usually appears larger-headed and bull-necked, partly due to black cap extending more onto sides of neck. Also has slightly rounded tail, with paler outer feathers. Juveniles of the 2 species rarely distinguishable.

Willow Tit

Marsh Tit

◁ Willow's head plumage often looks more untidy and loosely textured; in good light, adult's cap dull, matt black, not glossy. Willow's cheeks whiter, forming clear-cut boundary with rear of black crown, and bib larger, more diffuse.

▷ Female excavates new nesthole each year, although may be other apparently suitable holes nearby – even in same rotting tree stump. May use nestboxes, filled with woodchips or polystyrene for female to excavate. To add to difficulty of distinguishing between the species, Marsh Tits sometimes take over a Willow Tit's old nesthole.

BLUE TIT *Parus caeruleus*

14

male summer

female winter

KEY FACTS

Length: 11.5cm. **Wingspan:** 17.5-20cm. **Weight:** 9-12g. **Habitat:** woods (especially open oak and birch woods), parks, orchards, gardens, hedges, breeding wherever there are suitable holes in mature trees (or nestboxes). In winter occasionally in scrub, reedbeds etc. **Movements:** basically sedentary, with only local movements; some immigrants of slightly larger, brighter Continental race *caeruleus* late Sep-Apr (mainly late Sep-late Oct), especially S and E Britain; occasionally large numbers involved after build-up of Continental population; last major invasion 1957. **Population:** *c*4.4 million pairs breed. **Diet:** chiefly insects and spiders, also seeds, fruits and buds outside breeding season. **Voice:** most common of many calls are thin, repeated 'tsee-tsee-tsee' contact call, more forceful 'tsee-tsee-tsee tsit' in late winter and spring, and rapid, harsh, scolding 'churrr-rr-rr' of alarm or excitement, more slurred than similar call of Great Tit. Song usually 2-3 silvery 'tsee' notes followed by fast liquid trill. **Nest:** cup of moss, grass and plant fibres, lined with hair, wool, feathers, usually in hole in tree but also in holes in walls and other artificial sites such as lamp-posts and bus stops; readily uses nestboxes. **Eggs:** 7-16, white with reddish-brown spots. **Incubation:** 12-15 days, by female. **Fledging:** 16-22 days. **Broods:** 1. **Maturity:** 1 year. **Confusion species:** Great Tit (opposite).

J	F	M	A	M	J	J	A	S	O	N	D

▷ Short-distance flight quick, fluttery and direct, stopping abruptly at perch; higher, more erratic and undulating over longer distances. Male has gliding butterfly-like display flight in spring.

△ One of our most familiar and best-loved birds, and the commonest and most widespread of the tits, found from the tiniest of city gardens to remote rural areas everywhere except the highest mountains and many of the outer Scottish islands, though densities lower in upland areas. Distinctly smaller than Great Tit, with proportionately larger, squarer head, dumpy, box-shaped body, shorter tail. Particularly acrobatic, able to feed on lightest outer twigs unlike heavier Great Tit. Adults have most complex pattern on upperparts of any of our tits: blue crown and white face, with black eyestripe and black bib joining black collar; whitish spot on blue nape; greyish-green back, dark blue wings with narrow white wingbar and dull white tips to inner flight feathers (tertials); yellowish-green rump, blue tail. Underparts yellow, often showing variable narrow dusky band down belly. Males brighter than females, especially in fresh breeding plumage.

juvenile

◁ Juveniles have same basic plumage pattern as adults, but are much duller, with greener cap, hindneck and back, yellow, not white, on face and nape, and no bib.

▷ Like Great Tit, regularly raids doorstep milk bottles; prefers full cream milk. At bird feeders, can be very belligerent for its size. As many as 200 individuals may visit a well-stocked bird table in a single day, and possibly as many as 1000 over the course of a whole winter.

Readily take to nestboxes, which should be sited facing away from hot sun and out of reach of cats and other predators. Blue Tits may lay as many as 16 eggs in a single clutch, maximizing the chance of survival from a single brood.

male

female

△ Largest of the tits, much bulkier and longer than Blue Tit; only a little smaller than House Sparrow. Heavily built, with more rounded head and quite long tail. Adults have striking head pattern: black crown, bib and collar surround white cheeks, and bold black band extends from bib down bright sulphur-yellow underparts; yellowish spot on nape. Back distinctly green; wings mainly blue-grey, but also some black, greenish-yellow and white, with white wingbar; tail blue-black with white outer feathers. Male has blue gloss to black head, brighter, bluer edges to wing feathers than female's, and broader, glossy black band down underparts, widening between legs; female duller, with black areas sooty, not glossy.

juvenile

◁ Juvenile distinctly duller than adults, with sooty-brown rather than black cap, yellowish cheeks, brown tinge to back, and duller yellow underparts with less distinct, dull greyish-black belly stripe.

▷ Spends much more time on ground than Blue Tit and most other tits, especially in autumn and winter, when it searches among leaves and tears up moss and fungi to find food. Hacks noisily into tough hazel nuts with strong bill. Often drives off other tits when feeding or competing for nestholes; rarely, may even kill and eat other small birds.

male

◁ Flight stronger, less fluttering and jerky than other tits', more like warblers'. Spend much of autumn and winter roaming woods in family parties and in mixed flocks with different tit species and other small woodland birds.

KEY FACTS

Length: 14cm. **Wingspan:** 22.5-25.5cm. **Weight:** 16-21g. **Habitat:** wide range of wooded habitats, from urban gardens to remote forests, especially open deciduous woodland; less ubiquitous than Blue Tit in winter.
Movements: basically sedentary, with local movements, e.g. away from high ground in Scottish Highlands; some immigration of slightly slimmer-billed Continental birds of race *major*, especially in years with poor beechmast crops; last major irruption was 1957.
Population: *c*.2.2 million pairs breed. **Diet:** mainly insects, especially caterpillars and beetles, also spiders; seeds, fruits and nuts important in autumn and winter, especially beechmast.
Voice: remarkably varied, with huge vocabulary of different calls. Most common are loud, ringing 'chink chink chink', loud piping 'tui tui tui', harsh, scolding churr (slower than Blue Tit's), slurred 'tchae tchae' (rather like Marsh Tit's), and thin 'tsee-tsee-tsee' like other tits. Usual song distinctive, loud, rhythmic 'teacher teacher teacher', with emphasis on 1st syllable (unlike Coal Tit's sweeter song). **Nest:** cup mainly of moss, with some grass and plant fibres, lined with wool, hair, but not feathers, usually in hole in tree, but also in holes in walls, drainpipes etc. Of all tits, most readily uses nestboxes, preferring them to natural sites. **Eggs:** 5-11, white with reddish spots. **Incubation:** 12-15 days, by female.
Fledging: 16-22 days.
Broods: usually 1, but sometimes 2 in pine woods.
Maturity: 1 year. **Confusion species:** Blue Tit (opposite) smaller, with blue and white face and white separating crown from bill.

J	F	M	A	M	J	J	A	S	O	N	D

NUTHATCHES
Family Sittidae

Superficially resemble miniature woodpeckers, with powerful, chisel-like bills and large, strong feet, but unlike woodpeckers (and treecreepers), descend trees headfirst, as well as climbing upwards and sideways, and do not use short tails, which lack stiffened feathers, as props. Some species reduce size of nesthole entrance using mud. Loud, ringing calls and songs. Eat insects, seeds and nuts. Sexes very similar. A single species breeds here.

NUTHATCH *Sitta europaea*

male　　*female*

△ Small, with odd proportions, due to combination of long spike of a bill, large, long head, sleek body, deep flanks and short tail. Moves jerkily on trees, headfirst, downwards as well as upwards and sideways. Blue-grey upperparts, with long black eyestripe; lower face and upper throat white; flight feathers blackish; buff underparts; flanks chestnut, darker on male; undertail splashed chestnut; tail has black outer feathers, with white spots near tip. Very lively and noisy bird, moving restlessly about through trees and with long jerky hops on ground. Bobs body, sways head and flicks wings. Not at all shy; may be inquisitive. Often in pairs, and regularly joins mixed flocks of tits etc in winter. Visits bird feeders, especially for nuts, sunflower seeds and fat.

▷ Wedges hazel nuts, beechmast and acorns into crevices in bark of branch and hammers at them with audible blows of powerful, dagger-like bill to break them open and obtain food within.

male

female

◁ Female usually plasters up entrance to nesthole with mud, which soon dries hard to prevent entry of predators and rivals for the nesting site.

▷ Juvenile has brown tinge to upperparts; dingy eyestripe, narrower than adult's; and duller flanks and undertail.

juvenile

◁ Flight over any distance fast, darting, undulating. Distinctive silhouette: spear-shaped bill/head, broad wings and very short rear end.

KEY FACTS

Length: 14cm. **Wingspan:** 22.5-27cm. **Weight:** 20-25g. **Habitat:** mature deciduous woods, especially large oakwoods; wooded parks and gardens. **Movements:** extremely sedentary. **Population:** *c*130 000 pairs breed in Britain. **Diet:** chiefly insects, also hazel nuts, acorns, beechmast and other nuts and seeds in autumn and winter; often visits bird feeders. **Voice:** commonest calls are loud, ringing 'chwit chwit', sharp 'pseet pseet pseet' or 'tsit tsit tsit', given most intensively in spring and autumn; also shrill, trilling 'tsirrrr' and urgent 'twet twet twet' of alarm; song a rapid loud whistling 'quee quee quee' or faster trill. **Nest:** thick pile of bark flakes or dead leaves; usually in hole in tree, often old woodpecker hole, sometimes in wall. **Eggs:** 6-9, white with dark reddish-brown spots. **Incubation:** 14-15 days, by female. **Fledging:** 23-25 days. **Broods:** 1. **Maturity:** 1 year.

| J | F | M | A | M | J | J | A | S | O | N | D |

TREECREEPERS
Family Certhiidae

Small, very active tree-dwelling birds with long, slender, downcurved bills. Climb tree trunks in spirals, using short but strong legs with long toes and claws, and stiff, pointed tail feathers, used as a prop. Plumage soft and thick, camouflaged with speckled browns above, mainly white below. Nest well hidden on tree trunk, behind loose bark, in crevice or among tangled vegetation. A single species breeds here.

Certhia familiaris TREECREEPER

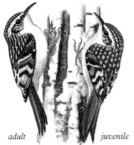

adult *juvenile*

Slim-bodied little bird, with slender, pointed, downcurved bill; spends its life on trees, creeping up trunks and branches with very distinctive, jerky, mouse-like shuffling action, using stiff, frayed-looking tail feathers as prop (though sometimes hangs beneath branch using feet only).

△ Upperparts brown, intricately streaked white and buff; long whitish eyebrow and 2 dull buff-white wingbars edged blackish on both sides; rufous rump. Underparts silvery-white, with variable buff wash on flanks, rear belly and undertail; can look darker below, as soft, loose feathers pick up dirt easily from bark. Juvenile duller, with greyer upperparts peppered with buff spots, less rufous rump and dull white underparts with small brown or greyish flecks on breast/flanks; bill shorter.

△ Feeding action highly distinctive: creeps up bark of tree in rapid spurts, starting near base and progressing in spirals round trunk and branches, alternately disappearing from view and reappearing. Searches for insect food as it climbs, flicking wings restlessly; then, at any stage in its ascent, flits down to next tree and resumes process.

▷ In winter, often roost communally behind loose bark, heads tucked into soft, dense lower back feathers.

◁ Flight light, flitting, erratic and undulating. Bursts of fluttering wingbeats alternate with glides or sideslips. Pale wingbars on quite long, paddle-shaped wings.

KEY FACTS

Length: 12.5cm. **Wingspan:** 17.5-21cm. **Weight:** 8-12g. **Habitat:** confined to trees, mainly broadleaved, in woods, parks, gardens, hedgerows. **Movements:** extremely sedentary. **Population:** 245 000 pairs breed. **Diet:** insects and spiders, also some seeds in winter. **Voice:** high-pitched, thin and sibilant; main calls are shrill 'tsieeew' and softer 'tsit'. Song a series of high 'tsee' notes, thin and tremulous at first, then accelerating and descending in pitch to fuller and surer finish with final flourish. **Nest:** flattened cup of rootlets, moss, grass, bark strips on often bulky foundation of twigs, dead ivy stems etc, lined with bark, feathers, hair, usually squeezed behind dead bark or ivy against tree trunk, sometimes in cracks or split trunks. **Eggs:** 5-6, white with reddish-brown spots. **Incubation:** 14-15 days, by female. **Fledging:** 14-16 days. **Broods:** 1. **Maturity:** 1 year.

| F | M | A | M | J | J | A | S | O | N | D |

SHRIKES
Family Laniidae

Small to medium-sized, with large heads, powerful, sturdy, sharply hooked bills and long tails, which are often waved from side to side and fanned; behave like miniature birds of prey, watching from vantage points, then pouncing on prey on or near ground, frequently after gliding or hovering; feed mainly on large insects, but also kill small lizards, birds and mammals. Surplus prey stored in 'larder', impaled on thorns or barbed wire. Plumage pattern often bold. Sexes almost alike, except for Red-backed. Harsh calls but song contains melodious notes. Found mainly in bushy scrub, commons, heaths, open woodland. Nest in bushes or trees. Most species in Africa; only two species regular but rare here.

GREAT GREY SHRIKE *Lanius excubitor*

98

Much larger than Red-backed Shrike (Blackbird-sized), this scarce winter visitor frequently first seen as distant but conspicuous pale speck on bare branch, wire or post, waving its long tail. However, occupies large winter feeding territory and often difficult to find.

adults   *1st-winter*

△ Powerful, aggressive-looking, with quite long, thick, hooked bill on large, rounded head, and smart grey/white/black plumage; perches upright or at an angle, with long, graduated tail frequently waved, fanned or angled to one side. Adults have grey forehead and crown, white eyebrow, prominent black patch through eye, grey back, separated by long white band from black wings. Females usually show faint brown barring on breast in winter. Juveniles have faintly barred brownish upperparts, paler, drabber, brownish eyepatch, and brown-tinged wings, much smaller, duller eyebrow, and faintly barred brownish-white underparts. 1st-winter birds like adult female but with juvenile brown-tinged greater wing coverts.

Linnet

△ Flight strongly undulating over any distance, with bursts of rapid wingbeats, alternating with glides on closed wings; usually glides steeply upwards to land on perch. Big head and long, graduated tail give it lengthy appearance; tail often fanned or waved in flight. Bold though narrow white wingbars distinctive. Sometimes hovers; pounces from perch down onto voles and other prey; also chases birds in flight, often taking them by surprise like Sparrowhawk.

KEY FACTS

Length: 24-25cm.
Wingspan: 30-34cm.
Weight: 60-65g. **Habitat:** winters here in open country with scattered trees/bushes, including heaths, downs, marshes, farmland, coasts.
Movements: winter visitor from N Europe (Oct-Apr).
Population: probably fewer than 75 birds winter here each year, after recent decline.
Diet: large insects (especially beetles), small mammals; mainly small birds during severe weather. **Voice:** chief call a hoarse, often monotonously repeated 'schroik' or 'schek-schek', sometimes extended into Magpie-like rattle; also long, nasal 'eeeeh' and clear, ringing 'schrrea'; song, rarely heard here, a mixture of harsh notes with more musical, chattering, trilling and squeaking notes. **Maturity:** 1 year. **Confusion species:** Red-backed Shrike (opposite).

J F M A M J J A S O N D

288

Lanius collurio RED-BACKED SHRIKE

male

female

Length: 17cm. **Wingspan:** 24-27cm. **Weight:** 25-30g. **Habitat:** breeds in dry heaths, downs, neglected hedgerows and scrub with gorse, other thorny shrubs; on passage seen chiefly along coasts. **Movements:** very rare summer visitor (May-Sep), wintering E Africa; scarce but regular spring/autumn passage migrant from Continent, May-Jun, Aug-Oct. **Population:** has suffered long-term decline in NW Europe, for reasons unknown, especially in Britain where species on edge of its range. From 300 pairs in 1952 and 80-90 pairs in 1971, has now declined to 1 or 2 pairs. **Diet:** mainly large insects; also small rodents, birds, lizards. **Voice:** commonest call a harsh, grating 'schack'; also nasal 'chee-uk', almost like call of Snipe. Song, not often heard, a long stream of mixed, quiet, melodious warbling notes and harsh scratchy notes, with jerky rhythm, interspersed with mimicry of other bird sounds. **Nest:** cup of grass, moss, wool and feathers, often incorporating coloured paper, string, cloth etc, lined with fine grass, rootlets, hair and down; built in dense, thorny bush. **Eggs:** 5-6, very variable in colour, cream, buff, greenish, with dark spots at blunt end. **Incubation:** 13-16 days, probably entirely by female. **Fledging:** 14-15 days. **Broods:** 1. **Maturity:** 1 year. **Confusion species:** Great Grey Shrike (opposite) much bigger, with grey/white/ black plumage, no chestnut on back and white wingbar.

Common and widespread here until late 19th century, now virtually extinct in Britain as breeding bird, occurring in small numbers only on spring and autumn passage. Small (smaller than Starling), slim, with sturdy, slightly hooked bill and long tail. Can be shy and elusive, but conspicuous when hunting from obvious lookout position. Perches upright, scanning for prey with head down; when excited, flicks tail or swings it from side to side; also partially fans it. Male striking, with pale blue-grey crown and rump separated by bright chestnut back, blackish flight feathers with chestnut edges, broad black mask, white throat, pale pink underparts, and black tail with white outer feathers, especially at base. Females quite variable, a few with duller version of male's head pattern, but most with dull reddish-brown upperparts, tinged grey on nape and rump, dark brown tail, with less white on sides than male, and cream underparts; sides of throat, breast and flanks marked with dusky-brown crescents.

juvenile

Juvenile resembles female but has less variable buff-brown or reddish-brown upperparts, marked with close blackish crescents, and dull cream underparts, more completely marked with greyish crescents.

Over short distances flight strong, fast, direct, generally low, with whirring beats of rather short, broad-based but quite pointed wings; long tail. Dashes out from perch to catch large insect or even small bird in flight, or pounces on prey on ground; sometimes glides and hovers, especially when hunting along side of hedge. Swoops down from one perch and up to same perch or another. Flight undulating over longer distances. Looks clumsy on ground, hopping on short legs and often opening wings and flirting tail. Frequently stores surplus prey in 'larder' by impaling it on thorns or barbed wire.

| J | F | M | A | M | J | J | A | S | O | N | D |

male, catching grasshopper

CROWS
Family Corvidae

Largest perching birds, with black or boldly patterned plumage; seven regular British species. Mostly conspicuous and often noisy, with mainly harsh calls. Powerful, longish bills and strong legs and feet. Take extremely wide range of foods; some hoard surplus in autumn. Sexes look alike. Nest in trees, on cliffs, in holes etc.

● Note: Jay and Magpie easily identified; black crows less distinctive: look for overall size, size/shape/colour/base of bill, presence/absence of grey in plumage, wing and tail shape, flight action; listen for calls.

JAY *Garrulus glandarius*

76

adult

juvenile

KEY FACTS

Length: 34-35cm.
Wingspan: 52-58cm.
Weight: 140-190g. **Habitat:** mainly woods, especially oakwoods, both broadleaved and coniferous, also orchards, parks, well-wooded gardens, from remote rural areas to large cities. **Movements:** basically highly sedentary, but some influxes of presumed Continental birds into SE England; occasionally major large-scale movements after failure of acorn crop, as in autumn 1983, when huge movements into S and E England. **Population:** c160 000 breeding pairs in Britain, c10 000 Ireland; c600 000-650 000 birds in winter. **Diet:** very wide range, chiefly insects, especially beetles and caterpillars, in summer; acorns staple food in winter; also small mammals, birds, eggs, carrion, scraps, fruit, seeds. **Voice:** far-carrying, harsh 'skaaak'; also barking 'kah' and Buzzard-like mewing 'peee-ow'; often mimics other birds; quiet song a medley of weak gurgling, bubbling or clicking sounds. **Nest:** cup of sticks, lined with roots, usually fairly low down in tree or in shrub. **Eggs:** 4-5, pale bluish-green, with very fine brown speckles. **Incubation:** 16-17 days, by both sexes. **Fledging:** 21-22 days. **Broods:** 1. **Maturity:** 1 year.

J F M A M J J A S O N D

△ Stocky, with stout bill; hops and leaps awkwardly but jauntily on ground and along branches, jerking long tail up and down or from side to side. Except where used to humans in parks, very wary, dashing off into cover with loud raucous screech; this far-carrying call often first clue to presence. Usually seen singly in open, but often in pairs or small noisy flocks in woods. Hides acorns in autumn. Brightest of our crows, mainly pinkish-brown, darker above than below; crown streaked black and white, often raised; gleaming pale blue eye and broad black moustache. Bright blue, black-barred patch on primary coverts below bend of wing and black flight feathers, with prominent white patch; undertail and rump white, contrasting with black tail. Juvenile's crown less streaked, body more reddish, underparts fluffy; tail shorter.

△ Flight variable: fast and low when escaping into cover, or slower, more laboured, floating, unsteady and often at good height over longer distances; level at first, then undulating. Flight action with bursts of slow, irregular, deep, floppy beats of broad, rounded wings below line of body. White rump contrasting with black tail most striking feature from above in flight; blue and white patches on wings also distinctive.

Pica pica **MAGPIE**

KEY FACTS

Length: 44-46cm (over half is tail). **Wingspan:** 52-60cm. **Weight:** 200-250g. **Habitat:** farmland and other open country, especially grassland, with dense hedges, scattered trees and bushes; increasingly in gardens, parks, etc. **Movements:** extremely sedentary. **Population:** c910 000 breeding pairs. **Diet:** very wide range, from caterpillars, worms and frogs to bread and other discarded food, but chiefly insects, especially in spring and summer, and fruits and seeds in autumn/winter; also some small mammals, birds and eggs etc. **Voice:** commonest call a rapid, loud, harsh, chattering 'chak-chak-chak-chak' or 'chaka chaka chaka'; also yelping, chirping and squawking calls, and song of quiet musical babbling and piping notes. **Nest:** large, usually domed structure of sticks, lined with mud and fine roots, high in trees or thorny bushes. **Eggs:** 5-8, pale greenish, spotted grey and dark brown. **Incubation:** 17-18 days, by female. **Fledging:** 22-27 days. **Broods:** 1. **Maturity:** 1 year.

| J | F | M | A | M | J | J | A | S | O | N | D |

△ Unmistakable, with boldly pied plumage and long tail. Medium-sized, slim body, only length of Jay's or Jackdaw's, but tail, accounting for over half total length, makes it look bigger, especially when fully spread into diamond shape in flight. Large white patches on shoulders, white belly and flanks; rest of plumage black, in sunlight glossed bluish-purple on head, breast and back, bluish-green on wings, and brilliant bronze-green, with bands of bluish, greenish and reddish purple, on tail. On ground, walls, roofs etc, moves with confident, high-stepping walk and rapid, often sideways, hops and leaps, usually with tail held up and closed. Often perches upright in trees and bushes, where moves much more clumsily due to long tail. Usually wary. Often seen in small groups, especially in winter, when the birds chase one another noisily among branches. Very distinctive loud, harsh chattering call.

Although Magpies will occasionally eat songbirds, their young and eggs, these form only very small proportion of diet. Much maligned by landowners, gamekeepers, gardeners and some 'bird lovers', though cats (and Sparrowhawks!) kill far more small birds, and Magpies eat many insect pests.

▷ Builds large, domed nest of sticks, usually high up in tree or deep within thorny bush; highly visible in winter but well hidden by foliage when in use. Like squirrel's drey which, though, is denser, more compact.

juvenile

◁ Juvenile much shorter-tailed than adult at first, and duller, with less contrastingly pied sooty-black and dirty-white plumage; gloss only on wings and tail.

◁ Flight very distinctive: weak, laborious and hesitant over distance, with quite rapid beats of short, rounded, fan-like pied wings alternating with brief, stalling glides, and long tail dragging behind; often looks as if struggling to keep up. Despite this, frequently flies well above tree height and for considerable distances. Over short distances, flight much more confident, with tail often spread as rudder as it dashes with great agility through dense cover.

CHOUGH *Pyrrhocorax pyrrhocorax*

adult

juvenile

239

△ Our rarest crow, restricted to the wilder W fringes of Wales, the Isle of Man, Islay, Colonsay and Jura, and S, W and N Ireland, where there is traditional, low-intensity farming, chiefly along coasts. Larger than Jackdaw, with all-black plumage and smaller head, tapering to distinctive long, downcurved, strikingly red bill; equally bright vermilion legs also unique feature among adult crows. Juvenile has shorter, less downcurved, duller, orange bill and orange to red legs. Adult's plumage very glossy, with brilliant blue and purple iridescence on body, green on upperwings and silvery-grey on underside of flight feathers. Juveniles have glossy wings, but dull brownish-black bodies, with purplish gloss only on tips of feathers. Long ringing calls distinctive and far-carrying; though now usually pronounced 'Chuff', name may once have been rhymed with 'cow' in imitation of its commonest call.

Choughs

Jackdaw

Choughs

△ Sociable birds, usually in pairs, family parties or larger flocks, sometimes with Jackdaws or Rooks. Wary, excitable, flicking wingtips and flirting tail, especially when calling. Perch on cliffs and rocks, rarely in trees. Obtain most of insect food by probing with bill into short, rabbit- or sheep-cropped turf of coastal heaths and clifftop pasture. Also break open dried cow, sheep or horse dung to obtain insects.

△ Superb, graceful flyers, with strong, buoyant, bouncing action; perform dramatic aerobatics around cliffs on broad wings, wingtips much less pointed than Jackdaw's and widely splayed, giving ragged look; head/curved bill look long and tapered, tail either quite short and squared or slightly wedge-shaped. Soars, glides, dives at breakneck speed down sheer cliff faces with almost closed wings, suddenly pulling out and shooting back up again on upcurrents of air.

KEY FACTS

Length: 39-40cm.
Wingspan: 73-85cm.
Weight: 280-360g. **Habitat:** in British Isles, chiefly sea-cliffs and close-cropped grassy clifftops; few inland in mountains, quarries, mainly Wales. **Movements:** basically highly sedentary, though young birds in particular make local movements, especially in winter. **Population:** long-term decrease in Europe but Irish population increasing slightly; c300 pairs breed Britain, c830 pairs Ireland. **Diet:** soil-dwelling insects, other invertebrates, especially ants, fly larvae and beetles; also earthworms, sandhoppers among rotting seaweed and carrion; some cereal grains in winter. **Voice:** loud, far-carrying, long, high 'chweee-ow', clearer, higher-pitched, more explosive than Jackdaw; also deeper, gull-like 'kaah' and 'kwuk-uk-uk', loud, harsh 'kwarr' of alarm. **Nest:** cup of sticks, lined with wool, hair, some grass and feathers. **Eggs:** 3-5, buffish, mottled grey and brown. **Incubation:** 17-18 days, by female. **Fledging:** 38 days. **Broods:** 1. **Maturity:** 1 year. **Confusion species:** Jackdaw (opposite) smaller, without red curved bill and red legs, and with grey 'shawl'; shorter, more pointed wings without splayed 'fingertips' of Chough. 'Kyow' calls of juvenile Jackdaws similar to Chough's but usually gruffer.

J	F	M	A	M	J	J	A	S	O	N	D

△ Smallest British crow, compact, dapper, with short bill. Shorter legs give more ground-hugging impression than larger crows. Bustles about on ground with head held high when looking for food; also in trees, on cliffs, quarries and ruins, on roofs, chimneys etc. Black, with grey 'shawl', clear-cut on nape but merging into dusky ear coverts and throat; pale greyish-white eye stands out strikingly. Plumage slightly glossy in good light: crown purplish, back bluish and wings greenish and bluish. As plumage wears through summer, male's head tends to become paler, more silvery than female's. Juvenile much duller, often brownish-black with little gloss, and brownish, hardly contrasting nape; eye dull brown.

Jackdaw adult
Jackdaw juvenile
Rook adult
Starling

△ Associates with other crows; often in mixed flocks with Rooks, not only when feeding, but also when travelling to and from roosting sites in trees or migrating; also often feeds with Starlings. Moves faster on ground than other crows, with jaunty, waddling walk and forwards or sideways jumps. Sometimes a flock will take off suddenly, flying up into air with loud calls, then breaks up and circles back to ground.

Jackdaws
Rook

△ Flight light, rapid, direct, with wings set well forward. Flight action rather pigeon-like, with quick, flickering beats of tapering, backward-pointing wings; short blunt head and quite narrow, shortish tail. Over cliffs, around ruins, glides and soars with tail spread, and dives and tumbles in dramatic aerobatics. When seen together with Rooks in flight, looks distinctly smaller. Noisy birds, particularly flocks in flight.

KEY FACTS

Length: 33-34cm.
Wingspan: 67-74cm.
Weight: 220-270g. **Habitat:** farmland, mature woodland, parks, from rural areas to town centres; need tree holes, chimneys, ruined castles etc, inland cliffs/quarries and sea-cliffs and rabbit burrows for breeding. **Movements:** largely sedentary, but young birds disperse in autumn, moving W and S, many to Ireland; also immigrants from Continent to E and S coasts in winter. **Population:** *c*600 000 pairs breed. **Diet:** wide range, chiefly insects, other invertebrates, seeds, fruits, carrion, scraps; also eats some small mammals and small birds and their eggs. **Voice:** short, sharp, high 'tjak', often given by flocks in flight when may be extended into chuckling cackles; also short, gruff or shrill 'kyow' and various cawing and yelping sounds. **Nest:** cup or (especially in chimneys) large, messy pile of sticks, often with layer of mud or animal dung, lined with rootlets, stalks, moss, hair, rotten wood, paper etc in treehole, cliff crevice, chimney, on ledge of old stone ruins, bridges etc, also in rabbit burrows. **Eggs:** 4-6, pale bluish-green lightly streaked/spotted dark brown. **Incubation:** 17-18 days, by female. **Fledging:** 30-35 days. **Broods:** 1. **Maturity:** 1 year. **Confusion species:** Chough (opposite).

| J | F | M | A | M | J | J | A | S | O | N | D |

ROOK *Corvus frugilegus*

KEY FACTS

Length: 44-46cm.
Wingspan: 81-99cm.
Weight: 460-520g. **Habitat:** farmland, parks with trees, not in most of uplands or in large city centres. **Movements:** mainly sedentary, though juveniles disperse for short distances in 1st winter; some Continental birds, especially from Baltic region and Netherlands, winter Britain, mainly in E. **Population:** *c*1.37 million pairs breed; *c*4 million birds in winter. **Diet:** chiefly insects and other invertebrates, especially cranefly larvae (leatherjackets), beetle larvae and earthworms, cereal grain, roots, potatoes, berries. **Voice:** main call well-known harsh, cawing 'kaaah', longer, higher, flatter, less raucous, more nasal, hoarser than Carrion Crow's similar call, and given singly not in triplets as in Carrion Crow; various other calls include gull-like 'kee-ook', croaking and growling sounds; song a mixture of soft cawing, rattling, gurgling and crackling calls. **Nest:** bulky cup of sticks, lined with grass, moss, leaves etc, near tops of tall trees. Colonies (rookeries) vary from several pairs to a few thousand. **Eggs:** 3-6, pale bluish-green with dark spots. **Incubation:** 16-18 days, by female. **Fledging:** 30-36 days. **Broods:** 1. **Maturity:** usually 2 years, sometimes 1. **Confusion species:** Carrion Crow (see opposite and right). Raven (p296) much larger, with much heavier bill, shaggy throat feathers and, in flight, more projecting head and wedge-shaped tail.

J	F	M	A	M	J	J	A	S	O	N	D

△ Large, with all-black plumage. Slightly smaller than similar Carrion Crow; adult has more slender, pointed, whitish bill and bare whitish area on face, much steeper forehead and baggy 'trousers' formed by loose flank feathers above legs, which make body look deeper, more untidy, less sleek and powerful. Tail often looks fuller, frequently spread and angled downwards or upwards. When food storage pouch in throat is full, shows as distinct lump. Plumage much glossier than Carrion Crow's, with purplish iridescence, brilliant in strong sunlight, but also visible on duller days, giving pale sheen. Has more rolling walk; regularly probes soft ground. Calls differ.

Rook juvenile

Rook 1st-winter

Carrion Crow

◁ Juvenile lacks pale face and bill of adult and is duller, browner; very like adult and juvenile Carrion Crow, but has steeper forehead, slimmer bill, scraggier body, more feathered thighs; glossier plumage in good light. By 1st winter (Jan-Feb), chin and area between bill and eye bare, but face not fully bare until Apr-May.

▷ Much more gregarious than Crow; nest in colonies and fly, feed and roost in flocks (but Crows can form loose flocks). Birds at rookeries very noisy, jerking and fanning tails and flicking wings.

◁ Flight around rookery aerobatic, with much wheeling around nests and noisy squabbling. Otherwise slightly more laborious than Crow's, with faster, more regular wingbeats, and less gliding. Bill/face narrower, wings more pointed, with straighter rear edge; tail slightly rounded.

Rooks

Carrion Crow

Jackdaws

Both races breed and are present throughout the year

Hooded Crow

Carrion Crow

Carrion Crow

Hooded Crow

Carrion Crow (race *corone*) and Hooded Crow (race *cornix* British Isles) different races of single species. Large crow, all-black (Carrion) or black and grey (Hooded). Slightly larger than Rook, which is similar to Carrion Crow. Best distinctions: fully feathered black face and heavier, less pointed black bill feathered at base and with more curved top surface, larger head with much flatter forehead, and neater, sleeker plumage (with gloss visible only in strong sunlight), and thighs with small neat feathering, lacking Rook's loose, baggy 'trousers'. Tail squarer-ended. Hooded Crow has identical structure, but back, breast sides and rest of underparts, and underwing coverts, ash-grey (with dark streaks visible at close range). Crows usually perch less upright than Rooks, and have less waddling walk; like Rooks, also hop and jump. Calls different from Rook. Usually solitary or in pairs, but gather in loose flocks in autumn and winter and feed near other crows all year. Wary of humans.

hybrids

◁ A whole range of fertile hybrids occurs between the 2 races, many with isolated patches of black on back and breast. Narrow zone of hybridization in Scotland (darker areas on map); this has altered position over the years, but not increased in width, indicating that hybrids less successful at survival than pure birds of either race.

▽ Flight strong, usually slower, more deliberate than Rook's; head/ bill look shorter, wings often with more bulging rear edge; tail square-ended; sometimes hovers awkwardly, as when dropping shells onto beach to break them open. Often mobs' Buzzards and other birds of prey, as well as Grey Herons, twisting and turning and calling with short, angry rattles; in turn, mobbed by songbirds, nesting waders etc.

J F M A M J J A S O N D

Raven

Hooded Crows

Carrion Crow

RAVEN *Corvus corax*

adult

juvenile

△ Largest of all crows (and all perching birds), as big as or bigger than Buzzard, with longer wings, and over 30 per cent bigger than Carrion/Hooded Crow. Looks very powerful, with long, deep body, big head, massive, deep, arched bill, bristly, erectile throat feathers, long wings, long wedge-shaped tail and strong legs and feet. All-black plumage, with oily purplish and olive-green gloss in sunlight. Juvenile has browner, much less glossy plumage; body may look slightly mottled. Powerful, decisive walk; also jumps forwards and hops sideways. Looks very long and horizontal on ground or rocks, often more upright on branches and other perches; tail usually held level. Very distinctive loud, resonant, far-carrying croaking calls.

△ Most powerful predator of all crows, capable of killing hare or Rock Dove, but feeds mainly on carrion, especially of sheep. Rarely kills healthy lambs, but still persecuted by gamekeepers and some farmers, though bigger threat is afforestation of upland sheep-farming areas. Where common, large numbers may gather at good feeding sites, and non-breeders form small flocks, joining up at dusk in roosts of up to 100 birds or more, though during breeding season usually seen singly, in pairs or family parties.

Ravens

Raven, soaring

Carrion Crow

Ravens, diving

△ Superb flyer, with powerful, slow wingbeats; often flies at great height. Glides and soars more than any other crow; can look like large bird of prey at distance. All year, but especially early in breeding season, performs dramatic aerobatics, diving, tumbling and rolling over on back, accompanied by loud croaking calls. Looks far, far larger than Crow or Rook; cross-shaped silhouette, with projecting big head/long powerful bill, bulging throat, long wings with 'hands' quite tapered and angled backwards, and long, diamond-shaped tail.

KEY FACTS

Length: 64cm. **Wingspan:** 120-150cm. **Weight:** 800-1500g. **Habitat:** sea-cliff mountains, moorland, inland cliffs and crags, wooded valley sides, only in W and N in Britain. **Movements:** mainly sedentary, but some birds, especially non-breeders/young birds, quite nomadic in winter. **Population:** *c*10 500 pairs breed; up to *c*40 000 birds in winter. **Diet:** mainly carrion (especially dead sheep), sheep afterbirths, injured mammals and birds, food stolen from other birds; also some healthy birds and mammals, invertebrates, grain. **Voice:** distinctive deep, rather hollow croaking 'prruk prruk' or thinner, higher-pitched 'kok-kok-kok' in flight; also deep, resonant 'korronk'. **Nest:** very large cup of sticks, heather stems (and seaweed on coasts) with grass, moss, lined with wool, hair. On ledge or crevice in cliffs and quarries or in tall tree. **Eggs:** 4-6, pale bluish-green, spotted dark brown and grey. **Incubation:** 20-21 days, by female. **Fledging:** *c*45 days, young often leave nest before able to fly. **Broods:** 1. **Maturity:** 2-3 years. **Confusion species:** Rook and Carrion Crow (pp294-5) much smaller, with slimmer bills, no shaggy throat feathers, in flight have less splayed wingtips and lack Raven's wedge-shaped tail (although rounder tail of Rook can look similar). Calls also different.

J F M A M J J A S O N D

STARLINGS
Family Sturnidae

Large family of medium-sized birds; only one species occurs regularly here. Sharp-billed, strong-legged, very active, noisy, highly sociable. Most species nest in treeholes. Sexes very similar. Very adaptable; feed mainly on open ground, thrusting strong bills beneath surface and opening them there to seize insect larvae, earthworms and other prey.

Sturnus vulgaris **STARLING**

summer female

male, singing

male

winter

female

KEY FACTS

Length: 21.5cm. **Wingspan:** 37-42cm. **Weight:** 75-90g. **Habitat:** most habitats, from farmland and woods to largest cities, except in remote moorlands and mountains. **Movements:** British breeders mainly sedentary; many winter visitors/passage migrants from N/NE Europe (Oct-Apr). **Population:** at least 1.46 million breeding territories; probably over 30 million birds in winter. **Diet:** insects, especially cranefly larvae (leatherjackets) in breeding season, earthworms, seeds, berries, fruits. **Voice:** main call a grating 'tcheerr'; also long, musical 'tsoo-eee' or 'tsieuw' and harsh scream of surprise; song a throaty medley of whistles, gurgles, clicks, creaks and chirrups; some birds incorporate mimicry of other bird calls, e.g. Curlew or Buzzard, or artificial sounds such as ringing of telephones. **Nest:** bulky base of dry grass, straw, fine twigs, etc; cup lined with rootlets, moss, feathers, wool and other finer materials; in holes of all kinds, in trees, in walls and roofs of buildings, crevices in cliffs, nestboxes; in treeless areas in drystone walls and holes in ground; some among ivy. **Eggs:** 4-7, pale blue, sometimes white. **Incubation:** 12-13 days, by both sexes. **Fledging:** 20-22 days, but young leave earlier if disturbed. **Broods:** 1-2. **Maturity:** many females breed at 1 year, most males at 2 years. **Confusion species:** Waxwing (p236) in flight.

△ Medium-sized, with tapering front end due to sloping forehead and longish, pointed bill. Mainly blackish with green/purple gloss; brown on wings. Male in spring/summer has few or no spots, all-dark eyes and yellow bill with bluish base. Sings from prominent perches, with quivering wings and spiky throat feathers. Summer female has some buff and whitish spots, thin whitish ring around eye, and yellow bill with pinkish base. Winter male finely spotted buff above and whitish below; mainly brown bill. Winter female similar, but with more, larger, rounder spots.

juvenile

juvenile in moult

juvenile late autumn

△ Juvenile grey-brown, with blackish feathers between bill and eye, whitish throat and whitish streaks on underparts; buff edges to wing/tail feathers; bill brown. During moult Jul-Oct, looks very patchy, with some pale, faded head feathers, and some dark, glossy feathers on wings and on underparts, which become spotted. By late autumn, distinctively pale-hooded.

△ Flight fast, strong, direct, with rapid beats of triangular wings and brief glides; short, squared-off tail; arrow-shaped silhouette very distinctive. Hawks for flying insects. In winter, small groups join up at dusk to form huge flocks, which perform amazing aerobatic manoeuvres before going to communal roosts on trees, reedbeds, city ledges.

| J | F | M | A | M | J | J | A | S | O | N | D |

SPARROWS
Family Passeridae

Small, dumpy-bodied, rather short-legged, thick-billed birds. Plumage typically of browns and greys, often with dark-streaked back; males often have more boldly patterned head. Shortish tails unforked or only slightly forked. Gregarious. Most build untidy domed nests of grass, often in holes. Most feed on or near ground, mainly on seeds; young fed largely on insects. Sexes usually differ. Two species here, both occurring naturally right across Eurasia; highly adaptable House Sparrow introduced and spread almost throughout world.

TREE SPARROW *Passer montanus*

`50`

KEY FACTS

Length: 14cm. **Wingspan:** 20-22cm. **Weight:** 19-25g. **Habitat:** mostly in lightly wooded farmland/parkland; in Ireland mainly coastal areas. **Movements:** largely sedentary; some passage migrants and usually few winter visitors from N Europe (Sep-Apr); irregular large-scale irruptions. **Population:** irregular fluctuations; maximum of *c*900 000 breeding pairs 1965; now only 120 000-140 000 pairs. **Diet:** mainly seeds; also invertebrates and scraps; some leaves, shoots, buds etc. **Voice:** most calls like House Sparrow's, but various chirps higher-pitched, more metallic, less monotonous, more rhythmic; much more distinctive is hard 'tek tek' call in flight. **Nest:** untidy structure of straw and grass filling hole in tree or building; also in nestboxes or in base of nest of crows etc; sometimes in hedges, when domed. **Eggs:** 4-6, white to pale grey, heavily marked dark brown. **Incubation:** 11-14 days, by both sexes. **Fledging:** 15-20 days. **Broods:** 2-3. **Maturity:** 1 year. **Confusion species:** House Sparrow (opposite).

J F M A M J J A S O N D

House Sparrow adult male summer

Tree Sparrow adult

Tree Sparrow juvenile

△ Unlike House Sparrow, not closely associated with human habitation, though does visit large suburban gardens etc; despite scientific name, very much a lowland bird. Also unlike House Sparrow, nests mostly in tree holes. Smaller, neater, smarter; also shyer, more secretive. Unlike House, sexes similar; easily distinguished from female House, but males more similar. Tree identified by chestnut-brown crown and black cheek spot; also has white collar (may be hidden when bird hunched up), no white above eye, double white wingbars, smaller, neater black bib, brown (not grey) rump and warmer buffer underparts. As with House, bill black in summer, yellowish at base in winter. Juvenile has duller crown, less distinct cheek spot and bib, and buff wingbars.

◁ Flight faster, more agile than House Sparrow's, often shooting off high when disturbed. Double white wingbar. Very distinctive hard double flight call, not heard from House Sparrows.

△ Often mixes with flocks of finches and buntings to feed on grain in stubble fields. Hops more actively and jerkily than House Sparrow, with tail more often cocked; at distance dark head contrasts with white collar (like larger, longer-tailed Reed Bunting, p315).

Passer domesticus **HOUSE SPARROW**

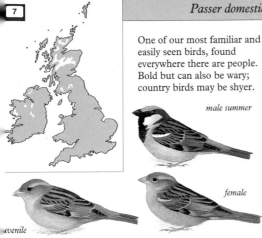

One of our most familiar and easily seen birds, found everywhere there are people. Bold but can also be wary; country birds may be shyer.

male summer

female

juvenile

△ Male has distinctive grey crown, untidy black bib, grey rump and greyish-white cheeks; small white streak over and behind eye; one short white wingbar and one indistinct buff wingbar further down wing. In spring/summer, nape chestnut, back chestnut streaked black, underparts greyish or slightly buffish-white. Urban birds often duller than those in rural areas. Bill black. Female much drabber, without male's striking head pattern; dull buff to olive-brown above, with darker streaks; indistinct pale buff streak behind eyes; 2 faint buff wingbars; dull buff below, often appearing little paler than upperparts at distance. Bill pale brown, yellowish at base. Juvenile like female, but crown and rump mottled brown, throat and belly whiter. Bill pinkish-brown or grey with paler tip.

▷ In winter, male has duller, browner crown and duller, less chestnut upperparts, smaller, mottled bib, and brownish or greyish bill.

male winter

House Sparrow adult female

Greenfinch juvenile

Reed Bunting juvenile

◁ Female/juvenile quite like juvenile Greenfinch, but latter has yellow panel on wings, streaked underparts and distinctly forked tail. Juvenile buntings have bolder head pattern, streaked underparts and longer, white-edged tails.

▷ Flight fast, direct, with rapid, whirring wingbeats. Flocks usually compact; birds do not change position or straggle, unlike finches. Male has chestnut shoulder and grey rump. Both sexes show single white wingbar in front of indistinct buff wingbar.

male summer

female

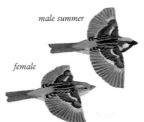

KEY FACTS

Length: 14-15cm.
Wingspan: 21-25.5cm.
Weight: 24-32g. **Habitat:** rarely far from human habitation, from city centres to farms in the remotest rural areas, including islands; most abundant in E Britain and E Ireland, preferring dryer conditions there; absent only from highest ground in Scottish Highlands and from some areas of C and W Ireland. **Movements:** most seem to be highly sedentary, though odd ringed birds have travelled over 400 km.
Population: decline in recent years, especially in suburbs; c3.4-6 million pairs breed; c8-14.5 million birds winter.
Diet: chiefly grain, also some other seeds, shoots, buds, berries; some insects and other invertebrates, especially for feeding to young nestlings; household scraps, peanuts etc, and animal feed on farms. **Voice:** loud, chirping: often monotonous 'cheer-eep', 'chissip', especially from males, very loud when given in unison from large flocks; abrupt 'cheu cheu', rattling twitters, and low, hoarse 'chreek' when taking flight. Song an irregular series of call notes. **Nest:** untidy structure of grass and straw, usually filling hole in building or other structure; also takes over nests of House Martins etc; some build domed nests in hedges. Increasing trend towards year-round nesting. **Eggs:** 3-7, white, greyish or greenish, speckled grey or blackish. **Incubation:** 11-14 days, by both sexes. **Fledging:** 11-19 days. **Broods:** 1-4. **Maturity:** 1 year. **Confusion species:** Tree Sparrow (opposite) similar to male, but smaller, neater, with chocolate-brown crown, black spot on white cheek, double white wingbar and different flight call. Juvenile Greenfinch and buntings (see above left).

| J | F | M | A | M | J | J | A | S | O | N | D |

FINCHES
Family Fringillidae

Large family of small birds with strong, conical bills which have internal grooves for husking seeds, which form main food. Bill shape adapted to precise diet: from delicate and tweezer-like in Goldfinch for eating light seeds of thistles etc, to massive in Hawfinch for cracking open very hard cherry stones; crossbills unique among birds, having crossed mandibles for extracting seeds from conifer cones. Many finches feed young on insects/invertebrates. Many have bright plumage, especially in males; sexes often differ.

● Note: head pattern; size of bill; presence/number/colour of wing patches; white on tail/rump; when overhead in distinctively undulating flight, look very similar in silhouette; structure may be useful but calls especially important.

BRAMBLING *Fringilla montifringilla*

male winter

male spring

female winter

77

KEY FACTS

Length: 14cm. **Wingspan:** 25-26cm. **Weight:** 22-30g.
Habitat: chiefly in beech woods and farmland on passage/in winter; breeds in birchwoods in N Europe.
Movements: passage migrant/winter visitor (late Sep-May) from N Europe.
Population: large fluctuations from year to year, depending on availability of chief winter food, beechmast; varies from 50 000 birds in poor year to perhaps 2 million birds in large-scale invasion year. Tiny numbers have bred Scotland and E England since 1920. **Diet:** mainly beechmast in winter, also seeds, berries; mainly insects in summer.
Voice: hoarse, metallic, twanging 'tsweek', louder, nasal, wheezing 'tseh-ep' of alarm; hard but subdued 'tchek' in flight, often repeated; song from spring males monotonous, repeated, nasal 'dzweee' very like Greenfinch's (p302), sometimes followed by harsh rattle. **Nest:** neat cup of grass, plant fibres, lichens, bark, lined with hair, feathers, in tree or bush. **Eggs:** 5-7, greenish to brownish, spotted dark brown. **Incubation:** 13-14 days, by female. **Fledging:** 13-14 days. **Broods:** 1.
Maturity: 1 year. **Confusion species:** Chaffinch (opposite).

J F M A M J J A S O N D

△ Similar shape to Chaffinch, but head looks larger, bill stubbier and chest slightly fuller; tail a bit shorter, more forked. Both sexes have orange-buff breast/shoulders, long, oval white rump and black tail, and white belly with black spots on flanks; lacks Chaffinch's white shoulders and outer tail feathers. Winter male's head/mantle blackish mottled buff, sides of neck greyish; winter female duller. Bill pale orange-yellow with black tip. By late winter/spring, males have striking black head/mantle; bold orange breast and shoulders; blue-black bill.

Goldfinch

Bramblings

Chaffinch male

Bullfinch male

male

male

female

△ White rump and black tail striking in flight; orange and white markings on wings (Chaffinch's are white only). Underwings show bright yellow 'armpits'. More compact than Chaffinch, with more erratic, bounding flight; often high. Bullfinch also has white rump/black tail, but rump broader, and bird much bulkier, with black cap, not shawl, and single white wingbar; does not form large flocks. Goldfinch has whitish rump/black tail, but is smaller and daintier, with broad yellow wing-bands; adult's head black, white and red.

Fringilla coelebs **CHAFFINCH**

17

One of our most abundant and widespread birds, and commonest finch. Stocky, with head often looking rather peaked; thick pointed bill; longish body, wings and tail, latter with shallow fork. Hops jerkily on branches but creeps along quite inconspicuously on ground.

female

male

summer

juvenile

KEY FACTS

Length: 14.5cm. **Wingspan:** 24.5-28.5cm. **Weight:** 19-23g. **Habitat:** woods, hedges, orchards, parks, gardens; British/Irish breeders winter in woods or near hedges, but Continental immigrants winter mainly in open fields. **Movements:** our breeders highly sedentary, except in very severe weather; passage migrants/winter visitors from Europe, especially N (late Sep-Apr). **Population:** c7.5 million pairs breed; c15 million birds winter here, plus c10-20 million immigrants from Europe. **Diet:** chiefly insects in breeding season, plus some other invertebrates (young fed almost entirely on invertebrates); mainly seeds at other times, with some berries and other plant matter. **Voice:** repeated, loud, rather metallic 'chwink' (Great Tit has similar call); penetrating 'tzit'; loud, clear 'wheet' from males in spring; low 'chip' in flight; song a series of about 12 cheerful, sweet, rattling 'chip-chip-chip...' notes ending in a flourish, 'tissi-chweeeoh'. **Nest:** neat cup of grass, plant fibres and lichens, lined with hair, feathers, in tree or bush. **Eggs:** 4-5, pale blue to brownish with purple-brown markings. **Incubation:** 12-13 days, by female. **Fledging:** 13-14 days. **Broods:** 1. **Maturity:** 1 year. **Confusion species:** Brambling (opposite).

△ Bold white shoulder patch and white wingbar very conspicuous; rump yellow-green; tail black with bold white outer feathers. Male summer acquires black forehead through feather wear; crown and nape blue-grey, mantle chestnut, cheeks and breast pinkish, rear underparts creamy-white; mainly black wings have faint greenish-yellow on secondaries as well as white shoulder patch and wingbar. Bill blue-grey. Female has olive-brown upperparts, with greyer crown and nape (especially in summer), paler greyish-brown face with darker cheeks, and pale greyish-brown underparts, often with pinkish tinge on breast; bill pale brown with dusky tip. Juvenile like female but with browner mantle, paler underparts, and duller, brownish-green rump.

males winter

△ In winter plumage, male has reddish-buff tinge to blue-grey crown and nape, duller mantle, cheeks and breast, and buff to pinkish bill with dark grey tip. Very gregarious in winter, feeding in fields with other finches; sexes often in separate flocks.

male

female

male

female

△ In cover, flies fast and level with tail often spread when turning or landing, but, over distance, flight undulating, as other finches, with wings closed after a few beats; long body and tail give different silhouette from smaller finches such as Linnet. White shoulder patch and white wingbar flicker boldly in flight, and white outer tail feathers distinctive.

J F M A M J J A S O N D

female

summer

male winter

male

KEY FACTS

Length: 15cm. **Wingspan:** 24.5-27.5cm. **Weight:** 25-32g. **Habitat:** open woodland, hedges, gardens, parks; winters in fields and gardens. **Movements:** mainly resident, though some move SW within Britain, and a few migrate to winter on Continent; some passage migrants/winter visitors from N Europe. **Population:** minimum of c690 000 pairs breed. Possibly as many as 3.5 million birds winter. **Diet:** almost entirely seeds, especially large and often hard ones, of 30 or more plants; few invertebrates in breeding season; feed young mainly on seeds, with some invertebrates. **Voice:** usual calls repeated brief 'chup chup' or 'teu teu'; repeated soft, quite lilting, Canary-like 'tsoooeeet' alarm call; main flight call a soft twittering 'chichichichichit', fuller, less metallic than Linnet's; territorial call of male in breeding season a long, nasal, wheezing 'dzweeeeeeer'; song a Canary-like twitter, mixed with calls, given from perch or in song-flight. **Nest:** sturdy cup of moss, grass and twigs, lined with finer grass, hair, feathers etc, in bush or tree, often conifers. **Eggs:** 4-6, white, greyish-white or pale beige, with sparse reddish or blackish markings. **Incubation:** 12-14 days, by female. **Fledging:** 14-15 days. **Broods:** 1 or 2. **Maturity:** 1 year. **Confusion species:** Siskin (opposite) smaller, slimmer, with bold double yellow wingbars and strongly streaked flanks, also black crown and bib in male. Only other British finches that look so heavy in flight are Hawfinch (p311), and crossbills (pp308-9), which are bigger, with different bills and plumage. Female and immature House Sparrow (p299) rather like juvenile, but lack yellow on wings.

△ Our largest green finch, with stocky, 'muscular' build; heav body, big head, short forked tail, short legs. Stout pinkish bill and small dusky mask in adults give 'frowning' expression. Yellow-green rump, striking yellow panel on wing and yellow patches at base of tail. Summer male bright olive-green above slate-grey on wings, bright greenish-yellow below. Brightening of plumage due to wear of feathers; older birds brightest. From autumn, after moult Jun-Aug, greyer above, especially on cheeks, with greyer flanks; tinged grey below. Female duller, browner above, faintly streaked, duller but still yellow tinged below, and less yellow on wings and tail than male. Legs pinkish. Solitary during breeding season, but forms flocks in winter, often mixed with other finches and buntings.

male, song flight

◁ In spring, male has distinctive bat-like song flight: circles round among or above treetops, singing constantly, with slow, deep, erratic wingbeats, showing off bold yellow patches in wings and tail.

▷ Juvenile duller, more streaked than female; greyish-buff above, including rump, yellow-grey below. Face has stronger pattern, with darker mottled ear coverts, paler chin. Yellow wing panel and tail sides duller, but still distinctive.

juvenile

Blue Tit   *males summer*

▷ Flight very undulating. Compact, stout body, short tail and long wings. Bright yellow patches at base of tail and yellow wing panels.

◁ One of our commonest garden birds, visiting bird feeders; especially fond of sunflower seeds. Aggressive when competing for food, driving off rivals of own species as well as tits and other small birds.

juvenile

male
summer

female summer

male
winter

KEY FACTS

Length: 12cm. **Wingspan:** 20-23cm. **Weight:** 12-18g.
Habitat: breeds in woodland, mainly coniferous, also birch and mixed woods; winters among alders and birches; in gardens, chiefly migrants, Mar-Apr; fond of streamsides.
Movements: mainly sedentary; some N breeders move S in winter; passage migrant/winter visitor from N/E Europe mid Sep-mid May.
Population: *c*360 000 pairs breed. Winter numbers vary, depending on numbers of Continental immigrants; could be as many as 500 000 birds in major invasion years. **Diet:** seeds, especially of conifers, alder, birch; some invertebrates in breeding season; feeds young on conifer seeds and invertebrates. **Voice:** clear, metallic 'tzu', quite wheezy 'tsu-eet' and hard twittering, often combined; shrill, clear 'tsewi' flight call; song, given in spring in circling, butterfly-like song-flight, a varied sweet twittering, often beginning with 'tluee' and ending with long nasal wheeze. **Nest:** small cup of twigs, grass and moss, lined with plant down, hair, sometimes feathers, usually high in conifer. **Eggs:** 4-5, pale blue, with pale red-brown spots. **Incubation:** 12-13 days, by female.
Fledging: 13-15 days.
Broods: 1-2. **Maturity:** 1 year. **Confusion species:** Greenfinch (opposite), Serin (right), Redpoll (p306).

J F M A M J J A S O N D

△ Very small, neat, slender finch, streaked green and yellow; quite plump body looks elongated due to fine, pointed bill, long wings and deeply forked tail. Usually in tree-tops, often with Redpolls, where very active and acrobatic, hanging tit-like from twigs. In early spring, attracted to bird feeders with string bags of peanuts. Male yellowish-green above, with faint streaks, heavier on flanks; crown and bib black (mottled grey in winter), wings mainly black, emphasizing 2 bright yellow wingbars, rump greenish-yellow; black tail with contrasting yellow patches at base. Female duller, greenish-grey above, without black on head, whiter below, more heavily streaked all over, including on duller yellow rump. Juvenile duller still, browner than female, with heavier streaks and streaked greyish rump.

males

females

△ Flight fast, direct and undulating after sudden ascent. Flocks tightly co-ordinated: burst from treetops, bound off, then swerve back to land in unison. Wings long and sharply pointed, with bold yellow bars and yellow in flight feathers, yellow rump and yellow patches at base of deeply forked tails.

female

juvenile

male
summer

male winter

Serins

△ **Serin** (*Serinus serinus*) annual visitor (mainly Feb-Jun, Oct-Nov) from Continent, rare breeder from 1967; chiefly coastal S England. Tiny (at 11cm only size of Blue Tit), with very short, stubby bill; summer male mainly bright canary-yellow, with darker, streaked greener wings/tail, whitish belly and dark streaks on flanks; after moult Aug-Sep, duller, greener; female even duller, browner, more streaked. Yellow rump distinctive (though paler in female), especially in fast, dancing flight; long dark wings, short, deeply forked tail. Lacks bold yellow wingbars and tail patches of Siskin. Juvenile brown-buff above, with slightly paler buff rump, faintly yellow-buff below, streaked darker overall. Distinguished from juvenile Siskin by size, bill shape and paler rump. Song a long, fast hissing jangle of twittering notes, mixed with Canary-like trills; calls include distinctive rippling 'tirrililit' and tinny 'tsooeet' of alarm. Escaped Canary larger, with longer tail; greyer above, yellower below.

female   *male*

summer

KEY FACTS

Length: 13.5cm. **Wingspan:** 21-25.5cm. **Weight:** 15-20g. **Habitat:** breeds mainly in gorse-covered heaths and commons, shrubby thickets and dense hedges, also in young conifer plantations, among dunes; winters chiefly in lowlands, in fields, waste ground, coastal marshes. **Movements:** British breeders mostly sedentary, though some winter as far away as W France/Iberia. Passage migrants/winter visitors from Scandinavia (Sep-Apr). **Population:** recent decline, especially Ireland, probably due chiefly to destruction of main food, weed seeds, by herbicides; *c*520 000 pairs breed Britain, *c*130 000 pairs Ireland. Perhaps 1 million or more winter. **Diet:** seeds, especially of arable weeds, also oilseed rape seeds; few invertebrates; young fed chiefly or almost entirely on insects. **Voice:** rather plaintive 'tsooeet' alarm call; rapid, soft, quite musical, twittering flight call, much less nasal than Twite's, much less metallic than Redpoll's. Song a very varied, sweet musical twitter, interspersed with scratchy or twanging notes, sometimes in chorus. **Eggs:** 4-6, pale bluish, with pink, purple and brown spots. **Incubation:** 11-13 days, by female. **Fledging:** 11-14 days. **Broods:** 2-3. **Maturity:** 1 year. **Confusion species:** Twite (opposite) very like winter male, female and juvenile Linnet, but more heavily streaked, with separate buff-white wingbar as well as thinner white edges to flight feathers; black (not grey) legs in adult; yellow bill in winter; male has pink rump. Redpoll (p306) smaller, daintier, more compact, more tit-like and agile, with heavier streaking; adults have red forecrown, black chin; rarely encountered far from trees.

| J | F | M | A | M | J | J | A | S | O | N | D |

△ Small, quite compact finch with rather flat-topped head, triangular, pointed bill and shortish forked tail. Nervous, difficult to approach outside breeding season, flocks bounding off into cover. Feeds in bushes in summer, on ground in winter. Gregarious, forming large flocks after breeding that roam about, often pausing briefly on tops of bush or hedge, uttering musical twittering. Less acrobatic than Redpoll or Siskin. Flicks wings and tail. Greyish bill; prominent white panels on blackish wings and white patches at base of black tail. From Apr, male has pale grey head, with pale crimson forecrown and breast, dark-streaked whitish throat and bright chestnut mantle; underparts whitish, with buff flanks. By Jul, some males even brighter, with paler head, whiter throat and deep crimson breast. Summer female much duller, lacking any red, and with less grey head, buffer throat and dark-streaked drab brown upperparts; underparts duller, browner, with breast and flanks heavily streaked brown.

male   *winter*   *female*   *juvenile*

△ Winter male (after moult Aug-Oct) much duller: brownish head, soft blackish streaks toning down brightness of chestnut mantle, pale buff, dark-streaked throat, and often no obvious red markings on crown or breast. Female changes little year round. Juvenile very like female, but more uniform, with narrower streaks; throat buff-white, almost unstreaked; often indistinct whitish wing panel, but white tail patches as adult.

winter   *males*   *female*

△ Flight fast and light, wavering over short distances, undulating when longer; frequent flights of feeding flocks can be more direct, almost sparrow-like or more bouncing; members of flock stay close together. White flashes in blackish wings and white patches at base of tail; white underwings.

winter

males

females

KEY FACTS

Length: 14cm. **Wingspan:** 22-24cm. **Weight:** 13-17g. **Habitat:** breeds on moors and mountains, rocky ground near coast; winters mainly on seashores, saltmarshes and coastal fields. **Movements:** some resident, but others move S along coasts, some as far as Continent. **Population:** most abundant on coastal moorland in Scotland and on grouse moors of S Pennines, but declining; *c*65 000 pairs breed Britain, *c*3500 Ireland; *c*250 000 birds winter. **Diet:** small seeds; young fed on seeds. **Voice:** very nasal, twanging 'tchwooeek' or 'twa-it' (hence common name); this, twittering flight call and song all harder, more metallic and penetrating than Linnet's; song less musical, with more twanging, dry chattering and hoarse jangling notes and slower, more disjointed phrasing. **Nest:** deep cup of twigs of heather, roots, grass, moss etc, thickly lined with wool/hair, among heather or bracken, in bush, bank, among rocks or in stone wall. **Eggs:** 4-6, blue with red-brown to purple-brown markings. **Incubation:** 12-13 days, by female. **Fledging:** 11-12 days. **Broods:** 1-2. **Maturity:** 1 year. **Confusion species:** female/juvenile Linnet (opposite) very similar, but paler, with streaked throat, more white in shorter wings and tail, and dark bill in winter; less metallic calls.

J F M A M J J A S O N D

△ Very like winter male/female/juvenile Linnet, but has stubbier (though sharply pointed) bill and longer tail, with darker, more tawny plumage. More ground-dwelling, feeding with Linnets and other finches and buntings on rough ground, saltmarshes etc in winter. Much scarcer than Linnet. At close range, distinguished by warm buff face and throat, less obvious white wing panel and tail patches, distinct buff-white wingbar; heavily streaked golden-buff of chest and flanks contrasting strongly with white belly and undertail; rump of male pink, though duller, streaked brown, in winter; legs of adults almost black, not brown as in Linnet; bill yellow in winter. Often best distinguished from Linnet by calls; winter flocks frequently give constant hard twittering.

male

summer

female

◁ In summer, nape and hindneck tinged grey, upperparts darker, underparts more strongly streaked and male's rump unstreaked, brighter pink. Bill pale grey, sometimes with yellow tinge.

▷ Juvenile very like female, but has slightly duller, greyer crown and nape, more rufous mantle, and more noticeably streaked, paler buff throat; underparts slightly paler, more streaked. Bill yellowish or pinkish-grey, yellow by Aug. Legs pale pink, turning browner; remain paler than adults' through 1st winter.

Twite juvenile

Linnet juvenile

male

female
winter

◁ Flight like Linnet's but longer tail noticeable. Flocks bound up when disturbed then fly down to disappear among ground vegetation. Pink rump of male distinctive, especially in summer, and less white on wings and tail; body and wing coverts darker, more streaked.

female

male

male

male

race cabaret *summer*

KEY FACTS

Length: 11.5-14.5cm.
Wingspan: 20-25cm.
Weight: 10-14g. **Habitat:**
breed mainly in open scrubby
woodland, also heathland,
hedges, parks, large gardens,
along rivers and streams,
especially with birches,
increasingly in young conifer
plantations; migrants often in
scrub/waste land, feeding on
weed seeds; also take birch
seeds from ground in spring.
Movements: some British
breeders migrate, many
wintering in Europe; passage
migrants/winter visitors of race
flammea from N Europe and
rostrata from Greenland etc.
Population: c230 000 pairs
breed; c250 000-750 000
birds in winter. **Diet:** mainly
seeds, especially of birch, also
weeds; invertebrates, mainly
in spring; young fed on seeds
and invertebrates. **Voice:**
most distinctive call, in flight
or perched, a hard, rattling,
staccato, stuttering 3- or 4-
note 'chuchu(chu)chuch' with
metallic echo (has buzzing
quality when in flock);
plaintive 'tsooeet' of alarm.
Song a long sequence of flight
calls mixed with buzzing trill,
given in song-flight. **Nest:**
cup of twigs, roots, grass,
moss etc, lined with plant
down, hair, wool, feathers, in
tree/shrub. **Eggs:** 4-6, pale
blue, marked rust-red to
purplish. **Incubation:** 10-12
days, by female. **Fledging:** 9-
14 days. **Broods:** 1-2.
Maturity: 1 year. **Confusion
species:** Linnet (p304) larger
(except for N immigrant
Redpolls), without double
buff wingbars and black/dusky
chin; Twite (p305) longer-
tailed, darker with orange-buff
throat; both these are longer,
less dumpy, and (especially
Linnet) have white in wings
and tail, unlike Redpoll. Siskin
(p303) also acrobatic in tree
tops, but more slender, with
double yellow wingbars and
yellow patches at base of tail.

J F M A M J J A S O N D

△ British/Irish race *cabaret* very small, dumpy-bodied, with
blunt face, small, triangular, sharp-pointed bill and short
forked tail. Very active and acrobatic, hanging upside-down
from tips of branches or clinging to stems of weeds; often with
Siskins in winter. Upperparts tawny-brown with blackish
streaks, 2 buff wingbars; dark-streaked flanks; straw-yellow
bill; blackish-brown tail with pale edges. Adults have red
forehead, black chin and black between bill and eye: males
have variably pink cheeks, throat, breast and upper flanks, all
brighter in summer, and dark-streaked pink rump; females
rarely show any pink and more heavily streaked below.

race flammea

race rostrata

△ N European race *flammea* ('Mealy Redpoll') passage migrant
and winter visitor (Oct-May), especially to E coasts, larger,
paler, greyer above with whiter wingbars and rump, and
glossier, brighter red forehead on adults, but very variable;
some males with worn plumage have almost white unstreaked
rumps. Greenland, Baffin Island and Iceland race *rostrata*,
occasional passage migrant and winter visitor to N and
W Scotland, even larger; has bigger bill, darker plumage with
heavy streaking (especially on flanks, which have 3 long
blackish streaks), pale wingbars and whitish rump. Both these
races, especially *rostrata*, have deeper flight calls than *cabaret*.

race cabaret
juvenile

◁ Juvenile lacks red on
forehead and has much more
indistinct dusky marking on
chin; more heavily streaked
above and below.

▷ Flight fast, undulating,
with light, bouncy, dancing
action, though birds in flock
tightly co-ordinated; hard,
dry chattering flight calls
distinctive. Spring song flight
of male circling, slow wingbeats alternating with glides.

males

females

Carduelis carduelis **GOLDFINCH**

18

male

female

KEY FACTS

Length: 12cm. **Wingspan:** 21-25.5cm. **Weight:** 14-17g.
Habitat: breeds in gardens, parks, orchards, hedges, woodland edges, in winter often on waste ground, rough grassland etc; needs seeding weeds for feeding.
Movements: most British breeders, especially females, migrate as far as SW France and Iberia, some to N Africa; probably immigrants from Continent some years.
Population: probably at least 275 000 pairs breed; perhaps fewer than 100 000 birds in winter. **Diet:** seeds, mainly softer, half-ripe ones of thistles, teasel, groundsel and other composite weeds; also few insects; young fed on some insects at first, then seeds.
Voice: main call a distinctive liquid, twittering 'switt-witt-witt' or harder 'tswitt'; also rather hoarse 'geez' and soft, whistled 'aah-i' of alarm. Song a Canary-like twitter, based on main call, with nasal, purring and rattling notes interspersed.
Nest: cup of rootlets, grass, wool, cobwebs, lined mainly with vegetable down and wool, in tree or tall shrub. **Eggs:** 5-6, very pale bluish, with reddish or purplish-brown markings.
Incubation: 11-13 days, by female. **Fledging:** 13-15 days.
Broods: 2, sometimes 3.
Maturity: 1 year. **Confusion species:** juvenile like juvenile Greenfinch (p302) and Siskin (p303), but has more black/yellow on wings.

J F M A M J J A S O N D

△ Unmistakable. Quite small, slender and dainty, with boldly patterned head, sharply pointed pale bill and bright golden-yellow band on black wings. Head red, white and black, with white spot on nape; nape and back rather greyish-brown, underparts whitish, tail black with white tip. In male, red extends slightly further back above and below eye; female has broader, greyer tips to lesser wing coverts. In winter, brighter, more cinnamon-brown above, with buff sides to breast.

▷ Juvenile lacks adults' bold face pattern, but has same black and yellow wings, though yellow duller. Greyish-buff body, paler below, with indistinct dull brownish spots and streaks. Attains adult plumage after moult from Aug to Oct.

juvenile

◁ In autumn and winter, flocks (aptly called 'charms') range widely in search of weed seeds. Specialize in feeding on those of thistle family, including thistles and teasels. Actions light and agile, swinging on seedheads and often feeding head down. They can be seen wherever such food plants abound, except in extensive areas of moors/mountains.

▷ Flight light, acrobatic, more dancing than any other finch, with deep erratic undulations; flocks stay together, seldom mixing with other finches. Golden-yellow bands contrast boldly with black of rest of wing, and whitish rump with black tail; white tips to flight feathers less noticeable. Face pattern distinctive from front or side.

CROSSBILL *Loxia curvirostra*

89

old male *juvenile*

old female *young male*

KEY FACTS

Length: 16.5cm. **Wingspan:** 27-30.5cm. **Weight:** 34-38g.
Habitat: conifers, mainly in woods or clumps, including plantations, but also in isolated trees, e.g. in parks and gardens, during 'invasion' years. Irrupting birds suddenly turn up in all sorts of habitats, but search out conifers for feeding and resting.
Movements: most breeding populations quite sedentary, but birds often elusive and unpredictable, leaving area when cones unavailable. During years of major cone crop failure in N and E Europe, large-scale eruptions of birds westwards, including to Britain. **Population:** fluctuates widely; probably fewer than 1000 birds in some years, but several times that number (possibly as many as 40 000) following major irruption. **Diet:** specialist feeder on conifer seeds, especially spruce, larch, pine; some seeds, berries, buds and shoots, and invertebrates.
Voice: distinctive, explosive, metallic 'chip chip' in flight, louder in alarm, also quieter 'choik choik' when feeding; song a mixture of short trills, loud creaking notes or musical warbling with several call notes. **Nest:** small cup of conifer twigs, moss, bark etc, lined with grass, hair, wool etc, high in conifer. **Eggs:** 3-4, cream to bluish-white, with sparse dark purplish markings. **Incubation:** 14-15 days, by female. **Fledging:** 20-25 days. **Broods:** usually 1, sometimes 2. **Maturity:** 1 year. **Confusion species:** Scottish and Parrot Crossbills (opposite).

J F M A M J J A S O N D

juvenile

△ Large, thickset, powerful-looking finch: big head, thick bill with mandibles crossed at tip (not visible at long range), thick neck, heavy body, short legs and sharply forked tail. Quite parrot-like in actions as well as shape, clambering about on or sidling along branches and often using strong bill as grappling hook. Also like parrots, uses one or both feet in feeding, to hold down conifer cones while it forces its crossed bill between the scales to prise them apart so that it can then extract the seeds with its tongue. Often snips off cone with bill and flies to perch to deal with it there. Agile and acrobatic, hanging from cones or fluttering from twig to twig. Noisy, calling frequently; first sign of a feeding party often sound of discarded cones dropping from trees. Spends most time high in trees, but often comes to water to drink; hops clumsily on ground. Breeds at any time of year, depending on abundance of food.

old male *young male* *old female* *young female*

△ Male mainly red, varying in richness, from greenish-yellow with only a few orange-red feathers or mainly orange-red in young males, to rose-red or bright crimson in old males; brighter on crown, rump and underparts; brightest in summer. Wings and tail black/brown, contrasting with rest of plumage, especially bright, pinkish-red rump. Female has mainly greenish-grey head and body, dusky wings and tail and paler underparts, with dark wings and tail; rump bright yellow-green. Older females in worn plumage much brighter and greener. In both sexes, dusky mottling and streaks visible at close range, and lower belly and undertail almost white.

◁ Juveniles have brownish or olive-grey heads and upperparts and whitish underparts, with heavy blackish streaks all over, including on dull rump; some have reduced streaking, with pale head and rump, others heavily streaked, with almost blackish head and body. Bill not distinctly crossed at first; can then look similar to female and juvenile Scarlet Rosefinch (p310).

> Flight strong, fast and undulating, with long swooping bounds, usually high up at tree level or above (though sometimes lower on migration). Bulky silhouette, with large oval head/bill and oval body, broad-based, leaf-shaped wings and short, strongly forked tail. Birds disturbed from drinking at puddles etc on ground shoot up quickly to tree canopy. Often call in flight.

males

females

Scottish Crossbills

male

female

juvenile

◁ **Scottish Crossbill** (*Loxia scotica*), for long regarded as merely a subspecies of Crossbill, now considered a distinct species – the only exclusively British bird species. Found only in N Scotland, in ancient Caledonian Scots pine forest and mature plantations with Scots pine. Extremely similar to Crossbill: virtually same length and with identical plumages, but has slightly larger head and deeper bill, adapted for dealing with Scots pine cones. Main call, 'chup', usually distinguishable from 'chip' of Crossbill. Hard to census, due to great difficulty of distinguishing it from Crossbill, which also occurs in same area (particularly following major invasions), variation in numbers due to fluctuating food supply, and nomadic behaviour of crossbills. Current population could be as low as 350 pairs or as high as 1300 pairs. Threats include continued decline of native mature pinewoods.

Parrot Crossbills

male

female

juvenile

▷ **Parrot Crossbill** (*Loxia pytyopsittacus*) longer (17.5cm) and bulkier than Crossbill/Scottish Crossbill, with deeper, more parrot-like bill than either; plumage same, except adults usually have paler, duller wings that contrast less with body. Like Scottish Crossbill, preferred food is Scots pine seeds, so usually found where these trees occur. Main breeding range in N Europe, from Norway E to Urals. After failure of cone crop there, irruptions as far as Britain occurred in autumn/winter of 1962-3, 1982-3 and 1990-1, with most leaving by spring but some remaining here; pair first recorded breeding 1984, in Norfolk; later breeding records from pairs in Scotland and Breckland, Norfolk/Suffolk border. Difficulty of distinguishing from Crossbill/Scottish Crossbill and crossbill habit of remaining high in trees mean that exact numbers of visitors hard to assess. During 1962-3 invasion, 85 birds reported, 61 of these from Fair Isle, Scotland; in 1982-3, minimum of 104 seen E Britain, from N Scottish islands to Norfolk; in 1990-1, over 200 reports, from Shetland to Kent. Otherwise, odd birds reported only occasionally.

BULLFINCH *Pyrrhula pyrrhula*

male

juvenile

female

20

△ Portly, neckless, with long, low head, short, deep, stubby black bill, quite long wings and longish, barely forked tail. Generally shy and secretive, mostly hidden in cover; best noticed by soft but far-carrying piping call. In pairs all year; family parties in autumn, occasionally small flocks in winter. Adults have long black cap, extending to face and chin, black wings with broad whitish wingbar, and prominent white rump contrasting with black tail. Male has blue-grey upperparts and pinkish-red underparts. Female has dull grey nape, olive-grey upperparts and pale pinkish-brown underparts. White lower belly and undertail in both sexes. Juvenile like female but lacks black cap; brown above, buff or yellowish-brown below. Wingbar buff and rump buff-white. Bill greyish.

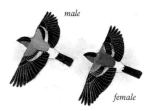

male

female

◁ White wingbar and, especially, white rump striking in flight, which is usually low, rather weak and flitting, bird soon disappearing into cover, but stronger, more bounding over distance.

▽ **Scarlet Rosefinch** (*Carpodacus erythrinus*) breeds in lightly wooded habitats, NE Europe, N Asia; major long-term expansion to W since 1930s; increasingly reported here as rare spring/autumn visitor (especially Sep). First bred here 1982 Scottish Highlands; several more since. House Sparrow-sized (14.5-15cm), but with shorter, deeper bill and longer, forked tail. Mature adult male (from 2nd summer) rare here; has scarlet head, breast and rump. Most are juveniles: warm olive-brown above, buffy-white below, softly streaked overall; females and 1st-summer males have colder, greyer tone. Rather dull and featureless; resemble female/juvenile House Sparrow, but dark beady eye stands out much more in plain face, bill darker, and usually indistinct double whitish wingbar (bolder, rusty-buff in juveniles). Call a soft, piping 'teu-eek'.

KEY FACTS

Length: 15cm. **Wingspan:** 22-26cm. **Weight:** 21-27g. **Habitat:** woods/gardens with trees and, especially, bushes/dense undergrowth; also visits orchards in late winter/spring. **Movements:** mainly sedentary; few immigrants from Continent of larger N race *pyrrhula* (males brighter, females paler). **Population:** large size of territories, combined with hard-to-define boundaries and bird's own shyness, makes estimates difficult; probably more than 200 000 pairs breed Britain, 100 000 pairs Ireland. **Diet:** seeds, berries, buds, shoots; a few invertebrates; young fed more invertebrates as well as some seeds. **Voice:** distinctive sad, low, piping 'deu', soft but penetrating. Song not often heard, a broken, quiet, creaky or wheezy warbling. **Nest:** cup of twigs, moss, lichen, lined with rootlets and grass, in dense bush or tree, often conifer. **Eggs:** 4-5, pale blue or greenish-blue with dark purplish-brown markings. **Incubation:** 12-14 days, by female. **Fledging:** 14-16 days. **Broods:** 2, occasionally 3. **Maturity:** 1 year.

J F M A M J J A S O N D

Scarlet Rosefinches

male

female

juvenile

male

Coccothraustes coccothraustes **HAWFINCH**

80

Very large, stout-bodied, bull-necked, parrot-like finch, with massive conical bill on big head, short, barely forked tail and short legs. Bill adapted for cracking hardest seeds and cherry stones, which other finches unable to eat; can apply force of over 50kg, equivalent to 60 tonnes in human!

male

female

male winter

summer

KEY FACTS

Length: 18cm. **Wingspan:** 29-33cm. **Weight:** 48-62g. **Habitat:** mixed and broadleaved woods, especially with hornbeam; also in trees in coppices, thickets, hedges, orchards, large gardens. **Movements:** mainly resident, with local wandering in winter in search of food; possibly a few immigrants from Continent. **Population:** recent decline in some areas; *c*3000-6500 pairs breed Britain; *c*6000-13 000 birds winter. **Diet:** mainly large tree seeds and fruit stones (especially of cherry); also tree buds and shoots, some invertebrates in breeding season; young fed mainly on invertebrates, also seeds. **Voice:** main call, used when perched and in flight, a short, explosive clicking 'pzik', like Robin's but more powerful. Also thin, long, harsh, whistling 'tzreee' and hoarse 'chi'. Song feeble, low, hesitant 'tchee... tchee... turr... whee... whee', more liquid and musical at end. **Nest:** cup of twigs, roots, moss, lichen, lined with rootlets and grass, in tree/shrub, especially old, shrubby oak or fruit tree, birch or hawthorn. Male often builds flimsy platform to entice female to mate. **Eggs:** 4-5, pale blue or grey-green, with blackish markings. **Incubation:** 11-13 days, by female. **Fledging:** 12-13 days. **Broods:** 1. **Maturity:** 1 year.

J F M A M J J A S O N D

△ Adult male has warm tawny-cinnamon head, with blue bill in summer, yellowish in winter, emphasized by black extending from base to eye and onto chin; nape pale pinkish-grey, contrasting with rich umber-brown mantle, shoulders and wing coverts; broad buff-white wing patch, glossy blue-black flight feathers, curiously notched at tips; rump yellowish-brown, tail mainly brown, with outer feathers black at base, and white tips, especially noticeable from below. Underparts pinkish-brown, with white undertail. Female slightly duller, with greyer crown and rump, duller, less extensive black on face, and pale grey panel along flight feathers, reducing impact of whitish wing patch.

▷ Juvenile has pale yellowish-brown head and breast, yellowish-buff bill, with narrow, dusky line around base, dull, mottled brown upperparts and paler, yellowish-buff underparts with bold dark bars.

juvenile

◁ Elusive, very shy and secretive, and difficult to see as usually remain in tops of trees. Most visible in autumn and winter, when roving flocks more often on ground, feeding beneath trees or along hedgerows. Very distinctive in silhouette, both perched and in flight.

▷ Flight fast, powerful, deeply undulating, usually above tree-tops, then sweeping into uppermost branches. Front-heavy silhouette with long, pointed wings and short tail. Male has dramatic 'roller coaster' display flight.

summer

Large family of small birds, similar to small-billed finches but with longer, only shallowly forked tails. Feed chiefly on seeds on ground, though may perch on shrubs, trees, wires etc; young fed partly or mainly on invertebrates. Most live in open country with scattered trees and bushes, and avoid human settlement. Mostly rather poor songsters. Nest in trees, bushes, on ground or in crevices. Flight quite fast and bounding. Sexes usually differ. Many species have white outer tail feathers.

● Note: often striking head patterns in breeding males. Females, winter males and juveniles mainly brownish, streaked; many difficult to identify. Look for colour of bill/legs/wing coverts, distinctness of wingbars, degree of streaking on underparts, colour of rump.

CORN BUNTING *Miliaria calandra*

52

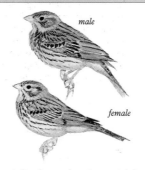

male

female

KEY FACTS

Length: 18cm. **Wingspan:** 26-32cm. **Weight:** 38-55g (male up to 20 per cent heavier than female). **Habitat:** arable farmland, downs, coastal scrub. **Movements:** sedentary. **Population:** once widespread, now virtually extinct SW England, Wales, much of Scotland and Ireland; c100 000 territories Britain, under 30 Ireland. **Diet:** mainly seeds, especially cereals, also invertebrates, particularly in breeding season; young fed on both. **Voice:** short rasping 'chip' contact call in breeding season; flight call a loud, low 'quit', rather liquid at start but with hard, clicking ending. Distinctive song a discordant, rising jangle, like rattling of bunch of keys. **Nest:** loosely built, deep cup of grass and roots, lined with fine grass, rootlets, hair, often in scrape in soil, also among grass, weeds or at base of shrub. **Eggs:** 3-5, very variable, usually very pale blue or buff with dark markings. **Incubation:** 12-14 days, by female. **Fledging:** 9-13 days; often leave nest before able to fly. **Broods:** 1-2, rarely 3. **Maturity:** 1 year. **Confusion species:** female and juvenile House Sparrow (p299), Scarlet Rosefinch (p310) smaller, slighter, with smaller bills; Skylark (pp220-1, see also right).

J F M A M J J A S O N D

△ Our largest bunting, much larger than House Sparrow: bulky body, large round head and heavy bill, with distinct tooth on lower mandible; shortish tail. Looks rather sparrow-like, especially on ground. Males bigger than females. Large dark eye prominent. Nondescript: grey-brown above, streaked blackish; whitish-buff below, streaked more finely from sides of throat to flanks, most densely in centre of breast, often forming dark smudge; at close range, slight head pattern formed by pale eyebrow and surround to cheeks, and dark stripe on side of chin joining dark patch on breast. Bill yellowish, legs bright pinkish to straw-yellow. Juvenile paler and brighter, more yellowish than adult, with fewer streaks on flanks and more contrasting pale buff fringes to wing coverts.

▷ From spring to early autumn, males perch on fence post, wire or other prominent position to sing unique jangling song.

male, singing

song flight   *Skylarks*

Corn Bunting

◁ Male sometimes sings in fluttering flight; unlike similarly sized Skylark, often dangles legs; also, Skylark flies higher and has white outer tail feathers and white trailing edges to wings.

males

winter

females

female

male

△ Large bunting with much white in wings and white underparts. Sturdy but long body; long wings, which, with short legs, give distinctive low-slung profile on ground, where moves with odd clockwork-like run or shuffling gait. Deep but stubby bill and distinctly forked tail. In winter, highly gregarious and usually very approachable, often preferring to run when disturbed. Flight fast, strong, deeply undulating, on long, pointed wings, which are largely white with black tips. Birds in constantly moving feeding flock make short leap-frogging flights over their companions, calling to one another. Flocks fly up suddenly, often quite high, resembling a flurry of snowflakes with their dancing flight as they descend, flashing white in wings and tail, then drop suddenly to ground.

KEY FACTS

Length: 16-17cm.
Wingspan: 32-38cm.
Weight: 30-40g. **Habitat:** breeds in Scotland on high mountain tops among scree and boulders (otherwise on rocky wastes and tundra in Arctic); in winter on moors and mountains in N Britain, also in coastal stubble and turnip fields, on saltmarshes, among marram grass on sand dunes, on shingle beaches.
Movements: passage migrant/winter visitor from Greenland/Iceland/Scandinavia mid Sep-Mar. **Population:** up to *c*50 pairs breed; perhaps *c*10 000-15 000 birds winter; marked variation from year to year. **Diet:** mainly seeds, also some insects when breeding and sandhoppers on coast in winter; forages for scraps around skiing sites; young fed entirely on invertebrates.
Voice: distinctive flight call a soft, rippling 'tirririripp'; other calls include short, soft, sad, whistling 'peeu', louder, high-pitched 'tweet' and rasping chorus from flocks. Song loud, fast, clear, fluty ventriloquial trill 'turee-turee-turee-turitui'. **Nest:** cup of moss, lichen and grass, lined with finer grass, hairs, feathers, in rock crevice.
Eggs: 4-6, pale blue or greenish, with reddish-brown to purplish-black markings.
Incubation: 12-13 days, by female. **Fledging:** 12-14 days. **Broods:** 1-2.
Maturity: 1 year.

winter

female

male

△ In winter, sexes similar, with warm tawny-buff crown, cheeks and smudgy breast band, more extensive on females. Black feathers of back and shoulders almost obscured by pale buff and rusty-buff fringes; large white panel in wings, bordered by black primary feathers. Bill bright straw-coloured, legs black.

▷ Male summer has white head and large white wing panel; rump and most of tail white; back, primary wing feathers and central tail feathers black. Bill and legs black. Female summer has streaked crown, cheeks and nape, buff or blackish patch on side of breast, grey or brown fringes to back and wing coverts, duller, less contrasting wings and tail.

male

summer

female

juvenile

male
1st-winter

◁ Juvenile mainly buffish-grey, with black streaks and mottling on upperparts and softer markings on underparts. Wings much less boldly patterned than adults', with little or no white, especially in females.

LAPLAND BUNTING *Calcarius lapponicus*

male

female

winter

△ Big, bulky, lark-like bunting, with large head, rather stubby pale bill, long, heavy body, long wings, short legs and shortish forked tail. Mostly on ground, when looks squat, creeping mouse-like, running quickly and jerkily or hopping. Gregarious, forming flocks, often with Skylarks, Shorelarks, Snow Buntings or finches. Winter male has sandy-buff face, with crown mottled blackish, black edges to cheeks, faint black moustache stripe, whitish throat; nape rufous, finely flecked with buff, separated from head by whitish band. Back has black feathers bordered rusty and yellowish-buff; wings blackish, with chestnut on coverts; tail black with white outer feathers. Breast with smudgy blackish necklace; flanks streaked and spotted black; underparts otherwise white. Winter female duller, with little or no chestnut on nape and less black on crown and flanks. Bill pale brown to pinkish-grey with dusky tip.

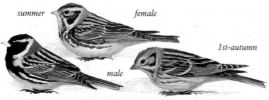

summer *female*

1st-autumn

male

△ Summer male striking: black head, throat, breast extending onto foreflanks, where broken into streaks; separated from chestnut nape/upper mantle by zigzagging pale cream band from behind eye, becoming white below cheek. Upperparts boldly streaked black/chestnut. Summer female duller, with mottled brown/black crown and cheeks, buff eyebrow extending to bill and around rear of cheeks to join whitish throat, and mottled black/brown of flanks and breast extending up onto throat as thin line. Bill yellow with black tip. 1st-autumn like adult winter, but has more yellow-buff head.

△ Flight fast, undulating, with flickering beats of long wings, often quickly gaining height; can look very like Skylark, its frequent winter companion, at distance, but has blunter head due to shorter bill and does not hover before landing; outer wings longer, more oval and tail shorter, well forked. Also resembles Snow Bunting, but flight less undulating.

male

Lapland Buntings winter

female

Skylark

KEY FACTS

Length: 15-16cm.
Wingspan: 25.5-28cm.
Weight: 20-30g. **Habitat:** in autumn, very scarce passage migrant to W coasts and islands, few on farmland etc inland, in winter on saltmarshes, rough grassland or stubble fields along E coasts; breeds on hummocky tundra in Arctic.
Movements: passage migrant/winter visitor (late Aug-early May) from Scandinavia and Greenland.
Population: perhaps average *c*200-500 birds winter, many more in peak years, more on passage. First known to have bred Scotland 1974, with few further pairs up to 1981.
Diet: mainly seeds in winter; invertebrates, especially flies, in breeding season; young fed mainly on flies. **Voice:** distinctive fast, dry, rattling trill, usually ending in hard 'tr-r-r-ik' and soft, fluting 'teu'. Also rich, piping 'teuw' and sharp 'zit'. Song, in circular display flight, a repeated short warbling rather like Skylark's. **Maturity:** 1 year. **Confusion species:** female/juvenile Reed Bunting (opposite) smaller, with smaller head, less distinct pale central crown stripe, less 'open' face pattern, shorter wings, and longer tail with bolder white outer feathers. Can look very like Skylark, especially in flight (see left). See also Little Bunting (opposite).

| J | F | M | A | M | J | J | A | S | O | N | D |

Emberiza schoeniclus **REED BUNTING**

summer

winter

male

female

male

female

KEY FACTS

Length: 15-16cm.
Wingspan: 21-26cm.
Weight: 15-22g. **Habitat:**
breed mainly in wet areas,
from reedbeds and marshes to
banks of rivers and flooded
gravel pits, also increasingly in
dry habitats such as young
conifer plantations, scrub and
farmland. Winter mainly in
farmland, coastal scrub,
gardens etc though still roost
communally in marshes.
Movements: mainly
sedentary. Passage migrant/
winter visitor from Continent
(late Sep-May). **Population:**
*c*350 000 pairs breed.
Probably over 1 million birds
winter. **Diet:** mainly
invertebrates in breeding
season; young fed only on
them; chiefly seeds otherwise,
with some other plant
material. **Voice:** main call a
plaintive, descending 'tseeu';
also very thin, high 'tseee',
loud 'tzeek', metallic 'chink'.
Song a brief, monotonous,
repeated, metallic 'tzeek-
tzeek-tzeek-tzizzizzick'. **Nest:**
substantial cup mainly of
sedges, grasses, lined with
rootlets, fine grass, some hair,
on or near ground in sedge/
grass tussocks, shrubs. **Eggs:**
4-5, very pale lilac or olive,
with purplish-black markings.
Incubation: 12-15 days, by
both sexes. **Fledging:** 10-12
days. **Broods:** usually 2,
occasionally 3. **Maturity:** 1
year. **Confusion species:**
Little Bunting (right),
Lapland Bunting (opposite).

△ Quite big, long, with longish tail that often has untidy look.
Male's head pattern makes him look big-headed; short,
bulbous bill. Often perches upright on longish legs on tall stem
or wire, flicking and fanning tail nervously, displaying bold
white outer feathers. Summer male striking, with black head,
white moustache and white collar; upperparts brown, streaked
blackish, with rufous shoulders and grey-brown rump;
underparts whitish, with fine dark streaks on flanks. Summer
female much duller, with chestnut mottling on blackish crown
and cheeks, buff eyebrow and dark moustache stripe reaching
bill; dull grey collar; much browner rump; underparts buffier,
with streaks on breast as well as flanks, densest on sides of
neck, often forming dark blob. Winter male much drabber,
with buff fringes obscuring black on head; throat blackish and
moustache buff-white; underparts buffier, with flanks less
streaked. Female winter even duller, with less obvious head
pattern, no trace of collar; juvenile very similar but more
boldly streaked, yellower-buff body.

▷ Flight jerky, with erratic
bursts of uneven wingbeats;
long, loose tail trails behind,
frequently looking thick-
ended. Often stays low, but
may rise up when disturbed
before diving down into cover.

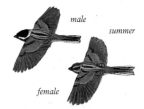

male

summer

female

▽ **Little Bunting** (*Emberiza pusilla*) rare but annual passage
migrant, mainly autumn (especially late Sep-Oct), to
Shetland, E coast Britain and Scilly; few spring (especially
Apr-May), well scattered, including inland; very few in winter;
has bred several times in Scotland recently. Smaller than
House Sparrow (13-14cm), neat, compact, neckless, with
sharp bill and quite short, slender tail. Mostly on ground,
shuffling along and flicking wings and tail, like Dunnock.
Often feeds with finches. Small female/immature Reed
Buntings very similar; Little best distinguished by hard 'tic'
call and face pattern: rufous crown bordered by blackish
stripe, rufous cheeks with blackish border that does not extend
to bill, creamy eyering; also straight, not convex, upper surface
to bill, brown, not rufous, shoulders and shorter tail.

adult winter

Little Buntings

1st-winter

YELLOWHAMMER *Emberiza citrinella*

53

male, singing

summer

female

KEY FACTS

Length: 16-16.5cm.
Wingspan: 23-29.5cm.
Weight: 24-30g. **Habitat:** most open country with shrubs, hedges, roadsides, scattered trees, especially farmland, heaths, scrub, bracken-covered slopes, young conifer plantations; often in stubble fields and farmyards in winter. **Movements:** mainly sedentary, though local movements as it leaves high ground in winter; probably small passage of Scandinavian birds along E coast (Sep-May). **Population:** decline, especially Ireland; *c*1.2 million pairs breed Britain, *c*200 000 Ireland; *c*2 million birds winter. **Diet:** mainly seeds, especially cereals and grasses, also invertebrates in breeding season, main food of young. **Voice:** main call a short, metallic 'tzit'; also high-pitched 'see' of alarm, slurred 'twitick' in flight. Song distinctive, a rapid, rhythmic 'tzi tzi tzi tzi tzi... tzeee', easily remembered as 'little-bit-of-bread-and-no cheese'; final long note often omitted. **Nest:** bulky cup of straw, grass, moss, lined with hair and fine grass, often with 'doorstep' added, in base of hedge, bank, shrub, clump of weeds. **Eggs:** 3-5, whitish to pale reddish with few dark spots and scribbles. **Incubation:** 12-14 days, usually by female only. **Fledging:** 11-13 days. **Broods:** 2-3. **Maturity:** 1 year. **Confusion species:** female/juvenile Cirl Bunting (opposite) very similar, but have greyish-brown (not chestnut) rump, clearer head pattern, less yellow underparts with finer streaking, and different call. Male's song also differs.

J	F	M	A	M	J	J	A	S	O	N	D

male   summer

female

△ Our commonest and most widespread bunting. Slightly larger than Chaffinch, with longer tail. Full-chested but slim, with long rear body and long forked tail; flat forehead, small eye and short, sharp bill. Often upright on overhead wire, bush or other prominent perch, flicking tail and calling; male has very distinctive song. Feeds on ground, adopting horizontal stance. Has distinctive plain chestnut rump in all plumages. Summer male has brilliant lemon-yellow head and underparts, with a few olive streaks on face, chestnut wash on sides of breast and flanks, with few blackish streaks; varies in brightness. Summer female duller, with more markings on head and throat in untidy pattern, much less yellow underparts and more heavily streaked flanks.

male winter

▷ After moult Aug-Oct, male duller, with more head markings, duller chestnut breast sides and flanks, and greenish-yellow fringes to wing feathers. Female slightly duller, less clearly streaked. Juveniles very variable, usually darker, more streaked than female; many have very little yellow.

juvenile

▽ Gregarious in winter, forming flocks, often mixing with other buntings and finches to feed on stubble. If disturbed, flocks fly straight up into bushes or trees and return in ones and twos when danger has passed.

◁ Flight fast and direct, usually with few undulations; take-off long and steep; often follows long, circular path, returning to same or nearby perch. Unstreaked, bright chestnut rump and white on sides of long tail conspicuous.

54

male, singing

juvenile

female

summer

KEY FACTS

Length: 15.5cm. **Wingspan:** 22-25.5cm. **Weight:** 20-28g. **Habitat:** small fields with weeds, dense hedges and tall trees; most near coast/in river valleys. **Movements:** mainly sedentary. **Population:** Mediterranean species at edge of range here; not discovered as British bird until 1800, in Devon; expanded range in 19th century to become widespread breeder N to Midlands and Wales. Massive decline, especially since late 1950s, probably due to modern farming methods and climate changes. Tiny population hangs on in SW England, almost all in Devon; c400 pairs breed. **Diet:** seeds, mainly grasses and cereals, also invertebrates in summer; young fed mainly on invertebrates. **Voice:** thin, quiet 'sip' or more melancholy 'tzepe'; chattering chorus from flock in flight. Distinctive song a short, fast, rattling trill, like 2nd part of Lesser Whitethroat's song but more metallic; shorter, quieter version in winter. **Nest:** untidy cup of stalks, roots, grass, leaves and moss, lined with fine stems and hair, hidden low in shrub, tree, hedge or creeper. **Eggs:** 3-4, greyish, with dark brown spots/scribbles. **Incubation:** 13-14 days, by female. **Fledging:** 11-13 days. **Broods:** 2, often 3. **Maturity:** 1 year. **Confusion species:** Yellowhammer (opposite).

J F M A M J J A S O N D

△ Slighter, more compact than Yellowhammer, with more drooping bill. Dull greyish-olive (male) to greyish-brown (female/juvenile) rump. Distinctive voice. Male summer unique: black-streaked olive-green crown, black and yellow striped head, black throat with yellow collar; olive-green breast band; chestnut back/shoulders; underparts buffish-yellow, much less yellow than male Yellowhammer's. Female much duller, but still with paler version of face pattern, so head more strongly striped than female Yellowhammer's; chestnut only on shoulders; less yellow, more finely streaked, below. Juvenile like female, but more strongly streaked below, less buff.

males

winter

female

△ After moult Aug-Oct, male duller, with black and chestnut partly obscured by buff tips to feathers; chest band greyer. Dull rump still distinctive (especially in flight). Spend winter in pairs or in flocks, roaming stubble fields or fields with weeds, but unlike Yellowhammers stay near hedges, often hidden by low vegetation. Rarely with other buntings/finches.

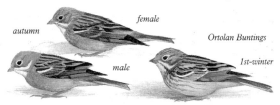

female

autumn

Ortolan Buntings

male

1st-winter

△ **Ortolan Bunting** (*Emberiza hortulana*) scarce but annual passage migrant from Continent, Aug-early Nov (especially late Aug-Sep), chiefly S coast England; few Apr-Jun (especially May), chiefly E coast Britain. Similar size (15.5-16.5cm) to Yellowhammer, but more compact, with shorter tail. Distinctive pale eyering around large eye, brown rump. Adults have greenish-grey head and breast, curving pale yellow moustache, pale yellow throat, chestnut-buff underparts, yellowish-brown rump; female duller with dark streaks on head, throat and breast; pink bill, pinkish legs.

COMMON NAMES

SCIENTIFIC NAMES